THE OXFORD HISTORY OF THE

COMPANION SERI

Written by specialists from various fields, this edited volume is the first systematic investigation of the impact of imperialism on twentieth-century Britain. The contributors explore different aspects of Britain's imperial experience as the empire weathered the storms of the two world wars, was subsequently dismantled, and then apparently was gone. How widely was the empire's presence felt in British culture and society? What was the place of imperial questions in British party politics? Was Britain's status as a global power enhanced or underpinned by the existence of its empire? What was the relation of Britain's empire to national identities within the United Kingdom?

The chapters range widely from social attitudes to empire and the place of the colonies in the public imagination, to the implications of imperialism for demography, trade, party politics and political culture, government and foreign policy, the churches and civil society, and the armed forces. The volume also addresses the fascinating yet complex question of how, after the formal end of empire, the colonial past has continued to impinge upon our post-colonial present, as contributors reflect upon the diverse ways in which the legacies of empire are interpreted and debated in Britain today.

Andrew Thompson's previous publications include *The Empire Strikes Back? The Impact of Imperialism on Britain from the Mid-Nineteenth Century* (2005) and *Empire and Globalisation. Networks of People, Goods and Capital in the British World, c.1850–1914* (2010). He is currently Chief Executive of the UK's Arts and Humanities Research Council, and is writing a new history of the international humanitarian system for OUP: *Humanitarianism on Trial. How a Global System of Aid and Development emerged from the end of Empire.*

THE OXFORD HISTORY OF THE BRITISH EMPIRE

Volume I. *The Origins of Empire*
EDITED BY Nicholas Canny

Volume II. *The Eighteenth Century*
EDITED BY P. J. Marshall

Volume III. *The Nineteenth Century*
EDITED BY Andrew Porter

Volume IV. *The Twentieth Century*
EDITED BY Judith M. Brown and Wm. Roger Louis

Volume V. *Historiography*
EDITED BY Robin W. Winks

THE OXFORD HISTORY OF THE BRITISH EMPIRE
COMPANION SERIES

Scotland and the British Empire
John MacKenzie and Tom Devine

Black Experience and the Empire
Philip D. Morgan and Sean Hawkins

Gender and Empire
Philippa Levine and Wm. Roger Louis

Ireland and the British Empire
Kevin Kenny and Wm. Roger Louis

Missions and Empire
Norman Etherington

Environment and Empire
William Beinart and Lotte Hughes

Australia's Empire
Deryck Schreuder and Stuart Ward

Settlers and Expatriates: Britons over the Seas
Robert Bickers

Migration and Empire
Marjory Harper and Stephen Constantine

THE OXFORD HISTORY OF THE BRITISH EMPIRE

COMPANION SERIES

Wm. Roger Louis, CBE, D. Litt., FBA

*Kerr Professor of English History and Culture, University of Texas, Austin
and Honorary Fellow of St Antony's College, Oxford*

EDITOR-IN-CHIEF

Britain's Experience of Empire in the Twentieth Century

EDITED BY

Andrew Thompson

OXFORD
UNIVERSITY PRESS

OXFORD
UNIVERSITY PRESS

Great Clarendon Street, Oxford, OX2 6DP,
United Kingdom

Oxford University Press is a department of the University of Oxford.
It furthers the University's objective of excellence in research, scholarship,
and education by publishing worldwide. Oxford is a registered trade mark of
Oxford University Press in the UK and in certain other countries

© Oxford University Press 2012

The moral rights of the authors have been asserted

First published 2012
First published in paperback 2016

Published in the United States of America by Oxford University Press
198 Madison Avenue, New York, NY 10016, United States of America

British Library Cataloguing in Publication Data
Data available

Library of Congress Cataloging in Publication Data
Data available

ISBN 978–0–19–923658–9 (Hbk.)
ISBN 978–0–19–879464–6 (Pbk.)

FOREWORD

The purpose of the five volumes of the Oxford History of the British Empire was to provide a comprehensive survey of the Empire from its beginning to end, to explore the meaning of British imperialism for the ruled as well as the rulers, and to study the significance of the British Empire as a theme in world history. The volumes in the Companion Series carry forward this purpose. They pursue themes that could not be covered adequately in the main series while incorporating recent research and providing fresh interpretations of significant topics.

Wm. Roger Louis

CONTENTS

CONTRIBUTORS

JEFFREY COX (PhD, Harvard University) is Professor of History at the University of Iowa. His major publications include *The English Churches in a Secular Society: Lambeth, 1870–1930* (1982), *Imperial Fault Lines: Christianity and Colonial Power in India, 1818–1940* (2002), and *The British Missionary Enterprise since 1700* (2008). He is now at work on a book entitled *European Religion/American Religion: Why the Difference?*

KRISHAN KUMAR (PhD, London School of Economics) is University Professor, William R. Kenan, Jr., Professor and Chair, Department of Sociology, University of Virginia. He was previously Professor of Social and Political Thought at the University of Kent at Canterbury. Among his publications are *Utopia and Anti-Utopia in Modern Times* (1987), *1989: Revolutionary Ideas and Ideals* (2001), *The Making of English National Identity* (2003), and *From Post-Industrial to Post-Modern Society* (2nd edn. 2005).

PHILIP MURPHY (DPhil, Oxford) is Director of the Institute of Commonwealth Studies and Professor of British and Commonwealth History at the University of London. He is the author of *Party Politics and Decolonization: The Conservative Party and British Colonial Policy in Tropical Africa 1951–1964* (1995) and *Alan Lennox-Boyd: A Biography (1999)*, and the editor of *British Documents on the End of Empire: Central Africa* (2005). He co-edits the *Journal of Imperial and Commonwealth History*.

ANDREW THOMPSON (DPhil, Oxford) is Professor of Modern History at the University of Exeter. He has published widely on the relationship between British history and Imperial history, and is author of *The Empire Strikes Back? The Impact of Imperialism on Britain from the Mid-Nineteenth Century* (2005). His recent book, *Empire and Globalisation. Networks of People, Goods and Capital in the British World, c.1850–1914* (2010), co-authored with Gary Magee, blends insights from the social sciences, economics, and history to provide an analysis of the cultural economy of Britain's empire. He is a Council member of the Arts and Humanities Research Council.

JIM TOMLINSON (PhD, London School of Economics) is Bonar Professor of Modern History at the University of Dundee. He has published widely on twentieth-century British history, especially on the history of economic policy, most recently *Jute No More: Transforming Dundee* (2011), edited with Chris Whatley. He is currently working with Ben Clift of Warwick University on historical and comparative developments in economic policy in Britain and France and on projects on 'Managing the economy, managing the people: Britain 1940–1997', and on the history of the jute industry.

WENDY WEBSTER (PhD, Cambridge) is Professor Emeritus of Contemporary British History at the University of Central Lancashire. She has published widely on questions of migration, ethnicity, gender, imperialism, and national identity including *Imagining Home: Gender, Race and National Identity* (1998), *Englishness and Empire, 1939–1965* (2005), and (with Louise Ryan) *Gendering Migration: Masculinity, Femininity and Ethnicity in Post-War Britain* (2008). Her current projects are on Englishness and Europe 1939–72 and on the multiethnic, multinational, and multilingual population of Second World War Britain, and have been supported by fellowships from the Leverhulme Trust and the Australian National University.

RICHARD WHITING (DPhil, Oxford) is Professor of Modern British History at the University of Leeds. His publications include *The Labour Party and Taxation: Party Identity and Political Purpose in Twentieth-Century Britain* (2001). He is currently writing a history of trade unions and British politics, and has recently co-edited, with Robert Crowcroft and S. J. D. Green, *The Philosophy, Politics and Religion of British Democracy: Maurice Cowling and Conservatism* (2010).

PREFACE AND ACKNOWLEDGEMENTS

In redrawing the intellectual map of British imperial history, considerable emphasis has rightly been placed over the last twenty or so years on bringing Britain itself back into the story of empire, and on integrating metropole and colony in a single analytic frame. However, notwithstanding a rapidly expanding historiography, the chronological focus of much of this 'new' scholarship has been upon the eighteenth and nineteenth centuries. With this current volume of the *Oxford History of the British Empire* Companion Series, I am grateful for the opportunity to redress the balance by exploring how imperialism reached back into the life of the British peoples, and how their identities were constituted through connections to empire, during *the twentieth century*. In short, how was Britain's own 'domestic' history shaped by its extensive imperial involvements at a time when the empire was weathering the storms of the two world wars, was subsequently dismantled, and then (apparently) was gone?

As general editor of the *OHBE*, special thanks go to William Roger Louis—a source of warm encouragement and sage advice from the project's beginning to end. John Darwin kindly hosted and chaired a very stimulating workshop at Nuffield College, Oxford, at which contributors were able to present and discuss early drafts of their chapters; he subsequently provided extremely helpful comments on the manuscript as a whole. David Omissi's suggestions for the 'Introduction' and 'Afterword' were characteristically perceptive, as were his comments on my own chapter. Further thanks go to Saul Dubow, Kent Fedorowich, Richard Grayson, Peter Mandler, Stuart Ward, and Richard Whiting for reading and commenting on parts of the text.

Meaghan Kowalsky showed considerable resourcefulness in gathering many of the materials for my chapter. She also took on much of the responsibility for liaising with the contributors, for which I am indebted to her. William Jackson provided some much-needed editorial support towards the end of the project. While working on this volume, Jan Franklin and Helen Wilson were my personal assistants, respectively as Faculty Dean and Pro-Vice Chancellor for Research, and thanks therefore go to both of them.

My team of contributors were a real pleasure to work with, and I am grateful for the way they responded so positively to my comments on drafts of their chapters. In the middle of the project I suffered a family bereavement and their understanding during this time was much appreciated. My editor at Oxford University Press, Stephanie Ireland, was tremendously supportive, particularly in the final stages of preparing the manuscript for submission.

Finally, thanks are also due to my wife, Sarah Lenton, who took a far greater interest in this volume than one could reasonably have expected, and who will no doubt be pleased to see it in print.

Andrew Thompson

University of Leeds
April 2011

1

Introduction

Andrew Thompson

I

This volume is the first systematic investigation of the impact of imperialism upon twentieth-century Britain.[1] Because of their broader remit, the
five volumes that comprised the main series of the *Oxford History of the
British Empire* did not set out to provide the reader with a detailed focus
upon the ways in which the empire was experienced in Britain, whereas this
volume aims to do exactly that.[2] In pursuit of this goal, its contributors
range widely across various aspects of British private and public life. They
consider societal responses to the empire, and the place of the colonies in
the public imagination, alongside imperialism's more tangible effects upon
demography, trade, party politics, government policy, the churches and civil
society, and the armed forces. The time frame adopted by the volume is also
distinctive. Studies of Britain's 'imperial experience' deal mainly with the
eighteenth and nineteenth centuries.[3] The twentieth century, including the

---

[1] There are, however, several important studies of the effects of empire upon Britain during
and after the Second World War. See esp. S.Ward (ed.), *British Culture and the End of Empire*
(Manchester, 2001); S. Rose, *Which People's War: National Identity and Citizenship in Britain,
1939–1945* (Oxford, 2004); and W. Webster, *Englishness and Empire, 1939–1965* (Oxford, 2005).

[2] Of particular relevance to this Companion volume is Wm. R. Louis and J. M. Brown (eds.),
The Oxford History of the British Empire (*OHBE*), iv. *The Twentieth Century* (Oxford, 1999).
Chapters in that volume by Ronald Hyam ('The British Empire in the Edwardian Era'), David
Fieldhouse ('The Metropolitan Economics of Empire'), Stephen Constantine ('Migrants and
Settlers'), Nicholas Owen ('Critics of Empire in Britain'), and John MacKenzie ('The Popular
Culture of Empire in Britain') are all relevant and helpful to the present enquiry. For a review of
OHBE iv, see A. S. Thompson, 'Is Humpty Dumpty Together Again? Imperial History and the
Oxford History of the British Empire', *Twentieth Century British History* (*TCBH*), 12 (2001),
511–27.

[3] For the 18th and 'long' 19th centuries, see K. Wilson, *A New Imperial History: Culture,
Identity and Modernity in Britain and the Empire, 1660–1840* (Cambridge, 2004); L. Colley,

interwar era and so-called 'wars of decolonization', has attracted much less
scrutiny, while the twilight decades of the 1960s and 1970s, when the
majority of the British people began to evaluate the loss of empire, are
barely mentioned at all. Given that a major motivation for rediscovering the
imperial past is the belief that it has been a formative influence upon our
'postcolonial' present, this neglect of the twentieth century is distinctly
puzzling. It is this neglect which the present volume seeks to redress.

The move of empire from the sidelines to the centre stage of British
historiography, however weighted towards the Hanoverian and Victorian
periods, is now so well established that it is worth reminding ourselves of
the situation which had previously pertained. In the wake of decolonization,
academic study of the empire was directed overwhelmingly towards its so-
called periphery in Africa, Asia, and the Pacific. 'Empire' was something
that was judged to have happened overseas; although originating in Britain,
imperialism remained marginal to the lives of most British people. This
view that Britain's 'domestic' history was relatively impervious to foreign
and imperial influences prevailed for at least thirty years, if not longer. It
was held by the majority of British historians, whatever their period of
specialization—indeed, just as the acquisition of colonies was little more
than a matter of superficial pride, so too their loss was felt to be only
temporarily disconcerting.[4] It followed that imperial history could justifi-
ably be held at arm's length from national history as a largely separate
branch of enquiry.

It would be a long time before historians of modern Britain were to
seriously reconsider this marginalization of the empire. This development
owed much to the launch of John MacKenzie's Manchester University Press

Captives: Britain, Empire and the World, 1600–1850 (London, 2003); C. Hall, *Civilising Subjects:
Metropole and Colony in the English Imagination* (Chicago, 2002); B. Porter, *The Absent-Minded
Imperialists: Empire, Society and Culture in Britain* (Oxford, 2004); A. S. Thompson, *The Empire
Strikes Back? The Impact of Imperialism on Britain from the Mid-Nineteenth Century* (Harlow,
2005).

[4] P. Calvocoressi, *The British Experience, 1945–1975* (London, 1978), 245. For the view that the
empire was on the whole an irrelevant factor in the lives of most Britons, see M. Beloff, *Imperial
Sunset*, i (London, 1969), 19; G. Elton, *The English* (Oxford, 1992), 234; J. Morris, 'The Popular-
isation of Imperial History: The Empire on Television', *Journal of Imperial and Commonwealth
History (JICH)*, 1/1 (1972), 113–18. For the revival of 'Little Englander' history at the end of the
20th century, see D. Cannadine, 'British History as a "New Subject": Politics, Perspectives and
Prospects', in A. Grant and K. J. Stringer (eds.), *Uniting the Kingdom: the Making of British
History* (London, 1995), 12–13, 27–8.

series, 'Studies in Imperialism', over a quarter of a century ago in 1984. The early volumes in the series, especially those written or edited by John MacKenzie himself, challenged the then prevailing assumption that imperialism was of little relevance to Britain's domestic history, and gave fresh impetus to the study of how the empire was represented in British popular culture—indeed, few facets of the media and entertainment industry were left untouched.[5] Since then, MacKenzie's series (shortly to reach a hundred volumes) has vigorously promoted the idea that imperialism was as much a cultural as a political, military, or diplomatic phenomenon. It has been highly influential in establishing the view that empire had 'as significant an effect on the dominant as on the subordinate societies', and should therefore be considered as an integral part of Britain's own history. Many 'Studies in Imperialism' titles are accordingly cited by contributors to this volume.

Alongside, and intersecting with the 'Studies in Imperialism' series, the late twentieth and early twenty-first centuries also witnessed a marked 'cultural turn' in the field of British history, a turn closely tied to the challenge of bringing the empire back into the story of the making of modern Britain.[6] Influenced by postmodernist and feminist theory, a group of scholars, loosely labelled 'new' imperial historians, have changed the ways in which both academics and a wider public think about Britain's imperial past, and the reversal of the colonial encounter has been among their chief concerns.[7] Particular emphasis has been placed upon the (contested) terminology of empire and the multiple meanings attributed to the concepts of 'imperialism' and 'colonialism'; the gender dynamics of Britain as a colonizing power, and the relationship between sexual experiences in the colonies and notions of masculinity and femininity 'at home'; and the ideological underpinnings of imperial power—especially the ways in which British discourses of 'otherness', race, and miscegenation were fashioned in

---

[5] See esp. J. M. MacKenzie, *Propaganda and Empire: The Manipulation of British Public Opinion, 1880–1960* (Manchester, 1984); id. (ed.), *Imperialism and Popular Culture* (Manchester, 1986); and id. (ed.), *Popular Imperialism and the Military, 1850–1950* (Manchester, 1992).

[6] For the contribution of postcolonial perspectives to 'bringing Britain itself back into the story of empire', see Dane Kennedy's insightful essay, 'Postcolonialism and History', in G. Huggan (ed.), *The Oxford Handbook of Postcolonial Studies* (Oxford, forthcoming).

[7] For some acute observations on the 'new' imperial history, including how the term needs to be approached in the plural rather than the singular, see S. Howe (ed.), *The New Imperial Histories Reader* (London, 2009), esp. 1–4.

response to the requirements of the so-called 'civilizing mission'.[8] Again, however, it bears repeating that much of this new work focuses upon the eighteenth and nineteenth centuries. The repercussions of empire for Britain in the twentieth century, both during and between the two world wars, and continuing into the era of decolonization, have received much less attention, while the 'after-effects' of empire—its longer-term legacies and contemporary resonances—have been discussed and debated much more by cultural studies scholars working in the field of postcolonial studies than by historians themselves.[9]

What were the effects of imperialism on Britain's 'domestic' history as the empire weathered the storms of two world wars, was subsequently

---

[8] From a wide literature, on sex and gender broadly see A. Burton (ed.), *Gender, Sexuality and Colonial Modernities* (London, 1999); P. Levine (ed.), *Gender and Empire, Oxford History of the British Empire Companion Series* (Oxford, 2004); A. Woollacott, *Gender and Empire* (Basingstoke, 2006). On masculinity, see J. Tosh, *Manliness and Masculinities in Nineteenth Century Britain* (Harlow, 2005), 173–214; Webster, *Englishness and Empire*, 184–217. On race and gender within Britain itself, see A. Burton, *At the Heart of Empire: Indians and the Colonial Encounter in late-Victorian Britain* (Berkeley, 1998); S. Lahiri, *Indians in Britain: Anglo-Indian Encounters, Race and Identity, 1880–1930* (London, 1999). On the development of racial discourse, see D. Lorimer, 'From Victorian Values to White Values: Assimilation and Exclusion in British Racial Discourse, c.1870–1914', in P. Buckner and D. Francis (eds.), *Rediscovering the British World* (Calgary, 2005). On the specific issue of miscegenation see L. Bear, 'White Women and Men of Colour: Miscegenation Fears in Britain after the Great War', *Gender and History*, 17 (2004), 29–61.

[9] One issue that *has* attracted significant attention is how the empire is publicly remembered. See, for example, the reception of the work of two Harvard historians, Niall Ferguson and Caroline Elkins. Ferguson, whose view of the British empire can be surmised from the subtitle to his book (and accompanying TV series), *Empire: How Britain Made the Modern World* (London, 2003), has been criticized for failing to recognize the violent and exploitative aspects of the British empire as well as the agency of non-Europeans. Ferguson dismisses these criticisms as left-wing polemic. For further discussion, see J. E. Wilson, 'Niall Ferguson's Imperial Passion', *History Workshop Journal*, 56 (2003), 175–83. A related controversy has surrounded the British military response to the Mau Mau uprising in Kenya, examined in Elkins's book, *Britain's Gulag: The Brutal End of Empire in Kenya* (London, 2005). Here debate has focused on the precise numbers of Kikuyu killed as a result of the Emergency, as well as the total number incarcerated in British internment camps. For further discussion, see Richard Drayton, 'The British Empire and Kenya Deaths', *The Guardian* (16 June 2010). A more wide-ranging assessment of Elkins's work is provided by Daniel Branch's *Defeating Mau Mau and Creating Kenya: Counterinsurgency, Civil War and Decolonisation* (Cambridge, 2009). For an excellent comparative essay on the historiography of decolonization, which sets the reception of Ferguson's and Elkins's books in a wider context, see R. Aldrich and S. Ward, 'Ends of Empire: Decolonizing the Nation in British and French Historiography', in S. Berger and C. Lorenz (eds.), *Nationalising the Past: Historians as Nation Builders in Modern Europe* (Basingstoke, 2010).

dismantled, and then apparently was gone? What sort of interpretative framework might help us to make sense of the shifting role of empire in British culture, society, and politics across a century that saw profound changes in the ways in which culture functioned and society and politics were organized? In their respective fields of expertise, the contributors to this volume were each asked to reflect on these questions in order to build up a better picture of the 'domestic' repercussions of empire for Britain in the twentieth century.[10] The result of their efforts is the first volume in the *Oxford History of the British Empire* Companion Series to compare and contrast the effects of empire across different facets of British public and private life. By focusing on the twentieth century, moreover, the contributors to this volume were drawn to the fascinating yet complex question of what type of challenges the imperial past presents for contemporary Britain. Their reflections upon how the empire's legacies are being experienced, interpreted, and debated in Britain today are drawn together and developed further at the end of this book.

II

The chapters that follow provide the reader with a variety of insights and perspectives into Britain's experience of empire during the twentieth century. They were written by specialists from various fields—including political, economic, and religious history; foreign policy and international relations; and histories of race, gender, identity, and popular culture. Yet although they pursue different lines of enquiry, it is nonetheless possible to pick out several recurring themes. Among the most striking of these is the degree to which many people in Britain continued, even after the so-called 'high noon of empire', to be involved in a wider British world to which they often had a direct functional connection. The empire's presence was, therefore, widely

[10] Chapters in *OHBE* iv which touch most directly upon the present volume's concerns, include: David Fieldhouse on 'metropolitan economics', Stephen Constantine on 'migration and settlers', John Mackenzie on 'popular culture', and Nicholas Owen on 'critics'. Meanwhile, several chapters in other *OHBE* Companion volumes, including Barbara Bush's 'Gender and Empire: the Twentieth Century' in *Gender and Empire*, Winston James's 'The Black Experience in Twentieth Century Britain' in *Black Experience and the British Empire*, and Alvin Jackson's 'Ireland, the Union, and the Empire' in *Ireland and the British Empire*, illuminate aspects of the present enquiry. See also the Companion volume on *Scotland and the British Empire*, edited by John MacKenzie and Tom Devine (2011).

felt across British society: it was far from being the exclusive domain of the privileged few who ran it, as is sometimes suggested or implied.[11] In this volume the reader will encounter diverse groups of Britons for whom the empire was often close to their everyday thoughts—national servicemen, as well as regular soldiers, who fought in the colonies during the two world wars and subsequent counter-insurgency campaigns; the family and friends of emigrants to the empire who kept in close contact with their loves ones overseas; a wide spectrum of the professional middle classes who sought to advance their careers within the British world; several of Britain's major industrialists, such as the Lancashire cotton mill owners, Dundee jute barons, and shipping magnates, whose fortunes were tied to the availability of raw materials in the colonies and the accessibility of colonial markets; and several other branches of trade in which the workforce as well as management would have been acutely aware of the fact that their prosperity depended upon Britain's ability to ensure the free flow of goods and capital around (and beyond) the empire. In their own ways, all of these social groups engaged with the empire, and, to varying degrees, their interests and identities were defined by it. The prospect of a significant shift in the basis of Britain's relations with the outside world thus carried real and tangible consequences for people across many walks of British society.

Societal responses to empire were not, of course, forged only through travel, trade, emigration, or warfare. They were also mediated through the realm of the imagination. In fact, it may well be that as many people in Britain encountered the empire through imperial imagery circulated by the mass media as they did through the more tangible types of connection described above. The twentieth century witnessed the advent of exciting new technologies which had the power to transport ordinary people out of their day-to-day lives to exotic foreign destinations. These technologies were actively harnessed for propagating and publicizing the empire.[12] Moreover, the appeal of empire through later Victorian and Edwardian literary influences also proved remarkably persistent, lasting until at least

[11] See e.g. Thompson, *The Empire Strikes Back?*, 3–5, 9–11, 239–41.

[12] S. J. Potter, *News and the British World: The Emergence of a British Press System* (Oxford, 2003); S. Nicholas, '"Brushing Up Your Empire": Dominion and Colonial Propaganda on the BBC's Home Service, 1939–1945', *JICH* 31 (2003), 207–30; C. Kaul (ed.), *Media and the British Empire* (London, 2006); J. Richards, *The Age of the Dream Palace: Cinema and Society in Britain 1930–1939* (London, 1984); On the wider impact of the new media, see J. Gardiner, *The Thirties: An Intimate History* (London, 2010).

the 1950s, and arguably beyond.[13] It was the disillusioned former colonial policeman turned critic of empire in India, George Orwell, who once claimed that most people were 'influenced far more than they would care to admit by novels, serial stories, films and so forth, and that from this point the worst books are often the most important, because they are usually the ones that are read earliest in life'.[14] Adventure stories, children's fiction, and missionary literature established in the public mind an association, however vague, between 'black people', superstition, and savagery—an association that underpinned the view that the British presence in places like Kenya and Malaya, whatever resistance it encountered, was nonetheless a 'civilizing' one against incurably 'backward' peoples. As Wendy Webster's and Andrew Thompson's chapters explain, these messages were reinforced and spread more widely during the interwar and post-war periods by the cinema and radio, as imperialists also tried to persuade the public that the empire could be accommodated to the desire for greater social improvement at home.

Another theme to emerge clearly from this volume is the extent to which the empire enveloped the British people's outlook on the rest of world for much of the twentieth century. (The shadow it casts on today's 'post-imperial' age is addressed separately in Chapter 9, 'Afterword'.) Krishan Kumar rightly cautions against the temptation to read empires teleologically—'to see their end as somehow foreordained'. In fact, there was little sense or anticipation among British politicians or a wider public of a retreat from empire until after the 1956 Suez Crisis. People in Britain lived with colonial rule and expected it to continue. Only a few years after the shock of the loss of Singapore, the Labour Party was busy promoting a new social democratic vision of empire, the counterpart to the welfare state at home. Singapore did indeed deal a severe psychological blow to the British, with a Mass Observation survey of 1942 recording that the public were questioning both the circumstances in which the colonies had previously been acquired and those under which they might subsequently be governed

---

[13] On literature and empire see Thompson, Ch. 7 in this volume. From a growing body of works, see also R. Anderson, *The Purple Heart Throbs: The Sub-Literature of Love* (1974); D. Bivona, *British Imperial Literature, 1870–1940: Writing and the Administration of Empire* (Cambridge, 1998); P. Lassner, *Colonial Strangers: British Women Writing the End of the British Empire* (New Brunswick, NJ, 2004); D. S. Mack, *Scottish Fiction and the British Empire* (Edinburgh, 2006); J. Richards (ed.), *Imperialism and Juvenile Literature* (Manchester, 1989); J. Rose, *The Intellectual Life of the British Working Classes* (New Haven, 2001).

[14] G. Orwell, *The Complete Works*, ed. P. Davison (London, 1998), ii. 74.

after the war.[15] Yet by 1947 a new sense of the possibilities of colonial development was emerging, in which a progressive yet still paternalistic empire would uplift the peoples of the colonies via the development of trade unions, cooperatives, and local government.[16] Looking back on the 1950s, the October 1956 attempt to seize control of the Suez Canal now seems like an act of utter folly. At the time, however, Britain's attempts to secure the canal did not necessarily seem like that at all. Indeed, it is conceivable that, had military operations been successful (and, crucially, had they been supported by the United States), the invasion might well have been enthu-siastically supported at home.[17]

This determination to act on a global scale, even as Britain's international economic standing declined, is conveyed powerfully by contributors to this volume. They explore how contemporary conceptions of the country's world role shifted over time, in response both to developments in British society, and to the momentous changes in the realm of international affairs. The resolve to maintain imperial rule in Asia, even while Hitler was seeking to dominate Europe, was shared by most British politicians. Their disagree-ments were really about the means—whether to make timely concessions on matters of less consequence in order to hold on to the levers of power, or, alternatively, to adopt a 'no surrender' approach in imperial affairs. This mindset was not effectively challenged until some years after the Second World War. Suez did of course eventually reveal Britain's great power pretentions as a fraud—in that sense the satirists of the 1960s were kicking at an open door when they derided the British establishment's conviction that Britain could and should remain a leading player on the world stage. However, the related belief among a post-war generation of political and military leaders that government entailed more than ensuring the nation's stability and prosperity, and that the experience of empire had equipped them with the expertise to resolve certain kinds of conflicts and thus assume a leading international role, persisted for some time after the shock of 1956.[18]

---

[15] Thompson, *The Empire Strikes Back?*, 209.

[16] See e.g. R. Hyam, 'Africa and the Labour Government, 1945–1951', *JICH* 16 (1988), 148–72, and P. Kelemen, 'Modernising Colonialism: The British Labour Movement and Africa', *JICH* 34/ 2 (2006), 223–44.

[17] For a subtle reading of the public mood at this juncture, see P. Lewis, *The Fifties* (London, 1978), 144–5.

[18] For the way in which this belief may have been reinforced by the 'moral authority' conferred by the presumed superiority of Britain's parliamentary, industrial, and cultural achievements,

Harold Wilson's claim that 'Britain's frontiers are on the Himalayas' certainly appears more grandiose in retrospect, but, as Philip Murphy suggests, it is a claim arguably no more grandiose than those made more recently by Margaret Thatcher or Tony Blair.

The British people's habit of viewing the world through the eyes of their empire was deeply ingrained. It was also reinforced by factors that lay beyond the military, diplomatic, and intelligence spheres. Take correspondence, for example. With different rates for colonial and foreign letters, 'the formal British empire was consistently more privileged than other clearly less fortunate parts of the world'.[19] The imperial penny post, introduced in 1898, had a marked impact on the volume of imperial mail, which more than doubled within five years, at a time when letters and postcards were still being transported by ships and trains.[20] Later, in 1934, the Empire Air Mail Scheme was inaugurated. It, too, sponsored the growth of the imperial mail. By the outbreak of the Second World War, Imperial Airway's ton-mileage figure for letters and parcels (a multiple of the commercial load over the distance it travelled) was over twenty times greater than what it had been at its inception, thereby helping to keep families in even closer touch with loved ones in the colonies.[21] Travel to and from the colonies likewise needs to be taken into consideration. The effects of spending a period of time in the colonies are of course too many and varied to be reduced to a simple sentence. But if we narrow our gaze to particular groups of people, such as journalists and politicians, it is clear that the 'imperial' mobility of the professional middle increased considerably during the first half of the twentieth century, and was formative in shaping their views of the empire and what it meant for Britain.[22] (Interestingly, the above trends in

which overlapped but by no means were synonymous with empire, see J. Darwin, *The Empire Project: The Rise and Fall of the British World System, 1830–1970* (Cambridge, 2009), 612.

[19] K. Jeffery, 'Crown, Communication and the Colonial Post: Stamps, the Monarchy and the British Empire', *JICH* 34 (2006), 45–70, at 50.

[20] Ibid. 52; Thompson, *The Empire Strikes Back?*, 58–60.

[21] Imperial and Foreign Mails. Summary of Main Developments of Air Mail Services up to 31st December 1935, Post 50/7, Post Office Archives, Reference No. P 5/6/05. See also P. Ewer, 'A Gentlemen's Club in the Clouds: Reassessing the Empire Air Mail Scheme, 1933–1939', *Journal of Transport History* 28 (2007), 75–92, who notes the huge pressures on the scheme technically resulting from its 'mass popularity' [p. 86]; R. Higham, *Britain's Imperial Air Routes, 1918 to 1939: The Story of Britain's Overseas Airlines* (Hamden, Conn., 1960).

[22] Thompson, *The Empire Strikes Back?*, 144–9; N. Kirk, *Change, Continuity and Class: Labour in British Society, 1850–1920* (Manchester, 1998); On journalism, see Potter, *News and the British*

correspondence and communication are mirrored in the volume of today's telecommunication traffic, where, measured in minutes, Britain is the leading partner of Australia and South Africa, second only to the USA in Canada, and third equal, with the United Arab Emirates, in India.[23])

International sport also shaped perceptions of a wider world and Britain's place within it. It was shortly after the Australian cricket team were whitewashed by South Africa in 1969 that Wilson's government decided to put considerable pressure upon the Test and County Cricket Board to pull out of South Africa's impending tour of England.[24] The catalyst for the cancellation occurred a year earlier, when South Africa refused to let Basil D'Oliveira, a South African-born 'Cape-Coloured' cricketer and member of the Marylebone Cricket Club (MCC), play on its soil. Apartheid South Africa had insisted that touring teams were composed only of whites. In the face of unrelenting pressure from the anti-apartheid movement, an upsurge in left-wing student activism, and the young South African exile Peter Hain's 'Stop the Seventy Tour', it soon became clear that there was likely to be considerable disruption to the South African test. In an ITV interview, Wilson himself denounced the decision to invite the South Africans, remarking that they had placed themselves 'outside the pale of civilised cricket'. He was later hit in the face by an egg thrown in protest over the cancellation of the tour.[25]

That cricket was a truly imperial game was never in doubt.[26] Played against the 'dependent' colonies and self-governing dominions—Canada excepted—the name of the body that controlled international cricket says it all: the Imperial Cricket Conference (ICC). Founded in 1909 by England, Australia, and South Africa, the ICC's membership was expanded in 1926 to include New Zealand, India, and the West Indies, and later Pakistan in 1952.

World, and B. Griffin-Foley, '"The crumbs are better than a feast elsewhere": Australian Journalists on Fleet Street', in C. Bridge, R. Crawford, and D. Dunstan (eds.), *Australians in Britain: The Twentieth Century Experience* (Melbourne, 2009).

[23] B. Harrison, *Finding a Role: The United Kingdom 1970–1990* (Oxford, 2010) 46–7.

[24] B. K. Murray, 'The Sports Boycott and Cricket: The Cancellation of the 1970 South African Tour of England', *South African Historical Journal*, 46 (2002), 219–49.

[25] On Basil D'Oliveira, see P. Oborne, *Basil D'Oliveira: Cricket and Conspiracy: The Untold Story* (London, 2004).

[26] B. Stoddart and K. A. P. Standiford (eds.), *The Imperial Game: Cricket, Culture and Society* (Manchester, 1988). Canada fits less comfortably: cricket was played enthusiastically by its expatriate population, but not so much by native-born Canadians. I am grateful to Kent Fedorowich for this observation.

Moreover, it is worth remembering that, prior to the 1950s, England played little part in international sporting competition in football—it did not even play in the World Cup tournaments of 1934 (hosted by Italy) or 1938 (hosted by France). England first participated in the World Cup in Brazil in 1950. Aside from the Olympics, the main form of international sporting competition before this date was either with other cricketing countries, or at the Commonwealth (previously British Empire) Games, first held in 1930 in Hamilton, Ontario. For the first half of the twentieth century, therefore, cricket contributed to the sense that the colonies had a special relationship to Britain; they were 'like us', unlike France, Germany, and even the United States, that played 'other' games.[27]

There were, however, powerful counter-currents, which ran contrary to more expansive views of Britain. Perhaps the most important, if somewhat elusive, of these is the complex relationship between the fortunes of the empire and the rise and fall of a popular commitment to militarism. A brief backlash against the jingoism of the South African War (1899–1902) was an early and evident sign of the public revulsion that could be provoked by more authoritarian strains of imperialism. The war paved the way for the landslide Liberal victory of 1906, and gave greater credence to internationalist modes of thinking. It also fed the determination of many politicians and journalists to distinguish between a tolerant British 'patriotism' and exclusivist German nationalism in the years prior to the First World War.[28]

That said, it was the interwar years that saw aspects of British culture become most noticeably insular and inward-looking. The years of brutal conflict from 1914 to 1918 tempered people's enthusiasm for extending British ideals of civilization to other societies, while 'deepening the

[27] On sport and the British Empire see B. Stoddart, 'Sport, Cultural Imperialism, and Colonial Response in the British Empire', *Comparative Studies in Society and History*, 30 (1988), 649–73, and the essays collected by J. A. Mangan (ed.), *The Cultural Bond: Sport, Empire, Society* (London, 1992).

[28] I am grateful to Peter Mandler for sharing his thoughts with me on the relationship between imperialism and militarism. On this point specifically, see Mandler, *The English National Character: The History of an Idea from Edmund Burke to Tony Blair* (New Haven and London, 2006), 131. For anti-war opinion more generally, see S. Koss (ed.), *The Pro-Boers: the Anatomy of an Antiwar Movement* (Chicago, 1973); A. Davey, *The British Pro-Boers, 1877–1902* (Cape Town, 1978); R. Price, *An Imperial War and the British Working Class: Working-Class Attitudes and Reactions to the Boer War, 1899–1902* (London, 1972); and P. Laity, 'The British Peace Movement and the War', in D. E. Omissi and A. S. Thompson (eds.), *The Impact of the South African War* (Basingstoke, 2002), 138–56.

consciousness of national difference'.[29] The widely remarked-upon 'femini-
zation of British culture' during the 1920s and 1930s is also thought to have
produced a much greater focus on non-imperial issues.[30] This is not to
suggest that imperial consciousness diminished at this time—the chapters
in this volume show that, in many respects, like the empire itself, it may
have grown. For example, expressions of popular sentiment surrounding
the monarchy between the wars—notably the 1935 silver jubilee, and the
1937 coronation of George VI—were clearly imperial as well as royal occasions, while the image of empire as the supplier of Britain's foodstuffs and
raw materials may have reached its apogee at this time.[31]

Nonetheless, the fact that domestic politics were the priority after the
First World War is clearly reflected in attitudes expressed towards Britain's
new imperial commitments. While in tropical Africa, there were signs of 'a
more thoughtful defence of colonial rule and a more critical view of its
actual practice',[32] in the Middle East there was evident hostility, even if
briefly displayed, towards Britain's recently acquired responsibilities. Previously there had been little public interest in Britain's involvement in this
region—the mandates in Iraq, Transjordan, and Palestine, the 'veiled' pro-
tectorate in Egypt, the real protectorates in the Persian Gulf, and a colony in
Aden were apparently not the stuff out of which most imperialists felt that a
vision for the future of the empire could be fashioned. As one scholar has
recently noted, there were few of the humanitarian or religious impulses in
the Middle East that brought tropical Africa to the attention of the public
and the press. Ignorance and indifference, if not outright antagonism,
typified British public attitudes towards the Islamic world, notwithstanding
the romance of T. E. Lawrence and the travel opportunities offered by

[29] J. Lawrence, 'Forging a Peaceable Kingdom: War, Violence and the Fear of Brutalisation in
Post-First World War Britain', *Journal of Modern History*, 75 (2003), 557–89, and 'The Transformation of British Public Politics after the First World War', *Past & Present*, 190 (2006), 186–216.
[30] A. Light, *Forever England: Femininity, Literature and Conservatism between the Wars*
(London, 1991).
[31] On stamps see Jeffery, 'Crown, Communication and the Colonial Post'. On consumption
see Stephen Constantine, *Buy and Build: The Advertising Posters of the Empire Marketing Board*
(London, 1986) and 'Bringing the Empire Alive: The Empire Marketing Board and Imperial
Propaganda, 1926–1933', in MacKenzie (ed.), *Imperialism and Popular Culture*. See also
A. Ramamurthy, *Imperial Persuaders: Images of Africa and Asia in British Advertising* (Manchester, 2003).
[32] Darwin, *The Empire Project*, 414.

Thomas Cook.[33] The major—and significant—exception to the marginality of the Middle East in popular conceptions of empire was the short-lived yet intense post-war controversy in the popular press over military expenditure, and government 'waste' more generally, led by the Beaverbrook papers. Indeed, it is easy to forget that many of our current preoccupations with British foreign policy in Iraq and Afghanistan—including whether Britain should get involved in quixotic foreign wars, and, if so, what repercussions heavy spending abroad might have for the economy 'at home'—greatly concerned our predecessors too. The interwar years were, then, not a time of mass public indifference to the empire. Yet they do seem to have been a period of greater introversion and even exhaustion, when 'English' (if not 'British') values and the 'imperial mission' were no longer so clearly or so comfortably aligned.[34]

As contributors explore different facets of Britain's world role, the country's diplomatic, military, economic, and demographic ties to the United States are widely reflected upon in this volume. At the start of the twentieth century, the Anglo-American relationship was already the subject of debate. In certain quarters of society, intensifying commercial competition—partly focused on the colonies—fuelled a feeling that what had previously been regarded as a friendly offshoot of Britain was now to be viewed with a measure of jealousy and suspicion. Anglo-American relations were further strained in the 1920s as a result of pressures from America for Britain to change its diplomatic policy (by not renewing the Anglo-Japanese treaty) and naval policy (by conceding parity with the US).[35] As Philip Murphy strikingly quotes, the head of the American Department of the Foreign Office could reflect in 1928 that 'war is not unthinkable between the two countries'.

Yet we must also be mindful of the 'underbelly' of Anglo-American relations—the bonds of language, literature, kinship, and intermarriage which all retained their importance well into the twentieth century. On

---

[33] Ibid. 385. On Thomas Cook in the Middle East, see W. Hazbun, 'The East as an Exhibit: Thomas Cook and Sons and the Origins of the International Tourist Industry in Egypt', in P. Scranton and J. F. Davison (eds.), *The Business of Tourism: Place, Faith and History* (Philadelphia, 2007).

[34] Mandler, *English National Character*, 147.

[35] See S. Roskill, *Naval Policy between the Wars*, i. *The Period of Anglo-American Antagonism, 1919–1929* (London, 1968); I. Nish, *Alliance in Decline: A Study in Anglo-Japanese Relations, 1908–1923* (London, 1972).

top of this, the influence of American inventions, the growth of travel between the two countries, and the long-term presence of several wealthy American families in London, further worked to forge a stronger positive consciousness of America in British society. In fact, there was an astonishing increase in popular knowledge of America among the British people in the opening decades of the twentieth century, at the very same time as mutual mistrust and suspicion of US motives entered into the realm of high politics as a result of diplomatic, commercial, and naval disagreements.

With that wonderful thing called hindsight, we can now see that, after America's entry into the Second World War, Britain would gradually have to adjust from its position as the world's pre-eminent power to that of junior partner of an emerging superpower destined to dominate international affairs. To some extent, the Anglophone alliance (and Britain's 'residual empire') eased this transition and allowed Britain to shore up its international influence and status: America's strategy for containing communism depended partly on Britain retaining its overseas bases, as well as the two countries sharing intelligence with each other. Yet in other ways the Anglophone alliance made this transition more complicated, especially in terms of Britain's accession to the European Economic Community (EEC). Here, as has frequently been observed, the perception of America as Britain's principal ally was a major complicating factor.

Contributors to this volume also draw attention to a progressive attenuation in the pluralistic meanings of empire. In particular they show how the further one moves into the twentieth century, the more the concept of empire begins to shrivel. Although there was no general reaction against, or widespread disaffection with, Britain's imperial role, residual reservations were more easily seen. In some ways, of course, the interwar years served to strengthen the bonds of empire, partly as a result of a fundamental shift in government policy which sought to persuade British migrants to relocate to the dominions, rather than the United States, and deployed state finances to this end. Yet even in the 1920s and the 1930s there are signs that, in some quarters of society, the concept of 'empire' was beginning to lose some of its appeal. Among churchgoers, for example, Jeffrey Cox's chapter traces how the image of the missionary as a heroic, itinerant evangelist, preaching the gospel in far-off places, gradually gave way to that of the institution builder, who created schools, hospitals, and training institutions, from which it was hoped, yet never guaranteed, that Christian values would emanate. Under the influence of liberal theology, moreover, ethnocentric perceptions of other cultures were to be challenged and then increasingly displaced by Christian universalist ideas about race.

In the realm of trade and investment, as Jim Tomlinson's chapter reveals, the notion of the empire as 'privileged economic space' lasted some while longer. The doctrine of 'constructive imperialism', thrice rejected by the Edwardian electorate, was revived after the First World War. An imperial preference clause in the 1919 budget was an initial step towards the Ottawa tariff agreements of 1932, which established a (limited) system of imperial preference, and were widely hailed as a triumph for the Chamberlain school of imperialism. Sterling-area exchange controls were a further expression of this preferential mode of policy-making which continued to influence economic thinking and planning well after 1945.[36] By the 1960s and 1970s, however, even the notion of empire as 'privileged economic space' had lost much of its purchase, as Britain was pulled ever further into the orbit of European, American, and East Asian markets. To be sure, the Labour Party in the 1950s and early 1960s was attracted to the notion of the Commonwealth as a new trading entity, a source of sympathetic votes in the United Nations, and more generally as a progressive force in the world which might allow the party to reconcile its socialism with the country's global ambitions. Yet, as Tomlinson argues, the assumption of economic complementarity proved just as problematic for the 'new' Commonwealth as it did for the 'old'. During the interwar years, colonial economic development policy strove to square the circle of relieving British unemployment while simultaneously addressing colonial underdevelopment. As is the case today, however, ultimately what mattered most for Britain's poorer colonies was access to the markets of the rich which were in no way synonymous with the empire.

Demographic trends tell a similar story. As Thompson's and Webster's chapters make clear, for the first half of the twentieth century the word 'Commonwealth' evoked in the public mind principally the colonies of settlement. Among many British politicians, and by no means only those on the Right, these colonies provided the basis for what was considered to be a more democratic view of empire. Among a wider public, meanwhile, many of those who had family and friends who had migrated to Australia,

---

[36] In addition to Tomlinson's chapter, see the essay by Charles Feinstein, 'The End of Empire and the Golden Age', in P. Clarke and C. Trebilcock (eds.), *Understanding Decline: Perceptions and Realities of British Economic Performance* (Cambridge, 1997).

New Zealand, Canada, and South Africa would have been acutely aware of
the way in which these migrants continued to think and speak of Britain as
'home'.[37] All this changed with the arrival of people from the Caribbean and
Indian subcontinent after the Second World War. Suddenly the Commonwealth, in its 'new' guise, became equated with the 'problem' of non-white
immigration. The word 'immigrant', previously used mainly to mean 'Jews',
now increasingly meant a 'coloured' (rather than 'colonial') person. Then,
as now, much frustration with immigration was directed towards the
chronic housing shortage that bedevilled post-war Britain.[38] The origins
of this shortage were not directly the result of immigration, for, as the
government acknowledged, immigrants were moving to areas where over-
crowding was already a problem. Yet it was evident that in some parts of the
country 'coloured' immigrants were collectively being blamed for the problem, even if in parliament the political parties were careful not to play the
'race card' over the housing question. Thus in 1964 Deptford local council-
lors went so far as to claim that:

to re-house coloured tenants over the heads of the long white waiting list would
be political dynamite . . . The Deptfordian rank and file regard the immigrants as a
plague, the local Labour establishment as a political problem, the administrators
as a social problem. All unite in seeing them as a problem to be contained . . . and
words like 'integration' and 'assimilation' are used only by outsiders.[39]

That race was now a contentious and potentially decisive political issue was
demonstrated to MPs in the general election of 1964 when a Labour seat in
Smethwick was won by a Conservative candidate campaigning on an overtly
anti-immigration platform against a nationwide swing to Labour. By 1965, the
Labour Party, which had initially opposed controls on 'new' Commonwealth
immigrants as racist, had joined the Conservatives in favour of such controls.[40]

[37] A. Woollocott, '"All this is Empire I told myself": Australian Women's Voyages "Home" and
the Articulation of Colonial Whiteness', *American Historical Review*, 102 (1997), 1003–29; C. Bridge
and K. Fedorowich (eds.), *The British World: Diaspora, Culture and Identity* (London, 2003).

[38] See esp. the excellent essay by John Davis, 'Rents and Race in 1960s London: New Light on
Rachmanism', *TCBH* 12 (2001), 69–92.

[39] See E. Passmore and A. S. Thompson, 'Multiculturalism, Decolonisation and Immigration: Integration Policy in Britain and France after the Second World War', *Revue française de
civilisation britannique*, 14/4 (2008), 37–49.

[40] R. Hansen, *Citizenship and Immigration in Post-War Britain: The Institutional Origins of a
Multicultural Nation* (Oxford, 2000); K. Paul, *Race and Citizenship in the Postwar Era* (Ithaca,
NY, 1999).

There were, moreover, other reasons why public sentiment towards the empire became more ambivalent at this time. As Andrew Thompson's and Richard Whiting's chapters explain, once India had achieved independence, and the 'white' dominions were no longer so widely thought of (or referred to) as part of the empire, what remained were in many ways its least appealing and most troublesome parts. For example, Whiting observes how, during the era of decolonization, older languages of imperialism had to be refurbished in order to help British politicians to negotiate the transfer of sovereignty. 'Responsibility', he argues, emerged as one of the keywords in party and popular politics during the last days of empire. However, such talk of a 'watching brief' over territories 'in the process of becoming themselves' coexisted with a sense of unease over the policing and military side to empire. In the face of a growing body of colonial protest and dissent, the unpleasant and uncomfortable fact of repression may have been understood to have ensured some kind of order. Yet even for those politicians and officials steeped in notions of racial superiority, the human cost of suppressing dissent could easily give rise to a feeling of distaste.[41] To some extent, after 1945 silence and denial, whether through the careful management of news by officials, or self-censorship by the press, could help to hide the more egregious and embarrassing aspects of counter-insurgency operations, just as they had before. Alongside this, there was also a campaign in the post-war years to reinvent the empire as a more egalitarian, welfare-oriented entity. Both of these strategies, however, had to vie with what actually was happening in Kenya and Malaya during the 'emergencies', and the realities of an empire rooted in power and coercion. Efforts to emphasize the more progressive or democratic aspects of British rule were therefore to a significant extent undercut by the close (and increasingly unwelcome) association in the public mind between imperialism and the military. Stripped of much of its romance, invincibility, and moral validity, the imperial relationship during the 1950s, 1960s, and 1970s offered significantly more scope for disappointment, as several of the chapters in this volume clearly reveal.

A more specific example of the growing public ambivalence towards the empire that slowly emerged in the years after the Second World War is

---

[41] See e.g. Harold Nicholson in Jan. 1960: 'You know how I hate the Negroes. But I hate injustice more…' quoted in J. Lewis and P. Murphy, '"The Old Pals' Protection Society"? The Colonial Office and the British Press on the Eve of Decolonisation', in C. Kaul (ed.), *Media and the British Empire* (Basingstoke, 2006), 56.

provided by public perceptions of Winston Churchill. After 1945, Churchill
came to be viewed as the 'saviour of Britain'—the man who set his stamp on
world affairs by thwarting the global ambitions of Hitler and defeating Nazi
Germany. Yet Churchill himself had been very heavily implicated in the
politics of empire in the first half of the twentieth century, most notably as
Under-Secretary of State for the Colonies (1905–8) and Colonial Secretary
(1921–2), as the moving force behind the creation of Iraq, the bitter opponent of self-government for India, an enemy of Gandhi, yet friend of Smuts,
and as an ardent pro-Zionist.[42] These were the things with which Churchill
would have been associated in the public mind before war broke out in 1939.
Indeed, it is worth remembering that his departure from government in
1929 was provoked by his opposition to self-government in India. And it was
Churchill who famously declared in his November 1942 speech to the
Mansion House that 'I have not become the King's first minister in order
to preside over the liquidation of the British empire'. Yet Churchill's memoirs of the Second World War sought to manipulate the way he would be
remembered. He deliberately downplayed his involvement in the empire,
especially in India and the Far East, emphasizing instead the cause of
anti-appeasement, resistance to Hitler in 1940, and his relationship with
Roosevelt and Stalin.[43] In this way, there was a gradual erasing of empire from
the public memory of a politician and statesmen whom, to this day, many
people continue to regard as the country's greatest ever Prime Minister.

Another potential source of disappointment with the empire for the post-
war generation was the consequences of decolonisation for the United
Kingdom and for relationships between its constituent parts. To what extent
did the empire hold the United Kingdom together? And, if it did, was the
inevitable consequence of the loss of that empire the further devolution if
not break-up of the Union under the umbrella of Europe? Krishan Kumar's
chapter tackles these questions head-on. Of particular interest is Kumar's
claim that the empire impacted differentially on the nations of the United

[42] Albeit as Chancellor of the Exchequer from 1924 to 1929, Churchill had implemented
severe cuts to the building of the Singapore naval base. See I. Hamill, 'Winston Churchill and the
Singapore Naval Base, 1924–1929', *Journal of Southeast Asian Studies*, 11 (1980), 277–86;
W. D. McIntyre, 'The Strategic Significance of Singapore, 1917–1942: The Naval Base and the
Commonwealth', *Journal of Southeast Asian History*, 10 (1969), 69–94.
[43] D. Reynolds, *In Command of History: Churchill Fighting and Writing the Second World War*
(London, 2005); R. Toye, *Churchill's Empire: The World That Made Him and the World He Made*
(London, 2010).

Kingdom. The English, he suggests, tended to play down their English identity to allow them to be an 'imperial people'. When their overseas connections contracted, therefore, they were left without a clear sense of who they are, as there was no developed tradition within English thinking of nationality. Meanwhile for the Scots, the Irish, and the Welsh, the empire was a force for convergence, enabling the creation of an overarching sense of British identity that they, as much as the English, could embrace. Yet, at the same time, the considerable contribution of the Celtic nations in Britain's imperial project could also serve to strengthen the sense of their distinct national identities.[44] To varying degrees, the Scottish, the Irish, and the Welsh were to find in the empire a form of self-affirmation that helped them to better contend with the political and cultural challenges they were facing.[45] Once people had begun to lose confidence in the 'imperial mission', the way was then opened for these communities to imagine different places for themselves within the United Kingdom, and even to ask the question whether they were better off without it. In the case of Scotland, a growing public indifference to empire may actually have pre-dated decolonization. By the interwar years, Scotland was already facing a significant loss of colonial markets for its heavy industries, and the consequent collapse of its international trade; the empire simply no longer seemed so relevant to many people's working lives.[46] Moreover, as Kumar reminds us, Irish, Welsh, and Scottish nationalisms had all begun to stir well before the end of empire. For these reasons it would be misleading to posit too simple a relationship between the end of empire and the future of the Union. Rather, alongside the receding memory of joint victory in war, a diminished pride in a shared political system, and rapidly waning economic prosperity, the loss of empire was one of several reasons why, in the 1970s, the UK seemed less of a 'going concern'.[47]

[44] For this view, see esp. John MacKenzie, 'Empire and National Identities: The Case of Scotland', *Transactions of the Royal Historical Society* (*TRHS*), 8 (1998), 215–32, and 'Essay and Reflection: on Scotland and the Empire', *International History Review* (*IHR*), 15 (1993), 661–88. See also MacKenzie's forthcoming *OHBE* Companion volume, co-edited with T. M. Devine, *Scotland and the British Empire*.

[45] Thompson, *The Empire Strikes Back?*, 200.

[46] T. M. Devine, 'The Break-Up of Britain? Scotland and the End of Empire', *TRHS* 16 (2006), 174–80.

[47] Harrison, *Finding a Role?*, 460.

To summarize: the 1950s, 1960s, and 1970s—pivotal decades in Britain's post-war history—saw the concept of empire increasingly shorn of many of its more positive meanings. Empire, as a collection of colonies or overseas 'possessions', gradually shaded back into that much more diffuse thing from whence it had first emerged, namely 'great powerdom'. Was there, however, a particular juncture or a 'tipping point' when the public realized that it was neither possible nor desirable to prevent the dissolution of the British empire?[48] The chapters in this volume suggest not. Instead, they point to a series of 'disruptive' moments, which ushered in underlying, discursive shifts in imperial discourse and rhetoric. The two world wars, or more accurately their aftermaths, stand out as periods when the shape of Britain's imperial future, and by implication the meaning of its past, were brought into open public forum and debated more extensively and intensively than hitherto. But, in addition to these global conflicts, contributors to this volume also highlight the effects on the public mind of the South African War (1899–1902), the Amritsar massacre in 1919, the Irish War of Independence (1916–21), the fall of Singapore in 1942, the independence and partition of India (1947–8), the expulsion of missionaries from China in 1949, the Suez Crisis of 1956, the revelations of brutality in Kenya and Nyasaland in 1959, the Commonwealth Immigrants Act (1962), Rhodesia's Unilateral Declaration of Independence in 1965, and the Defence Review of the following year, Enoch Powell's 'Rivers of Blood' speech in 1968, Britain's entry into the EEC in 1973, and the Falklands War of 1982. With the possible exception of Suez,[49] however, which did arguably call into question the viability and value of empire,[50] the above

---

[48] The idea of 'tipping points' derives from the work of the sociologist Morton Grodzins, who took from epidemiology the idea that there occurs a moment at which a virus reaches critical mass. Transferring this idea to the world of human social interaction, Grodzins suggested that ideas and behaviours can move through a population in just the same way as a disease. Hence, in his view, there have been moments in human history when change becomes unstoppable and qualitatively different; not gradual, but dramatic and revolutionary. More recently, the idea of tipping points has enjoyed another lease of life from the popular *New Yorker* writer Malcolm Gladwell. See here M. Grodzins, *The Metropolitan Area as a Racial Problem* (Pittsburgh, 1958); and M. Gladwell, *The Tipping Point* (London, 2000).

[49] Even in the case of the Suez Crisis, however, it can be argued that the 1950s, as a decade, were a time when the 'exceptional atmosphere of unity and relative self-satisfaction' born of the years 1939–45 gradually began to dissipate, and when a new mood of 'national self-criticism' crept in; the international humiliation of 1956 was simply the most distilled expression of these developments: see Mandler, *English National Character*, 215.

[50] See e.g. Darwin, *The Empire Project*, 605.

events would seem to be better understood either as catalysts for, or the crystallization of, changes in the public mood rather than their sole or sudden causes.

III

Today's historians are more open and alert to the ways in which Britain's own history may have been shaped by its long imperial involvement. They nonetheless disagree—sometimes acrimoniously—about the demands that the empire made upon British society. Recent publications thus arrive at very different conclusions regarding how entrenched imperial values and beliefs actually were. A particularly contentious matter has been whether the 'new' imperial history may have overcompensated for the previous neglect of empire in metropolitan culture by exaggerating its impact—for example, by expanding the definition of 'imperialism' to include phenomena only loosely or tangentially associated with Britain's colonies, if at all. There has also been concern with the 'new' imperial history's emphasis on the social and cultural, seemingly at the expense of less fashionable branches of history (especially economic, military, and political history) and the study of the empire's more material repercussions.[51] Lurking behind the debate about the extent to which Britain was in fact 'imperialized'—neatly if not entirely accurately labelled the 'maximalist' and 'minimalist' schools—are therefore some sharply conflicting methodological perspectives and conceptual difficulties.

Historical debates are often at their fiercest when scholars disagree over the treatment of evidence, and the 'new' imperial history has been no exception. Exposés of 'extravagant' and 'sweeping' claims of the extent to which British society was imperialized have been vigorously countered by accusations of an 'austere' empiricism stemming from a narrow preoccupation with the records and concerns of the state.[52] How, then, are we to

---

[51] Foremost among them has been Bernard Porter's *Absent-Minded Imperialists*. On the merits of Porter's analysis, see reviews by John Darwin in the *Times Literary Supplement* (18 Feb. 2005); Ian Phimister in the *English Historical Review*, 120 (2005), 1061–3, and Stephen Howe in *The Independent* (14 Jan. 2005). On similar debates in France, see J.-M. Bergougniou, R. Clignet, and P. David, *'Villages noirs' et visiteurs africains et malgaches en France et en Europe 1870–1940* (Paris, 2001).

[52] For further reflections on the debate, see S. J. Potter, 'Empire, Cultures and Identities in Nineteenth and Twentieth Century Britain', *History Compass*, 5 (2007), 51–71, and S. Ward, 'Echoes of Empire', *History Workshop Journal*, 61 (2006), 264–78.

establish the empire's effects on Britain? Should the focus of enquiry be on how people in the past understood and acknowledged the influences of imperialism upon their lives? Or should more thought be given to the world of inference and assumption, and how people's lives could be shaped by forces which they themselves did not apprehend?

There is, moreover, the semantic challenge of defining core concepts in this debate, including the very term 'imperialism' itself. As far back as 1940, the Australian historian, and student of Commonwealth relations, Keith Hancock (1898–1988), remarked that imperialism 'is no word for scholars'.[53] Yet we can hardly dispense with it. 'New' imperial historians have responded by trying to get to grips with the shifting meanings of empire in past social and political usage, and by tracing the evolution of the concept over time 'as indicative of broad shifts in historical under-standing'.[54] In so doing, they have sought to show how public responses to British overseas expansion were conditioned by the particular form of expansion in question.[55] The specific connotations of words like 'imperial', 'imperialist', and 'imperialism', it is argued, stemmed from the context in which they were conceived. Such studies further highlight the pitfalls of diluting terminology to the point where 'empire' is only very loosely connected to the processes of conquest and colonization, or, conversely, of focusing on certain types of expansion—military, bureaucratic, com-mercial—and thereby denying other, less obvious registers of British power—religious, intellectual, and cultural. More broadly, in analysing the discursive realm of empire, scholars have shown how the problems and possibilities presented by British expansion were constructed linguis-tically, such that people's responses to, say, the Amritsar massacre in India in 1919, or the Hola camp massacre in Kenya in 1959, were conditioned not

[53] W. K. Hancock, *Survey of British Commonwealth Affairs*, ii (London, 1940), 1–2. See also J. Davidson, *A Three-Cornered Life: the Historian W. K. Hancock* (Sydney, 2010).

[54] See e.g. A. S. Thompson, 'The Language of Imperialism and the Meanings of Empire: Imperial Discourse in British Politics, 1895–1914', *Journal of British Studies* (*JBS*) 36 (1997), 144–77; Bridge and Fedorowich, 'Introduction', in *The British World*; and D. Gorman, *Imperial Citizenship: Empire and the Question of Belonging* (Manchester, 2006).

[55] On this point, see especially Saul's Dubow keynote address to the British World Confer-ence in Bristol, published as: 'How British was the British World? The Case of South Africa', *JICH* 37 (2009), 1–27.

just by these events themselves but by the way they were represented in the British media.[56]

How, then, do contributors to this volume grapple with this array of methodological and conceptual difficulties? One problem they draw to our attention is that arising from Britain's overlapping international and imperial involvements. What influences can be attributed specifically to the empire, and what influences are better understood as stemming from Britain's wider role as a global power? Philip Murphy's chapter on the relationship between empire and Britain's status as a great power emphasizes how Britain entered the twentieth century as a country with a uniquely global orientation, whose interests and priorities reached far beyond her formal empire.[57] Meanwhile Jim Tomlinson, examining British economic thinking and policy, draws on new research on the relationship between empire and globalization to explain how Britain worked with the grain of a global (not just imperial) economic system that it had itself played a key role in shaping and sustaining.[58]

If Britain was transformed by the business of empire, therefore, it was rarely to the exclusion of other influences. These influences were several. First, there was the global power of the Royal Navy. Second, there were Britain's large-scale foreign investments. Third, there were the important markets of Europe, the USA, and Latin America. Fourth, there was the role of sterling as a reserve currency. Fifth, there was the marked external focus of protestant religion. We must, therefore, be mindful of the difficulties of disentangling what are specifically 'imperial' from wider 'international' phenomena.[59] Indeed, taken together, Murphy's and Tomlinson's chapters suggest that the empire was indeed a key facet of Britain's international relations, yet by no means the only one. It tended to reflect and reinforce

[56] See S. Carruthers, *Winning Hearts and Minds: British Governments, the Media and Colonial Counter-Insurgency, 1944–1960* (1995); and D. Sayer, 'British Reaction to the Amritsar Massacre, 1919–1920', *P&P* 131 (1991), 130–64.

[57] See also P. K. O'Brien, 'The Costs and Benefit of British Imperialism, 1846–1914', *P&P* 120 (1988), 163–200.

[58] A. G. Hopkins (ed.), *Globalization in World History* (London, 2002); A. G. Hopkins (ed.), *Global History: Interactions between the Universal and the Local* (Basingstoke, 2006); G. B. Magee and A. S. Thompson, *Empire and Globalisation: Networks of People, Goods and Capital in the British World, c.1850–1914* (Cambridge, 2010).

[59] L. Colley, 'The Difficulties of Empire: Present, Past and Future', *Historical Research*, 79 (2006), 367–82, at 375; ead. *Captives*, 376; T. M. Devine, 'The Break-Up of Britain? Scotland and the End of Empire', *TRHS* 16 (2006), 163–80, at 174; Thompson, *The Empire Strikes Back?*, 6.

Britain's interests and involvement in the wider world rather than to stand
apart from them. Richard Whiting goes further. He claims that 'international relations' loomed larger than 'empire' in popular consciousness in
Britain. He then goes on to suggest that this explains why the public could
evince seeming indifference to imperial withdrawal yet continue to support
the defence of Britain's international role, albeit increasingly as America's
subordinate ally.

All of the chapters in this volume also have to grapple with the seemingly
bewildering variety of influences that came from the colonies. The view that
the empire worked unevenly and inconsistently upon Britain emerges from
the recent literature on this subject. There is greater appreciation of the way
in which an intense (and intensifying) pluralism on the part of British
society makes it difficult to generalize about the affect of imperialism on
the 'home' or 'metropolitan' society.[60] This volume goes further. In particular, its contributors convey the sheer scale of the empire, and the huge
range of potential influences emanating from it, when compared to the size
of Britain. Understood in this way, it is hardly surprising that the empire
featured in many aspects of the private and public life of what was a small
and relatively well-integrated country. However, there was nonetheless a
certain diffidence with which the empire was regarded, as it was not always
perceived to sit comfortably with the prevailing culture in Britain and many
of the issues it raised were, by their very nature, divisive. So the impact of
imperialism upon Britain was pervasive, but Britain's embrace of that
empire more tentative.[61]

Take the subject of emigration, which nicely illuminates how the sinews
of empire worked their way multifariously into British life. For most of the
twentieth century, migration to the colonies continued to play a tremendous social and imaginative role in British society. Complex patterns of
correspondence, return migration, and remittances bound British society
at home to the overseas 'British' societies of Australia, New Zealand,
Canada, and South Africa—demographic ties which retained their significance well into the twentieth century, as the ethnic basis of dominion
populations diversified much later than that other major recipient of British

[60] For a shrewd commentary on the literature, including the question of the 'social penetra-
tion of empire', see Ward, 'Echoes of Empire', 264–78. On the question of class differences
specifically, see Porter, *Absent-Minded Imperialists*, pp. xiv–xv.
[61] I am grateful to Richard Whiting for these observations.

emigrants—the United States. Yet migrants from Britain were attracted to the colonies for different reasons and, indeed, with very different results. Some made their fortunes, others failed miserably. In between these extremes there were perhaps as many experiences as there were people who left Britain's shores. The impressions of the colonies that filtered back to the 'mother country' through migrant networks therefore defy easy generalizations.[62]

Wendy Webster and Jeffrey Cox reflect upon a different if related type of complexity, namely that pertaining to racial thinking. Webster explains why the hostility and prejudice directed against people of colour from the 'new' Commonwealth needs to be read against a much longer history of anti-alienism previously directed towards immigrants from Ireland and Eastern Europe. She is also careful to distinguish between the expectations and experiences of people arriving in Britain from the Caribbean and from South Asia, for what differentiated migrants from the 'new' Commonwealth was arguably as significant as what they held in common. In a similar vein, the shifting ethnocentric figures of speech deployed by missionaries about non-Christian peoples are considered by Jeffrey Cox. Although these discourses originated in previous centuries, some of them—especially those regarding the treatment of women—had remarkable staying power; in fact, Cox shows how they continue to provide political capital for Hindu nationalists and Muslim radicals today. Yet he also describes how other strains of liberal theology and Christian universalism, based upon feelings of racial equality and sisterhood, came much more to the fore in the 1920s and 1930s, with the Student Christian Movement and the International Missionary Council taking up anti-racism as a central cause during these decades, and the World Council of Churches later providing a focus for opposition to South African apartheid after the Second World War.

Cumulatively, therefore, what emerges from these (and other) chapters is a strong sense of the variety of vectors along which influences and ideas from the colonies might be carried back to Britain, as well as the intricate systems of 'indigenous' British social and political thought through which these influences and ideas were then filtered.

---

[62] K. Fedorowich, 'The British Empire on the Move, 1760–1914', in S. Stockwell (ed.), *The British Empire, Themes and Perspectives* (Oxford, 2008); and M. Harper and S. Constantine, *Migration and Empire: Oxford History of the British Empire Companion Series* (Oxford, 2010).

Several of the contributors to this volume point to the hidden, implicit, and everyday existence of empire in the lives of the British people.[63] Kumar's chapter on identities coins the phrase 'banal imperialism' to explore how collective beliefs, whether revolving around 'nation' or 'empire', could enter into people's consciousness in so routine and ordinary a fashion as to go virtually unnoticed, or at least be taken largely for granted. Other contributors reveal how imperial influences have been rendered invisible simply by the passage of time. Cases in point include the all-too-often overlooked religious and missionary foundations of today's international development charities,[64] which continue to provide a major vehicle for the collection and distribution of overseas aid; the colonial origins of the modern conservation movement, which date back to the game reserves, national parks, and moves towards wildlife protection of interwar East Africa; and the expectations of today's asylum seekers arriving from Britain's former colonies (which, according to a recent Home Office report, differ from those seeking asylum from other parts of the world). It was perfectly possible therefore for people's lives to be affected by empire without them realizing it, or indeed having any real sense of attachment to it. Indeed, it can be argued that some of the salient social features of Britain today are those that have arisen, in whole or part, from Britain's long imperial involvement, even if the imprint of empire upon them has all but been eroded.[65]

The empire, moreover, emerges from this book as much as a symbolic as a substantive force in British public life. This seems to be particularly true during the 1950s, 1960s, and 1970s—a period when Britain was retreating psychologically as well as culturally from empire, and when, like today, it was embroiled in several protracted counter-insurgency operations in overseas territories. For the British, the process of comprehending the loss of their colonies soon became entangled in wider debates about the current state or condition of the country. Why was Britain not yet a recognizably 'modern' society, as a growing number of journalists and politicians now claimed? How far would the process of divesting itself of what was

[63] See also Hall and Rose, 'Introduction', 2–3, 21, 28–9, 30–1.

[64] More broadly, one might trace British aid policy back to the Colonial Development Act of 1929, which was succeeded by the Colonial Development and Welfare Act of 1940. See M. Havinden and D. Meredith, *Colonialism and Development: Britain and its Tropical Colonies, 1850–1960* (London, 1993).

[65] B. Porter, 'An Imperial Nation? Recent Work on the British Empire at Home', *Round Table*, 96 (2007), 225–32.

increasingly perceived as a hierarchical, aristocratic, and over-extended empire accelerate the updating of its industrial base and social structure? Was an emergent emphasis on personal needs, and the legitimacy of their fulfilment, fundamentally incompatible with what were widely perceived to be 'imperial' values, such as authority, duty, loyalty, and self-sacrifice? To what extent was the feeling that the country's economic problems were part of a long-run and deep-seated 'decline' exacerbated by the loss of its great power and imperial status? And did the loss of confidence in imperial values simply reflect or actually serve to reinforce the 'dissolving certainties' of the British peoples in their shared identity, and future of their Union, in the later twentieth century? These questions—framed during the decades of decolonization—were part and parcel of social and political debate about Britain's future. They tell us less about public feelings towards particular colonies, and more about how the concept of 'empire', more loosely defined, had come to serve as a foil against which key aspects of the national character could be defined. In the words of Richard Whiting, 'by the 1970s, the chance for what was essentially a "decolonized" state to turn inwards upon its own concerns, was fulfilled'.

Whiting also provides a fascinating illustration of how the debate about empire—specifically, the 'settler interest'—might fruitfully be conceived as a debate about Britain's own political culture and the sometimes incompatible elements within it. Part of his chapter considers the influence of the so-called 'diehard' forces in the interwar Tory Party. The 'diehards' saw white settlers as having a special claim on the loyalty of the British government, and, politically, were the main source of metropolitan support for the more coercive strands of British rule. Yet, as Whiting explains, their influence was curtailed by moderate Conservatism's strategy for ensuring domestic political stability by destroying the Liberal Party and encouraging a constitutionalist Labour Party. These 'domestic' goals of moderate Conservatives in turn required, or at the very least encouraged, an accommodation with the forces of anti-colonial nationalism and an acceptance, however gradual and reluctant, of the trend towards self-government. Hence Baldwin's willingness to repeatedly throw himself behind the cause of Indian reform from 1929 to 1934, while portraying his diehard opponents as the real threat to empire.[66]

---

[66] P. Williamson, *Stanley Baldwin: Conservative Leadership and National Values* (Cambridge, 1999), 243–76.

Throughout this volume one is further struck by the degree to which the 'imperial' and 'domestic' in British private and public life were closely entwined, sometimes so closely as for it to be very difficult to separate them for the purposes of historical analysis.[67] For example, there is much scope for further consideration of the interplay between social welfare policies 'at home' and 'abroad'. In the decade before the First World War, legislation passed in the settler colonies concerning old age pensions, the resolution of labour and wage disputes, and legally enforced minimum wages have recently been shown to have contributed to the development of debates on these issues in Britain.[68] Conversely, after both world wars, it is clear that ideas about welfare reform that were generated 'domestically' within Britain can be shown subsequently to have spread to parts of the empire.[69] But more work remains to be done to understand how influential and important these connections actually were.

One field in which the 'imperial' and 'domestic' were very closely inter-woven is religion. Jeffrey Cox's 'empire of Christ', which spanned regions of 'formal' and 'informal' British rule, conveys this point very clearly. 'The empire of Christ' often sat uncomfortably with official conceptions of empire. Moreover, within the empire, over time, missionary activity came to focus more on Africa and Asia as the settler colonies chose to recruit their own clergy and lay workers locally. Yet if the 'imperial culture' forged by missionary activity was in many ways specific to the churches, it was none-theless a 'culture' that was widely diffused. As Cox contends, under constant pressure to justify its work to home supporters, it was the missionary arm of the imperial enterprise that was often able to penetrate grass-roots society most effectively. Missionaries, indeed, could sustain themselves and their work only by imbuing their cause in the religious life of countless local congregations.[70]

---

[67] Thompson, *The Empire Strikes Back?*, ch. 6; Hall and Rose, 'Introduction', 17.

[68] E. Rogers, 'International Transfer of Ideas in Historical Perspective: The New World in British Economic and Social Debates from the Late 19th Century to the First World War', *Policy & Politics*, 37 (2009), 353–61.

[69] S. Constantine, *The Making of British Colonial Development Policy, 1914–1940* (London, 1984); L. Butler, *Britain and Empire: Adjusting to a Post-Imperial World* (London, 2002).

[70] For the 19th century, see S. Thorne, *Congregational Missions and the Making of an Imperial Culture in Nineteenth-Century England* (Stanford, 1999); for the 20th century, see J. Cox, *The British Missionary Enterprise since 1700* (London, 2008), pts. III and IV.

A further example of this interpenetration of the 'imperial' and the 'domestic' is provided by Philip Murphy. His chapter on Britain's role as a global power highlights the importance of the empire, both in terms of its requirements and its resources, to the organization of British military power in the twentieth century. More specifically, Murphy explains how colonial policing provided the Royal Air Force (RAF) with a vital peacetime role.[71] The very survival of the RAF in its early years was tied to the cheap but effective contribution the service made to colonial counter-insurgency campaigns in British Somaliland, Iraq, Aden, Kurdistan, India's North-West Frontier, Palestine, and the Sudan.[72] It was this contribution that enabled the Chief of the Air Staff, Air Marshal Sir Hugh Trenchard, to prove the service's worth in Whitehall.

Finally, the way in which notions of 'space' and 'place' shaped the public imagination of empire—an emerging theme in the 'new' imperial history— is explored at several points in this volume. Spatial terminology—'metropolis', 'periphery', 'ex-centric', 'bridgeheads', and 'contact zones'—has of course long proved popular with historians of empire. Not until the mid-1990s, however, did scholars working at the interface of history and geography start to explore what have been called new 'relational' approaches to colonization.[73] In addition to showing how metropolitan and colonial spaces were 'mutually constitutive', this scholarship also sought to generate a greater awareness of the variety of connections—imaginative as well as material—that linked together the empire's peoples, practices, and places.[74]

Several contributors to this volume highlight how experiences of empire could be mediated as much through the locality and region as through the nation, and how space and place were therefore 'repositories of social

---

[71] D. E. Omissi, *Air Power and Colonial Control: The Royal Air Force, 1919–1939* (Manchester, 1990); J. Cox, 'A Splendid Training Ground: The Importance to the Royal Air Force of its Role in Iraq, 1919–1932', *JICH* 13 (1985), 157–84; J.Sweetman, 'Crucial Months for Survival: The Royal Air Force, 1918–1919', *Journal of Contemporary History*, 19 (1984), 529–47.

[72] Omissi, *Air Power and Colonial Control*, 37–8.

[73] See e.g. A. Lester, *Imperial Networks: Creating Identities in Nineteenth Century South Africa and Britain* (London, 2001); D. Lambert, *White Creole Culture, Politics and Identity during the Age of Abolition* (Cambridge, 2005); D. Massey, *For Space* (Los Angeles, 2005); and R. A. Butlin, *Geographies of Empire: European Empires and Colonies, c. 1880–1960* (Cambridge, 2009).

[74] For the interconnectedness of empire, see esp. N. Dirks (ed.), *Colonialism and Culture* (Ann Arbor, 1992); Hall, *Civilising Subjects*; T. Ballantyne, *Orientalism and Race: Aryanism in the British Empire* (Cambridge, 2002); A. Burton, *After the Imperial Turn: Thinking With and Through the Nation* (Durham, NC, 2003); Thorne, *Congregational Missions*.

meaning'.[75] Take the notion of 'imperial cities'. Belfast, Bristol, Glasgow, Dundee, Liverpool, and Manchester all carved out particular niches in the overall economy of empire, which brought them considerable prosperity for the first part of the twentieth century, but stoked up big problems for the future.[76] Although colonial sources of raw materials, export markets, and overseas trading networks did not necessarily determine the performance of the British economy as a whole, they could nonetheless be vitally important for the economic fortunes of major urban centres. Imperial decline in these places was thus keenly felt, as greater exposure to competition from the colonies deprived staple industries of customers, skilled workers of opportunities for overseas employment, and shipping companies of monopolies. As Tomlinson's chapter shows, the idea of the empire of 'privileged economic space', which had considerable purchase among some parts of the Tory Party and business community until the 1940s, had to give way during the 1950s to the principles of economic liberalism and the (perceived) need for significant structural readjustments for the United Kingdom's economy. Again this may help to explain why large swathes of British society reacted to the end of empire with such apparent indifference—despite the vigorous lobbying of settler groups, it simply no longer seemed so necessary for many people's livelihoods or security.

IV

The twentieth century was an era when much of the world was under various types of imperial control, when Europe itself was convulsed by two world wars, and when the legitimacy of established empires was challenged by India, China, and Japan. Just as the reality of British imperialism waxed, mutated, and eventually waned, according to the shifting balance of wealth and power in East Asia and Europe, so too the imperial 'idea' or 'project' had continually to be refashioned in the public mind. As recent writing has emphasized, the fate of British rule was never simply determined by the internal dynamics of Britain's imperial system: however

[75] The phrase is taken from R. Kingston, 'Mind Over Matter? History and the Spatial Turn', *Cultural and Social History*, 7 (2010), 111–21, at 112. See also Alan Lester and David Lambert's 'Introduction' to their excellent edited collection, *Colonial Lives Across the British Empire: Imperial Careering in the Long Nineteenth Century* (Cambridge, 2006).

[76] See esp. Tom Devine's analysis of the impact of the 'imperial economy' on Scotland: 'Break-Up of Britain?', 168–9, 175–80.

successfully British rulers in the colonies developed strategies to shore up local support or to contain local resistance, they were repeatedly reminded of the fact that there was much that 'they might hope to influence but could hardly control'.[77] Moreover, it was the world-system, in which Britain's empire was embedded, which ultimately determined its fate. Developments in the Asiatic empires of Turkey, Persia, India, China, and Japan—including the large-scale movement of people across them—massively complicated Britain's ability to project its power overseas and to bring to heel its distant peoples.

The student of Britain's twentieth-century 'imperial experience' must therefore be alert to the intricate interplay between what was happening 'domestically' within Britain and what was happening 'externally' in the wider British (and non-British) worlds. After the South African War (1899–1902), the British people's perceptions and understandings of their imperial (and wider international) involvements were never simply a reflection of changes in their own society, but of the ways in which the world around them was changing too. The First World War, for example, may have enhanced the empire's sense of common purpose, and extended imperialism into people's daily lives through the mass media, entertainment industry, and domestic consumption. In the immediate aftermath of the war, however, a battery of revolts in India, Egypt, and Iraq tested the public's appetite for imperial rule, as policy-makers in Whitehall and officials in the colonies struggled to balance the imperative of controlling the costs of overseas rule upon the taxpayer in Britain with the need to secure support from so-called 'moderate' indigenous groups who could then act as a counterweight to more radical nationalist forces.[78] Similarly, after the Second World War, public belief in a very meaningful imperial relationship had increasingly to coexist with a deepening sense of unease over the policing and military side to empire, coupled with a growing antagonism to the arrival in Britain of 'coloured' people from the colonies, and the unsettling effects of the contraction of Britain's influence in the world. Indeed, it is only by bringing together an understanding of the dynamic nature of British society, with the equally dynamic nature of Britain's colonies (and the world around them), that we can properly explore how far the empire mattered to

[77] Darwin, *The Empire Project*, esp. 649–55.

[78] J. Gallagher, 'Nationalisms and the Crisis of Empire, 1919–1922', *Modern Asian Studies*, 15 (1981), 355–68; K. Jeffery, *The British Army and the Crisis of Empire, 1918–1922* (Manchester, 1984).

people in twentieth-century Britain, why it mattered to them, and the resulting demands it made upon their lives. The chapters in this volume seek to do precisely that, and, moreover, to convey its logical corollary, namely, the highly protean nature of Britain's relationship with its empire, which, however inconveniently, frequently refuses to be reduced to big or broad generalizations, but rather constantly requires us to be mindful of the specificities of (social) class, of place, and, above all, of time.

2

Britain as a Global Power in the Twentieth Century

Philip Murphy

The remark by former US Secretary of State, Dean Acheson, in 1962 that Great Britain had 'lost an Empire and has not yet found a role' has become a rather weary cliché in the history of twentieth-century British foreign policy.[1] Nevertheless, it is difficult to hear British ministers and military chiefs discussing their country's place in the international community without being reminded of Acheson's words. Their regular insistence that Britain requires the necessary military firepower to exert influence across the world is rarely matched by a cogent explanation of why such a global reach is necessary or even desirable. Instead, one can expect to hear phrases about the importance of Britain 'securing a place at the top table' and 'punching above its weight', and, conversely, of avoiding the temptation to 'crawl back into its shell' or to 'batten down the hatches'. Indeed, early twenty-first-century British politicians are still capable of invoking the image of their country as 'an outward-looking island race'.[2] This emphasis on Britain's continuing global 'mission' clearly does owe something to the concrete legacy of its maritime history, not least the UK's continued responsibility in the early twenty-first century for the defence of a string of dependent territories in the West Indies, the mid- and south Atlantic, the Mediterranean, and the Indian Ocean. Yet the almost instinctive desire to project power on a global scale, combined with an apparent inability to articulate why this should be in the national interest, might appear to be a

---

[1] The author would like to thank Matthew Jones and Kent Fedorowich, who read earlier drafts of this chapter.

[2] This from the Conservative defence spokesman, Gerald Howarth, on the Radio 4 news, 20 Dec. 2008.

psychological legacy of empire; proof of Acheson's accusation that the British failed to make the mental adjustment to the loss of the greater part of their overseas territories.

It is certainly the case that Britain's determination to play a leading role in international affairs outlasted rapid decolonization and, indeed, seemed remarkably little affected by it. Yet the reason for this may owe less to imperial nostalgia and more to the fact that British global interests always transcended formal empire. These interests included large-scale foreign trade and investment, the roles of sterling as a leading reserve currency and of the City of London as a global trading centre, and the broader cultural and political affinities of the anglophone world which helped to provide Britain with access to the resources not just of the Commonwealth but of the United States in two world wars. There is a further objection to Acheson's jibe, namely that for the final six decades of the twentieth century, Britain had a remarkably clear and consistent image of its role: that of being the principal ally of the United States (although, as the British more slowly and grudgingly acknowledged, decidedly the junior partner in that relationship). These two central themes in British foreign policy—the desire to play a leading, independent role in global affairs, and the willingness to subordinate its interests to those of the US—might initially appear mutually inconsistent. Yet as we shall see, it would have been difficult for British policy-makers not to have concluded, on the basis of the history of the period from 1900 to 1940, that the latter was the best guarantee of the former.

The resources of the empire, both military and economic, had proved of questionable value to the UK. At no point in the twentieth century did the British empire-Commonwealth have the potential to become a self-sufficient military or economic bloc, although arguably its existence encouraged Britain to remain aloof from developments that might have provided it with more effective guarantees of security and prosperity. The two world wars demonstrated that the empire could be mobilized for war with great success (albeit with near-fatal long-term consequences). Yet in neither case was this a foregone conclusion and many believed, not unreasonably, that the empire would disintegrate under the pressure of war. Indeed, in the prelude to the Second World War, there were genuine doubts about whether the dominions would support the UK in a European conflict. As such, empire in the first half of the twentieth century was an uncertain and unstable geopolitical resource, of limited value as a deterrent to Britain's potential enemies and

poorly understood by British policy-makers themselves. Against that background the interrelated resources of the Anglo-American alliance and
nuclear weaponry appeared to offer Britain not merely a degree of security
unprecedented in its modern history but also the means to reassert its
power in the world.

Empire and British Defence Policy to 1918

As the twentieth century dawned, Britain faced a number of challenges to its
traditional strategy of avoiding European continental alliances and commitments, and relying on the power of its navy. Naval construction by rival
powers threatened the supremacy of the Royal Navy. This threat was
amplified by the emergence of the powerful *Dreadnought* class of battleship
in the 1900s. Despite the adoption of 'a two-power standard' in the 1889
Defence Act, under which Britain's navy would be maintained at the
combined strength of the two next largest fleets, the advent of the *Dreadnought* appeared to render much of Britain's existing fleet obsolete in this
new arms race.[3] The rise of a united Germany, equipped with a mass
conscript army, promised to upset the balance of power in Europe. Meanwhile, major improvements in land transport on the continent of Europe,
principally in the form of railway construction, threatened to undermine
the effectiveness of naval blockade as an instrument of war, while at the
same time leaving India increasingly vulnerable to attack from a Russian
army which could be moved rapidly towards the Afghan border.[4] These new
conditions suggested that the army was likely to have an enhanced role in
future British military strategy. Yet the Second Boer War had exposed the
inadequacy of Britain's army, as well as demonstrating the effectiveness of
irregular forces employing guerrilla tactics. As one of the world's leading
economies, Britain might have been expected to have had little difficulty in
equipping itself for the new military challenges of the twentieth century. Yet
the very success of the British economy may, as has recently been argued,
have made it more difficult for Britain to build up its army. With domestic

[3] A. S. Thompson, *Imperial Britain: The Empire in British Politics c. 1880–1932* (Harlow, 2000),
111–12.

[4] D. M. Rowe, D. H. Bearce, and P. J. McDonald, 'Binding Prometheus: How the 19th
Century Expansion of Trade Impeded Britain's Ability to Raise an Army', *International Studies
Quarterly*, 46/4 (2002), 553.

civilian wages rising, it was expensive to encourage high calibre volunteers
to join the armed forces, while any system of conscription which removed
workers from comparatively well-paid employment would have been politically unpopular.[5]

These new threats were rendered all the more acute by the extraordinary
extent to which the British economy was externally orientated. Yet the focus of
this external orientation was not, principally, the empire. While Britain contributed 44 per cent of the total overseas lending by the main creditor countries
in 1914, most of this investment was directed outside the empire.[6] In 1909,
Britain's trade with the United States was greater than its combined trade with
the non-American dominions, and with its possessions in Asia, West Africa,
China, and Central America.[7] As one commentator has recently noted, the two
world wars proved that 'Britain could live without trading with most of its
empire. It could not live without trade with the United States and South
America.'[8] In his study of how Britain's overseas resources ultimately contributed to victory in the First World War, Avner Offer extends his focus well
beyond the British empire, speaking variously of the 'British Atlantic orientation' and the 'English-speaking peoples'.[9] This points to elements of continuity
in British foreign policy across the twentieth century, which the rapid liquidation of the British empire has tended to obscure. It was essential to Britain not
merely to defend the empire but to preserve the global trading system as a
whole. This is a crucial point, and one that goes a long way to explain why the
insistence by British policy-makers that their country's defence capability
should have a global reach did not end with post-war decolonization.

A growing sense of vulnerability dispelled any illusions British policy-
makers may have retained that their nation could remain aloof from international alliances. Britain entered into ententes with France in 1904 and with
Russia in 1907, and in 1902 it formed an unprecedented alliance with an
emerging Asian power: Japan. Correlli Barnett's dismissive verdict on the
Anglo-Japanese alliance was that 'Britain had already reached the paradoxical
situation where she could not find the resources to defend the Empire that

---

[5] Ibid. 551–78.

[6] K. Neilson, '"Greatly Exaggerated": The Myth of the Decline of Great Britain before 1914',
International History Review (*IHR*), 13/4 (1991), 707.

[7] P. Payson O'Brien, 'The Titan Refreshed: Imperial Overstretch and the British Navy before
the First World War', *Past & Present* (*P&P*), 172 (2001), 153.

[8] Ibid. 152–3.

[9] A. Offer, *The First World War: An Agrarian Interpretation* (Oxford, 1989), 404.

was supposed to be the prop of her world power'.[10] Certainly, such alliances both demonstrated the limits of Britain's global power and restricted its freedom of action in the world. Britain's decision in 1921 to terminate the alliance it had made with Japan in 1902 owed much to the tensions that had long been apparent in that relationship, focusing on Japan's ambitions in China and Siberia and on her indulgent attitude towards Indian revolutionaries.[11] Indeed a significant part of the rationale for the alliance had disappeared by 1907 with Russia's defeat in the 1904–5 war against Japan and the subsequent signing of the Anglo-Russian entente. Ironically, perhaps the strongest argument for retaining the alliance, as British Foreign Secretary Edward Grey explained to the 1911 Imperial Conference, was that it served to restrain Britain's most dangerous potential rival in Asia—Japan itself.[12]

How useful, then, were the resources of the empire in enabling Britain to defend its interests against the new threats of the twentieth century? Britain's Indian empire has been described as a 'bank of military power', its own revenues capable, from the second half of the nineteenth century onwards, of supporting an army of 140,000 men and a British garrison of about half that size.[13] Yet British military planners in the opening years of the century had proved highly pessimistic about their capacity to withstand a Russian attack on India without massive reinforcements.[14] Indeed, throughout the second half of the nineteenth and the first half of the twentieth centuries, the maintenance and deployment of the Indian army presented significant problems for British policy-makers. Following the Indian Revolt of 1857, London ensured that the number of Indian troops was not more than twice that of the British troops stationed on the subcontinent, so that the forces available to suppress any future sepoy rising were proportionately sufficiently large.[15] Concerns about the discipline and morale of Indian troops also made the British cautious about deploying them in conflicts

[10] C. Barnett, *The Lost Victory: British Dreams, British Realities, 1945–1950* (London, 1995), 10.

[11] A. Best, 'The "Ghost" of the Anglo-Japanese Alliance: An Examination into Historical Myth-Making', *Historical Journal*, 49/3 (2006), 811–31.

[12] K. Neilson, 'The Foreign Office and the Defence of Empire, 1919–1939', in G. Kennedy (ed.), *Imperial Defence: The Old Wrld Order 1856–1956* (London, 2007), 36.

[13] J. Darwin, 'Imperial Twilight, or When did the British Empire End?', in P. Buckner (ed.), *Canada and the End of Empire* (Toronto, 2005), 18.

[14] Neilson, 'Greatly Exaggerated', 713–19.

[15] D. French, 'The British Army and the Empire, 1856–1956', in Kennedy (ed.), *Imperial Defence*, 93.

where they might sustain heavy losses. Although Indian troops were sent to
France in 1914, they were withdrawn by the end of 1915, and for the rest of
the war they were mostly deployed to the less murderous battlegrounds of
Africa and the Middle East. A mutiny in Singapore in February 1915 by
Indian troops from the 5th Light Infantry heightened fears in London about
the susceptibility of colonial troops to subversion by Britain's enemies.[16]
Indian forces made their most significant contribution to the Empire's war
effort in the Mesopotamian campaign of 1916. Yet here a further weakness
became apparent, one which would only increase over time. Britain's failure
to develop an industrial base in India or invest in the equipment of its
forces, meant that the Indian army was technologically antiquated, better
suited to internal policing operations than to twentieth-century warfare. As
we shall see, political developments in the interwar period would render the
deployment of the Indian army even more problematic.

In the case of the dominions, one of the most striking features of the Great
War was the contrast between pre-war anxieties on the part of policy-makers
in London about the comparatively low levels of military spending, and their
extraordinary contribution those countries actually made to the imperial war
effort. At the turn of the century, the cost of British naval forces in the Pacific
was borne predominantly by Britain itself. Britain contributed around £2
million, compared with £75,500 from Australia and £15,500 from New Zeal-
and.[17] Britain urged the dominions to make a greater contribution to imperial defence. Yet negotiations ran up against what was to become a recurring
issue: how and by whom were those forces to be controlled? In the case of
naval forces, the situation before the First World War was striking. The First
Lord of the Admiralty argued that it was essential for the Navy to be
concentrated rather than dispersed worldwide. By November 1907, Britain's
home or Atlantic fleets claimed forty-four of the country's battleships; the
remaining six were assigned to the Mediterranean. None were available for
service in the Pacific. Along with 100 per cent of Britain's battleships, European and Atlantic waters claimed 95 per cent of its destroyer strength, and 86 per
cent of its armoured cruiser strength.[18] This tendency to concentrate forces in
home waters increased further as the First World War neared. As First Lord of
the Admiralty, Winston Churchill was reluctant to have ships stationed as far

[16] See B. Kah Choon, *Absent History: The Untold Story of Special Branch Operations in Singapore 1915–1942* (Singapore, 2001), 3–60.
[17] O'Brien, 'Titan Refreshed', 149.   [18] Ibid. 150–2.

away from Britain as the Mediterranean.[19] Indeed, what was perhaps most striking about imperial defence on the eve of the First World War was the willingness of the Australian and New Zealand governments and the Malay States to finance the construction of vessels in British shipyards destined for deployment in European waters.

The threat to Britain appeared to come not just from German naval rearmament but from the prospect of Germany defeating France and thereby dominating the Channel ports. It was this, combined with Britain's dependence on the French Navy to protect its interests in the Mediterranean while it concentrated its forces in home waters, which helped to persuade the British government that it could not remain aloof from a European war. The fundamental question for British policy-makers was how they could engage effectively in any such conflict. A 1903 British army memorandum famously compared a fight between Germany and Britain to one between an Elephant and a Whale—the one with its mass conscript army pre-eminent on land, the other dominating the seas with its powerful navy.[20] Britain's army was clearly no match for that of Germany. Under those circumstances, the principal hope of British statesmen was that the Royal Navy and the British empire would act as a dual deterrent to German aggression against France. The Germans would surely be aware that a naval blockade would eventually stifle their ability to wage war. Meanwhile Britain would be able to harness the resources of its vast empire and the broader 'Atlantic world' behind its own war effort. Yet deterrence ultimately failed. It did so in large part because Britain failed to make clear to Germany until it was too late that it could not 'stand aside' from a European war. Another element, however, may well have been, as Avner Offer argues, that the *potential* military power of the Anglophone world was never sufficiently apparent to Britain's rivals (or, it might be suggested, even to the British themselves) to figure prominently in the labyrinthine calculations that were to engulf Europe in war. 'The Germans', in Offer's words, were 'victims of "intuitive reasoning" preferring the near, the available, the familiar, the vivid—and refusing to peer below the horizons of Europe'.[21] Their attentions had focused on Britain's domestic armed forces; and while the Royal Navy, concentrated in home waters, ruled out the possibility of an invasion of Britain, the British army appeared far less of a threat to German ambitions. Bismarck once joked

---

[19] Ibid. 165.   [20] Offer, *First World War*, 291.   [21] Ibid. 404.

that if it ever invaded Germany, he would send the police to arrest it.[22] In so far as the British empire featured in German planning, it was seen as a point of vulnerability, ripe for revolt, and considerable attention was devoted by Kaiser Wilhelm II and his military advisers to means by which Britain could be decoupled from its empire in the event of war. At the heart of Britain's problem was that its empire had never been moulded into an entity that had the conventional appearance of a modern great power.

When the First World War did break out, the contribution of the dominions to the imperial armed forces was out of all proportion to their size. Canada, Australia, New Zealand, and South Africa contributed 1,309,000 men, of whom 150,000 did not return. Australia lost more troops than did the United States.[23] This commitment owed much to a sense of explicitly racial solidarity, especially on the part of Britain's South Pacific dominions, encouraged by a sense of strategic vulnerability.[24] The war saw Britain utilizing the resources of its empire to allow it to act as a major power on the European continent in a way unprecedented in its history.[25] Yet mobilization for war placed immense strains on the empire. In the dominions, Afrikaner generals led a short-lived revolt about South Africa's involvement in the war in 1914, and the issue of conscription was defeated in two highly divisive referenda in Australia, and when introduced into Canada in 1917 led to riots by French Canadians in Quebec. Closer to home, the British faced a rising in Ireland in 1916, and a full-scale insurrection there once the war was over. The conditions of the war also fuelled insurrectionary nationalism in Egypt and India. Confronted with all these issues, and with the added responsibilities of administering former German and Ottoman mandates, Britain entered the interwar period displaying classic symptoms of 'imperial overreach'.

The Interwar Period

One solution to the new commitments and challenges that faced Britain following the First World War might have been to formalize the wartime

---

[22] P. Brendon, *The Decline and Fall of the British Empire* (London, 2007), 253.

[23] A. Stewart, *Empire Lost: Britain, the Dominions and the Second World War* (London, 2008), 3.

[24] See S. Ward, 'Security: Defending Australia's Empire', in D. Schreuder and S. Ward (eds.), *Australia's Empire* (Oxford, 2008), 242.

[25] Neilson, 'Greatly Exaggerated', 692.

systems of imperial cooperation and to transform the empire into something more immediately recognizable as a cohesive military power.[26] Yet the will to do so was lacking in both the UK and the dominions. Even under the circumstances of the war, cooperation had been hampered, on the one hand by the competing agendas of the dominion governments and the domestic political constraints upon them and, on the other, by Britain's reluctance to press for a formal structure of imperial policy-making.[27] With the war over, the dominions wasted little time in asserting their independence in the field of foreign affairs.[28] This autonomy, which was formally recognized in the 1931 Statute of Westminster, posed a dilemma to British policy-makers—while they could not count on the dominions for support in any military operations undertaken by the UK, the dominions continued to regard it as an integral part of the imperial compact that Britain would come to their aid were they ever attacked.[29]

Britain, for its part, was equally reluctant to have its freedom of manoeuvre limited by a cumbersome process of imperial consultation. There were certainly some interwar policy-makers like Leo Amery, the Secretary of State for the Colonies from 1924 to 1929 (and simultaneously for Dominions Affairs from 1925), who regarded this as a price worth paying for the proper mobilization of the strength of the empire. Amery claimed that Britain was 'not a part of Europe' and that the First World War had only been necessary 'because we had failed to make ourselves sufficiently strong and united as an empire to be able to disregard the European balance'.[30] Yet his counterpart at the Foreign Office, Austen Chamberlain, did not believe that Britain could insulate itself from the implications of the European balance of power and focused much of his energies on European affairs. For Chamberlain, imperial consultation threatened to place unacceptable constraints on the effective formulation of foreign policy. He argued that 'in a crisis the British

---

[26] Ibid. 691.

[27] R. Holland, 'The British Empire in the Great War, 1914–1918', in J. M. Brown and Wm. R. Louis (eds.), *The Oxford History of the British Empire* (*OHBE*), iv. *The Twentieth Century* (Oxford, 1999), 114–37.

[28] J. Darwin, 'A Third British Empire? The Dominion Idea in Imperial Politics', in *OHBE* iv., 68–9.

[29] A. Clayton, *The British Empire as a Superpower, 1919–1939* (Basingstoke, 1986), 5.

[30] R. S. Grayson, 'Imperialism in Conservative Defence and Foreign Policy: Leo Amery and the Chamberlains, 1903–1939', *Journal of Imperial and Commonwealth History* (*JICH*), 34/4 (2006), 511.

Empire must not be paralysed because nowhere in the Empire has anyone the right to speak or act on its behalf'.[31] At least in a negative sense, it was Chamberlain's approach which prevailed.

Ironically, while the dominions would prove, along with India, the most valuable parts of the empire in terms of providing Britain with the resources necessary to defeat the Axis powers, their role in the decade preceding the war was to add to the impression that Britain would not involve itself in a European conflict. With their economies badly damaged by the Depression, they were reluctant to sanction increased defence expenditure, and feared that a continental commitment on the part of Britain might lead them into war.[32] As before the First World War, low levels of defence spending by the dominions caused concern in London. In 1937–8, whereas the United Kingdom was spending about 5.6 per cent of national income on defence, Canada and Australia were spending about 1.0 per cent, New Zealand 0.8 per cent, and South Africa 0.4 per cent.[33] Indeed, India's defence budget of £34.5 million in 1937–8, was more than double the combined defence budgets of the dominions.[34] The Canadian Prime Minister, Mackenzie King, was even unwilling to agree to Arthur Tedder's proposal in 1936 for a Commonwealth aircrew training programme, and a scheme of this sort was not finally approved until April 1939.[35] Given the relatively meagre assistance that the dominions appeared able to provide, combined with the difficulty of achieving agreement between them, British policy-makers in the 1930s remained unwilling to seek any common imperial foreign and defence policy.[36]

As in the prelude to the First World War, the empire appeared to Britain's potential enemies too fractured and militarily weak to act as an effective deterrent. Hitler allegedly laughed when he heard that South Africa had declared war on Germany. Certainly, the bitter and very public controversy within the country following the parliamentary vote on 4 September 1939

[31] R. S. Grayson, 'Imperialism in Conservative Defence and Foreign Policy: Leo Amery and the Chamberlains, 1903–1939', *JICH* 34/4 (2006), 511.

[32] Clayton, *British Empire as Superpower*, 299.

[33] G. C. Peden, 'The Burden of Imperial Defence and the Continental Commitment Reconsidered', *Historical Journal* (*HJ*), 27/2 (1984), 416–17.

[34] Ibid. 418.

[35] J. S. Corum, 'Air Power and the Defence of Empire, 1918–1956', in Kennedy (ed.), *Imperial Defence*, 162.

[36] J. Darwin, 'Imperialism in Decline? Tendencies in British Imperial Policy between the Wars', *HJ* 23/3 (1980), 666.

which took South Africa into the war caused concern in Whitehall and gave little indication to the German government that Britain had gained a staunch ally.[37] The British government itself was far from confident that the dominions would rally to its cause in the event of Britain becoming embroiled in another European war. Towards the end of 1937, fearing that they might simply remain aloof, a senior official at the Dominions Office had raised the possibility of devising some sort of 'halfway house' for the dominions between outright neutrality and full military engagement.[38]

Far from acting as deterrent to Britain's enemies, the empire was itself highly vulnerable to foreign threats. By the interwar period, British power was facing challenges from increasingly assertive nationalist movements.[39] The fragile and provisional nature of colonial states clearly made them vulnerable to invasion (as was vividly demonstrated by the rapid collapse of British rule in Malaya and Burma in 1941–2). Yet even the *threat* of invasion, or indeed, the puncturing of the illusion of British military supremacy, could be profoundly destabilizing. If it was part of the imperial compact that Britain would protect its empire from foreign attack, doubts about its ability to do so could undermine confidence. Towards the end of December, in the wake of the attack by Japan on Pearl Harbor and its advance through South East Asia, Australia's Prime Minister, John Curtin, famously declared that his country looked to the United States, 'free of any pangs as to our traditional links or kinship with the United Kingdom'. In the dependent territories, the British worried that their ability to maintain the tacit cooperation of local populations might be undermined if the myth of British military superiority were punctured. These fears proved fully justified as the prospect of a Japanese invasion encouraged the Indian National Congress to press its political demand for independence and, ultimately, to launch the 'Quit India' movement.

There is certainly something to be said for Correlli Barnett's argument that, the 'myth' of the British empire as a great power was only sustainable so long as the empire itself was not under any significant threat of

---

[37] See A. Stewart, 'The British Government and the South African Neutrality Crisis, 1938–1939', *English Historical Review* (*EHR*), 123/503 (2008), 947–72.

[38] W. D. McIntyre, *The Britannic Vision: Historians and the Making of the British Commonwealth of Nations, 1907–1948* (Basingstoke, 2009), 268.

[39] J. R. Ferris, '"The Greatest Power on Earth": Great Britain in the 1920s', *IHR* 13/4 (1991), 734.

invasion.[40] By the 1930s this threat was extremely significant. Under these circumstances, it has been suggested, far from the empire being an asset in geopolitical terms, the need to defend it actually forced Britain to divert military resources which could have been directed against the threat from Germany.[41] Central to this argument were the repercussions of the defence review conducted in 1937 by Sir Thomas Inskip, the minister for coordination of defence. Its principal conclusion, endorsed by the cabinet, was that Britain's priorities should be first domestic air defence, second the protection of shipping routes, and third imperial defence. It was therefore decided that resources could not be spared to equip British troops for a European role. This decision was only overturned in February 1939.

Given the figures set out above, indicating that the UK shouldered a disproportionate part of imperial defence expenditure, it might appear self-evident that the empire was indeed a net liability to Britain. Nevertheless, on closer inspection, the situation was more complex than this. In the interwar period, lacking even the degree of security that had been provided by the Anglo-Japanese treaty, Britain proved no more willing than it had before 1914 to disperse its fleet to offer genuine protection to its empire. Perhaps the most striking symbol of the dilemmas faced by British policy-makers between the wars in the area of imperial defence was the construction of the heavily fortified naval base at Singapore. It was no coincidence that the project commenced in 1921. With the termination of the Anglo-Japanese alliance, some new strategy needed to be found to meet a potential Japanese challenge to British interests in the region. The base was intended to provide Britain with a citadel, capable of holding out against attack until the fleet arrived to reassert imperial power. Financial constraints had subsequently halted its construction, but this resumed in the wake of the Manchurian crisis of 1931, which had heightened British fears of Japanese aggression. The base was intended to convince not just Australia and New Zealand but also the United States that Britain was a valuable ally in the region.[42] Yet as tensions in Europe grew, the assumption underlying the construction of the base—that the fleet could rapidly be dispatched in time of crisis—looked

---

[40] Barnett, *Lost Victory*, 7, and 'Overstretched? The Making and Impact of the UK's Defence Reviews since 1957', Churchill College Archives Centre, 25 Oct. 2007.

[41] Peden, 'Burden of Imperial Defence', 409.

[42] R. Hyam, *Britain's Declining Empire: The Road to Decolonisation 1918–1968* (Cambridge, 2006), 82.

increasingly unrealistic. Indeed, as early as 1932, Sir Robert Vansittart, the Permanent Under-Secretary at the Foreign Office commented, 'we are incapable of checking Japan in any way if she really means business'.[43] As Ronald Hyam notes, the Singapore base was 'essentially a bogus policy, a symbol of Britain's (unrealisable) commitment to protect Australia and New Zealand from Japanese attack, as a cardinal link in the Commonwealth geopolitical structure'.[44]

Meanwhile, if the army was being starved the resources necessary to allow it a European role, these resources were being diverted to air defence and not to imperial defence. Between 1934 and 1938, whereas War Office spending increased threefold, Air Ministry spending increased nearly eightfold.[45] There is also a danger in suggesting that the rejection of a continental commitment from 1937 to early 1939 was a necessary consequence of imperial defence commitments.[46] In July 1934 the War Office had been directed to construct a continental field force, a move that demonstrated Britain's commitment to be able to shape the balance of power in Europe. It was only the succession to the premiership in 1937 of Neville Chamberlain, who had long opposed a British continental military presence, which led to the notion of a field force being abandoned.

The development of the Royal Air Force (RAF) after 1918 sheds instructive light on this broader debate. Given London's close proximity to the European mainland, the emergence of bomber aircraft as weapons of war left Britain vulnerable to attack. The response of Air Marshal Hugh Trenchard, who assumed control of the RAF at the end of the First World War, was to stress the notion of deterrence: that Britain should be in a position to inflict overwhelming destruction from the air on any power that threatened it.[47] Yet in the wake of the First World War, with no immediate threat to the UK, resources were not made available to construct an effective deterrent. Indeed, the very future of the RAF as an independent force was under threat. Against this background, Trenchard identified colonial counter-insurgency as an area in which he could prove the value of his service to

---

[43] R. A. C. Parker, *Chamberlain and Appeasement: British Policy and the Coming of the Second World War* (Basingstoke, 1993), 37.

[44] Hyam, *Britain's Declining Empire*, 81–2.

[45] Peden, 'Burden of Imperial Defence', 414–15.

[46] See B. J. C. McKercher, 'Deterrence and the European Balance of Power: The Field Force and British Grand Strategy, 1934–1938', *EHR* 123/500 (2008), 98–131.

[47] Clayton, *British Empire as a Superpower*, 3, 25.

Whitehall. An early opportunity arose in 1919–20 in British Somaliland, where the authorities faced a small-scale rebellion. Whereas the British government had anticipated a protracted campaign, costing over £1 million, the RAF was able to suppress the rising at a cost of £77,000.[48] Trenchard was able to present the RAF as the solution to the dilemma of how an expanded empire could be policed at a time of financial stringency. Between the wars, the RAF operated against risings in Aden, Kurdistan, India's North-West Frontier, and Palestine.

Yet if colonial policing actions provided the RAF with an essential rationale, it could hardly be suggested that vital resources were being diverted into imperial defence. The poorly armed nature of their internal adversaries meant that, between the wars, the RAF were able to operate in the colonies with aircraft, often inherited from the First World War, that would have been obsolete in any European conflict. Partly as a consequence, these operations consumed a relatively small share of the service's overall budget.[49] Furthermore, the defence of key strategic points within the empire from *external* attack was also under-resourced. Despite the significant increase in spending on the RAF initiated in 1935 in response to the threat from Germany, new aircraft were concentrated almost exclusively at home. In 1939, Singapore, Malaya, the Middle East, and the Mediterranean were still defended with obsolete aircraft, and Malta with none.[50] In this respect, although imperial defence did not divert significant resources away from home defence, it might be argued that for much of the interwar period the RAF, like the British intelligence community, maintained a capacity and orientation better suited to combating internal resistance to imperial rule than external threats.

If the empire was not, therefore, necessarily a drain on British defence in the interwar period, it remained a highly uncertain military resource, and as such failed to pose a sufficient deterrent to Britain's potential enemies. Indeed, as the possibility grew that Britain might face a triple challenge from Germany, Italy, and Japan, the empire itself appeared increasingly vulnerable. What made it all the more so, was Britain's failure to construct alliances that might provide a substitute deterrent. Mindful of the tangle of

---

[48] J. S. Corum, 'Air Power and the Defence of Empire, 1918–1956', in Kennedy (ed.), *Imperial Defence*, 154.

[49] Ibid. 157.

[50] Ibid. 158–9.

agreements that appeared to many interwar observers to have propelled Europe into the slaughter of the Great War, British policy-makers were instinctively reluctant to enter into any such commitments. At the same time, profound differences in their approach to Germany effectively ruled out any chance of an alliance with France. The Soviet Union, another possible ally against a rearmed Germany, was seen by many in the British establishment as a greater threat than the Nazis.

Meanwhile, British relations with the United States underwent some serious strains. The nostalgia with which the Anglo-Japanese treaty was increasingly viewed by some British politicians and policy-makers from the 1920s, owed much to a sense that Britain had gained little from the United States in return for having terminated the treaty, and to resentment at American attempts to achieve reductions in the relative strength of the Royal Navy. From the point of view of the Admiralty, the fact that Britain was far more heavily dependent than the United States on the importation of food and raw materials made it essential that further reductions in the relative strength of its navy be resisted. It therefore turned its face against US proposals, put forward at the disarmament conference which opened in Geneva in July 1927, that Britain concede parity with the United States in all classes of ship in its navy, not just in capital ships (as had been agreed at the 1921 Washington Conference). The Chancellor of the Exchequer, Winston Churchill, supported the Admiralty's position, claiming: 'There can be no parity between a Power whose Navy is its life and a Power whose navy is only for prestige.'[51]

In the wake of the collapse of the Geneva talks, Anglo-American relations reached a low ebb. In 1928, the head of the American Department of the Foreign Office urged the need to concentrate on improving relations with the US since 'war is *not* unthinkable between the two countries. On the contrary, there are present all the factors which in the past have made for war between States.'[52] The London Naval Treaty of 1930 finally seemed to establish the basis for Anglo-American cooperation in international affairs. Yet its impact was undermined by the drift towards protectionism in the United States, which the election of Roosevelt in 1932 did nothing to check. Indeed, his administration's measures to improve economic conditions at home, particularly the devaluation of the dollar, appeared to Neville

---

[51] K. Burk, *Old World, New World: The Story of Britain and America* (London, 2007), 468.
[52] Ibid. 471.

Chamberlain, the British Chancellor of the Exchequer, as an unpardonable retreat from the vital task of reviving the global economy as a whole. Chamberlain carried this distrust of the United States with him when he entered Downing Street in 1937.[53] As the 1930s progressed, the growing perception of a shared external threat from Japan might have been expected to revive cooperation. Again, however, British strategy in South East Asia was coloured by a mistrust of the United States, and a fear that, if it came to full-scale confrontation with Japan, Britain had far more to lose than the United States.[54]

The Second World War and Its Aftermath

When the Second World War broke out, the mass mobilization of the British empire proved vital to Britain.[55] Indeed, the success of this mobilization served to revive an interest in empire among British policy-makers. It gave rise to the illusion that Britain's remaining territories in Africa and South East Asia could be reinvigorated as the basis for a continuing great power role.[56] Yet the war placed extraordinary strains on the fragile systems of consent and collaboration that held the empire together and ultimately delivered a death-blow to Britain's pretentions to great-power status.

During the Second World War, as in the First, the Indian army underwent a massive expansion, from 189,000 to 2.3 million. Indian troops took part in the North African campaign, in the invasion of Italy in 1943, and in the recapture of Burma in 1944–5. Yet the costs of a vastly expanded Indian army had important repercussions for Britain's future relations with the subcontinent. Between the wars, the British authorities, although determined that the Indians themselves should bear the expense of the military establishment, had nevertheless been cautious about raising taxation to a level that might provoke fresh unrest. During this period, Indian troops were an important resource for British operations in North Africa, the Middle East, and the Far East. Yet faced with nationalist protests at having to shoulder the expense of deploying Indian troops outside the subcontinent,

[53] Holland, *Pursuit of Greatness*, 123, 134.
[54] Ibid. 140–1.
[55] See Ashley Jackson, *The British Empire and the Second World War* (London, 2006).
[56] Ibid. 529.

Britain began, from 1933, to subsidize the defence budget of India.[57] As the Second World War approached, Britain belatedly committed itself to a significant programme of investment to address the Indian army's poor standard of equipment and India's lack of defence industries. This, combined with a relatively generous settlement between the Treasury and the Government of India at the outbreak of the war, meant that, whereas in the First World War, India had borne the entire cost of its military contribution, in the Second, Britain shouldered an ever greater proportion of Indian military expenditure. By 1941–2, Britain was contributing around two-thirds of India's defence budget. It paid for this by transferring sterling into the Government of India's account in the Reserve Bank of India in London.[58] By the end of the war, India had become Britain's largest creditor after the United States, fundamentally altering the financial balance of power between the two. At the same time, with British industry unable to meet its needs, the Indian army became increasingly dependent on the United States for its equipment, a process that led to a further weakening of imperial ties.

The dominions, for all their earlier reluctance to embroil themselves in another European war, once again provided a disproportionate contribution to the imperial war effort in terms of their overall populations. Even South Africa provided 200,000 personnel, around half of whom were Afrikaans-speakers. New Zealand, the population of which included only 335,000 males of ages 18–45, had mobilized 129,000 by the end of 1943. Among the Allied powers, only the Soviet Union had a higher proportion of casualties in relation to its population.[59] Yet although the contribution of the dominions exceeded Britain's pre-war expectations, the alliance was always a fragile one. Holding it together was the responsibility of the Dominions Office, a department which remained throughout its existence very much in the shadow of the Foreign Office. Whereas the Foreign Office liked to present itself as the true champion of British global interests, the Dominions Office was frequently accused of siding too closely with the dominions in their disputes with the UK.[60] Yet the Dominions Office had a uniquely clear understanding within Whitehall that the Commonwealth

---

[57] French, 'British Army and Empire', 102.

[58] Wain Wright, *Inheritance of Empire: Britain, India and the Balance of Power in Asia, 1938–1955* (Westport, Conn., 1994), 20.

[59] Stewart, *Empire Lost*, 165–6.

[60] Ibid. 9.

could only act together on the basis of compromize and conciliation. This sensitive task was not made any easier by the rapid turnover of the department's secretaries of state during the war, or by the fact that other senior ministers, most notably Churchill himself, still inhabited a mental universe in which the 'British empire' would meekly accept London's lead.[61]

As in the First World War, Britain was able to draw on the economic as well as the human resources of the empire-Commonwealth. Yet this was not enough to save it from virtual bankruptcy by the winter of 1940–1. Its salvation came in the form of the US Lend-lease Act passed in 1941. As the war progressed, Britain's indebtedness both to the United States and to the empire mounted. One underlying lesson of the war, however, was that while Britain remained in a position to exploit its overseas possessions, its relationship with the United States offered a far better guarantee of its longer term survival. The US had the manufacturing base that the empire, outside Canada, so conspicuously lacked. Whereas by 1943, the value of armaments production in Britain was around $11 billion, in the United States it was $37.5 billion. In financial terms, Britain did not just benefit from the scale of lend-lease itself, which represented a subsidy from the United States of around $22 billion. It also benefited from the fact that the US was ultimately prepared to write off all but around 3 per cent of this debt, presenting Britain with a final bill of only $650 million.[62] While Britain could successfully throw itself on the mercy of the US, it could not do so with its imperial creditors. It succeeded in obtaining the cancellation of only about 1 per cent of its sterling liabilities (concessions made by Australia and New Zealand). Whereas John Maynard Keynes had proposed cancelling 33 per cent of these debts, the political sensitivity of doing this to the balances of dependent territories effectively ruled the option out. Hence, by 1946 India's sterling balances stood at £1,300 million, a factor that fundamentally altered the relationship between London and Delhi.

Having rescued Britain from financial disaster during the war, the US stepped in to rescue it from bankruptcy once the war was over with a $3.75 billion loan agreed in December 1945. This was supplemented by a $1.25 billion loan from Canada, comparatively a very significant gesture given that the Canadian economy was about a tenth of the size of that of the US.[63] Yet

---

[61] Stewart, *Empire Lost*, 164.
[62] P. Clarke, *The Last Thousand Days of the British Empire* (London, 2007), 402.
[63] Ibid. 401.

the Canadian loan could not disguise the fact that it was the United States rather than the empire-Commonwealth that was now underwriting Britain's ability to play a significant geopolitical role. This, combined with the sense of financial crisis which would continue to grip London for many years to come, and the massive dislocation which the war had caused, particularly in Asia, called for a major reappraisal of British overseas commitments. With the need to feed and administer its occupation zone in Germany adding to its perennial problem of 'imperial overreach' it was clear that Britain lacked the forces simultaneously to suppress nationalists in India, Zionists in Palestine, and Communists in southern Europe. As a consequence, February 1947 witnessed three decisions in quick succession by the British government which would have profound repercussions for the post-war world: to refer the Palestine mandate to the United Nations; to withdraw British troops from Greece; and to quit India.

Yet its 'will-to-global-power', far from being diminished by the Second World War, was reinforced by Britain's self-perception as the saviour of the world from fascism. The successful mobilization of the empire had raised hopes that the colonies might, if properly developed, form the basis for a revival of great-power status. An acceptance of India's destiny as a self-governing member of the Commonwealth was accompanied by a deluded belief that it would continue to follow Britain's lead in foreign affairs, enabling the vast military resources of the subcontinent to form an essential element of a global system of Commonwealth defence.[64] Cooperation with the US was initially viewed as a temporary expedient while the essential task was undertaken of reconstructing the British empire-Commonwealth. As, however, it gradually became apparent that the Commonwealth could never serve this purpose, so too, in the eyes of British policy-makers, did the intrinsic value of the American alliance. Ultimately, Britain had gained genuine security in the first four decades of the twentieth century neither from its empire, nor from its attempts at cooperation with other powers. With the experience of wartime cooperation behind them, and with the emergence of the United States as the pre-eminent economic power in the world, Britain found the role of the United States' key ally an increasingly conducive one.

[64] A. Inter Singh, 'Imperial Defence and the Transfer of Power in India, 1946–1947', *IHR* 4/4 (1982), 568–88.

British leaders also recognized in the new phenomenon of atomic weaponry a further opportunity to revive their country's great-power status. Even before the first atomic bomb had been successfully tested, Churchill had told General Charles de Gaulle: 'Colonies are today no longer a pledge of happiness or a sign of power... Modern [air] squadrons are worth more than overseas territories.'[65] Squadrons equipped with atomic bombs promised to compensate strategically for the loss of India (although, as we shall see, the Chiefs of Staff continued to regard some colonial outposts as a vital source of secure bases). The goal of becoming a major nuclear power was inextricably bound up with the Anglo-American alliance. On the one hand, British leaders recognized that they needed to re-establish collaboration with the US in the field of nuclear military technology. The British and Americans had worked closely together on the Manhattan Project, which had created the first atomic bomb. This collaboration had, however, been abruptly terminated by the Americans following the passage of the McMahon Act in 1946. It was not until 1958 that Harold Macmillan managed to reach agreement with the Americans for the repeal of the Act, and its replacement with the Atomic Bilateral Agreement, which restored close Anglo-American cooperation in this field. On the other hand, Britain believed that only by virtue of it being a nuclear power would the United States be compelled to listen to its voice in international affairs and support it in any crisis (since the US had little chance of escaping Soviet retaliation in any nuclear conflict involving the United Kingdom).[66] Suspicion of US motives helped to persuade some of the Labour Left, most notably Aneurin Bevan, that it was essential for Britain to remain a nuclear power. Despite the withdrawal of American cooperation, Britain pressed ahead unilaterally with its nuclear programme, exploding its first atomic bomb in October 1952, and from 1954 pursuing the development of the hydrogen bomb.

It is easy to suggest that the so-called Anglo-American 'special relationship' was as much an illusion on the part of post-war British policy-makers as the notion of the Commonwealth had been.[67] Yet this tends to underestimate the extent to which the United States genuinely valued British support. As the US became embroiled in a Cold War of global proportions,

[66] Ibid. 252–3.
[67] For a trenchant treatment of this theme, see S. Haseler, *Sidekick – Bulldog to Lapdog: British Global Strategy from Churchill to Blair* (London, 2007).

the global reach of Britain's empire increased the importance of this relationship. A State Department policy statement of June 1948 argued: 'The United Kingdom, the Dominions, Colonies and Dependencies, form a world-wide network of strategically located territories of great military value, which have served as defensive outposts and as bridgeheads for operations. Subject to our general policy of favouring eventual self-determination of peoples, it is our objective that that the integrity of this area be maintained.'[68] Nevertheless, British policy-makers undoubtedly had unrealistic expectations of the extent to which the relationship with the US could revive Britain's great-power status. As the Second World War reached its close, ministers and officials at the Foreign Office retained an explicitly imperial outlook. In March 1945, the Foreign Secretary, Anthony Eden, told his cabinet colleagues that a continued British presence in the Middle East was 'a matter of life and death to the British Empire'.[69] The perceived Soviet threat to British influence in the Middle East and the Mediterranean was at least as significant as the spread of Communist influence over Eastern Europe in precipitating the breakdown of wartime cooperation between Britain and the USSR.[70] This threat also persuaded the British that cooperation with the US to prevent Soviet incursions was essential, at least until Britain was able to shoulder the burden itself.

The leader of the Labour Party, Clement Attlee, who assumed the premiership in July 1945, was sceptical about Whitehall's traditional emphasis on the strategic value of the Mediterranean and the Middle East. At least in the early years of his premiership, his outlook was firmly internationalist. At the beginning of September 1945, he told his cabinet colleagues that the British empire could 'only be defended by membership of the United Nations Organisation'.[71] Yet his Foreign Secretary, Ernest Bevin, continued to adhere to Eden's more orthodox sense of strategic priorities and was strongly supported in this by the Chiefs of Staff. As the nuclear deterrent became ever more central to British military planning, so did the RAF's strategic bomber force. While the Chiefs of Staff argued in general terms for the importance of the British military presence in the Middle East and the

[68] Burk, *Old World, New World*, 578.
[69] J. Kent, 'The British Empire and the Origins of the Cold War, 1944–1949', in A. Deighton (ed.), *Britain and the First Cold War* (Basingstoke, 1990), 167.
[70] Ibid. 168–9.
[71] R. Smith and J. Zametica, 'The Cold Warrior? Clement Attlee Reconsidered 1945–1947', *International Affairs*, 61/2 (1985), 243.

Mediterranean as a bulwark against the spread of communism, as early as 1946 they also highlighted the need to maintain bases in these areas which would enable the RAF to launch strikes against the Soviet Union.[72]

Britain's deepening economic crisis, far from convincing Bevin of the need to shed commitments, provided him with further ammunition against Attlee's internationalism. In September 1947 he told Attlee that Britain could only 'pull our weight in foreign affairs' once it was free of financial dependence on the United States. That could not be achieved purely through an export drive, but by fully mobilizing the economic resources of colonial Africa.[73] The same month, Bevin held talks with French foreign minister Georges Bidault to discuss economic cooperation in Africa. Bevin did his best to dress what might have appeared a scheme for the exploitation of Africa in progressive terms, arguing that Britain could enhance its global position, not merely by mobilizing the 'material resources' of its colonial empire, but by organizing and consolidating 'the ethical and spiritual forces inherent in this Western civilisation of which we are the chief protagonists'.[74] In March 1948, the suggestion was still being made in cabinet that Anglo-American cooperation was merely a temporary necessity and that if Britain developed Africa, the US, which lacked essential mineral resources of its own, would be 'eating out of our hand in four or five years'.[75] Yet the disastrous East African groundnut scheme would shortly illustrate the difficulties of mobilizing Africa for the purposes of Britain's economic recovery. Nor was there much serious prospect of turning the continent into a significant military resource. The continuing poverty of Britain's African colonies made it impossible for them to raise a significantly greater number of troops to compensate for the loss of India in 1947.[76]

Running counter to Bevin's reversion to a quasi-imperial policy was the demand from the Treasury for cuts in defence expenditure in line with the post-war weakness of the British economy. The aim of boosting production in industry and agriculture required a scaling-down of the proportion of the British workforce in the armed forces. Yet Bevin's reluctance to reduce Britain's overseas commitments meant that it was only after the sterling

[72] Corum, 'Air Power and the Defence of Empire', 167.
[73] Kent, 'British Empire and the Origins of the Cold War', 178.
[74] Hyam, *Britain's Declining Empire*, 137–8.
[75] Kent, 'British Empire and the Origins of the Cold War', 178–9.
[76] French, 'British Army and Empire', 101–3.

crisis in July 1947 that the cabinet agreed to a reduction in the armed forces from 1,217,000 to 713,000 by March 1949.[77] Even this modest economy, however, would be swept away by the massive rearmament programme introduced in the wake of the outbreak of the Korean War in June 1950. Britain's growing dependence on the United States, particularly after the introduction of the Marshall Plan in 1947, served to tie it ever more firmly to the American camp in the nascent Cold War.[78] Under these circumstances, there was a widespread desire across Whitehall to prove Britain's value as an ally by increasing military spending; and this was felt as keenly by officials in Whitehall's economic planning sections as in the Foreign Office. The rearmament programme was, of course, undertaken against the background of very real fears that another world war was imminent. In December 1950, following talks in Washington, the Chief of the Imperial General Staff, Field Marshal Sir William Slim reported that 'The United States were convinced that war was inevitable, and that it was almost certain to take place within the next eighteen months'.[79] Between July and December 1950 plans for a major rearmament programme were agreed and then revised upwards on three occasions. The defence budget was finally set at £4,700 million for three years from 1951–2. As a proportion of British gross domestic product, defence spending rose from 5.8 per cent in 1949–50 to 8.7 per cent in 1952–3, a figure higher than in 1938–9.[80]

The reaction of British officials responsible for economic planning tended to focus more on the benefits of the rearmament programme for Britain's relations with the US, and hence its geopolitical status, than on the immediate damage it might do to its domestic economy. Sir Leslie Rowan, Economic Minister to Washington, encapsulated this gung-ho spirit when he suggested in July 1950 that there was 'a good chance for Britain to be treated as partners if we did our stuff'.[81] While urging the importance of maintaining dollar-earning export production, the Treasury and the Board

[77] G. Peden, 'The Treasury and the Defence of Empire', in Kennedy (ed.), *Imperial Defence*, 84.

[78] For a discussion of the changing alignment of Britain in the Cold War during this period see P. Weiler, 'British Labour and the Cold War: The Foreign Policy of the Labour Governments, 1945–1951', *Journal of British Studies*, 26/1 (1987), 54–82.

[79] Burk, *Old World, New World*, 594.

[80] Peden, 'Treasury and Defence of Empire', 85.

[81] J. Park, 'Wasted Opportunities? The 1950s Rearmament Programme and the Failure of British Economic Policy', *Journal of Contemporary History*, 23/3 (1997), 359.

of Trade were ready to concede that defence might have to take precedence. Only when the last increase had been agreed in December did officials begin to express any concerns that the cost might not be sustainable. These concerns were vindicated by the summer of 1951 when it became clear that the rearmament programme had had a far more serious impact on Britain's balance of payments than had been anticipated due, in part, to a greater-than-expected rise in the cost of imports. While Robert Hall of Whitehall's Economic Section subsequently blamed everyone else for the crisis, from 'weak' ministers to ruthless military negotiators, it is clear that he and his fellow officials in the economic planning sections exerted remarkably little restraining influence on the escalation of defence spending.

There can be no question about the heavy economic price the British paid for their rearmament programme, in terms both of the boost it gave to inflation and of its role in diverting energies away from exports at a moment when British goods had been made more competitive by the 1949 devaluation of the pound.[82] Ultimately, however, it presented only a temporary obstacle to Britain's economic recovery. Longer-term impediments were offered by some other imperial legacies which continued to shape the outlook of British politicians and officials. One was the failure to recognize the need to reorient British trade towards the non-sterling countries of the Organization for European Economic Cooperation (OEEC), and a corresponding faith in the Commonwealth's ability to recover some of its previous value as a market for British exports.[83] Another was the priority given to the balance of payments over economic growth so as to preserve the international value of sterling and hence its role as an international reserve currency.[84] Nevertheless, the failure to achieve significant defence cuts in the late 1940s, and the escalation of defence spending in the early 1950s, left British policy-makers with the problem of attempting to bring defence spending in line with the capacity of Britain's faltering economy.

At the same time, it quickly became clear that the idea that British support for the United States over Korea would help to underwrite Britain's great power status was ill-founded. Aside from the damage that was done to the British economy, the military engagement in Korea placed a further strain on Britain's armed forces, which were already struggling to cope with

---

[82] Holland, *Pursuit of Greatness*, 233–4.
[83] Park, 'Wasted Opportunities?', 368–9.
[84] Ibid. 370–1.

a series of major commitments around the world, not least the Malayan Emergency. Furthermore, if the affair had strengthened Anglo-American relations, the two sides had quite distinct differences of approach to international politics. If Attlee's successful appeal to Truman in December 1950 to refrain from the use of the nuclear bomb in Korea appeared to represent a victory for British influence over the US, there were to be few comparable examples in the post-war era. Indeed, writing in 1983, Anthony Verrier described this (at the risk both of exaggerating the impact of Attlee's appeal and of denigrating subsequent British diplomacy) as 'the last time an American President took the advice of a British Prime Minister'.[85] Conversely, the notion that the Americans might have been prepared to expose Britain to a nuclear attack by the Soviet Union in retaliation for a US attack on China left a legacy of suspicion in Anglo-American relations.[86] Fears that its close relationship with the US might be an obstacle to British foreign policy gained further ground in May 1951, when Prime Minister Mosaddeq of Iran nationalized the Anglo-Persian Oil Company. No longer able to call upon the Indian army, and with its 80,000 troops in the Suez Canal Zone lacking the logistical support to enable it to be easily deployed elsewhere, the military options open to Britain were severely limited. Both the British Foreign Secretary, Herbert Morrison, and the Minister of Defence, Emanuel Shinwell, favoured an invasion to protect British interests. Yet faced with the knowledge that the US opposed armed intervention, Attlee vetoed the plan in cabinet.[87]

Under the administrations of Churchill and Eden, Attlee's immediate successors, two stark realities—Britain's subordination to US power, and the crippling economic burden its global military commitments were imposing on the British economy—became ever more apparent. Churchill's belief that he could recreate his wartime negotiating position as leader of one of the 'Big Three', and mediate between the US and the Soviet Union, was regarded as a nostalgic illusion even by some of his own cabinet colleagues. Eden, his Foreign Secretary, did demonstrate through his skilful handling of German entry into the North Atlantic Treaty Organization (NATO) in 1954 and of

---

[85] A. Verrier, *Through the Looking Glass: British Foreign Policy in the Age of Illusions* (London, 1983), 92.

[86] Holland, *Pursuit of Greatness*, 235.

[87] W. R. Louis, *Ends of British Imperialism: The Scramble for Empire, Suez and Decolonization* (London, 2006), 735–6.

the Geneva conference on the future of South East Asia, that Britain could still exert a constructive and relatively independent role in global affairs. As Prime Minister, however, Eden notoriously overreached himself in attempting to defy American wishes in the Middle East. He told the cabinet in October 1955 that Britain should not feel 'restricted overmuch by a reluctance to act without full American concurrence and support'.[88] The following year, the failure of the Anglo-French invasion of Egypt brutally exposed the folly of this sentiment.[89] At the same time, the Churchill and Eden governments were provided with ever more stark warnings that Britain's global commitments were out of all proportion to its economic means. In June 1956 a ministerial Policy Review Committee considered a paper on 'The future of the United Kingdom in world affairs', drawn up by officials from the Treasury, the Foreign Office, and the Ministry of Defence. It contained the stark conclusion that Britain had 'ceased to be a first-class power in material terms', and warned that ever since the war 'we have tried to do too much – with the result that we have only rarely been free from the danger of economic crisis'.[90]

In practice, however, strong arguments could be, and were, made that any sudden reduction in Britain's overseas commitments could have damaging repercussions, many of which would adversely affect Britain itself. Powerful voices around the cabinet table were always on hand to outline these consequences. The Foreign Secretary and the Chiefs of Staff could point both to the political and strategic dangers of weakening Western defence by any reduction in Britain's commitment to NATO and to its other overseas military responsibilities, and to the economic dangers of losing control of vital supply routes and commodity-producing areas.[91] The Commonwealth Relations and Colonial Secretaries could point to the damage that would be done to British prestige, and to the instability that would be generated by any precipitate withdrawal from its existing commitments. The Chiefs of

---

[88] Reynolds, *From World War to Cold War: Churchill, Roosevelt and the International History of the 1940s* (Oxford, 2006), 204.

[89] It is worth noting, however, that in his new biography *Harold Macmillan* (London, 2009), C. Williams suggests there is little convincing evidence to support the conventional view that the US used its economic leverage at the World Bank to put economic pressure on the UK during the time of the crisis.

[90] D. Goldsworthy, *British Documents on the End of Empire: The Conservative Government and the End of Empire, 1951–1957*, pt.1 1 (London, 1994), pp. xxviii–xxix.

[91] Ibid. pp. xxvi–xxvii.

Staff were in a particularly powerful position to put the political, strategic, and economic case for the maintenance of high levels of defence expenditure. Despite the creation of the Ministry of Defence in 1946, the ability of ministers to exercise effective control over defence spending was hampered by powerful navy and air force lobbies at Westminster, by the direct access of the service chiefs to the cabinet, and by the fact that the three service budgets were negotiated separately.[92] While Correlli Barnett's attacks on the 'nostalgic self-delusion' of British policy-makers, determined to act as 'house prefects to the world', clearly have some force, he arguably underrates the concrete institutional impediments to dramatic cuts in British overseas expenditure.[93]

The determination of the Chiefs of Staff to maintain Britain as a leading military power coexisted increasingly uneasily with what was probably the government's central global objective in the twenty years after the end of the Second World War. The June 1956 paper on 'The future of the United Kingdom in world affairs', argued that the preservation of the international value of sterling was 'the greatest single contribution we can make to the maintenance of our own position in world affairs and to the success of the policies which the free world is seeking to pursue'.[94] The government proved determined to defend sterling parity with the dollar at the $2.80 level it had been set in 1949. During Churchill's second administration, 'ROBOT', a radical scheme supported by the Treasury and the Bank of England to 'float' the pound, was defeated not least because of fierce criticism from the Foreign Office.[95] Parity with the dollar was viewed as essential in order to maintain sterling as a reserve currency and to protect the sterling area. The government was reluctant to see a running-down of sterling balances, even though, once they became largely convertible in 1955, they left the pound highly vulnerable to speculative attacks.[96] Its fixation with sterling and the maintenance of parity also left it heavily dependent on the United States. In the Suez Crisis of 1956, these two points of vulnerability—the risk of speculative attacks and dependence on the US—combined to undermine Britain's reassertion of imperial power. As James M. Boughton notes: 'If devaluation

---

[92] Reynolds, *From World War to Cold War*, 210.

[93] Barnett, *Lost Victory*.

[94] Goldsworthy, *British Documents on the End of Empire*, pp. xxviii–xxix.

[95] J. Darwin, *The Empire Project: The Rise and Fall of the British World-System 1830–1970* (Cambridge, 2009), 584–5.

[96] Reynolds, *From World War to Cold War*, 209.

or floating had been viable, the United Kingdom could have resisted external financial pressures for long enough to wage what would likely have been an effective military campaign against Egypt.'[97] In the wake of Suez, as before, the continued defence of sterling parity was the Exchequer's justification for demanding major cuts to the defence budget.[98] Yet ironically, this same British obsession with the value of sterling was also to be used as a lever by the US in the 1960s in their attempts to persuade Britain to retain a military presence East of Suez. Strong hints from the US that their willingness to support sterling might be weakened by a British withdrawal from Asia, was a factor which limited British freedom of manoeuvre prior to devaluation in 1967.

The shock administered by the Suez Crisis in the autumn of 1956 provided ministers and officials with an opportunity to question some of the well-worn assumptions behind British foreign policy. One product of this reassessment was the Defence White Paper of 1957, which signalled a move away from a conscript army towards a greater reliance on nuclear deterrence. Another was the audit, conducted by British officials in 1957 at Macmillan's instigation, of the financial benefits and burdens entailed by colonial possessions. It has been suggested that the latter marked a shift away from the 'evolutionary' approach of Alan Lennox-Boyd as Colonial Secretary from 1954 to 1959, to the 'radical' one of his successor, Iain Macleod.[99] Arguably, however, this underestimates the underlying pragmatism of both Lennox-Boyd and Macleod. It also fails to acknowledge the extent to which, even before Suez, the British recognized that the goodwill engendered by an amicable transition to independence was a better guarantee of British economic interests than the preservation of colonial rule in the face of growing opposition.[100] At the same time, Suez certainly did not cause British policy-makers to renounce their aspirations to great-power status. Although Britain shed the greater part of its remaining territorial responsibilities under the Macmillan governments, a strong determination survived in Whitehall during these years that Britain should remain a global

[97] James M. Boughton, 'Northwest of Suez: The 1956 Crisis and the IMF', *IMF Staff Papers*, 48/3 (2001), 435.

[98] Reynolds, *From World War to Cold War*, 211.

[99] T. Hopkins, 'Macmillan's Audit of Empire, 1957', in Peter Clarke and Clive Treblicock (eds.), *Understanding Decline: Perceptions and Realities of British Economic Performance* (Cambridge, 1997), 234–60.

[100] P. Murphy, *Alan Lennox-Boyd: A Biography* (London, 1999), 169–70.

power. Britain would retain a string of bases, 'our Gibraltars' as Macmillan put it, stretching across the Mediterranean, Africa, the Indian Ocean, and the Far East, which would continue to give the UK a genuinely global military reach.[101] It was envisaged that even former colonies would play a role in this strategic formation, and treaties guaranteeing Britain ownership of or access to bases were incorporated in the independence settlements of Ceylon, Cyprus, Malaya, and Nigeria. When Ceylon received its independence in 1948, for example, it granted the Royal Navy the use of Trincomalee, which became Britain's East Indies Station. Even when the station was disbanded in 1958 and British forces departed, responsibility for the area was simply divided between the Far East Command, the Atlantic and South American Command, and the Arabian Seas and Persian Gulf Station. As Ashley Jackson notes, the example of Ceylon 'reveals two enduring British defence themes: on the one hand, the desire never to abandon a commitment, even when that commitment was being scaled down; on the other hand, the habit of stretching resources (some would say overstretching) to continue to meet those commitments'.[102]

Europe, Decolonization, and the 'Special Relationship'

The principal foreign policy objective of the incoming Macmillan government was to repair relations with the United States. The Macmillan years are generally seen as one of the smoother periods of that relationship, between the Suez debacle of 1956 and tensions over British withdrawal from East of Suez in the second half of the 1960s. Even then, however, behind an apparently successful record of Anglo-American cooperation in the Middle East and elsewhere in the developing world, lay profound differences in the ways in which British and American policy-makers analysed international affairs.[103] Over the Belgian Congo and British Guiana, UK and US policy-makers were positively at odds with one another, and the American cancellation of the Skybolt missile system in 1962 provoked a crisis in Anglo-American

---

[101] W. R. Louis, 'The Dissolution of the British Empire', in *OHBE* iv. 344.

[102] Jackson, 'Imperial Defence in the Post-Imperial Era', in Kennedy (ed.), *Imperial Defence*, 309–10.

[103] N. J. Ashton, 'Anglo-American Revival and Empire during the Macmillan Years, 1957–1963', in M. Lynn (ed.), *The British Empire in the 1950s: Retreat or Revival* (Basingstoke, 2006), 167.

relations that was only resolved by the swift decision of Kennedy to offer Britain the Polaris nuclear delivery system.

Meanwhile the perception of Great Britain as being America's principal ally in Europe provided a complicating factor in a new dimension of Britain's foreign policy: its relationship with the European Economic Community (EEC), which came into existence on 1 January 1958. At the beginning of June 1950, Britain had declined an invitation to take part in talks on the Schuman Plan for a European coal and steel community, the predecessor organization of the EEC. The immediate impediment for Britain had been its reluctance to give an undertaking in advance of talks to accept some pooling of sovereignty.[104] Yet a number of other factors fed into this decision, factors that were to continue to shape British attitudes towards European integration. The first was a sense that membership of some form of European union would compromise Britain's key political relationships with the Commonwealth and the United States. The second was a belief that Britain's economic alignment was principally with the sterling area rather than with Europe. Certainly in 1949, continental Europe still took only a quarter of Britain's exports compared with the half that went to sterling area countries.[105] With the dramatic recovery of the economies of the EEC member states, the significance for Britain of trade with Europe steadily increased. Nevertheless, by 1960 the Commonwealth was still taking over 40 per cent of British exports, and it was only in the following year that British exports to Europe overtook those to the Commonwealth.[106] The third factor in British calculations was a misguided belief that the six founder members first of the European Coal and Steel Community and then of the EEC would not be able to reach agreement or make their chosen form of association work.

Related to this was an equally misguided belief that the Six would be prepared to embrace some alternative scheme put forward by Britain which would enable the latter both to preserve its preferential trading agreements with the Commonwealth and to gain access to the growing European market. This led first, from July 1956, to the British government's 'Plan G', a scheme for a free trade area which would include the Six and other OEEC nations, and then, when that did not prove acceptable to the Six, to a plan

[104] J. W. Young, *Britain and European Unity, 1945–1992* (Basingstoke, 1993), 28–35.
[105] Reynolds, *From World War to Cold War*, 193.
[106] Ibid. 222; Young, *Britain and European Unity*, 76.

for a separate free trade area running parallel to the EEC. Yet by the time the agreement for the latter scheme, known as the European Free Trade Area (EFTA), was signed in October 1959, the obvious success of the EEC and fears on the part of British manufacturers that they might be excluded from this vibrant market, were placing increasing pressure on the Macmillan government to consider seeking full membership of the EEC.[107] By July 1961, when the cabinet decided to apply, it was clear that neither the Commonwealth nor EFTA could compensate for the effects of Britain's continuing exclusion from the EEC.

Yet the Macmillan administration's desire to bring the UK into the EEC ultimately proved impossible to reconcile with the British government's other, longer-standing priorities of strengthening the Anglo-American alliance and maintaining an 'independent' nuclear deterrent. The 'American factor' was not a wholly negative one in Britain's attempts to negotiate entry. Australia, for example, was keen that Britain should retain a military presence in South East Asia, and was therefore suspicious of Britain's decision to apply for membership of the EEC, fearing that this would lead to the termination of preferential trading arrangements with the Commonwealth and might herald a general realignment of the UK towards Europe. Yet given that British membership of the EEC was a significant foreign policy objective of the US, Australia's Prime Minister, Sir Robert Menzies, was reluctant to cast himself in the role of an obstacle to that goal.[108]

Ultimately however, Britain's relationship with the US was to prove fatal to Macmillan's European ambitions. The Nassau Pact on the supply of the Polaris system to the UK confirmed de Gaulle's suspicions that Britain would be a 'Trojan horse' of American influence within the EEC, and in January 1963 he effectively vetoed the British application for entry. Thereafter, along with fears that British entry would undermine plans for a Common Agricultural Policy (CAP) favourable to the interests of French farmers, the UK's strong links with the US continued to be a key factor in de Gaulle's opposition to British membership of the EEC. De Gaulle, who removed France from the command structures of NATO in March 1966, envisaged a French-led EEC which would be able to mediate between the US

---

[107] Young, *Britain and European Unity*, 69.

[108] A. Benvenuti, 'Australian Reactions to Britain's Declining Presence in Southeast Asia, 1955–63', *JICH* 34/3 (2006), 421–2.

and Soviet-led blocs in the pursuit of détente. The inclusion of a British government closely allied to the US would have undermined that objective.[109] De Gaulle vetoed Britain's second application for membership in November 1967, and it was only his resignation in 1969 that left the way open for a third, successful application for entry under the Heath administration. At the same time, the failed first application for EEC membership under Macmillan may have hastened the process of political and cultural estrangement between Britain and the Commonwealth. In the case of Australia, its political leaders were conscious of the degree to which the Commonwealth had proved an obstacle to these negotiations and were convinced that Britain would be far more ruthless in any future application in pursuing narrowly national interests.[110]

Although the leader of Labour Party, Harold Wilson, was ultimately to accept the logic of Macmillan's application to the EEC, on becoming Prime Minister in 1964, Wilson still appeared to hold some distinctly 'traditional' notions of Britain's global destiny. He told the House of Commons in December 1964 that Britain could not afford to relinquish its world role, and notoriously announced the following June that 'Britain's frontiers are on the Himalayas'.[111] His early decisions to resist a devaluation of sterling and to maintain Britain's nuclear deterrent both appeared to signal a determination that Britain should maintain its global influence in finance and defence. Wilson also envisaged an enhanced role for the Commonwealth. Yet as with the Attlee administration, his government could not resist placing a socialist gloss on these global ambitions. Britain's leadership was to be based on 'progressive' values—demonstrating to its foreign and Commonwealth partners that the UK was 'at one with them in the things that matter to them—in fighting oppression and racialism'.[112]

In practice, however, the Wilson administration was to oversee perhaps the most comprehensive realignment of British foreign policy in the postwar era. Ironically, it was the widespread sense that Wilson was failing to fight 'oppression and racialism' in Southern Rhodesia, which illegally declared its independence in November 1965, that rapidly soured relations

[109] See H. Parr, 'Saving the Community: The French Response to Britain's Second EEC Application in 1967', *Cold War History*, 6/5 (2006), 425–54.

[110] For a discussion of this theme see S. Ward, *Australia and the British Embrace: The Demise of the Imperial Ideal* (Melbourne, 2001).

[111] Holland, *Pursuit of Greatness*, 318–20.

[112] Hyam, *Britain's Declining Empire*, 332.

with the Commonwealth. Wilson found himself harangued over Britain's failure to take stronger measures against Rhodesia by his fellow Commonwealth prime ministers when they met in September 1966. Two months later, his new Foreign Secretary, George Brown, spoke of 'developments in the Commonwealth that may make it more difficult for us to exercise worldwide influence as the central nation in that multi-racial community'.[113] The Rhodesian crisis in turn had a dual impact on the Wilson government's attitude to the EEC. On the one hand, membership appeared to offer the chance to offset the damage that might be done to the British economy by mandatory sanctions against Rhodesia. On the other, growing friction with the Commonwealth served to convince Wilson that it would not provide an effective basis for British global power.[114] By the late 1960s it was becoming clear that even within the old dominions, the traditional cultural and constitutional ties to the metropole, based around a shared sense of 'Britishness' and a common allegiance to the Crown, were steadily eroding.[115] The Wilson government's estrangement from the Commonwealth was further encouraged by domestic political pressures. In the 1964 general election, Wilson's prospective Foreign Secretary, Patrick Gordon Walker, was defeated in his Smethwick constituency after an explicitly racist campaign by his Tory opponent which delivered the largest swing to the Conservatives in any seat in the country. A determination not to be out-flanked on the right over the issue of Commonwealth immigration persuaded the Wilson government to tighten controls in 1965 and again in 1968.

The most dramatic indication of Britain's changed role in the world came with the announcement by Wilson in January 1968 that British forces would be withdrawn from their bases 'East of Suez' by the end of 1971. This was not, as recent research has made clear, a sudden rejection by Wilson of his earlier support for Britain's continued global role.[116] As early as 1961, the government of Harold Macmillan had identified South East Asia as an area

[113] P. Alexander, 'A Tale of Two Smiths: The Transformation of Commonwealth Policy, 1964–1970', *Contemporary British History* (*CBH*), 20/3 (2006), 309.

[114] Hyam, *Britain's Declining Empire*, 341.

[115] A. G. Hopkins has recently argued that the focus in the historiography of British decolonization on the emergence of the 'new Commonwealth' has distracted attention from the parallel process of cultural and political estrangement from Britain in the 'old Dominions'. See 'Rethinking Decolonization', *P&P* 200 (Aug. 2008), 211–47.

[116] For the best overview of this subject see S. Dockrill, *Britain's Retreat from East of Suez: The Choice between Europe and the World?* (Basingstoke, 2002).

in which British forces could be substantially reduced.[117] Three years later, the prospect of achieving a major cut in the costs of British military activity in the region appeared no less attractive. By that stage, however, the development of the Indonesian confrontation with Malaysia and the escalating US engagement in Vietnam meant that the Americans were keen that the British military presence in the region should be maintained. Indeed, the Foreign Office Planning Staff concluded that 'we need to maintain our effort in the area if we are to keep our position as a world power and the United States' principal partner'.[118]

The ending of the confrontation with Indonesia in 1966 considerably expanded the government's freedom of action. Wilson's Defence Review, published in February 1966, noted that Britain's involvement in conflicts around the world had shown little indication of diminishing, with forces being despatched to eight trouble spots in 1963, sixteen in 1964, and seventeen in 1965.[119] The Review's conclusion, that defence spending should be cut from 7 to 6 per cent of GDP by 1969–70, signalled a clear determination to reduce the scope of those commitments. The Wilson government continued to face considerable US pressure to preserve the British presence in South East Asia. Yet this provided Wilson with a useful bargaining chip in his negotiations with the Johnson administration. When urged to send British troops to Vietnam, Wilson's ministers could claim that Britain was already making an important contribution to fighting the Cold War in South East Asia through its presence in Malaysia. Indeed, even the application for membership of the EEC was deployed by Wilson in the cause of keeping Britain out of Vietnam. In the face of Johnson's hostility to the notion of British withdrawal from South East Asia, Wilson suggested to him in April 1967 that the UK was shifting its role to providing leadership in the European Community, as the United States had long been urging. Wilson later rather disingenuously told the cabinet that the only alternative to British membership of the EEC was to join the Americans in Vietnam.[120]

[117] M. Jones, 'A Decision Delayed: Britain's Withdrawal from South East Asia Reconsidered', *EHR* 117/472 (2002), 575.

[118] Ibid. 578.

[119] D. Sanders, *Losing an Empire, Finding a Role: British Foreign Policy since 1945* (Basingstoke, 1990), 228.

[120] H. Parr, 'Britain, America, East of Suez and the EEC: Finding a Role in British Foreign Policy, 1964–1967', *CBH* 20/3 (2006), 412.

The deterioration in Anglo-American relations that was sparked by Wilson's decision to withdraw troops from East of Suez continued after 1970 under the premiership of his Conservative successor, Edward Heath. Heath's instincts represented a unique alignment for a post-war British prime minister, combining a commitment to Europe with a hostility to the Commonwealth and a remarkable indifference to Britain's relationship with the United States. The first of those features found momentous expression when in 1973 Heath succeeded in bringing Britain into the EEC. The final feature was also apparent in 1973, when Heath aligned Britain with other Western European leaders in refusing to make base facilities available to the Americans in their operation to supply Israel in the Yom Kippur war.[121] Indeed, in retrospect, the 1970s as a whole can appear as a marked hiatus in Britain's global ambitions, with the virtual completion of the process of decolonization, a belated recognition among British policymakers of Britain's European identity, and with Anglo-American relations at their most distant for decades. On this latter point, the process of détente clearly reduced the significance of the Anglo-American relationship to the US, just as the advent of the 'second Cold War' from the late 1970s served to increase it. One historian of the period claims that 'by 1974, Britain's world role had been almost completely abandoned'.[122] This was certainly the impression given by some official pronouncements at the time. The Wilson government's 1975 Defence White Paper referred to Britain's 'former aspirations to a world-wide role'.[123]

The Durability of Britain's Global Responsibilities and the 'Special Relationship'

There is, however, a danger of exaggerating this retreat from a global role and missing the continuities in British policy. First, Britain's attitude towards its European identity remained distinctly ambivalent. Despite the clear victory of the pro-European camp in Wilson's 1975 referendum on continued EEC membership, anti-European rhetoric remained a prominent feature of British political discourse. This owed much to the timing of British entry. By 1973 the EEC had developed a set of policies geared far more closely to the economies of its original member states than to that of the UK with the unusually small proportion of its workforce employed in

---

[121] Sanders, *Losing an Empire*, 177.   [122] Ibid. 229.   [123] Ibid.

agriculture and its heavy dependence on food imported from outside Europe. British entry into the EEC also coincided with the onset of the global economic crisis sparked by the Arab–Israeli conflict of October 1973. As David Reynolds notes, Britain joined the Community 'at the worst possible moment, when the basic institutions were set to its detriment, and when economic recession minimised both the chances of institutional reform and also the opportunities presented by the enlarged common market'.[124] Yet there was also, arguably, a more fundamental mismatch between the principles of reciprocity and solidarity which underlay the EEC and the British desire to use membership as the instrument for a specifically national revival.[125]

Secondly, Heath's downgrading of Britain's Atlantic and Commonwealth ties proved remarkably short-lived. When Labour returned to power in 1974, Wilson signalled 'business as usual' with the appointment as Foreign Secretary of the staunchly Atlanticist James Callaghan. As with previous and future Labour governments, the Wilson and Callaghan administrations of the 1970s found it remarkably easy to reconcile a traditional vision of Britain's global responsibilities with the morally charged rhetoric of socialist internationalism. This was partly achieved through an emphasis on Britain playing a constructive role in international organizations including the UN and the Commonwealth.[126] Tensions remained between the British and US positions, not least over their analyses of the Soviet Union. With their long experience of dealing with Russia, Callaghan and Wilson were more inclined than the Americans to believe in the possibility of constructive engagement. Nevertheless, this was combined with a firm belief that détente could best be achieved by the West negotiating from a position of strength. It convinced them of the need to maintain a strong British contribution to NATO, to keep pace with developments in weapons technology, and to replace the Polaris nuclear missile system. In its dying days, the Callaghan government was close to reaching a decision to buy the American-built Trident missile

[124] Reynolds, *From World War to Cold War*, 246.

[125] For an exploration of this theme see C. Lord, *British Entry to the European Community under the Heath Government of 1970–1974* (Aldershot, 1993).

[126] A. Lane, 'Foreign and Defence Policy', in A. Seldon and K. Hickson (eds.), *New Labour, Old Labour: The Wilson and Callaghan Governments 1974–1979* (London, 2004), 155–6. Lane concludes that 'Labour came to office [in 1974] with a much bigger view of the world and of Britain's potential for a role in it in the future than had been the case during the Heath administration'.

system. In the event, it would be Callaghan's Conservative successor, Margaret Thatcher, who took this decision, one that would further underline Britain's heavy dependence on the United States in the area of defence.[127]

This commitment to the defence of Europe, obliged the Labour governments of the 1970s to find savings elsewhere. It is a mark of the incomplete nature of the so-called withdrawal from 'East of Suez', that the defence review of 1974 and the Defence White Paper of March 1975 were able to identify further cuts in this region.[128] Indeed, as Ashley Jackson notes, the range of British commitments that continued into the 1970s was impressive.[129] Britain played a role in the South East Asia Treaty Organization (SEATO) until 1977, and in the Central Treaty Organization (CENTO) until 1979. Although Britain's Far East Command in Singapore was dissolved in 1971, Britain maintained a presence there through the Australia–New Zealand–UK (ANZUK) Force which lasted from 1971 to 1974, and through the establishment in 1971 of a Five Power Defence Arrangement (FPDA) between Australia, Britain, Malaysia, New Zealand, and Singapore. As well as creating an Integrated Air Defence System for the Malayan peninsula, the FPDA provided a framework for intergovernmental consultations and joint military exercises. Even with the loss of bases in Singapore and Aden, Britain continued to operate from a series of smaller bases across the Far East, the Indian Ocean, and the Mediterranean, such as Gan Island in the Maldives until 1986 and Mauritius until 1976. Indeed, one by-product of the adoption of the sea-based Polaris missile system was to increase the navy's interest in 'imperial fragments' which could provide transponder stations for maintaining communications with their submarines.[130] Oman provided an important base for British intervention in Kuwait in 1991, and it continued to support British military operations elsewhere in the Middle East. Britain rented military facilities on Malta until 1979, and still, of course, has facilities on Gibraltar and the sovereign bases of Cyprus (the latter providing the largest RAF base outside Britain). An important aspect of the creation of the British Indian Ocean Territory from the Chagos Archipelago in the 1960s, was not just to provide the US

---

[127] Ibid. 161.

[128] A. Jackson, 'Empire and Beyond: The Pursuit of Overseas National Interests in the Late Twentieth Century', *EHR* 123/499 (2007), 1350–66.

[129] Jackson, 'Imperial Defence in the Post-Imperial Era', 311–20.

[130] J. Black, *The British Seaborne Empire* (New Haven, 2004), 337.

with a base in the Indian Ocean, but also to allow Britain itself continuing access to military facilities in the region if other bases were closed down. Britain established the Armilla Patrol in the Gulf in 1979. Meanwhile, in a struggle as Jackson nicely puts it 'always uncomfortably located somewhere in the interstices between colonial and domestic history', British forces in Northern Ireland sought to apply counter-insurgency techniques developed in Malaya, Kenya, and Cyprus.[131]

The areas of intelligence and nuclear weaponry provided an 'underground stream' of routine day-to-day cooperation which gave reality to the 'special relationship' with the US even at times when relations between the two governments were ostensibly relatively cool. A report by the US State Department's Bureau of Intelligence and Research in advance of Harold Wilson's visit to Washington in February 1968 commented that 'the most concrete proof that the United States and the United Kingdom are each other's favoured partner is found in the fields of nuclear weaponry and intelligence. Each government provides the other with material and information that it makes available to no one else'.[132] Again, Britain's 'residual empire' provided an important element in intelligence liaison. Despite, for example the divergence between British and US policies towards the People's Republic of China, access to the British-controlled territory of Hong Kong provided the CIA with an invaluable 'watchtower on China' during this period.[133] In return, of course, intelligence liaison offered Britain important support in the defence of its residual empire. An example of the way in which intelligence provided an invisible thread running through the 'special relationship' was the Falklands conflict of 1982. While the United States sought to maintain a public pretence of neutrality, largely for Latin American consumption, its transmission of satellite intelligence to London was an important element in Britain's ultimate, close-run victory.[134]

---

[131] Jackson, 'Empire and Beyond', 1363.

[132] R. J. Aldrich, '"The Value of Residual Empire": Anglo-American Intelligence Co-operation in Asia after 1945', in R. J. Aldrich and M. F. Hopkins, *Intelligence Defence and Diplomacy: British Policy in the Post-War World* (Ilford, 1994), 227. Aldrich has recently noted (GCHQ (London, 2010), 289) that in 1973, as a mark of its frustration with the UK, the Nixon administration sought to suspend some aspects of intelligence liaison. Even then, however, it is not clear that the US agencies fully complied.

[133] Ibid. 232–6.

[134] Sanders, *Losing an Empire*, 180.

By that stage, of course, the climate of Anglo-American relations had again changed. The election of Margaret Thatcher in 1979 and Ronald Reagan in 1980 put politicians into power in Downing Street and the Oval Office with remarkably similar instincts in foreign and domestic policy. In the foreign policy sphere, this manifested itself in a determination to challenge Communism across the globe, which encouraged, in its turn, a shared attitude to another of Britain's imperial legacies—the problem of South Africa. The logic of Cold War confrontation encouraged both Thatcher and Reagan to resist the imposition of economic sanctions on South Africa.[135] In a broader sense, the advent of the 'Second Cold War' had begun to strengthen Anglo-American ties, and with them Britain's sense of a renewed global role even before Reagan had come to power. The Soviet invasion of Afghanistan in 1979 had created a new, extra-European focus in the Cold War. In January 1980, at the beginning of the Carter administration's final year in office, Britain's decision to accept the deployment of cruise missiles on its soil marked a significant reassertion of the UK's role as America's principal ally in Europe.[136]

NATO, which since 1949 had involved Britain in an unprecedented commitment to the defence of continental Europe, had a paradoxical impact on the country's strategic priorities. On the one hand, it increasingly allowed the army to take priority over the navy in the allocation of the defence budget. On the other hand, the very success of NATO in deterring Soviet aggression, combined with Britain's economic vulnerability to the disruption of global trading routes and its continuing commitment to the defence of a string of dependent territories, meant that actual conflicts were more likely to erupt outside Europe, with the consequent need for a maritime capability.[137] This paradox made itself felt in the 1980s. In 1982, British defence spending of around $27 billion a year was about the same in absolute terms as France or West Germany. As a proportion of GDP, however, it was much higher—5.2 per cent, compared with 4.2 per cent for France and 3.4 per cent for West Germany.[138] Even the Thatcher government, with its strong commitment to defence, recognized that cuts in this area were inevitable. Since the defence of Europe and Britain's status as a

---

[135] Ibid. 182–3.
[136] Ibid. 178.
[137] H. Strachan, 'The British Way in Warfare Revisited', *HJ* 26/2 (1983), 449.
[138] Reynolds, *From World War to Cold War*, 277–8.

nuclear power were regarded as sacrosanct, it was the Royal Navy which was
the principal target for cuts when the government's Defence White Paper
was published in June 1981. Yet the outbreak of the Falklands conflict the
following year provided a stark and unexpected warning of the vulnerability
of British dependencies, and offered naval chiefs an opportunity to assert
the value of their service.

Having seen how divisive the 1981 review had been amongst their own
backbenchers and how quickly it had been overtaken by the repercussions of
the Falklands crisis, Conservative ministers shied away from full-blown
defence reviews for the rest of the decade. They subsequently undertook
the more limited 'Options for Change' exercise in 1990–1, and the 'Defence
Costs Study' in 1994, which focused on support services.[139] The broad policy
concerns of the Major government on the issues of defence and foreign
policy strongly resembled those of British governments in previous decades
and in turn helped to shape the Blair government's Strategic Defence Review
of 1998. On the one hand, there was considerable pressure from the Treasury
for reductions in the burden of defence expenditure, particularly in the light
of the ending of the Cold War. The desire for a 'peace dividend' was such
that by 1997, the defence budget represented a smaller proportion of GDP
than at any time in the twentieth century, and the size of the armed forces
was smaller than it had been since the 1930s. Nevertheless, Conservative
ministers displayed little inclination to shed responsibilities and continued
to stress Britain's global role. Writing in 1991, Adrian Smith noted that
Britain still retained 'a unique range of post-imperial strategic commitments'. Indeed, 'No other advanced industrial nation (including France and
the United States) has its defence programme—and framework for defence
decision making—so clearly determined by its past'.[140] With the dramatic
reduction of the threat of a major war in Europe, however, there was a new
emphasis on the need for more flexible forces, capable of being deployed
quickly to areas away from those where British troops had traditionally been
based, yet able to engage in major conflicts and not merely 'low-intensity'
operations. While this was a relative novelty in the post-war area, it was in a
sense, a return to a longer tradition of British military organization.

[139] C. McInnes, 'Labour's Strategic Defence Review', *International Affairs*, 74/4 (1998), 824.
[140] A. Smith, 'Command and Control in Postwar Britain: Defence Decision-Making in the
United Kingdom, 1945–1984', *Twentieth Century British History*, 2/3 (1991), 232.

Determined not to be portrayed as 'soft on defence' as it had been in the 1980s, Labour came to power in 1997 broadly committed to the defence policies of the Major government including a commitment to NATO and the transatlantic alliance and to the retention of the Trident nuclear missile system. Hence, having promised a review of defence policy in its manifesto, its room for manoeuvre was distinctly limited. The 1998 Strategic Defence Review (SDR) stressed the centrality of NATO and envisaged no expanded military role for Britain in European Union-based structures. It also spoke of a new series of global threats and promised two new aircraft carriers, to be deployed after 2012, to replace three smaller carriers with the aim of facilitating the projection of Britain's global power. As the Major government had done, Labour's SDR insisted that troops should be equipped to fight in a variety of scenarios including 'high-intensity' ones. Like the Attlee and Wilson governments before it, however, the Blair administration felt the need to put a progressive gloss on what might have appeared to be a very traditional assertion of Britain's self-image as a global power. It stated:

The British are, by instinct, an internationalist people. We believe that as well as defending our rights, we should discharge our responsibilities in the world. We do not want to stand idly by and watch humanitarian disasters or the aggression of dictators go unchecked. We want to give a lead, we want to be a force for good.

Blair took up this theme in his now famous speech to the Economic Club of Chicago in April 1999. The address, major parts of which were drafted for the prime minister by Lawrence Freedman, Professor of War Studies at King's College, London, came against the backdrop of Anglo-American intervention in Kosovo. Setting out an agenda of liberal interventionism, Blair claimed: 'We are all internationalists now, whether we like it or not. We cannot refuse to participate in global markets if we want to prosper. We cannot turn our backs on conflicts and the violation of human rights in other countries if we want still to be secure.'[141] The 'moralising internationalism' which Correlli Barnett had long ago identified as a characteristic of British foreign policy-making was clearly alive and well. It certainly fitted comfortably alongside the neo-conservative agenda of the administration of George W. Bush, to which the terrorist attacks on America in September 2001 gave a renewed sense of mission and licence. For a British government which had been anxious about its 'special relationship' with the US being

---

[141] J. Kampfner, *Blair's Wars* (London, 2003), 52.

usurped by Germany, the aftermath of the 9/11 attacks provided a Korea-like opportunity to demonstrate its value as an ally by 'doing its stuff' in the subsequent occupations of Afghanistan and Iraq.

The 1998 SDR contained another familiar element: there was a commitment to cut the size of the defence budget—so that it would be £915 million lower in real terms by 2001–2. Yet there was no corresponding promise to reduce defence commitments.[142] Nor did it contemplate a greater specialization of UK forces, which would have restricted Britain's ability to act alone (despite its already heavy reliance on the US in areas such as satellite navigation and technical support for Trident). Instead, it relied on efficiency gains in areas such as procurement and the restructuring of existing forces to achieve the necessary savings.

In April 2007, shortly before Tony Blair stepped down as Prime Minister and just after the Commons had endorsed his government's decision to proceed with a replacement for the Trident missile system, the Cabinet Office published a policy statement on British foreign policy, *Building on Progress: Britain in the World*. With British forces engaged in major operations in Iraq and Afghanistan, the rhetoric of a 'force for good' was accompanied by some less than apologetic references to Britain's history of international engagement. In his Forward to the document, Blair sought to suggest that his own distinctly interventionist approach to foreign affairs emerged from a far longer tradition in national policy: 'Britain is an island nation whose role in the world has, for centuries, been global. We recognise that what happens beyond our borders can have a dramatic impact on our citizens and national interests.'[143] Responding to those who urged Britain to 'remain out of the fray', Blair claimed that this was 'not a policy that has been in Britain's best interests throughout our history, nor do I believe that it is the right course for our future'. Britain's specifically imperial record was skated over in the policy document (despite the quaintly New Labour reference to 'our historic and people-to-people links across the globe'). Meanwhile, its international role was discussed primarily in the context of joint action with the United States and the European Union, with the Commonwealth relegated to a brief paragraph. Nevertheless, lurking behind the managerial euphemisms and talk of promoting shared values was the

---

[142] McInnes, 'Labour's Strategic Defence Review', 840–1.

[143] Prime Minister's Foreword to *Building on Progress: Britain in the World* (Prime Minister's Strategy Unit, Cabinet Office, Apr. 2007).

distinct sense of an imperial power reconnecting with its past. The document suggested that, whereas in recent years Britain's military role had been envisaged in terms of relatively brief engagements, its experiences in Iraq and Afghanistan had demonstrated that future operations were 'likely to involve protracted periods of peace enforcement activity delivering long-term security solutions through stabilisation, reconstruction and re-establishment of the rule of law'.

The future sounds oddly familiar.

Select Bibliography

K. Burk, *Old World, New World: The Story of Britain and America* (London, 2007).

P. Clarke, *The Last Thousand Days of the British Empire* (London, 2007).

A. Clayton, *The British Empire as a Superpower* (Basingstoke, 1986).

J. Darwin, *The Empire Project: The Rise and Fall of the British World System, 1830–1970* (Cambridge, 2009).

D. Dockrill, *Britain's Retreat from East of Suez: The Choice between Europe and the World?* (Basingstoke, 2002).

R. Holland, *The Pursuit of Greatness: Britain and the World Role, 1900–1970* (London, 1991).

A. G. Hopkins, 'Rethinking Decolonization', *Past & Present*, 200 (Aug. 2008), 211–47.

R. Hyam, *Britain's Declining Empire: the Road to Decolonisation 1918–1968* (Cambridge, 2006).

A. Jackson, *The British Empire and the Second World War* (London, 2006).

J. Kampfner, *Blair's Wars* (London, 2003).

G. Kennedy (ed.), *Imperial Defence: The Old World Order 1856–1956* (London, 2007).

Wm. R Louis, *Ends of British Imperialism: The Scramble for Empire, Suez and Decolonization* (London, 2006).

D. Sanders, *Losing an Empire, Finding a Role: British Foreign Policy since 1945* (Basingstoke, 1990).

A. Stewart, *Empire Lost: Britain, the Dominions and the Second World War* (London, 2008).

A. Verrier, *Through the Looking Glass: British Foreign Policy in the Age of Illusions* (London, 1983).

J. W. Young, *Britain and European Unity, 1945–1992* (Basingstoke, 1993).

3

From the Empire of Christ to the Third World: Religion and the Experience of Empire in the Twentieth Century

Jeffrey Cox

The year 1910 is remembered as one of political crisis in Great Britain. Two general elections produced a political stalemate over Ireland that spiralled into a constitutional crisis. Uncertain of the role of the new monarch, George V, some people looked back to the crisis of 1830–2, and wondered if Britain would once again face the prospect of a constitutional breakdown, or even the graver possibility of civil war in Ireland. The issues that Britain faced in the decade following 1910—sovereignty in Ireland and suffrage at home, the role of trade unions and the prospects of a socialist government, global war that involved both Europe and the empire, a vastly expanded government committed to both global intervention and domestic welfare—defined the issues that have dominated public debate throughout the twentieth century. They are secular issues. With the exception of Ireland, they do not concern directly the constitutional or social role of religion in the life of Britain.

Although little noticed by historians of the twentieth century, 1910 was also notable for another event that received major attention in the press and in public debate at the time, an assembly of dignitaries from the major Protestant churches of the world at the World Missionary Conference in Edinburgh. By 1910, due to the global expansion of Christianity, the Protestant churches were no longer confined to their European and European settler heartland of Great Britain, Germany, and North America, but were spread throughout Africa, South Asia, China, and Latin America. The members of those churches were overwhelmingly non-white, but the leaders—or at least the leaders who could afford to travel to Edinburgh—were overwhelmingly white.

At the World Missionary Conference global affairs received close attention, although the European and imperial balance of power, and state and maritime security, were neglected. Since the beginnings of Protestant global expansion in the eighteenth century, British men and women with a religious point of view had put forward a distinctive interpretation of the historical role of the British empire. Critics of empire often assumed, and still assume, an identity of interests between the agents of British imperial expansion and the agents of British ecclesiastical expansion. Throughout the empire and Commonwealth in the twentieth century students encountered an exam question: 'The flag followed the cross, or the cross followed the flag. Discuss.' The close association of the two was not in question, only the order of advance.

When British Christians turned their eyes to the rest of the world, they often used language that we recognize as imperialistic, i.e. a combination of global universalism and triumphalist aggression. Congregational hymn-singing was at the heart of worship in many of Britain's churches. They sang 'Onward Christian soldiers, marching as to war; with the cross of Jesus going on before'. Where were Christians marching? Among other places, 'From Greenland's icy mountains, from India's coral strand; Where Afric's sunny fountains roll down their golden sand.' The Christian churches constituted the single most important voluntary institution in early twentieth-century Britain, enrolling the voluntary participation of millions of British people. The World Missionary Conference was a celebration of the international character of those institutions.

Despite the widespread assumption of a straightforward identity between Britain's imperial advance and the global expansion of Christianity, the empire of Christ could never be equated in any simple and straightforward way with the empire of Britain. The relationship between the cross and the flag was full of contradictions. Unlike the rulers of the Spanish and Portuguese empires, who had justified imperial expansion as a divine obligation to Christianize the world, British imperial rulers rarely thought of the British empire as an instrument of Christianization, or (except in Ireland) as a means of imposing on others a national state church. The military revolt of 1857 in India had prompted an uncharacteristically systematic explanation of Britain's imperial religious policies, Queen Victoria's proclamation of 1858: 'Firmly relying ourselves on the truth of Christianity, and acknowledging with gratitude the solace of religion, we disclaim alike the right and desire to impose our convictions on any of our subjects.'[1]

Like Britain's imperial rulers, British church leaders did not for the most part regard the British empire as a Christian empire. It was, instead, analogous to the pagan Roman empire, which had opened the door for the spread of the gospel. St Paul made use not only of his Roman citizenship but had at his disposal the convenience of safe Roman roads and Mediterranean sea lanes. The British empire, like the Roman empire, could never be treated as the empire of Christ, but as a providential convenience. Along with the spread of global capitalism and Western technology, it represented a glorious open door for those who wished to engage in voluntary efforts to Christianize the world.

However much church leaders hoped to live in a parallel universe known as the empire of Christ, they could hardly ignore the empire of Britain. The British empire provided an open door, but it was a door that imperial rulers could slam shut, which they in some times and places did. Furthermore church leaders were very much aware, from the days of Captain Cook onwards, that the British empire was an instrument of far more than political control. It was an agent of what we might now call cultural imperialism as well as global economic expansion and technological advance. Imperial rule could be a force for good or an obstacle to good. Western cultural and economic expansion could be a force for good, or a force for evil.

Basing their optimism on more than a century of Christian globalization, the pulpit rhetoricians of the World Missionary Conference surveyed a world that had been unified through Western imperial and economic expansion much as the Mediterranean world had been unified by Rome. They were speaking at a time not only of imperial expansion, but also of ecclesiastical expansion in the Protestant world. The governments of the world, including imperial governments, were judged by universal standards at Edinburgh. Did they allow Christian missionaries to operate, or not? What was their stance towards the three great social evils of the modern world—opium, alcohol, and forced labour? As they peered into the future, they saw in the signs of the times evidence of a movement towards the

---

[1] A. T. Embree, 'Christianity and the State in Victorian India: Confrontation and Collaboration', in Davis and Helmstadter (eds.), *Religion and Irreligion in Victorian Society: Essays in Honor of R. K. Webb* (London, 1992), 151.

conversion of Japan, China, and India to Christianity, a development that would go hand in hand with the rise of anti-imperialist nationalism and fundamentally change the religious dynamics of the world.

Britain's missionary leaders were very much aware that the analogy with the Roman empire implied, sooner or later, decline and fall. They hoped to construct an empire of Christ that would survive the empire of Britain. From the very first days of the missionary enterprise in the eighteenth century, missionaries in principle worked towards the goal of creating indigenous churches that would survive the end of the British empire. In the words of the influential Victorian missionary theorist Henry Venn, their goal was to create non-Western churches that would be 'self-supporting, self-governing, and self-extending'. In some ways that goal was achieved in the course of the twentieth century, but not in ways that anyone at the Edinburgh Conference could have foreseen. No one could have anticipated that in less than a century the Anglican archbishops of Nigeria and Uganda, nations with far more Anglicans than Europe and North America combined, would use their influence to have the American Episcopal Church temporarily suspended from the World Anglican Communion.

The early twentieth century was the apogee of a distinctive phase of religious history that Britain shared with Europe, lasting from the eighteenth century to the late twentieth century, one that marked the decline and transformation of a distinctively European form of religion. From the imposition of Christianity as the official religion of the Roman empire to the last great pagan state funeral in Europe, that of the Grand Duke of Lithuania in 1385, the transformation of Europe into a Christian region had been a slow and arduous process based on elite initiative. What had been created by that time was Christendom, a form of Christianity that was territorial, parochial, and controlled by elites, a religion for the people rather than a religion of the people.

Most of Europe had experienced a slow Christianization of time and space weather, culminating in the near universal adoption of the Christian sacraments as rites of passage for families and individuals. As to individual belief, it is no doubt true that on the eve of the Reformation almost all Europeans other than Jews were Christian believers of some sort. The alternatives were the sanctioned or covert continuation of pre-Christian practices, often in ways that we would label magic or 'luck', and private and in some cases communal indifference to Christian teaching. Christian religious officials certainly believed they were in a permanent war with both the widespread practice of magic and endemic popular indifference.

Hugh McLeod has identified the three most important decades in European religious history of the last half millennium as the 1520s, the 1790s, and the 1960s. Christendom was fragmented into competing Christianities at the time of the Reformation, but with marginal exceptions the major Christian churches retained a fundamental principle i.e. that religion was a matter for elites and ruling officials to provide for the people. The early sixteenth century to the late eighteenth century was the age of confessional Christendom. Europe became a patchwork of Protestant, Catholic, and Orthodox principalities.[2]

Although important elements of the old confessional forms of religion remained intact in early twentieth-century Britain, they had been by that time transformed almost beyond recognition by the emergence and growth of new forms of Christianity since the eighteenth century. The rules governing religion changed fundamentally, first in the eighteenth century, and then throughout Europe in the wake of the French revolutionary upheavals. Under the 'confessional' religious settlements of early modern Europe, religion in its public aspect was a matter for political and social elites to settle for those under their jurisdiction. Under the 'voluntarist' religious settlement in modern Europe and North America, public forms of religion are treated as consequences of the conscientious choices of individual believers, which could only happen in the context of some degree of religious toleration.

Britain emerged from the seventeenth century with a ruling class that was unwilling or unable to impose religious uniformity in the form of universal adherence to one of Britain's state churches. It was in the context of relative religious toleration that Britain's Christian institutions began to grow and multiply in the eighteenth and nineteenth centuries. The best known religious entrepreneur of the modern age was John Wesley, but church growth was much broader than Methodism or the distinctive theology that marked 'the evangelical revival'. The old state churches of Scotland and England retained many features of the old confessionalism, notably their near monopoly on the rites of passage of baptism, marriage, and funeral. By 1851, though, roughly half of Britain's churchgoing population

[2] H. McLeod, *The Religious Crisis of the 1960s* (Oxford, 2007).

practised outside the established churches.[3] They found themselves required to compete for the allegiance of the people, and that is what they did, transforming themselves over many decades into voluntary societies committed to persuasion, and scrambling to assemble voluntary contributions and public resources in the form of both taxes and government grants, especially for education.

As a result of the ecclesiastical revival of the eighteenth and nineteenth centuries, early twentieth-century Britain was blanketed with churches, staffed by hundreds of thousands of professional and volunteer church workers. It was impossible to walk down an urban street, or enter a village, without seeing a church or chapel, or several of them. By 1910 the number of church buildings of the established churches of England and Scotland constituted nearly 20,000; Baptists and Congregationalists together supported another 9,000 churches (still referred to as 'chapels' in some circles) and the various Methodist groups more than that. Roman Catholic churches, which served more persons per building than the Protestants, numbered 2,000 and growing. The church buildings were at the centre of a large penumbra of other kinds of Christian institutions, with paid and volunteer staff numbering in the hundreds of thousands. The Church of England alone boasted 24,000 ordained clergy in 1911; the Church of Scotland and its major rival, the United Free Church of Scotland, over 3,500 between them. The principal Nonconformist denominations supported in England alone over 9,500 ordained ministers and an impressive 46,000 recorded lay preachers, and those are just the men.[4]

These clergymen and ministers maintained Sunday church services for the hard core of committed Christians, and rites of passage for the large majority of the people of Britain. Sunday worship attendance was waning in the early twentieth century, although services still drew numbers that would be considered very large if the churches were simply considered another voluntary social institution rather than the heirs of a universal Christendom. Christian baptism, confirmation, marriage, and burial on the other hand were practices followed by a large majority of the people of Britain. As

[3] The best statistical treatment of the 1851 Religious Census, the basis of this assertion, remains W. S. F. Pickering, 'The 1851 Religious Census: A Useless Experiment?', *British Journal of Sociology*, 18/4 (1967), 382–407.

[4] R. Currie, A. D. Gilbert, and L. Horsley, *Churches and Churchgoers: Patterns of Church Growth in the British Isles since 1700* (Oxford, 1977).

late as the 1930s 70 per cent of all live births were followed by baptism in the Church of England, a figure that might have been an all-time high for the modern period.[5] Roughly 80 per cent of all marriages were conducted in a church or chapel in 1911, although it is important to remember that the 20 per cent married in the Registry Office were often Nonconformists rather than secularists. Despite the efforts of the Rationalist Associations and Ethical Societies, it was virtually impossible to avoid a Christian burial without considerable foresight and planning.

Local parishes and chapels in the early twentieth century sponsored or were affiliated with a vast array of religious and social welfare institutions staffed largely by paid or volunteer women. They included mothers' meetings, maternity societies, slate clubs, friendly societies, thrift societies, boot and clothing clubs, savings banks, literary societies, debating societies, girls clubs, gymnasiums, adult and children's temperance societies, uniformed organizations including the Boys' Brigades and Church Lads' Brigades, Christian Endeavour societies, vocational education classes, Bible classes, and sports clubs. Hundreds of thousands of men and women, religious activists, sustained parishes and chapels and their associated organizations. The distinctions we make in the twenty-first century between religion and philanthropy simply did not apply to many church activities in the early twentieth century. They were both part of one large project, the Christianization of Great Britain, a task that could no longer be left up to elite patronage and force of law.

Many of these institutions were directed to the young, but one in particular was virtually universal in the early twentieth century, the Sunday school. Churches recorded the enrolled Sunday scholars, and the two established churches counted a million and a half in 1911, while the principal Nonconformist denominations of England counted over 3 million, with the Wesleyan Methodists alone accounting for nearly a million children. The Free Church of Scotland added another quarter of a million, and the Presbyterian Church of Wales nearly 200,000 more. Sunday school enrolments began to fall in the early twentieth century largely because the age structure was changing, but as late as the 1930s roughly a quarter of all children in the appropriate age cohort in England were enrolled in the Sunday schools of the Church of England alone. In the early twentieth

[5] *Facts and Figures about the Church of England* (London, 1965).

century it was almost impossible for a young person of any social class to avoid Sunday school.[6]

Two centuries of voluntarist Christian activity had sustained a Christian Britain, although one that little resembled the Christendom of the early modern period. Studies of local communities have shown that families that were regarded as lost to the churches, largely because adult working-class males would have little to do with Sunday church attendance, were none-theless enmeshed in Christian institutions through the efforts of working-class mothers. They depended on Sunday schools and local churches and chapels for help in seeing their children grow into sober and responsible young adults. Although rational assent to the theological doctrines of Christianity was vague, there was a 'diffusive Christianity' prevalent even in those neighbourhoods where levels of Sunday church attendance were very low.[7]

Unless they write ecclesiastical history, historians of twentieth-century Britain for the most part, whatever their religious views, share a secular outlook when writing history. It is important to establish the importance of Christianity in early twentieth-century Britain, both as a system of belief and as a set of institutions that involved a majority of the population, because of the presumption of marginality that dominates the history of the twentieth century. Secular intellectuals, although deeply engaged with religious issues in the late nineteenth century, regarded religious debates as a stage in the dismantling of religion in humanity's inevitable progress to-wards a secular future. The master narrative of secularization served, and still serves, as a key to understanding history. A person who consulted the 1910 edition of the *Encyclopedia Britannica* on the state of religion would discover the definitive words of T. H. Huxley: 'That...Christianity is doomed to fall is, to my mind, beyond a doubt; but its fall will neither be

---

[6] Currie, Gilbert, and Horsley, *Churches and Churchgoers*. On the pervasiveness of Sunday schools in the early 20th century see S. J. D. Green, *Religion in the Age of Decline: Organisation and Experience in Industrial Yorkshire, 1870–1920* (Cambridge, 1996). Figures such as these are the basis for Callum Brown's designation of the Edwardian Age as 'a Faith Society' in his *Religion and Society in Twentieth-Century Britain: Religion, Politics, and Society in Britain* (New York, 2006).

[7] On the pervasiveness of religious institutions at the local level, and the diffusion of Christian belief, see J. Cox, *The English Churches in a Secular Society: Lambeth, 1870–1930* (Oxford and New York, 1982) and S. C. Williams, *Religious Belief and Popular Culture in Southwark, c.1880–1939* (Oxford and New York 1999).

sudden nor speedy.'[8] It was not very long into the twentieth century when large sections of the British educated and professional classes began to assume as a matter of course that the fall of Christianity had indeed been rapid since the Victorian age.

Only recently have historians began to take the role of religion in twentieth-century Britain seriously, in part because of a new awareness in the late twentieth century of the importance of religion in the rest of the world, including the modern industrialized world outside of Europe. Some scientists have felt the need to respond to intellectual challenges to the hegemony of a particular scientific view of natural history, especially in the United States. The presence of significant numbers of Muslims in Britain thrust unfamiliar religious issues to the centre of public debate. By the late twentieth century, those who continued with Huxley to accept the view that Britain had been thoroughly secularized in the twentieth century found themselves facing intellectual difficulties in sustaining the view that the decline of Christian belief and practice is inevitable, rather than a peculiarity of recent European religious history.

Two historians who have done the most to bring twentieth-century British religion into focus are Hugh McLeod and Callum Brown, and both have concentrated on the 1960s as a crucial decade in the history of British Christianity.[9] A relatively simple change in chronology often serves as a powerful tool of historical revisionism. Once the 1960s is defined as a significant period of transition, an entirely new field of inquiry opens up for the history of the first two-thirds of the twentieth century, a period before the decade that Brown labelled the time of 'the death of Christian Britain'. Even when one turns to the history of parliament and government, looking for the importance of religion, one finds an extraordinary degree of parliamentary time devoted to religious issues in the years before and after the First World War, issues such as the regulation of public worship in the Church of England, the disestablishment of the Church in Wales, and a hard-fought political war over how the government should organize and fund the teaching of religion in the schools. As voluntary social institutions, the British churches arguably reached their peak level of influence in the early twentieth century.

---

[8] *Encyclopedia Britannia* (11th edn.), vol. xiv.

[9] C. G. Brown, *The Death of Christian Britain: Understanding Secularisation, 1800–2000* (New York, 2001); McLeod, *Religious Crisis of the 1960s*.

If religion has been shoved to the margins of the history of twentieth-century Britain, empire has been marginalized in the histories of British religion. The traditions of British ecclesiastical history are insular, in more than one sense of the word. The dean of modern church historians, Owen Chadwick, wrote his canonical two-volume history without mentioning the second most important project of the Victorian churches.[10] The first was creating a generation of young people who were more Christian than the last generation, mainly through Sunday schools. The second was the missionary enterprise, which was among other things a consequence of the expansion of the British empire, and the means by which church and chapel people in Britain encountered the British empire. Following in the Chadwickian tradition, Callum Brown in his recent survey of twentieth-century British religion devotes only a very few pages to missionaries.[11]

The presumption of the marginality of missionaries is testimony to the power of the distinction between British and foreign. I am as guilty of unthinking adherence to that binary distinction as other historians. When ploughing through church and chapel records for a history of the decline of the churches in early twentieth-century Lambeth, I came across abundant evidence of the importance of missionaries in local parishes in chapels. Failing to recognize the interpenetration of the imperial and the domestic, I set that evidence aside on the grounds that it happened overseas.[12] Reinforcing the marginality of the missionary enterprise in British ecclesiastical history was a long tradition dating from the eighteenth century of treating missionaries as figures of fun. Missionary activists to this day smart at the Revd Sydney Smith's description of the early Baptist missionaries to Bengal as 'little detachments of maniacs'.[13] By the early twentieth century there was an extensive body of comic literature about missionaries, who often appeared in cartoons being cooked in a pot by cannibals.

The missionary enterprise though was treated with great seriousness by men and women in Britain's churches, and attracted the time, effort, and money of some of the most high-minded religious activists across all social classes. Although organized into national or regional organizations, some

---

[10] O. Chadwick, *The Victorian Church: An Ecclesiastical History of England* (New York, 1966).

[11] C. G. Brown, *Religion and Society in Twentieth-Century Britain: Religion, Politics, and Society in Britain* (Harlow, 2006).

[12] J. Cox, *The English Churches in a Secular Society: Lambeth, 1870–1930* (New York, 1982).

[13] S. Smith, 'Indian Missions,' *Edinburgh Review*, 12 (Apr. 1808), 151–81.

purely denominational but many drawing from several denominations, the
missionary enterprise was rooted in local congregations. There was hardly a
neighbourhood in Britain without a church or chapel, and where there was
a church or chapel, there was a missionary society. By the beginning of the
twentieth century all but the tiniest congregations had either an associated
local missionary organization, or at least one individual missionary activist
who collected funds for a missionary society or for a particular overseas
congregation or Anglican diocese. A large, well-funded urban parish might
support dozens of missions. In south London, the evangelical parish of
Christ Church, Gipsy Hill, supported as a matter of course the evangelical
Church Missionary Society, but also solicited funds for South American
Missionary Society, St Mary's Southwark Aid Fund, the Religious Tract
Society, Moravian Missions, Mission to Seamen, Mission to Lepers, Mission
to Deep Sea Fisherman, London Jewish Society, London City Mission, Italian
Church Reform Association, Irish Society, Irish Church Missions, the
Industrial Society, Dr Barnardo's Homes, the Colonial and Continental
Church Society, the Church Pastoral Aid Society, the Church of England
Waifs and Strays Society, the Church of England Zenana Mission, and the
bishop of Sierra Leon's Fund.[14]

In 1910 there were roughly 175 national missionary societies or missionary
society auxiliaries independently collecting funds in England, Scotland, and
Wales for work overseas, although some of them did domestic mission and
Christian literary work as well.[15] Some of the largest societies were asso-
ciated with recognized denominations: The Church Missionary Society
(evangelical Anglican), the Society for the Propagation of the Gospel
(SPG, high Anglican), the Wesleyan Methodist Missionary Society, the
Baptist Missionary Society, and the London Missionary Society (mostly
Congregationalist). Others societies raised funds for a particular diocese,
such as the Association in Aid of the Diocese of Capetown, the Rangoon
Diocesan Mission Association, the Meshonaland Association, and the
Union of the Bishop of North Queensland's Auxiliary in England. Even
small denominations with a theology that one would expect to work against
missionary effort organized mission societies, the ultra-Calvinist Strict

[14] Cox, *English Churches*, 41.
[15] World Missionary Conference, *Statistical Atlas of Christian Missions* (Edinburgh, 1910),
27–37.

Baptists supporting both the Strict Baptist Mission and the Strict Baptist Missionary Society.

Edwardian Britain became a centre for global denominational networks that sprawled across the British empire and beyond. London was the site of the third Methodist Ecumenical Conference in 1901, and the Baptist World Alliance was founded at Exeter Hall in 1905. The Third International Congregational Council was held that year in the United Free Church Assembly Hall in Edinburgh. The Archbishop of Canterbury had presided over decennial global gatherings of Anglican bishops at Lambeth Palace since 1867. The fifth Lambeth Congress of 1908 was preceded by a Pan-Anglican Congress focused on the presence of that denomination in mission fields, and with broad participation from women and lay supporters of missions as well as the usual bishops. The concluding service of prayer and thanksgiving in St Paul's resulted in contributions of £350,000 towards sustaining the Anglican global mission.[16]

The great enthusiasm in Britain for the Pan-Anglican Congress demonstrates the extent to which local parishes and chapels were more fully engaged with their mission churches than with their fellow denomination-alists in the European settler colonies and the United States. One obvious reason for this contrast lies in clerical and ministerial recruitment. The large majority of missionaries recruited in Britain were sent for the most part to work with people of different races, and often provided pastoral care for their mission churches. The major British denominations of the mid-Victorian period also created specialized missionary societies to supply clergy and ministers to the white settler churches of the empire. By the early twentieth century the white Congregational, Methodist, Baptist, and Anglican churches in Canada, South Africa, New Zealand, and Australia were able to recruit locally their own white clergy and lay female workers. The white settler denominations had organized their own array of mission-ary societies. Although they continued to cooperate with and support the metropolitan foreign missionary societies, they also recruited personnel from their respective settler communities, often to work with indigenous peoples in their own country.[17]

[16] E. Stock, *The History of the Church Missionary Society, Supplementary Volume, the Fourth* (London, 1916), 551.

[17] Hilary M. Carey (ed.), *Empires of Religion* (Basingstoke, 2008).

Also working against global denominational solidarity in Britain were a range of pan-denominational missionary societies including the 'faith missions', sometimes referred to as 'Matthew X' missions in honour of Christ's command to go forth without visible means of support. Faith missionaries in practice did no such thing, but raised funds in local parishes and chapels in competition with the established denominational societies. The largest of the faith missions, including the China Inland Mission and the Heart of Africa Mission, competed not only for funds but for personnel with the established missions, and along with the rapidly growing Salvation Army, they undermined denominational solidarity and contributed to the long-run polarization of all the major Protestant churches into liberal and evangelical factions. Collecting societies also existed in Britain for missionary societies based in other countries, including the London Association in the Aid of Moravian Missions which sent funds to the Moravians in Herrnhut, Saxony, and the London Committee of the Barotsi Mission of the Paris Evangelical Missionary Society. Roman Catholic missions had always been run for the most part in multinational orders with their own parochial and diocesan networks (making the distinctively British, or Irish, contribution almost impossible to count), although Roman Catholics had created their own distinctively English missionary society, St Joseph's Foreign Missionary Society in Mill Hill.

All but the smallest missions produced a periodical, sometimes more than one, for distribution through churches and chapels, Sunday schools, and individual supporters. Those of any size produced additional newspapers directed to women, children, or the better educated (e.g. the SPG's *East and West*). Their numbers and circulation appear to be unquantifiable. The most widely circulated were the *Missionary Herald* (Baptist), the *Zenana Missionary Herald* (Baptist), *The Mission Field* (SPG), the *Church Missionary Review*, the *Church Missionary Gleaner*, the *Foreign Field* (Wesleyan), the *Zenana* (Zenana Bible and Medical Mission), *India's Women and China's Daughters* (Church of England Zenana Missionary Society), the *Chronicle* (London Missionary Society), *All the World* (Salvation Army), and the extremely successful and widely read organ of the China Inland Mission, *China's Millions*. These found their way into millions of households in the early twentieth century, and it is likely that they were read simply because they contained such readable and compelling stories of missionary heroism and good works, illustrated with exotica from the non-Western world.[18] Even the smaller periodicals, directed to a highly specialized audience, were well edited, although it is very difficult to determine what readers concluded about the British empire or the world in general from *The Delhi Mission News* (Cambridge Mission to Delhi), *Open Doors* (Palestine and Lebanon Nurses' Mission), or the *Quarterly Paper* of the South African Church Railway Mission.

The regular periodicals were a part of a much larger body of literature produced by the missionary societies, and also by denominational Sunday school societies and the ecumenical Sunday School Union, much of it directed to households and children. Illuminated cards, texts, and calendars were produced at the Mildmay 'Illuminating Depot' in north-east London, and the larger missionary societies organized local groups to generate their own illuminated texts with a focus on their particular work. Sunday school children were supplied with posters of children in foreign lands, cut out dolls to dress up with exotic clothing, postcards with pictures of little children around the world, and texts for pageants in which children could dress up as Africans or Indians and put on performances for their enthusiastic (or reluctant) parents.

Perhaps most important of all were the short biographical studies of missionary heroes, most of them Victorian, held up to children and young people as role models. In the nineteenth century the Baptist Missionary Society published a series focused on Baptist missionary heroes, but others ranged across denominational lines. In the twentieth century the London Missionary Society published a successful series of lives of mission heroes, not all of them white, including titles on John Williams of the South Seas, Robert Moffat of South Africa, Sundar Singh of India, Henry Martyn of India, Samuel Pollard of China, C. E. Tyndale-Biscoe of Kashmir, Father Jackson of Burma, Clifford Harris of Iran, William Carey of India, Mary Slessor of Africa, John Vanderkemp of South Africa, David Hill of China, David Livingstone of Africa, Albert Schweitzer of Africa, Bishop Crowther of Africa, Mary Bird of Persia, Bishop Bompas of the Arctic, and Frederick Booth-Tucker of India. For good measure, they added to the list non-missionary heroes who, like missionaries, were doing God's work in the

---

[18] On this genre see Anna Johnston, *Missionary Writing and Empire, 1800–1860* (Cambridge, 2003).

world: William Penn, John Wesley, William Wilberforce, Elizabeth Fry, Abraham Lincoln, Florence Nightingale, and Madam Chiang Kai-shek.[19]

Young people were not limited to reading books in order to be introduced to missionary heroes. They could meet them in person. The better-funded missionary societies expected their missionaries to go on furlough every few years in Britain, touring the country and raising funds. The kind of missionary that a young person met might reasonably be called a hero, but failed to resemble the heroes that were featured in missionary biography. The missionary movement had worked hard in the nineteenth century to transform the image of a missionary. By the time the heroic explorer and enemy of the slave trade David Livingstone was buried in Westminster Abbey, missionaries were no longer sent out as little detachments of maniacs, but as social reformers who were feted for devoting their lives to making the world a better place.[20] The image of David Livingstone, though, was no guide at all to what missionaries actually did in the field. They were not heroic itinerant evangelists in pith helmets moving from place to place preaching the gospel under a palm tree. They were instead institution builders, creating Christian schools, hospitals, and training institutions on the assumption that Christian values would emanate from them. Even those missionaries who went out as 'faith missionaries' with the China Inland Mission, and who claimed to reject the missionary strategy of building institutions, in practice built Christian institutions in China.[21]

David Livingstone was atypical in another respect: he was a man. The missionary enterprise was distinctive among the British enterprises that sent people to work overseas in that it was predominantly female. In 1916 there were roughly 7,500 British Protestant missionaries at work overseas, a number that had doubled in the previous quarter of a century, and 58 per cent of them were female. In some parts of the world, notably India and China, the female percentage was closer to two-thirds. The Protestant overseas work force continued to grow after the First World War, reaching its peak at some point in the 1930s. The heyday of British missions was not

---

[19] The Eagle Books series was published by Edinburgh House Press, London.

[20] On the making of the Livingstone myth see Dorothy O. Helly, *Livingstone's Legacy: Horace Waller and Victorian Mythmaking* (Athens, Ohio, 1987); for its persistence in the 20th century see National Portrait Gallery (Great Britain) and Scottish National Portrait Gallery, *David Livingstone and the Victorian Encounter with Africa* (London, 1996).

[21] Rhonda Anne Semple, *Missionary Women: Gender, Professionalism, and the Victorian Idea of Christian Mission* (New York, 2003).

reached during Livingstone's Victorian itinerations, but in the interwar period, when the British empire achieved its greatest territorial reach. Throughout the nineteenth century Britain had sent more Protestant missionaries overseas than any other nation. By the early twentieth century Britain had been surpassed by the United States, but remained the second largest sending nation throughout the twentieth century, only to be surpassed by South Korea in the very early twenty-first. British missionaries were stationed in all parts of the world, not only those under British imperial rule. The impact of imperial influence can be seen nonetheless in the disproportionate deployment of British missionaries, when compared to the number of Americans, in areas of British imperial control, Africa and South Asia. American missionaries outnumbered the British in areas of American overseas influence, East Asia and Latin America.[22]

In addition to churches and chapels, universities became important sites for missionary recruitment in the late nineteenth and early twentieth centuries. The Student Christian Movement (SCM), founded in Britain as the Student Volunteer Movement in 1889 and renamed in 1905, encouraged university students to pray daily for missions, and commit their lives to the service of Christ. Their handbook was John Mott's *The Evangelization of the World in this Generation* (1900), published in a cheap edition and sold to the general public. The SCM claimed to have persuaded 1,621 students to commit themselves to missionary work in the 1890s, with more than 500 of them actually setting sail. It was the SCM's goal to make the missionary profession a mainstream enterprise, associated not only with piety and moral commitment, but with high standards of academic respectability and professional training. Although the student Christian organizations were beginning to fragment along theological lines, the SCM remained unified and national in its scope in the pre-war years, attracting 1,640 delegates from university branches to a national conference in Liverpool in 1908 under the slogan 'That They May All Be One'.[23]

Churches and chapels, Sunday schools, and university student organizations recruited missionaries, but most important of all was the encouragement that young people, especially young women, received in their homes.

---

[22] J. Cox, *The British Missionary Enterprise since 1700* (London, 2008), fig. 5.
[23] For the early history of the SCM. see Tissington Tatlow, *The Story of the Student Christian Movement of Great Britain and Ireland* (London, 1933).

If a typical missionary were to be chosen from the early twentieth century, it would perhaps be someone like Dr Ellen Farrer. Raised in a prosperous Nonconformist family in Hampstead, a member of the Heath Street Baptist church, she was encouraged to take advantage of the educational opportunities opening up for women. It was her mother who suggested to her that her academic success might be a providential sign that God intended her to make the world a better place through the missionary enterprise. This involved some agonizing choices, including the decision to train as a medical doctor and to forgo a proposed marriage in order to travel to India in 1891, where she spent the next forty years as a physician and surgeon in the Punjabi town of Bhiwani.

Surviving decades of both physical and political storms in Punjab, Farrer was a publicist as well as a skilled physician, writing hundreds of letters a year as well as the mandatory reports sent back to the Baptist Missionary Society, which published selections from them. She returned to London regularly, and on her first furlough in 1897 addressed the annual breakfast of the Baptist Zenana Mission with an account of the significance of her work. Medical missionaries were often accused of proselytizing, but the accounts of Farrer show that she was first and foremost a doctor. The significance of her work lay in where she was doing it, bringing the benefits of Western surgical practice and the germ theory of disease to help people in ways that were almost impossible to challenge. The effectiveness of Western medical skills justified her presence in a foreign land, but so did her sense of religious calling. Facing criticism that her work was essentially practical in nature, resulting in few conversions, she claimed to be using her education and her professional skills in the service of God. When faced with the prospect of violent nationalist attacks on her mission, she was incredulous.[24]

As the missionary enterprise reached its peak of influence in the early twentieth century, its supporters justified the mission presence abroad by reference to the admirable character of missionaries, who were at their best heroes and in their everyday work men and women who were making the world a better place. Missionaries worked in Christian institutions that

---

[24] Ellen Farrer's personal diaries are held by the Angus Library, Regents Park College, Oxford. Although her mission work was covered regularly in Baptist Missionary Society publications through the 1930s, she has neither a biography nor an entry in the *Oxford Dictionary of National Biography*. An account of her medical practice may be found in Imogen Siobhan Anderson, 'A Mission for Medicine: Dr Ellen Farrer and India, 1891–1933' (PhD, University of Durham, 1997).

provided a visual justification, in bricks and mortar, for the foreign ecclesiastical presence as long as the people of Britain could be persuaded that these institutions were doing good. The presence of hospitals and clinics, of schools and public health projects, of Christian churches and training schools for non-Western Christian workers, papered over the deep theological divisions within the churches. Evangelical Christians who believed that the ultimate purpose of the enterprise was the salvation of individual souls also believed that Christian influence would emanate from mission institutions, especially from those designed to train an army of indigenous ministers and church workers. Liberal Christians who believed that Christianity was best expressed in service to one's neighbours justified their work by reference to the self-evident good that Christian institutions were doing. When missionaries were accused of being handmaidens of imperial rule, colonizing the hearts and minds of imperial subjects, they could point to the liberal and humanitarian work that Christian missionaries were doing independently of any government, a work that was meant to endure beyond the end of any empire, including Britain's.[25] When missionaries were accused of racism, they could point out that Britain's 7,500 overseas missionaries were part of a multiracial Christian workforce in which whites were a minority. On the eve of the First World War, white missionaries from Britain were at work in Christian institutions that employed one way or another, by their own account, 43,000 non-Western employees of all sorts, a number that grew to more than 65,000 in the 1930s, constituting 89 per cent of the overseas missionary workforce.[26]

The issue of race caused insoluble problems for the churches overseas and at home. When building up their case for voluntary support for missions in the very early nineteenth century, missionary publicists deployed figures of speech about non-Christian peoples of the world that were rightly considered defamatory by critics. They did this in the face of intense scepticism about what they were doing, and also in the face of a surprisingly widespread belief, especially in the wake of Cook's voyages, in the uncorrupted nature of the noble savage, untainted by Western civilization. Others believed that there was much to admire in the ancient civilizations of the Middle East, India, and China, and that little detachments of poorly

[25] A. N. Porter, *Religion Versus Empire? British Protestant Missionaries and Overseas Expansion, 1700–1914* (Manchester, 2004).

[26] Cox, *The British Missionary Enterprise*, table 1.

educated missionaries had no right to meddle with them. The missionary counter-attack utilized synecdoche, i.e. they took an extremely offensive characteristic of a foreign people as characteristic of the whole. The earliest and apparently most effective synecdoche was cannibalism. If you could find evidence of cannibalism, whether in the South Seas or among the Caribs or later in Africa and even later in New Guinea (along with head hunting), you had to say very little more in order to justify the proposition that Christianity would be a better way of life. Accusations of sexual immorality, usually left up to the imagination as far as details go, were also widely used, especially against Hinduism. Any evidence of the mistreatment of women, from sati to foot-binding to purdah, was judged to be very effective when discussing the civilizations of India and China. In missionary literature Islam often appeared to be virtually defined by the seclusion of women.

These depictions continued well into the twentieth century, and were shared by feminists and social reformers and humanitarians beyond the churches.[27] Some of these depictions, especially wholesale condemnations of entire societies over their treatment of women, have had remarkable staying power in the West, and also the ability to stir up bitter resentment in non-Western societies. In India, Hindu nationalists continue to make political capital out of the missionary history of defamation, especially in the widely read works of Arun Shourie who does little more than quote directly from the works of nineteenth-century missionaries and missionary apologists.[28] To the extent that young British people of the early twentieth century received from churches and Sunday schools most of their information about what other people are like, including the people ruled by Britain, one effect of missionary literature must have been the reinforcement of ethnocentrism and, at least by implication, a strengthening of the case for British imperial rule, insofar as British rule allowed the propagation of Christianity.

Missionary literature by the early twentieth century was also marked by a waning of defamation of other cultures. The study of comparative religions led to a lower tolerance generally for wholesale attacks on foreign cultures. There had always been a wide gap between the use of defamatory

---

[27] Antoinette M. Burton, *Burdens of History: British Feminists, Indian Women, and Imperial Culture, 1865–1915* (Chapel Hill, NC, 1994).

[28] A. Shourie, *Missionaries in India: Continuities, Changes, Dilemmas* (New Delhi, 1994) and *Harvesting Our Souls Missionaries, Their Design, Their Claims* (New Delhi, 2000).

literature at home and the use of such rhetoric by missionaries in the field. Defamation of a whole culture was not the best way to persuade people from that culture to cooperate with you in the building of Christian institutions, which is what missionaries were doing. Non-white people had to be persuaded that missionaries were committed to interracial cooperation, to what the anthropologists Jean and John Comaroff refer to as 'the multiracial Christian commonwealth of missionary fantasy'.[29] Working together across racial lines was no fantasy in mission institutions, but a practical necessity, and missionaries drew on alternative narratives to those of defamation, particularly the theme of the universal brotherhood of man under the fatherhood of God. Furthermore missionaries not only had to justify their work to home supporters by defaming other cultures, they also had to persuade people at home that non-white peoples were potential equals in the empire of Christ. One of the most widely read missionary periodicals was *Our Indian Sisters*. David Livingstone drew the ire of the founders of the Anthropological Society because of his insistence, in the face of anti-black racists such as Richard Burton, on the innate capacities of the people of Africa.[30] That is one of the reasons why the arch-imperialist Livingstone is such a hero in African Christian circles today. Drawing on the images of sisterhood and racial equality, missionary literature stressed the great ability, intelligence, and industry of non-Western people, including their capacity to improve themselves by becoming Christian.

Based on Christian universalism, the theme of racial equality was carried through in missionary literature for children. The London Missionary Society published an attractive set of postcards with images of children from around the world. The text for the teachers instructed them to stress that, although other children may dress funny and look funny, children around the world are fundamentally the same, i.e. they like to play, they love

---

[29] J. and J. Comaroff, *Of Revelation and Revolution: Christianity, Colonialism, and Consciousness in South Africa*, 2 vols. (Chicago, 1991), i. 32. For a book that stresses even more than the Comaroffs the intrinsically imperialist character of missions, see T. O. Beidelman, *Colonial Evangelism: A Socio-Historical Study of an East African Mission at the Grassroots* (Bloomington, Ind., 1982). Works that stress the collaborative nature of the missionary enterprise include J. D. Y. Peel, *Religious Encounter and the Making of the Yoruba* (Bloomington, Ind., 2000) and J. Cox, *Imperial Fault Lines: Christianity and Colonial Power in India, 1818–1940* (Stanford, Calif., 2002).

[30] Dane Kennedy, *The Highly Civilized Man, Richard Burton and the Victorian World* (Cambridge, Mass., 2005), 131–63.

their parents, etc. Children were instructed not to colour African children black because they are instead a lovely golden brown.[31] The anti-racist 'Jesus loves the little children' was one of the most popular children's missionary hymns, composed in America but popular in Britain as well:

> Jesus loves the little children
> All the children of the world
> Red and yellow, black or white
> They are precious in His sight
> Jesus loves the little children of the World

In Sunday school children learned, or were taught, that there are some very bad things about some non-Christian cultures, but children around the world are happy and cheerful and in many ways, except for their colourful clothes, just like us, and that in the countries where missionaries work there are many people working hard to improve themselves and their neighbours.

Although twentieth-century missionary literature is characterized by a waning of defamation, certain ethnocentric narratives had more staying power than others. There is apparently an endless market for stories of cannibalism, particularly about missionary martyrs in the South Pacific who were alleged to have been eaten. The emphasis on racial equality, though, overshadowed the older defamatory tropes, which were also counteracted at a more formal theological level by the emergence of 'fulfillment theology.' Even before the emergence of liberal theology and the comparative study of religions in the nineteenth century, some missionaries had looked for the good rather than the evil in other religions, and stressed the 'intimations' of Christian belief that could be found even in Hinduism or Islam or Confucianism. In the early twentieth century this emerged as a full-scale, and highly controversial, treatment of other religions as stepping stones to Christianity. J. N. Farquhar's *The Crown of Hinduism*, a classic of liberal Protestant theology published in 1913, set off a storm of controversy and helped widen the already growing gap between evangelical and liberal wings of the missionary enterprise, but his arguments, and similar arguments, may be found scattered about in all sorts of missionary writings beginning in the nineteenth century.[32]

---

[31] Elsie Wood, *Children of Africa Post-Card Painting Book* (London, 1920).

[32] J. N. (John Nicol) Farquhar, *The Crown of Hinduism, by J. N. Farquhar* (2nd edn., repr., 1913; New Delhi, 1971); Eric J. Sharpe, *Not to Destroy but to Fulfil; the Contribution of J. N. Farquhar to Protestant Missionary Thought in India Before 1914* (Lund, 1965).

To treat Hinduism as a stepping stone to Christianity is of course to many Hindus just as offensive and ethnocentric as treating it as an unqualified source of moral evil, but the emergence of liberal attitudes towards other cultures and religions represents an important change in the perception of other cultures by the Christian churches of Britain. Liberal theology also helped to reinforce Christian universalism on questions of race. To read much of the literature on race in the late nineteenth and twentieth century, one would think that biological interpretations of race swept everything before them.[33] There is no doubt that scientific and biological arguments, and an enthusiasm for eugenics, were becoming more attractive in the early twentieth century, and there are some examples of missionaries adopting scientific racism as a justification for the maintenance of racial hierarchies in mission institutions. They were a small minority, though, for the missionary enterprise was for the most part a bastion of resistance to scientific racism and eugenics. Even at the height of the defamatory treatment of other cultures in the early nineteenth century, missionary hierarchies of race were rarely justified on scientific or biological grounds. The justification was almost always one of professional status, i.e. superior Western expertise in the areas of education, medicine, and religion. By the early twentieth century even the most conservative of missionary rhetoricians, even those who were deeply attracted to eugenic ideas, such as Bishop H. H. Montgomery, the head of the Society for the Propagation of the Gospel, found themselves compelled to justify miscegenation in the church on theological grounds, regardless of what the scientific consequences might be for humanity.

Having created a global network of multiracial Christian institutions, Britain's churches faced a serious dilemma. However much mission theorists might resist scientific racism, however much missionary societies were committed to creating a church that was self-governing, however much missionaries were committed to the creation of a multiracial Christian commonwealth, mission institutions were highly stratified by race. Non-white Christians had not been slow to point this out in the late nineteenth century, especially in the wake of the Church Missionary Society's appointment of a white bishop of the Niger Delta to replace their first African

---

[33] See e.g. John Marriott, *The Other Empire: Metropolis, India and Progress in the Colonial Imagination* (Manchester, 2003).

bishop, Samuel Ajayi Crowther.[34] Conflict around racial hypocrisy and the
reality of white privilege occurred at a less visible level in mission institutions almost everywhere, although it was largely ignored in missionary
literature.

Non-white Christians as well as missionaries found themselves in a
dilemma. Many of them were deeply indebted to mission institutions for
education and social advancement, and were equally grateful to those
people, white though they might be, who brought the gospel to their land.
Missionaries were important and respected people not only in mission
institutions around the world, but in the broader Christian communities
that were beginning to grow rapidly, especially in Africa. The missionary
movement had been the target of anti-Western and nationalist criticism, as
well as anti-foreign violence, in both India and China by the early twentieth
century, but even in those countries there was among some secular nationalists a strain of respect for missionary social reformers and educators and,
in the case of India, for missionaries such as C. F. Andrews who actively
promoted the nationalist cause.[35]

Despite all of this, non-white Christians ran up against the realities of
white privilege in their everyday interactions with missionaries, to whom
they were usually subordinate in the church and the workplace. The hierarchies of race in mission institutions and in churches were rarely justified
explicitly on grounds of race, but on the grounds of professionalism.
Missionary clergymen and teachers had the educational background that
was necessary to train clergymen and ministers in the appropriate way.
Missionary teachers of secular subjects such as science had experience and
training in those fields, and in the management of schools and training of
teachers. Missionary women knew how to run girls' schools, train nurses,
and educate women doctors. White privilege was a fact of life in mission
institutions, and critics were told to be patient.

Non-Western Christians who were associated with mission institutions
combined affection for missionaries with a keen sense of the hypocrisy of

[34] Emmanuel Ayankanmi Ayandele, *The Missionary Impact on Modern Nigeria, 1842–1914: a Political and Social Analysis* (London, 1966); cf. Andrew Porter, 'Cambridge, Keswick and Late-Nineteenth-Century Attitudes to Africa,' *Journal of Imperial and Commonwealth History* (*JICH*), 5/1 (1976), 23–46; Andrew Porter, 'Evangelical Enthusiasm, Missionary Motivation and West Africa in the Late Nineteenth Century: The Career of G. W. Brooke', *JICH* 6/1 (1977), 5–34.

[35] Daniel O'Connor, *Gospel, Raj, and Swaraj: The Missionary Years of C. F. Andrews, 1904–1914* (Frankfurt am Main, 1990).

the Western churches. This bubbled to the surface at the 1910 Missionary Conference in a now well-known address by an Indian Anglican clergyman, the Revd Samuel Azariah, who travelled halfway around the globe to appeal to the leaders of the missionary movement to confront the racial divide. At that time, despite the genuine commitment of the missionary societies to building up an indigenous Indian clergy, all of the bishops of the Anglican Church of India were Europeans. Azariah, who would later become the first Indian bishop of this Indian Church, did not complain about the lack of career advancement. He complained instead of the barriers of race in interpersonal relationships. To an audience that one observer described as 'broken...by a sort of subterraneous rumbling of dissent' from the white missionaries to India present, Azariah spoke of the need for racial reconciliation: 'This will be possible only from spiritual friendships between the two races...Through all the ages to come the Indian Church will rise up in gratitude to attest the heroism and self-denying labours of the missionary body. You have given your goods to feed the poor. You have given your bodies to be burned. We also ask for love. Give us friends!'[36]

Nineteenth-century arguments about race revolved around the missionary goal of developing self-governing, indigenous non-white churches; in the twentieth century, arguments about race increasingly focused on the need to eradicate racial prejudice within the churches, and then to eliminate the apartheid system in South Africa. In the aftermath of the Edinburgh conference, missionary activists created a global network of mission institutions, including the *International Review of Missions* in 1912. In 1921 J. H. Oldham, a former Scottish YMCA missionary to India, was instrumental in founding the International Missionary Council, which among other things organized international missionary conferences in Jerusalem in 1928 and Madras in 1938. The number of non-white delegates grew rapidly at each convention. By the 1920s there was an explicit political attack on racism in missionary circles, the influential text being Oldham's *Christianity and the Race Problem*, published by the Student Christian Movement in 1924.

By the time the Student Christian Movement and the International Missionary Council took up anti-racism as a central cause, though, the

---

[36] W. H. T. Gairdner, *'Edinburgh 1910': An Account and Interpretation of the World Missionary Conference* (Edinburgh, 1910), 109–10. On Azariah see Susan Billington Harper, *In the Shadow of the Mahatma: Bishop V. S. Azariah and the Travails of Christianity in British India* (Grand Rapids, Mich., 2000).

world situation had changed dramatically. The dreams of a global, united, multiracial Protestant Christianity leading the way to world unity, social reform, and social progress were shattered by world war, the rise of nationalism and communism, and the slow but inexorable decline of Britain's Christian institutions over the course of the twentieth century. The First World War in some ways affected the missionary movement obliquely. A few men became chaplains, and a few women enlisted as nurses, but overall levels of the British missionary workforce remained relatively stable during the war. The number of Christian personnel stationed overseas continued to grow after the war. However, the opening of new spheres of British influence in Africa and the Middle East under League of Nations mandates did little to provide new open doors for missionary advance. It was already clear by the 1920s that the Indian national movement was not going to move India in a Christian direction, and Indian Christianity, although growing rapidly, was contained within marginalized and oppressed social groups that could not provide the kind of elite leadership that church leaders had envisioned. The notion that Christianity would spread through a form of stratified diffusion, from elites downward, was deeply rooted in the structure of missionary institution building, which meant that only a few missionaries were paying close attention to the prospects of Christian growth in Africa. In China, though, hopes remained high for Christian growth and influence under the nationalist movement, only to be choked off entirely by the ultimate Communist victory. The expulsion of all missionaries in 1949 was the most traumatic event in twentieth-century missionary history. After 1948, the International Missionary Council was overshadowed as a means of global ecclesiastical cooperation by the World Council of Churches, which absorbed it in 1961.[37] By that time, world Christianity had become far more fragmented than it had been in 1910. The rapidly growing independent and pentecostal churches, far removed from the elite structures of mission and ecumenical Christianity, were beginning to come into their own.

By the interwar years the mainstream churches of Britain had to face up to the reality of long-term institutional decline. In 1910 the decline of regular Sunday morning church attendance was noticeable, although other statistics of religious participation were holding up or even improving.

---

[37] Ruth Rouse, Stephen Neill, and Harold Edward Fey, *A History of the Ecumenical Movement*, ed. Harold Edward Fey (Philadelphia, 1967).

Between 1906 and 1910, though, membership in the principal Nonconformist denominations—Methodist, Baptist, and Congregationalist—began to fall, and settled into a pattern of decline that has continued throughout the twentieth century. By the interwar period few Anglicans would deny that their churches were in decline as well, and by the late twentieth century the Roman Catholic Church began to conform to what appeared to be a general decline of British Christian institutions and Christian influence. Historians normally attribute this decline to a global process of secularization, and argue mainly about the timing of the inevitable, but it is possible to be more precise about the causes of the decline of the churches.

In the early twentieth century 'Nonconformity' was a major form of social identity in Britain.[38] Although under 10 per cent of the overall population, Nonconformists constituted well over a third of the regular churchgoing and Sunday school attending population. Nonconformist chapels were a pillar of national identity in Wales, where Nonconformists were a majority. Throughout England there were few places where 'chapel' did not exist down the road from the parish church and supply an alternative way of being English, one that became a major issue in the 1906 general election (to the great annoyance of secular liberals and Fabians). One of the most important social changes in twentieth-century Britain is the eclipse of Nonconformity, which lacks a historian. By the late twentieth century the word Nonconformist had come to mean something entirely different, conforming in Britain to its American usage, i.e. a strange or independent-minded person.

Like all institutionalized religions, Nonconformity recruited first and foremost from its own children, and there were fewer children per family in the early twentieth century. What is more important, though, is the difficulty Nonconformist parents faced in transmitting a sense of Nonconformist social identity to their own children. Many parents were theological liberals, who believed in allowing children to make up their own minds. Those who were evangelical often regarded evangelicalism as non-denominational, and were just as happy to see their children move to Anglican or independent evangelical congregations as remain Baptist or Congregationalist or Methodist. Furthermore, Nonconformist identity was based on a sense of grievance over social exclusion that had largely disappeared by the early twentieth

---

[38] David Bebbington, *The Nonconformist Conscience: Chapel and Politics, 1870–1914* (London, 1982).

century. By the mid-twentieth century, for instance, people from a
Nonconformist background were significantly over-represented among
academics, a profession from which they had been largely excluded for
much of the nineteenth century.[39] The Church of England might remain
the most snobbish church in Christendom in the twentieth century, but it
was difficult to persuade young Nonconformists that they were disadvan-
taged by it in any visible way.

As Nonconformity began to decline, all of the Protestant churches including the national churches of England and Scotland began to suffer from
a sense of declining social utility. People of all social classes participated in
and supported the churches largely because of a sense that they were
important social institutions, appealing to a public sense of altruism and
civic duty along with piety and respectability. By the 1920s, with the growth
of specialized, non-ecclesiastical voluntary organizations and the rapid
spread of what we now call the welfare state, it became more difficult to
argue that the churches were essential to the maintenance of social stability
and morals. The process of what sociologists call functional differentiation,
by which more and more specialized bodies take greater responsibility for
the maintenance of social cohesion, has been documented in numerous
studies of British religion. This occurred in a context in which sections of
the professional and educated classes had already been convinced that
there was something unsound about religious arguments. This point of
view was put economically by Evelyn Waugh in *Brideshead Revisited*, where
Charles Ryder is somewhat bemused to discover a family that takes religion
seriously:

I had no religion. I was taken to church weekly as a child, and at school attended
chapel daily, but, as though in compensation, from the time I went to my public
school I was excused church *in the holidays*. The view implicit in my education
was that the basic narrative of Christianity had long been exposed as a myth, and
that opinion was now divided as to whether its ethical teaching was of present
value, a division in which the main weight went against it.[40]

The utility of religion was the heart of the matter. In his *Autobiography*
(1873) John Stuart Mill described 'this age' as one in which 'real belief in any

[39] A. H. Halsey and M. A. Trow, *The British Academics* (London, 1971), 413–19.
[40] E. Waugh, *Brideshead Revisited: The Sacred and Profane Memories of Captain Charles Ryder* (London, 1944; repr. 1999), 85–6.

religious doctrine is feeble and precarious, but the opinion of its necessity for moral and social purposes almost universal'.[41] His view of belief was wishful thinking, since belief and utility are closely linked in modern religious history, but his identification of the importance of the reliance on religion for ethical teaching was correct. In the twentieth century the link between utility, ethics, and belief was broken as the churches lost their social responsibilities to governmental or non-religious bodies.

The churches were global as well as domestic institutions, and the same changes that affected their domestic work may be seen in their international connections and interests. By the late twentieth century the churches were just as involved in global concerns as they had been early in the century, but the focus had changed in fundamental ways. The empire of Christ had never coincided with the empire of Britain, but missionary work had been concentrated in the areas of imperial control and influence: South Asia, Africa, and China. The course of world events weakened and finally eliminated the imperial focus of the churches. Their fields became instead, for liberal Protestants, the 'Third World', and for evangelicals, 'unreached peoples'.

In the aftermath of the First World War, religious activists began to develop alternative non-missionary institutions to express their concern for mending the world. Social reform had been a spasmodic concern of the missionary enterprise throughout the nineteenth century: anti-slavery agitation, campaigns for indigo workers in Bengal, opposition to the opium trade, campaigns against brutality and forced labour in the Congo, all had important missionary dimensions. The primary focus of missions, though, had always been institution building rather than social reform. The horrors of the First World War brought in its train a concern to deal with the immediate humanitarian crisis through the provision of direct relief.

Eglantyne Jebb might have found her way into the missionary enterprise before the war. An Anglican, she became involved in humanitarian work during the war along with her sister Dorothy Buxton, who joined the Society of Friends in 1916. In 1919 the two of them founded the Fight the Famine Council, an emergency relief organization that later became the Save the Children Fund, one of the most prominent of Britain's secular charities with religious origins. Rather than disbanding the organization once the post-war crisis ended, Jebb and her associates transformed the

---

[41] J. S. Mill, *Autobiography* (1873), ed. John Robson (repr. London, 1989), 71.

organization into a permanent advocacy organization for children at risk world wide. In 1923 she drafted the Declaration of the Rights of the Child, a model human rights statement later taken up by the League of Nations and in subsequent forms by the United Nations. Jebb's motives, like the motives of missionary activists in the pre-war era, were a mixture of humanitarianism and religious faith, but the outcome was an organization that attracted religious activists on a non-denominational and non-religious basis. A recent biographer describes her motives as 'a complex interaction—impossible now precisely to recapture—between fluctuations in personal health, unhappiness in personal life, belief in woman's distinctive moral power, an almost obsessive preoccupation with the need to rectify injustice, and a religious commitment harnessed to what later seemed largely secular causes'.[42]

The story of the Save the Children Fund illustrates one of the features of twentieth-century religious history: the invisibility of liberal Protestantism. In the view of liberal Protestants, God has called men and women to do good in the world, whether inside or outside of explicitly Christian institutions. The most extreme example, perhaps, was the Revd C. F. Andrews, the former member of the Cambridge Mission to Delhi who in the 1920s proclaimed that Christ's work in the world was being performed by the Indian National Congress.[43] One did not have to go that far in embracing what appear to be secular institutions to repudiate, on liberal Protestant theological grounds, the distinction between the religious and the secular.

Churches rarely regard the advent of war as their fault, but as twentieth-century European history shows, they are easily annexed into almost any war effort. Not all churches are equally susceptible to militarism and nationalism, though. Although a few of the clergy were pacifists, speaking in broad terms the First World War posed few problems for the Church of England. Some parishes covered their prayer books in khaki, while others converted their crypts into rifle ranges. Church Missionary Society missionaries in India helped recruit a Punjabi Christian regiment to fight in Mesopotamia. Despite the anti-war and even pacifist heritage of some

[42] B. Harrison, 'Jebb, Eglantyne (1876–1928)', in *Oxford Dictionary of National Biography* (Oxford, 2004), URL: <http://www.oxforddnb.com>.

[43] Charles Freer Andrews, *The Testimony of C. F. Andrews*, ed. Daniel O'Connor (Madras, 1974); David M. Gracie (ed.), *Gandhi and Charlie: The Story of a Friendship* (Cambridge, Mass., 1989).

sections of the Baptist and Congregationalist denominations, most Non-conformists went along with the war effort, showing only modest sympathy or support for the handful of their own young men who declared themselves conscientious objectors. Instead they dutifully honoured their own war dead, putting up memorial plaques to them just as the parish churches did. The churches created the most widespread form of public memorial-ization of the dead in Britain.

There was an undercurrent of liberal internationalism within Noncon-formity that found expression at various times during and after the war. One of Congregationalism's leading liberal ministers, the Revd Bernard Snell, sent out a Christmas message in 1914 that was filled with despair: 'Our civilization bankrupt, our hopes shattered, our consciences shocked, impotent all of us.'[44] After the war this sentiment found an outlet in the League of Nations Union. By the early 1930s the overwhelming majority of the local branches of the union were associated with churches or chapels, and a large majority of them were Nonconformist chapels.[45] Missionary activists at the 1910 Edinburgh Conference looked forward to a world in which Christianity would provide the basis for international unity. Liberal Protestants of the interwar period, by way of contrast, put their hopes in the secular negotiators and imperial mandates of the League of Nations. In Nonconformist chapels throughout England in the 1920s, the local branch of the foreign missionary society was competing for funds and volunteers with a local branch of the League of Nations Union.

Few historians have noticed the religious foundations of the League of Nations Union or the Save the Children Fund. Liberal Christians became invisible to historians, their religious convictions diffused through institu-tions that can only be identified as Christian from a particular theological point of view when one examines closely their history and basis of support. This trend accelerated in the aftermath of the Second World War, which resulted in the closing of a vast field of missionary activity in China. Although it was not clear at the time, decolonization left India, Pakistan, and most of Africa open to missionary effort, at least for a few decades. The closing of China was so traumatic largely because of the high hopes that had been entertained during the nationalist period. The China Inland Mission was forced to regroup, redeploy its missionaries, and change its name.

---

[44] *Brixton Free Press* (25 Dec. 1914).
[45] Donald Birn, *The League of Nations Union 1918–1945* (Oxford, 1981), 137.

For those mission fields that remained open to British missionary effort, fewer missionaries were available. With fewer members, and even fewer young people due to a declining birth rate, it became more difficult for the Protestant churches to recruit missionaries. It is difficult to compare numbers across time because the definition of a missionary changed, but the decline in Protestant missionaries is evident however they are counted— from 8,500 in the 1930s to roughly 6,000 by 1980. By the latter date it is possible to estimate the number of Roman Catholic missionaries, defined as personnel from Britain posted abroad, as another 1,400. Despite the institutional decline of the churches, several thousand Britons were working overseas under explicitly Christian auspices in the late twentieth century.[46]

Britain's Protestant churches were increasingly polarized into evangelical and liberal wings. Christians concerned with global affairs were less likely to be working in explicitly Christian institutions either at home or abroad. Non-evangelical Christians, many with deep and sincere Christian motives, could often be found working in humanitarian organizations that appeared to be secular, or in Christian organizations whose work appeared to be virtually identical to non-sectarian and non-religious organizations. Of those working for missionary societies, more and more of them were evangelical. In the immediate post-war period a list of the largest missionary societies continued to have a denominational focus with the Anglican Church Missionary Society and Society for the Propagation of the Gospel joining the principal societies of the Methodists, Baptists, Congregationalists, and Church of Scotland in the top ten. By the end of the twentieth century the top ten list was entirely dominated by interdenominational evangelical societies, some of Victorian origins such as the Overseas Missionary Fellowship (the former China Inland Mission), others entirely new, such as Youth with a Mission, Operation Mobilization, and the Wycliffe Bible Translators.[47]

The relative success—if growth be a measure of success—of evangelical Protestantism has been much commented upon, especially by evangelicals. Some of its causes are not mysterious. Liberal Protestants were committed to institutional maintenance, in part because they inherited in Britain, as in much of Europe, the bulk of the institutional apparatus of Christendom, which is very expensive and time-consuming to maintain. Time spent by a

---

[46] Cox, *British Missionary Enterprise*, table 1.   [47] Ibid. table 2.

parish priest raising funds to prevent the roof from falling in on worshippers is time not spent in recruiting more worshippers. Furthermore, liberal Protestants, as already noted, give a religious significance to work that is to all appearances secular, including organizations of a vaguely liberal and internationalist variety such as the Save the Children Fund and the League of Nations Union. The pioneers in liberal Protestant global engagement were in some ways Britain's Quakers, who shared with American Quakers the 1947 Nobel Peace Prize awarded to the Friends Service Council in London and the American Friends Service Committee. Although very small in number, British Quakers turn up as founders or supporters of virtually every internationalist humanitarian organization in twentieth-century Britain with the exception of those limited explicitly to particular denominational or theological goals. The Nobel Prize Committee quoted a young Quaker who explained the theological significance of their work:

We weren't sent out to make converts. We've come out for a definite purpose, to build up in a spirit of love what has been destroyed in a spirit of hatred. We're not missionaries. We can't tell if even one person will be converted to Quakerism. Things like that don't happen in a hurry. When our work is finished it doesn't mean that our influence dies with it. We have not come out to show the world how wonderful we are. No, the thing that seems most important is the fact that while the world is waging a war in the name of Christ, we can bind up the wounds of war in the name of Christ. Religion means very little until it is translated into positive action.[48]

The outward and visible sign of mainstream liberal Protestantism in the post-war world was the World Council of Churches, founded in Amsterdam in 1948 as the institutional legacy of the international missionary conferences of the interwar period. Prominent in its founding were denominational leaders from Britain who had organized during the war the British Council of Churches, which became the affiliated national branch of the world council. The World and British Councils of Churches were committed, not to Christian expansion in the normal sense of the word, but to Christian unity. It is difficult now to recreate the widespread enthusiasm for global church unity found in Britain's churches in the 1950s and 1960s. Many church leaders believed that the fragmentation of

---

[48] *Friends' Quarterly* (Apr. 1948), 75, URL: <http://nobelprize.org/nobel_prizes/peace/laureates/1947/press.html>.

the churches was a scandal, and that a united church would grow and exert Christian influence simply by virtue of being united.

The World Council of Churches provided a focus for the most important international political intervention of Britain's churches in the post-Second World War period: opposition to South African apartheid. In this they were joined by the Student Christian Movement. Initially founded to recruit university students for the missionary societies, the SCM became a major focus for Christian young people to express their solidarity with the victims of apartheid, a system that was all the more infuriating because it was a legacy of British imperialism that was imposed by devout Christian settlers. One of the most prominent Christian anti-apartheid campaigners, Trevor Huddleston, arrived in South Africa 1943 as a High Church Anglican missionary. By 1956 his outspoken opposition to apartheid led to his recall to England, after which he became an Anglican bishop in Tanganyika, Stepney in east London, and in 1978 bishop of Mauritius in the Indian Ocean, a position he used as a base for a global campaign against apartheid.[49]

The imperial focus of the churches in the early twentieth century had by this time been replaced, for mainstream and liberal Protestants, by what might be called 'Third Worldism'. This took its most emphatic form in the SCM, which became a vehicle for Christian youth protest in the 1960s. Evangelical student societies had by the post-war period separated from the SCM into their own network of Christian unions. The SCM became increasingly radicalized in the 1960s and turned into one of the most important vehicles for student radicalism generally before disintegrating in internal political battles, and being reconstituted as a more moderate and mainstream organization for liberal Christians in the universities.[50]

New organizations founded in the postwar period also became vehicles for a broader, middle class form of Christian Third Worldism, although their Christian origins and basis of support were often invisible even to their contributors and supporters. Missionary societies had always done some famine and hunger relief, especially through the provision of orphanages, and also work that would later be labelled 'development', i.e. building vocational schools, digging wells, helping promote agricultural improvements, etc. In the post-First World War crisis, Christian activists founded

---

[49] Piers McGrandle, *Trevor Huddleston: Turbulent Priest* (London, 2004).

[50] Robin Boyd, *The Witness of the Student Christian Movement: 'Church Ahead of the Church'* (London, 2007).

the crisis-based Save the Children Fund which later launched a broad international programme of education and support for vulnerable children worldwide. In the even broader crisis following the Second World War, Christian activists at Oxford founded what later came to be called Oxfam.

Oxfam's founder was a former missionary, Canon Richard Milford, who provides a good example of the ways in which missionary enthusiasm came to be channeled into liberal Protestant global philanthropy. Active in the Student Christian Movement while at Magdalen College, Milford then taught in India at mission colleges in Travancore and Agra. He returned to England to become secretary of the SCM in Liverpool, then Vicar of St Mary's Oxford, the university church. In 1942 he acted on an idea first proposed by a Quaker friend of his, Henry Gillet, and organized the Oxford Committee for Famine Relief, which became Oxfam.

Although founded initially to provide relief for Greece, Oxfam expanded rapidly in the post-war era to become the primary agency of British concern for what eventually became known as the Third World. Unlike the League of Nations Union, Oxfam's local work was not rooted in local parishes and congregations. They created their own local support groups, 605 of them by 1970, and opened local shops which became familiar features of high streets around Britain, 258 of them by 1969, growing to 430 in the next two years. Oxfam stressed its secular nature and even-handed distribution of funds without any religious or political dimension, but it resembled a missionary society in more ways than one. Third World handicrafts and Christmas cards were sold in its shops and by mail, along with literature depicting Third World children in their indigenous costume.[51]

Oxfam was distributing overseas more than £17 million a year by 1970. Just as one has to look very closely at the work of the League of Nations Union in order to realize the religious character of its grass-roots support, one must read Oxfam's literature closely to realize that even as late as the 1970s much of their aid was being distributed through Christian missionary societies rather than the secular NGOs of the very late twentieth century. Oxfam had become by 1970 a collecting agency for a vast ecumenical array of foreign mission projects, including the White Fathers, the South American Missionary Society, the Salvation Army, the United Free Church of Scotland, the Regions Beyond Missionary Union, the Baptist Missionary

---

[51] Maggie Black, *A Cause for Our Times: Oxfam, The First 50 Years* (Oxford, 1992).

Society, the Sisters of Charity, the Worldwide Evangelization Crusade, and the World Council of Churches. In Kenya alone they provided funds to the Catholic Mission in Lodwar, the Africa Inland Mission, the Finnish Free Foreign Mission, the Bishop of Nakuru, the Loroguma Catholic Mission, the Nkubu Catholic Hospital, the Butala Catholic Mission Hospital, Catholic Relief Services, the Presbyterian Church of East Africa, the Bishop of Kutui, and the Kwangju Christian Hospital. The list for India was even longer and entirely Christian with the exception of the Ramakrishna Mission. Dahomey was exceptional in that all development projects were secular, but in the overwhelming majority of countries the grants went to Christian agencies.[52]

Although Oxfam had Christian origins, and in its first quarter of a century distributed funds to missionary organizations abroad, it was secular in its rhetoric, and when compared to the missionary societies recruited directly few British people to work overseas. That purpose was served by another organization, religious in origins yet secular in its rhetoric, Voluntary Service Overseas (VSO). Founded in 1958 by Alexander Graeme Dickson, VSO claimed to have recruited over 30,000 volunteers to serve in over seventy countries during the next half-century. The target here was not the mission fields of the world, but the areas where people needed help, i.e. the Third World. According to Dickson's 'Christian but non-denominational faith', everyone had a capacity for service to others, and that service was mutually beneficial to the provider and recipient alike.[53]

The older missionary societies continued their work in the postwar world, competing with and benefiting from the work of Oxfam, and under pressure from the newer evangelical missions whose institutional work resembled that of the liberal societies, but who were reluctant initially to adopt the rhetoric of Third World development. As the older mission societies were displaced as vehicles for overseas development in the Third World, and Oxfam and VSO raised funds and recruited volunteers on an explicitly secular basis, the Christian churches responded by developing their own explicitly Christian institutions committed to Third World development. The largest was Christian Aid, which evolved from the post-war

[52] Oxfam, *Annual Reports* (Oxford, 1969–2007), *1969–1970*. A newsprint supplement headed 'Total Grants Allocated by Oxfam May 1969 to April 1970'.

[53] H. C. Swaisland, 'Dickson, Alexander Graeme (1914–1994)' (Oxford, 2004), URL: <http://www.oxforddnb.com>.

relief efforts of the British churches. Known first as Christian Reconstruction in the British Isles, it was later reorganized in cooperation with the British Council of Churches and the World Council of Churches division of Inter-Church Aid and Refugee Services. It raised funds under the name 'Christian Aid', which became its official name in 1964.[54]

Never as large as Oxfam (its contributions ran 15–20 per cent of Oxfam's), its early work proceeded on a parallel track, with local support groups, used clothing shops, and a line of Christmas cards. One of its officials was Janet Lacey, who came from a Methodist background in the north of England. Employed by the YWCA, she adopted the social gospel theology of liberal Protestantism. After directing boys' and girls' clubs at a Dagenham community centre in the 1930s and 1940s, she was appointed youth secretary of the World Council of Churches, and later became the director of Christian Aid. Rooted in the churches, Christian Aid's political orientation was Third Worldist, promoting not only aid to the poor but nationalist resistance and popular revolt. For a meeting of the World Council of Churches, Lacey helped put together a play called *The Rebel* which included scenes from peasant revolts in Ireland and slave rebellions in the United States.

Lacey provided a thoughtful analysis of her own theological motivation for this kind of liberal Christian work, characteristically apologetic about any kind of dogmatism that might be associated with Christian views:

Was it Christian? I do not know. Something had to be done and I did it without considering why...I think I can claim to be a religious person at least in thought if not in deed, and I am an almost fanatical believer in the ecumenical movement in the deepest meaning of the word. The world desperately needs unity. I believe that Jesus taught the love for mankind that knows no bounds and that the Church or its equivalent is an essential body in any country. It is a necessity in our culture and part of our history even if it is not any more accepted as an essential of life by the majority of the population. I have always found the dogmas and generally accepted doctrines of the Church difficult to accept and mostly impossible to believe. But, even when I have felt isolated and most bored by the Church, I have never been able to dissociate myself from religion and the question for truth and the meaning of life.[55]

[54] Janet Lacey, *A Cup of Water: The Story of Christian Aid* (London, 1970).
[55] Ibid. 33–4.

What is evident in her soul-searching is a combination of genuine religious faith of a liberal Protestant variety with a determination, characteristic of liberal Protestantism, to disassociate herself from dogmatic forms of Christian theology. Christian Aid went even further, disassociating itself from the indigenous Christian churches in the Third World that were in part the fruits of the ongoing missionary enterprise. Christian Aid wished to reassure its Christian donors that their contributions were going to support agricultural training courses, hostels for girls, TB clinics, etc. 'Need not creed' was the Christian Aid slogan. Hoping to broaden their appeal to secular donors, the 1968 report reassured them that 'the relatively small amount of money used for the strengthening of needy minority churches comes from funds given by church people only'.[56]

The prestige of 'development' led the overseas aid agencies to distinguish themselves not only from the legacy of missionary work overseas, but from the legacy of 'famine relief'. The stature of 'development' was given a boost by the publication of the two reports of the World Bank's Brandt Commission, *North-South* (1980) and *Common Crisis* (1983). Increasingly embarrassed by the growing gap between the wealthy and the poor in the post-war capitalist world, European governments began treating 'development' as a panacea for the problems of global capitalism, and the British aid agencies and churches alike got on board.

By 1985 Oxfam's elaborate manual for their field directors conceded that sometimes direct famine relief was necessary, but subordinated that work to the greater goal of permanent economic development to raise the standard of living in the Third World.[57] Evangelicals and Roman Catholics established their own development agencies, the Evangelical Alliance Relief Fund (TEAR) and the Catholic Agency for Overseas Development (CAFOD), that followed in Oxfam's path, moving quickly from an emphasis on famine relief to development. Reading the literature of any Christian aid agency, one will soon encounter the most durable parable of Christian development work (sometimes identified as a Chinese proverb): 'Give a man a fish; you have fed him for today. Teach a man to fish; and you have fed him for a lifetime.' Christians had gone beyond the work of the Good Samaritan, they

[56] Christian Aid, *Annual Reports 1968–1969* (London, 1969–71), 3.
[57] Brian Pratt and Jo Boyden (eds.), *The Field Directors' Handbook: An Oxfam Manual for Development Workers* (4th edn., Oxford, 1985).

claimed, and were now engaged in a theologically based struggle to improve permanently the condition of humanity.

Oxfam was ostensibly secular in its orientation, and never bothered to call attention to the heavily Christian nature of its aid recipients, which they presumably hoped would escape the notice of secular donors. The Brandt Commission reports pointed the way to heavy government involvement in development work. After the 1980s, Oxfam moved decisively away from their dependence on Christian agencies to distribute their relief funds, and towards government and secular NGO funded local development agencies. By the early twenty-first century Oxfam received contributions from over half a million individuals in Britain, but £56 million of its £181 million dollar budget came from government agencies, and its top fifty list of recipient programmes contained not one that could be labelled religious.[58]

Oxfam continued to cooperate with explicitly Christian development groups, especially Christian Aid, in the promotion of the ideology of support for the Third World. In 1973 Oxfam and Christian Aid relaunched the *New Internationalist*, a readable, informative, and extremely moralistic magazine devoted to promoting Third World support among the people of Britain. Their fundamental task was to persuade readers that Oxfam was not just a charity that sells old clothes to buy food for hungry children. The first issue included a long interview with Kenneth Kaunda on development in Africa, an interview with Roy Jenkins claiming that only a united Europe could tackle the problem of world poverty, and an article predicting the imminent economic collapse of Bangladesh, along with letters of congratulation from (among others) Shirley Williams MP, Phillip Potter, General Secretary of the World Council of Churches, the Rt. Hon. Richard Wood MP, Minister for Overseas Development Administration, the Right Revd Trevor Huddleston, the Bishop of Stepney, Peter Hain, and Sir Bernard Braine MP, Member of the All Party Select Committee on Overseas Aid.[59]

In the 1990s Oxfam cooperated with Christian Aid, Save the Children, and the Catholic Agency for Overseas Development to create a poster pack for use in humanities courses in primary schools. Entitled *The Great Wave 1491–1991: An Alternative History of Encounter and Resistance in the Caribbean*, it marked the triumph of the transition from empire to Third World

---

[58] Oxfam, *Annual Reports* (Oxford, 1969–2007), 2004.

[59] *New Internationalist*, 1 (Mar. 1973).

among non-evangelical Christian groups in Britain.[60] By this time, the decline of Britain's mainstream Protestant churches had accelerated greatly, beginning with a striking loss of members and participation in the 1960s, especially on the part of young families, that continued into the early twenty-first century. The reasons for this sharp downward turn are now the subject of scholarly controversy, but it is important to recognize that decline is not the whole story of Britain's churches in late twentieth-century Britain. Part of the story is one of transformation, particularly by the growing importance in British Christianity of evangelical, pentecostal, and black churches, and the impact of Islam on British religious consciousness. Each of these changes involved religious engagement with either imperial issues or debates about imperialism in a formally post-imperial age.

In the interwar and immediate post-war period, evangelical Protestants went through a period of retreat into their own religious subculture, one that was not immune to the general decline in importance of the churches, but was more resistant to decline than the liberal or mainstream churches and chapels. The evangelical interest in recruitment was not always a success in producing church growth, but other things being equal, churches that are interested in recruitment are more likely to grow than churches that are more interested in institution maintenance, church unity, social service, or the exertion of a diffuse influence on society. Evangelicals were strongest among Anglicans, Baptist, and the Brethren; by 1962 75 per cent of all British overseas missionaries came from those three denominations. In the 1950s evangelical mission strategy was shaped by two controversial books of the 'church growth school', Donald McGavran's *The Bridges of God* (1955) and *How Churches Grow* (1959).[61] Although an American, McGavran's missionary experience came from the British empire, where he was a Disciples of Christ missionary to India. Published in Britain by the evangelical World Dominion Press, and recommended by Sir Kenneth Grubb, president of the evangelical Anglican Church Missionary Society (who had been promoting similar ideas for years), McGavran's books set off a vigorous debate in British mission circles. Liberal and mainstream Protestants built on the

---

[60] *The Great Wave 1491–1991: An Alternative History of Encounter and Resistance in the Caribbean,* a poster pack for humanities work in the primary school (CAFOD, Christian Aid, Oxfam, Save the Children, 1992).

[61] Donald Anderson McGavran, *The Bridges of God: A Study in the Strategy of Missions* (London, 1955) and *How Churches Grow: The New Frontiers of Mission* (London, 1959).

historical institutional emphasis of the missionary enterprise to create a gospel of social service and global ecumenicalism, utilizing the extensive bureaucracies of the British Council of Churches (and its successor body, Churches Together in Britain and Ireland) and the World Council of Churches. Rejecting the wholesale and indiscriminate broadcasting of the gospel, and also the entire missiological emphasis from the 1790s to the 1950s of building Christian institutions, McGavran argued instead for group conversion. Although McGavran's sociological and theological views were highly controversial, he reflected a new emphasis among evangelicals in a rejection of institution building, and a relentless focus on the recruitment of entire social groups that could be identified as potentially receptive to conversion.

As liberal Protestant religious commitment became diffused throughout the development and ecumenical agencies in Britain and the world, evangelical mission societies, whatever they thought of the theology of church growth, began to focus more on receptive peoples around the world, particularly those who in previous centuries would have been identified as 'uncivilized'. Now they were simply identified by evangelicals as 'receptive', or 'potentially receptive'. Alongside the evangelical outreach to 'unreached peoples' was the work of the Wycliffe Bible Translators, with headquarters in Dallas, Texas, which was committed to translating the Bible into every language in the world, and developing a written language for that purpose for those languages that had none. By 2001 Wycliffe was the fourth largest employer of British missionaries working overseas.

As the British churches declined, some evangelical chapels and parishes began to grow, many of them independent of the mainstream denominations. As a result of their missionary recruitment efforts, the number of missionaries remained relatively stable from the 1960s to the turn of the century, although the definition of a missionary was changing. While some missionaries devoted their life to professional translation work, others volunteered for very short term work, some of it in the more de-Christianized portions of Europe where the logistical problems of bringing in enthusiastic but untrained temporary workers were not as daunting as they were in the Amazon basin or New Guinea. Many short-term missionaries were either retirees or college students, and in 2001 the two largest missionary societies were Youth with a Mission and Operation Mobilization, entirely new and entirely evangelical organizations that specialized in short-term mission work. The focus of their work was neither the British empire, nor the

Third World, but unreached and receptive peoples anywhere they might be found, a strategy of promiscuous opportunism that was treated dismissively by mainstream and liberal Christians.

Evangelicals drew upon the most vibrant and growing sectors of British Christianity, which remained the largest voluntary organizations in Britain even after decades of decline. In 2001 there were 48,807 churches in the UK, including 18,608 Anglican, 5,139 Presbyterian, 6,531 Methodist, 4,693 Catholic, 3,338 Baptist, and 10,448 others. They were served by 35,265 Christian ministers including 3,931 women (11 per cent), a number that was growing rapidly.[62] British Christianity was also being reshaped by immigration, which is one of the most important variables in the growth or decline of Christianity in modern history, and in Britain the imperial legacy was highly visible in the presence of black Christian immigrants from the West Indies and Africa. The number of black people in Britain grew from roughly 10,000 early in the century to 1.2 million in 2001. Although a relatively small percentage of the total population, black people had a disproportionate effect on the Christian churches, not only by creating their own pentecostal and charismatic congregations and denominations, but by their presence in the pews of formerly all-white churches. Between the presence of several hundred highly visible black congregations, and new black church attenders in Baptist, Anglican, Methodist and other congregations, black churchgoers constituted 44 per cent of the church attenders on an average Sunday in inner London, with whites constituting only 41 per cent. The rest were South or East Asian.[63] In 2003 one of the leading contenders for the vacant seat of the Archbishop of Canterbury was the Bishop of Rochester, Michael Nazir Ali, formerly a bishop of the Protestant Church of Pakistan. In 2005 a new Archbishop of York of Ugandan descent, John Sentamu, was enthroned in York Minister at a service in which the new archbishop played African drums. The global nature of Christianity was not only evident in the highly visible non-white presence in British Christianity, but in the importance of links to now fully independent overseas churches. The overwhelming majority of the world's active Anglicans were Africans, and the archbishops of the Anglican churches of Nigeria and Uganda were sufficiently powerful

[62] Peter Brierley (ed.), *UK Christian Handbook: Religious Trends No. 7* (Swindon, 2008), 12:3.

[63] Peter Brierley (ed.), *UK Christian Handbook: Religious Trends. Analyses from the 2005 English Church Census* (Swindon, 2006), 12:46. Thanks to Callum Brown for this reference. See David Killingray, *Black Voices: The Shaping of Our Christian Experience* (Nottingham, 2007).

within global Anglicanism to have the American Episcopal Church de-
moted to second-class status for its liberal views on homosexuality in the
Church.

The British empire might have come to an end, but the conflicts over
race, sexuality, and theology in Britain's churches are only one of the visible
ways in which imperialism is far from over. Attempts by the Western
churches to promote liberal theology and ecumenicalism in Third World
churches have been resisted broadly as efforts to impose Western values on
indigenous, self-governing churches, although those churches are often
eager to take funds from the West to maintain their institutions. The
focus by evangelicals on 'unreached peoples' set off a sharp reaction against
the 'cultural imperialism' implicit in bringing Christianity and the Western
written word to people who had previously had little or no contact with
global capitalism or Western values. Evangelicals were somewhat taken
aback by this argument, since they steadfastly argue that Christianity is
universal not Western, and that Christianizing a people and providing them
with a written language is in fact a way to preserve their culture in the face of
the inevitable onslaught of consumer capitalism, mining companies, and
the sexual immorality and violence promoted by the Western media.
Anthropologists and Third World activists who defend indigenous peoples
on the other hand see missionaries working hand in hand with capitalism
and Western government to subjugate 'unreached peoples' to militarism
and capitalism.[64] Christopher Hampton's *Savages* first appeared on the
London stage in 1974, indicting evangelical missionaries not only for their
complicity in Brazilian militarism, global capitalism, and imperialism, but
for cooperation in genocide.

Some critics of religion regarded the assimilation of indigenous peoples
as an undesirable consequence of evangelical mission work. Others regarded
the alleged failure of South Asian immigrants to Britain to assimilate to
British culture as an undesirable consequence of Islam. As late as the 1970s
most people in Britain had never seen a mosque, but as the Muslim
population grew from under 25,000 in 1951 to over a million and a half by
2001, new mosques proliferated: 8 per year from 1964, 25–30 per year
from 1974, reaching 613 mosques by 1996, more than the total number
of wholly African-Caribbean pentecostalist congregations. Even before

---

[64] See Norman Lewis, *The Missionaries* (London, 1988).

terrorist attacks on British civilians had been linked to radical mosques, great concern was expressed about the failure of British Muslims to conform to secular normality, especially in matters of dress. Surveys showed that Muslims attended prayers at the mosque at a stunningly higher rate than Christians attended church. In one survey in the 1990s 74 per cent of Muslims claimed that religion was 'very important' in their lives compared to 11 per cent of self-described members of the Church of England.[65]

The presence of Muslims in Britain, the explosive growth of evangelical and pentecostal Christianity around the world, the emergence of the Christian Right in American politics, and the presence of 'scientific creationists' who challenged the hitherto unchallenged authority of certain kinds of scientific reasoning contributed to a general soul-searching about the place of religion in modern societies generally by the late twentieth century. Problems that had been regarded as solved appeared again as problems. Debates about religion and imperialism raged long after the end of the British empire. The secular path to modernity, modelled on a particular phase in the history of European Christianity, appeared to be called into question, leading to anxiety about the consequences of a resurgent global phenomena labelled 'fundamentalism'. Some defenders of scientific inquiry launched wholesale attacks on religion as a threat to the rational and scientific thinking that was the basis of civilization, recycling half-forgotten arguments of the late Victorian age. The self-confidence of Mill and Huxley and their twentieth-century heirs about the demise of Christianity no longer seemed so certain. Towards the end of the twentieth century Alan Gilbert peered into the future in his closing comments in *A History of Religion in Modern Britain*. He could contemplate as an alternative to secularization only a 'kind of demodernization which would radically reverse the process of secularization' and 'might prove catastrophic for civilization as a whole'.[66]

It is far from clear how Britain will manage the contentious religious issues inherited from an imperial past as the country stumbles towards a new twenty-first-century religious settlement. The British monarch has held the title of Defender of the Faith since the early sixteenth century, when the

[65] Lancashire Council of Mosques, *Islam in Britain*, URL: <http://www.%20lancashiremos ques.com>; *Islamophobia: A Challenge For Us All* (Runnymede Trust, 1997).

[66] A. Gilbert, 'Secularization and the Future', in S. Gilley and W. J. Shiels (eds.), *A History of Religion in Britain: Practice and Belief from Pre-Roman Times to the Present* (Oxford, 1994), 503–21, at 520.

faith being defended was Roman Catholicism. Prince Charles set off public controversy when he announced plans to request that parliament change his title to Defender of Faiths, a change that would presumably allow Hindus and Muslims to participate in his coronation. Since then he has expressed a preference for Defender of Faith.[67] Some secularists and religious people alike might find that unsatisfactory. However, the people and rulers of Great Britain, and the leaders of Britain's religious communities, have a long history of negotiating settlements among people with a wide variety of religious views, and no religious views at all. Insofar as history is a guide to anything, it appears to be unlikely that the results of any new religious settlement in Britain will be catastrophic.

Select Bibliography

E. AYANDELE, *The Missionary Impact on Modern Nigeria, 1842–1914: A Political and Social Analysis* (London, 1966).

D. G. BARRETT, T. KURIAN, AND T. M. JOHNSON (eds.), *World Christian Encyclopedia: A Comparative Survey of Churches and Religions in the Modern World* (Oxford, 2001).

T. BEIDELMAN, *Colonial Evangelism: A Socio-Historical Study of an East African Mission at the Grassroots* (Bloomington, Ind., 1982).

M. BLACK, *A Cause for Our Times: Oxfam, the First 50 Years* (Oxford, 1992).

R. BOYD, *The Witness of the Student Christian Movement: Church Ahead of the Church* (London, 2007).

P. BRIERLEY (ed.), *UK Christian Handbook: Religious Trends. Analyses from the 2005 English Church Census* (Christian Research, 2006).

C. G. BROWN, *The Death of Christian Britain, Understanding Secularisation 1800–2000: Christianity and Society in the Modern World* (New York, 2001).

—— *Religion and Society in Twentieth-Century Britain: Religion, Politics, and Society in Britain* (New York, 2006).

A. BURTON, *Burdens of History: British Feminists, Indian Women, and Imperial Culture, 1865–1915* (Chapel Hill, NC, 1994).

HILARY M. CAREY (ed.), *Empires of Religion* (Basingstoke 2008).

Church Information Office, *Facts and Figures about the Church of England* (London, 1965).

J. and J. COMAROFF, *Of Revelation and Revolution: Christianity, Colonialism, and Consciousness in South Africa*, 2 vols. (Chicago, 1991).

J. COX, *The British Missionary Enterprise since 1700* (London, 2008).

---

[67] Andrew Pierce, 'Prince Charles to be Known as Defender of Faith,' *Daily Telegraph* (13 Nov. 2008).

J. Cox, *The English Churches in a Secular Society: Lambeth, 1870–1930* (Oxford and New York, 1982).

—— *Imperial Fault Lines: Christianity and Colonial Power in India, 1818–1940* (Stanford, Calif., 2002).

R. Currie, A. D. Gilbert, and L. Horsley, *Churches and Churchgoers: Patterns of Church Growth in the British Isles since 1700* (Oxford, 1977).

N. Goodall, *A History of the London Missionary Society, 1895–1945* (London, 1954).

S. J. D. Green, *Religion in the Age of Decline: Organisation and Experience in Industrial Yorkshire, 1870–1920* (Cambridge, 1996).

S. B. Harper, *In the Shadow of the Mahatma: Bishop V.S. Azariah and the Travails of Christianity in British India* (Richmond, 2000).

E. G. K. Hewat, *Vision and Achievement 1796–1956: A History of the Foreign Missions of the Churches United in the Church of Scotland* (Edinburgh, 1960).

G. Hewitt, *The Problems of Success. A History of the Church Missionary Society, 1918–1942*, vol. i. *In Tropical Africa, the Middle East, at Home* (London, 1971).

—— *The Problems of Success: A History of the Church Missionary Society, 1918–1942*, vol. ii. *Asia, Overseas Partners* (London, 1977).

A. Johnston, *Missionary Writing and Empire, 1800–1860* (Cambridge, 2003).

D. Kennedy, *The Highly Civilized Man Richard Burton and the Victorian World* (Cambridge, Mass., 2005).

David Killingray, *Black Voices: The Shaping of Our Christian Experience* (Nottingham, 2007).

J. Lacey, *A Cup of Water: The Story of Christian Aid* (London, 1970).

D. M. Lewis, *Christianity Reborn: The Global Expansion of Evangelicalism in the Twentieth Century* (Grand Rapids, Mich., 2004).

N. Lewis, *The Missionaries* (London, 1988).

D. McGavran, *The Bridges of God: A Study in the Strategy of Missions* (London, 1955).

—— *How Churches Grow: The New Frontiers of Mission* (London, 1959).

P. McGrandle, *Trevor Huddleston: Turbulent Priest* (London, 2004).

H. McLeod, *The Religious Crisis of the 1960s* (Oxford, 2007).

J. Marriott, *The Other Empire. Metropolis, India and Progress in the Colonial Imagination* (Manchester, 2003).

D. Martin, *Pentecostalism: The World Their Parish* (Oxford, 2002).

National Portrait Gallery (Great Britain) and Scottish National Portrait Gallery, *David Livingstone and the Victorian Encounter with Africa* (London, 1996).

D. O'Connor, *Gospel, Raj, and Swaraj: The Missionary Years of C.F. Andrews, 1904–1914* (Frankfurt am Main, 1990).

—— *Three Centuries of Mission: The United Society for the Propagation of the Gospel 1701–2000* (New York and London, 2000).

J. Peel, *Religious Encounter and the Making of the Yoruba*, African Systems of Thought (Bloomington, Ind., 2000).

J. Pettifer and R. Bradley, *Missionaries* (BBC Books, 1990).

A. N. Porter, *Religion Versus Empire? British Protestant Missionaries and Overseas Expansion, 1700–1914* (Manchester, 2004).

A. Porter (ed.), *Atlas of British Overseas Expansion* (London, 1991).

R. Rouse, *The World's Student Christian Federation: A History of the First Thirty Years* (London, 1948).

—— S. Neill and H. E. Fey, *A History of the Ecumenical Movement* (Philadelphia, 1967).

R. A. Semple, *Missionary Women: Gender, Professionalism, and the Victorian Idea of Christian Mission* (Rochester, NY, 2003).

E. Sharpe, *Not to Destroy but to Fulfil: The Contribution of J. N. Farquhar to Protestant Missionary Thought in India Before 1914* (Lund, 1965).

B. Stanley, *The History of the Baptist Missionary Society, 1792–1992* (Edinburgh, 1992).

G. Studdert-Kennedy, *Providence and the Raj: Imperial Mission and Missionary Imperialism* (New Delhi, 1998).

T. Tatlow, *The Story of the Student Christian Movement of Great Britain and Ireland* (London, 1933).

K. Ward and B. Stanley, *The Church Mission Society and World Christianity, 1799–1999* (Cambridge, 2000).

S. C. Williams, *Religious Belief and Popular Culture in Southwark, c.1880–1939* (Oxford and New York, 1999).

J. Wolffe, *God and Greater Britain: Religion and National Life in Britain and Ireland, 1843–1945* (London, 1994).

4

The Empire Comes Home: Commonwealth Migration to Britain

Wendy Webster

In Philip Donnellan's documentary about Caribbean migrants in Britain—
The Colony shown on BBC 2 in 1964—a man shown working in a foundry
reflects:

Sometimes we think we shouldn't blame the people because it's we who have
come to their country and troubled them. On the other hand, we think if they in
the first place had not come to our country and spread the false propaganda, we
would never have come to theirs.[1]

In using the language of them and us—'their country', 'our country'—the
speaker suggests separation between metropolis and empire, but also connections, particularly through a traffic in people. Such connections were
summarized in a slogan used in campaigns against restrictions on the entry
of Commonwealth migrants to Britain in the 1960s: 'We're here because you
were there.'

In the first half of the twentieth century, the extensive traffic in people
between metropolis and empire was imbalanced, consisting mainly of white
British travelling to and from empire—as, for example, administrators,
traders, and missionaries. There was a sharp decline in emigration to the
USA, and emigrants went for settlement primarily to the dominions of
Australia, Canada, New Zealand, and South Africa. By comparison, the
traffic to Britain from empire was limited. In 1951, for example, British
census data showed that there were 30,000 Australians living in Britain,
whereas in 1946–51 alone, 140,000 people emigrated from Britain to
Australia under the Free and Assisted Passages Scheme. Migration to Britain

---

[1] *The Colony*, BBC TV (1964).

before 1945 was chiefly from Ireland and continental Europe: a pattern continued in the late 1940s as demands for labour were met by government schemes for settlement by Poles who had served in the armed forces in the war, for the recruitment of people from displaced persons camps in Germany and Austria, and for bulk recruitment from Italy. Although there was a long history of black and Asian migration to Britain, and this was extended during the Second World War as men and women were recruited from the Caribbean and India to serve in the armed forces and work in war industries in Britain, numbers were limited. Once the war was over, most servicemen and servicewomen were demobbed back home. Mass migration from the Commonwealth to Britain belonged to the post-war period, coinciding with decolonization, and reaching a post-war peak in 1961: a date by which the British empire was almost at an end.[2]

As the 30,000 Australians living in Britain in 1951 demonstrated, Commonwealth migrants to Britain always included white people from the dominions.[3] This traffic, dominated by white British emigrating to Australia, was often viewed as internal migration. Widely publicized celebrations of the millionth post-war migrant to Australia in 1955 featured a British migrant as the millionth—Mrs Barbara Porritt—and continually associated her with the idea of 'home'. In the Australian media, stories of her arrival made much of her former British home in Yorkshire and of Yorkshire's links with Captain James Cook, emphasizing the close ties between Australia and Britain.[4] Many Australian migrants and visitors making the reverse journey from Australia to Britain thought in terms of arrival at a place thousands of miles away that they had never seen before as 'going home'.[5] But in the post-1945 period, 'Commonwealth immigrants' were not associated with Australians or other white Commonwealth migrants but with black and Asian people arriving in Britain who were rarely viewed as internal migrants moving within a common British world from one part of

---

[2] By 1961 India, Pakistan, Ceylon, Ghana, Malaya, Nigeria, Sierra Leone, Tanganikya, and Cyprus had all gained independence and joined the Commonwealth, to be followed in the next five years by Jamaica, Trinidad and Tobago, Uganda, Zanzibar, Kenya, Malawi, Malta, Zambia, Gambia, Singapore, Guyana, Botswana, Mauritius, Lesotho, and Barbados.

[3] Very few Aboriginal people made the journey to Britain from Australia. See A. Woollacott, *To Try Her Fortune in London* (Oxford, 2001), 13.

[4] S. Wills, 'When Good Neighbours Become Good Friends: The Australian Embrace of Its Millionth Migrant', *Australian Historical Studies*, 36/124 (2004), 345–7.

[5] Woollacott, *To Try Her Fortune*, 143.

the empire to another. By the 1950s, despite substantial European migration to Britain as well as white migration from the Commonwealth, the term 'immigrant' was widely used to mean a black or Asian person, usually male.

Literature on migration to Britain generally focuses on groups that were visible as targets of racisms. Until recently most literature on migrants from Europe was on the period before 1945, when anti-alienism was directed against many European groups and in the post-1945 period followed the direction of racisms, shifting attention to black and Asian migrants from the Commonwealth and empire.[6] There is a dearth of work on white groups from the Commonwealth who had limited visibility in Britain throughout the century. Historians have produced substantial work on British policy-making on immigration, but mainstream history was slow to situate questions of migration, race, and ethnicity within a domestic context, especially by comparison with other disciplines—notably sociology, cultural studies, and, more recently, cultural geography.[7] Imperial history was also slow to take up questions about the impact of empire on the metropolis, including migration from empire to Britain. The volume of the *Oxford History of the British Empire* on the twentieth century, for example, makes almost no mention of such migration.[8] What have been named 'new imperial histories' developed since the 1980s, are notable for their challenge to the separation through which imperial history was generally sealed off from

[6] Recent work on post-1945 migration from Europe includes J.-Dieter Steinert and I. Weber-Newth (eds.), *European Immigrants in Britain 1933–1950* (Munich, 2003); T. Lane, *Victims of Stalin and Hitler: The Exodus of Poles and Balts to Britain* (Basingstoke, 2004); L. McDowell, *Hard Labour: The Forgotten Voices of Latvian Volunteer Migrant Workers* (London, 2005); K. Burrell, *Moving Stories: Narratives of Nation and Migration among Europeans in Post-War Britain* (Aldershot, 2006); K. Burrell and P. Panayi (eds.), *Histories and Memories: Migrants and Their History in Britain* (London, 2005); Inge Weber-Newth and Johannes-Dieter Steinert, *German Migrants in Post-War Britain: An Enemy Embrace* (London, 2006); E. Delaney, *The Irish in Post-War Britain* (Oxford, 2007); L. Ryan and W. Webster (eds.), *Gendering Migration: Masculinity, Femininity and Ethnicity in Post-War Britain* (Aldershot, 2008).

[7] A substantial literature was produced by sociologists from the early post-war period. See C. Waters, '"Dark Strangers" in Our Midst: Discourses of Race and Nation in Britain, 1947–1963', *Journal of British Studies* (*JBS*), 36/2 (1997), 207–38; M. Clapson, 'The American Contribution to the Sociology of Race Relations in Britain from the 1940s to the Early 1970s', *Urban History*, 33 (2006), 253–73. For contrasting perspectives on policy-making in the post-1945 period, see K. Paul, *Whitewashing Britain: Race and Citizenship in the Postwar Era* (Ithaca, NY, 1997); R. Hansen, *Citizenship and Immigration in Post-War Britain* (Oxford, 2000).

[8] J. Brown and Wm. R. Louis (eds.), *The Oxford History of the British Empire* (*OHBE*), iv. *The Twentieth Century* (Oxford, 1999).

domestic history in a separate subdiscipline. Those working in this area have been concerned to reconnect histories of Britain and empire, but have been preoccupied mainly with the nineteenth century. Their limited attention to twentieth-century history only rarely extends into the period of decolonization and transition to Commonwealth after 1945. There is nevertheless some important work on the connections between empire and migration to Britain.[9] This essay draws on this work in considering how far imperial connections and colonial mentalities shaped the reversal of the colonial encounter.

Why did campaigners who used the slogan 'We're here because you were there' feel the need to point up connections between their presence in Britain and the history of empire? Catherine Hall and Sonya Rose suggest that in the 1950s, 'the West Indians and South Asians who were arriving were thought of as postwar migrants rather than imperial subjects with a long history connecting them to Britain'.[10] Bill Schwarz, commenting on images of West Indians arriving in Britain in the 1950s, suggests that they portrayed only an 'immigrant', thus effacing Caribbean history: 'Immigrants, it seemed, had no past, coming into life only at that moment when they entered the line of vision of the native, "host" population.'[11] Kathleen Paul argues that while in the 1948 British Nationality Act the terms 'British subject' and 'Commonwealth immigrant' were interchangeable, the choice of the title 'Commonwealth Immigrants Act' instead of 'British Subjects Act' for legislation restricting entry to Britain in the 1960s meant that migrants' association with Britain 'was pushed into the background'.[12] As these comments suggest, British perceptions of black and Asian Commonwealth

---

[9] See esp. B. Schwarz, '"The Only White Man in There": The Re-Racialisation of England, 1956–1968', *Race and Class*, 38/1 (1996), 65–78; Shompa Lahiri, 'South Asians in Post-Imperial Britain: Decolonisation and Imperial Legacy', in Stuart Ward (ed.), *British Culture and the End of Empire* (Manchester, 2001), 200–16; B. Schwarz (ed.), *West Indian Intellectuals in Britain* (Manchester, 2003); B. Schwarz, 'Claudia Jones and the *West Indian Gazette*: Reflections on the Emergence of Post-Colonial Britain', *Twentieth Century British History*, 14/3 (2003), 264–85; A. Thompson, *The Empire Strikes Back* (Harlow, 2005); L. Tabili, 'A Homogeneous Society? Britain's Internal "Others", 1800–Present', in C. Hall and S. Rose (eds.), *At Home with the Empire: Metropolitan Culture and the Imperial World* (Cambridge, 2006).

[10] Hall and Rose (eds.), *At Home with the Empire*, 4.

[11] B. Schwarz, 'Crossing the Seas', in Schwarz (ed.), *West Indian Intellectuals*, 7.

[12] K. Paul, 'From Subjects to Immigrants: Black Britons and National Identity, 1948–1962', in R. Weight and A. Beach (eds.), *The Right to Belong: Citizenship and National Identity in Britain, 1930–1960* (London, 1998), 231.

migrants scarcely acknowledged the imperial history that connected them to Britain. There was very substantial ignorance in Britain about imperial histories and geographies. A survey in 1948 found that only 49 per cent of those questioned could name one colony.[13] Many migrants commented on such ignorance, especially by comparison with what they knew about Britain—far more than people in Britain knew about empire.

Despite scant acknowledgement of migrants' associations with Britain, examining Commonwealth migration as a legacy of empire reveals a range of ways in which policy, attitudes, and experiences were shaped by empire. This is most obvious in the case of policy-making, and policy-makers were one group who were well informed about imperial relations (which in the post-1945 period were generally renamed Commonwealth relations). Such relations were a major factor in shaping official policy on Commonwealth immigration. This was the case in the 1950s when any moves to restrict immigration were made covertly, not openly, because of the desire to maintain Commonwealth unity. It was also the case in the 1960s when the imposition of restrictions on entry to Britain coincided with a perception of the Commonwealth's fading importance to national identity and interests and Britain began a 'turn to Europe' through its first application to join the European Economic Community. A range of factors shaped wider attitudes and migrants' experiences, but empire was amongst these, sometimes bulking large. Loss of imperial power is an important context for understanding attitudes to black and Asian migrants after 1945, while migrants' own attitudes and experiences were shaped by empire especially in the case of Caribbeans. Like Australian migrants and visitors, Caribbean migrants thought of Britain as 'home' but encountered in Britain what Bill Schwarz has called 'the unhomeliness of the imaginary homeland'.[14]

The experience of Caribbean migrants draws attention to different versions of empire in metropolis and empire, and there were also different meanings within the metropolis as well as within different parts of empire. Peter Marshall has grouped British interpretations of empire from the mid-eighteenth century under what he calls 'two very crude headings': libertarian and authoritarian. He argues that the authoritarian interpretation of a manly and powerful nation, embodying the values of hierarchy and order ceased to be fashionable from the 1920s, and that the libertarian

---

[13] G. K. Evans, *Public Opinion on Colonial Affairs* (London, June 1948).
[14] Schwarz, 'Crossing the Seas', 8.

interpretation of an empire that embodied liberal values 'has been a far more powerful and ultimately much more enduring strain of imperial identity than the pomp and circumstance so often assumed to have been the only strain'.[15] During and after the Second World War this libertarian view was very apparent as the language of empire was displaced by the ideal of a Commonwealth of equal races and nations.

One story that developed around migrants in the 1950s and 1960s suggested that liberal values also found expression in attitudes to Commonwealth migration, and there was considerable investment in the idea that Britishness exemplified tolerance in contrast to racial attitudes in South Africa and the Southern States of America. The vision of a multiracial Commonwealth and the transition from empire to Commonwealth were generally uncontentious—surveys showing that a majority of people preferred the language of Commonwealth because it did not have imperialistic associations. But a libertarian approach to immigration in the 1950s and 1960s rarely extended to the advocacy of a multiracial Britain.[16]

Loss of imperial power undermined the authoritarian interpretation of a manly and powerful nation, and another story developed around migrants registered such loss through reversing many themes within the authoritarian view. In place of the vision of Britain bringing order to the colonies, black and Asian Commonwealth migrants were portrayed as bringing disorder to the metropolis. The story of migrants as a threat to Britishness showed Britons as vulnerable and embattled, often foregrounding female figures. While the themes of this story frequently clashed with a libertarian approach, there was also some convergence, particularly in a common focus on Commonwealth migration as a 'colour problem'—a focus that suggests how far white Commonwealth migrants were invisible. The story of Commonwealth migrants threatening Britishness appropriated libertarian ideas, increasingly portraying such migration as a development that would lead to racial violence and undermine Britain's identity as a decent and tolerant nation. In reworking narratives of the British under siege in colonial wars, including colonial wars of the 1950s, this story showed Britons as embattled and vulnerable not at the hands of the colonized but of migrants, and not in empire, but at home.

---

[15] P. Marshall, 'Imperial Britain', *Journal of Imperial and Commonwealth History*, 23/3 (1995), 389–90.
[16] W. Webster, *Englishness and Empire, 1939–1965* (Oxford, 2005), 53.

Stuart Hall writes of the 'tremendous paradox' involved in the timing of mass migration to Britain: 'the very moment Britain finally convinced itself it had to decolonise, that it had to get rid of the colonies, the colonised began flooding into England'.[17] The focus of this chapter on this moment, tracing the implications of substantial black and Asian migration in the 1950s and 1960s coinciding with increasing awareness of loss of imperial power, potentially obscures the history of anti-alienism against European migrants in Britain in the first half of the century. Legislation restricting migration to Britain was introduced at the beginning of the century in the Aliens Act of 1905, targeted primarily at limiting the entry of destitute Jewish immigrants, and the first of a series through which controls were successively strengthened. Anti-alienism was a strong thread in attitudes to Jewish and Irish migrants in Britain in the first half of the twentieth century, extending to European enemies in the First and Second World Wars. Imperial forces fought against Europeans in both wars, and empire propaganda showed black and Asian troops as part of an empire united across differences of race and ethnicity against a common enemy, while European enemies in Britain were subject to mass internment and the target of violence in rioting. Germany, displacing France as Britain's main twentieth-century European enemy, was an important 'other' against which Britishness was constructed. Reviewing this history, Robert Miles argues that 'theories of racism grounded solely in the analysis of colonial history and which prioritise the single somatic characteristic of skin colour have a specific and limited explanatory power'.[18]

The history of anti-alienism suggests how far there were different understandings of different migrant groups in Britain in different contexts and at different moments with attention to a 'colour problem' concentrated particularly in mid-century. While the term 'immigrant' was widely used to mean Jews in the early part of the century, after 1945 it increasingly came to mean a black or Asian person, producing a characteristic opposition between Britishness as white, and 'immigrants' as 'coloured'. This opposition obscured the history of immigration before 1945—predominantly Irish and Jewish—as well as the continuities between the pre-1945 and post-1945

---

[17] S. Hall, 'The Local and the Global: Globalization and Ethnicity', in A. McClintock, A. Mufti, and E. Shohat (eds.), *Dangerous Liaisons: Gender Nation and Postcolonial Perspectives* (Minneapolis, 1997), 176.

[18] R. Miles, *Racism After 'Race Relations'* (London, 1993), 148.

periods, both characterized by significant migration from Europe. In 1961, just before the passage of the Commonwealth Immigrants Act designed primarily to restrict black and Asian migration from the Commonwealth, the number of aliens resident in Britain, predominantly white Europeans, was larger than the number of those who had arrived from the Caribbean and the South Asian subcontinent. In the last quarter of the twentieth century, migrants from the white Commonwealth and the European Union outnumbered those from the Indian subcontinent and the Caribbean.[19] After 1945, European immigrants increasingly acquired the invisibility that characterized white Commonwealth migrants throughout the century, although they regained visibility in the new millenium.

Laura Tabili, writing about the history of migration to Britain suggests that 'Episodes of intense "othering", discrimination and violence remain[ed] better documented than everyday coexistence or conflict' while an emphasis on conflict, 'has allowed the most xenophobic and racist of historical actors to stand for all Britons'.[20] This chapter, focusing on Commonwealth migration at its high point in the mid-twentieth century, traces some of the diversity of racial thinking in a culture that was never monolithic or singular, considers the diversity of migrants' expectations and experiences, sets Commonwealth migration not only in the context of colonial history and decolonization but also in the context of the wider history of twentieth-century migration to Britain, and looks at the impact of Commonwealth migration on metropolitan culture and identity.

Official Policy

In September 1956, on the first birthday of *Panorama*, the prestigious BBC television current affairs programme, Christopher Chataway reported on the 'colour bar' at British Railways. He ended the report by editorializing:

What is disturbing, I think, is that the men at Smithfield, and at depots like it, should deprive West Indians of any chance to prove themselves simply because of their colour... If this colour prejudice persists, then there's going to be a great deal of unemployment of coloured men. The only other alternative is to ban West Indians from coming into this country, and if we ever decided to do that we

---

[19] J. Walvin, *Passage to Britain* (Harmondsworth, 1984), 111; E. Richards, *Britannia's Children: Emigration from England, Scotland, Wales and Ireland since 1600* (London, 2004), 274.
[20] Tabili, 'Homogeneous Society?', 63, 65.

should certainly have forfeited our right for good and all to criticise South Africa or the extremists in the Southern States of America. Good night.[21]

Chris Chataway's editorializing focused on characteristic concerns of a libertarian approach to migrants, condemning what he called 'colour prejudice' and distinguishing Britain from regimes which practised racial segregation in the Southern States of the US and apartheid in South Africa: a distinction that was widely used in the 1950s to advertise Britain's liberal credentials. However, the colour prejudice that he considered would make Britain unfit to criticize South Africa—a colour bar at British borders—was being actively considered at the time of his broadcast. A committee of ministers, set up by the Conservative government in 1955, was meeting in secret to look at the possibility of immigration controls. A similar committee had been set up by the previous Labour government in 1950 to review 'further means which might be adopted to check the immigration into this country of coloured people from British Colonial Territories'.[22] Before the passage of the first Commonwealth Immigrants Act in 1962 restricting immigration, both the Labour government, from 1950, and subsequent Conservative administrations used informal methods to discourage black and Asian migration to Britain, particularly through encouraging colonial governments to restrict the issue of passports and other travel documents.[23]

Australia was quite open in the 1950s about a White Australia immigration policy. Why were discussions about controls of immigration conducted secretly in Britain in the same period? When a parliamentary question from a Labour MP in March 1954 requested the Conservative government to set up a committee to look into immigration, the Home Secretary advised against the announcement of a committee because 'even to contemplate restricting immigration from the Colonies would be a step toward breaking up the Empire, and in other quarters it would be regarded as evidence that the Government are in favour of a colour bar'.[24] In the same year, Henry

---

[21] J. Dimblebly, *Richard Dimbleby: A Biography* (London, 1975), 278–9.

[22] K. Malik, *The Meaning of Race: Race, History and Culture in Western Society* (Basingstoke, 1996), 20.

[23] I. Spencer, 'The Open Door, Labour Needs and British Immigration Policy, 1945–1955', *Immigrants and Minorities*, 15/1 (Mar. 1996), 22–41; Hansen, *Citizenship*, 59; Lampiri, 'South Asians', 206; S. Brooke, 'The Conservative Party, Immigration and National Identity, 1948–1968', in M. Francis and I. Zweiniger-Bargielowska (eds.), *The Conservatives and British Society 1880–1990* (Cardiff, 1996), 147–70.

[24] Hansen, *Citizenship*, 68.

Hopkinson, Minister of State for Colonial Affairs, commented that 'In a world in which restrictions on personal movement and immigration have increased we still take pride in the fact that a man can say *civis Britannicus sum* whatever his colour may be, and we can take pride in the fact that he wants and can come to the Mother country'.[25] A public image of racial tolerance, advertised through the 'open door' policy, was considered important in order to avoid offending colonies and former colonies, strengthening colonial nationalist movements, or damaging Commonwealth unity.

A covert policy that attempted to restrict the entry of black and Asian people to Britain was not new in the 1950s. The Coloured Alien Seamen Order introduced in 1925 and renewed in 1938 and 1942 attempted to exclude black seamen from Britain by requiring those without documentary evidence of their British nationality to register as aliens. The Home Office responsible for the Order was aware that few black seamen possessed such evidence, and that its policy therefore converted British subjects who could not prove their nationality into aliens. As Laura Tabili's work demonstrates, although this policy received some publicity, particularly through public protests by seamen, it was implemented through confidential letters from the Home Office to Chief Constables and, as an Order in Council, never publicly debated.[26]

Kathleen Paul's pioneering work on policy-making after 1945 demonstrates continued concerns to restrict the entry of black and Asian people in the late 1940s. In a context of acute labour shortage, Paul contrasts initiatives taken to recruit a wide range of European groups to the labour market, as well as continued encouragement of Irish migration, with the limited and circumscribed entry of black and Asian migrants from the Commonwealth.[27] In discussions about the possibility of recruiting colonial labour, a government working party's 1948 report set out the range of Europeans recruited to the British labour market since the war, but of a proposal to bring in colonial labour, recommended only a very limited and experimental scheme for women to work as hospital domestics, noting that 'a large majority of any workers brought here would be coloured, and this fact has

[25] Quoted in Malik, *Meaning of Race*, 21.

[26] L. Tabili, '*We Ask For British Justice': Workers and Racial Difference in Late Imperial Britain* (Ithaca, NY, 1994).

[27] Paul, *Whitewashing Britain.*

been borne in mind throughout our discussions'.[28] Moreover, in an unprecedented move, and one that was never subsequently extended to any other
group of migrants, the Ministry of Labour set up a Committee on Publicity
for the Education of Popular Opinion on Foreign Workers and appointed a
Public Relations Officer to orchestrate such publicity.[29] In this way they
attempted to shape attitudes through interventions to secure favourable
publicity in the media for Poles in Britain under the Polish Resettlement
Scheme, European Volunteer Workers recruited from displaced persons
camps in Germany and Austria, and Italians who arrived under bulk
recruitment schemes.

White migrants from the dominions, while generally lacking visibility,
became visible in government discussions in the 1950s about restricting
Commonwealth migration which expressed the desire to preserve their
rights of free entry. The Labour committee in 1950 noted that 'it would be
difficult to justify restrictions on persons who are citizens of the United
Kingdom and Colonies, if no comparable restrictions were imposed on
persons who are citizens of other Commonwealth countries', and considered control of white Commonwealth migrants 'undesirable'. The Conservative secret committee was also unwilling to apply controls to white
migrants from the dominions. One reason for decisions to use informal
rather than legislative methods to discourage black and Asian migration in
the 1950s was concern that such rights could not be preserved without
conceding that legislation was designed to prevent what the Conservative
Committee of Ministers' report called 'a coloured invasion of Britain'.[30]
When legislation was eventually introduced in the 1960s, it did not concede
this, and was not overtly directed against black and Asian migrants,
although a memorandum by the Home Secretary, R. A. Butler, explained
that 'its restrictive effect is intended to, and would in fact, operate on
coloured people almost exclusively'.[31] Concerns to preserve the right of
entry for white Commonwealth migrants became more overt with the
passage of the 1971 Act which was distinguished by a 'patrial' clause where
rights to abode in Britain were confined to those with a parent or grandpar-

[28] Report of Working Party on Employment in the UK of Surplus Colonial Labour, 1948,
National Archives (NA) CO 1042/192.

[29] Publicity for the Education of Popular Opinion on Foreign Workers, Minutes of Committee Meeting, 5 Dec. 1947, NA, LAB 12/513.

[30] Hansen, *Citizenship*, 60, 76–8.

[31] Quoted in Paul, 'From Subjects to Immigrants', 236.

ent born in Britain—a requirement that many whites in Commonwealth could meet, but few blacks.

The 1962 Commonwealth Immigrants Act was controversial—opposed by the Labour Party and a range of newspapers. Hugh Gaitskell, the Labour Party leader, described it in parliament as a 'plain anti-Commonwealth measure in theory, and a plain anti-colour measure in practice'.[32] A leader in *The Times* commented: 'The damage, emotional, economic and political, which it is likely to do the already fragile fabric of Commonwealth can hardly be exaggerated.'[33] Some opponents saw such a measure in the terms Chataway had outlined in the 1956 *Panorama* programme—as forfeiting Britain's right to criticize South Africa. Gaitskell, speaking in the House of Commons, suggested that 'the Nationalists in South Africa would be rubbing their hands and say that the British were beginning to learn at last'. He concluded: 'Think, consult, inquire before you deal another deadly blow at the Commonwealth.'[34]

The concerns about the Commonwealth expressed by the Labour Party and *The Times* suggest the extent to which the debate about legislation restricting Commonwealth immigration was shaped by imperial connections. Many opponents of the legislation, including Gaitskell, were strongly attached to the ideal of a Commonwealth which they saw as representing all that was best in the libertarian tradition, giving Britain claims to moral leadership in the world, and an important aspect of the British identity that had received so much reinforcement in the Second World War: tolerant, decent, civilized. Those who supported the legislation were not necessarily anti-Commonwealth, but the timing of the Act coincided with an increasing perception that the importance of the Commonwealth to national identity had faded, as well as a turn to Europe expressed through the first bid to join the European Economic Community in 1961. In this context, despite the dangers of damaging the Commonwealth emphasized by opponents of the Act, concerns about Commonwealth reactions to British policy on immigration became less pressing. Indeed a major criticism that the Labour party levelled at the Conservative government was that it had done little to consult Commonwealth leaders about the Act.

The highly contested politics of immigration control in 1962, shaped by concerns about the Commonwealth and different perceptions of its

---

[32] *The Times* (17 Nov. 1961).   [33] *The Times* (15 Nov. 1961).
[34] *The Times* (17 Nov. 1961).

importance to British identity and interests, quickly gave way to consensus. In a leading article in February 1967 *The Times* reflected on the opposition to restrictions in 1962 which had included its own warnings about dangers to the fabric of the Commonwealth:

There were widespread misgivings at the passing of the Commonwealth Immigrants Act in 1962. A good many people were reluctant to believe that such restrictions were necessary. Since then it has become evident that they are essential.

The same leading article made clear that what it deemed 'essential' were limits on black and Asian migrants:

[...] the pretence has been made that while limitations are necessary, they have nothing to do with colour. This is cant. Commonwealth immigration into Britain has had to be curbed not because of the employment situation, or even because of the numerical pressure upon housing and welfare resources, but because of the danger of racial tension developing.[35]

The Labour Party recanted equally comprehensively on its 1962 position. In February 1965 the Labour Home Secretary Sir Frank Soskice, appearing on Independent Television News, denied the entire history of Labour opposition to the 1962 Act, stating that Labour had 'always been in favour of control'.[36] In March 1965, both Conservative and Labour MPs who had voted against the 1962 Act stated in parliament that they had been wrong.[37] When Labour came into government in 1964, far from repealing the Commonwealth Immigrants Act, they passed further legislation, notably the 1968 Act which was rushed through parliament in March, introducing quotas that allowed entry to only 1,500 British Asians per year. It was directed against the possible entry of large numbers of East African Asians, with British passports, who had been expelled from Kenya.

The increasing consensus about the need for controls on Commonwealth immigration suggests the limits of a liberal approach. Despite the use of the 'open door' policy in the 1950s to advertise Britain's libertarian credentials, the vision of a multiracial Commonwealth was rarely matched by any vision of a multiracial Britain. Most previous official policy had repudiated such a

---

[35] *The Times* (16 Feb. 1967).
[36] Quoted in P. Foot, *Immigration and Race in British Politics* (Harmondsworth, 1965), 170.
[37] *The Times* (24 Mar. 1965).

vision, although covertly, from the Coloured Alien Seamen Order, through the recruitment of migrants and refugees from continental Europe rather than the Commonwealth to solve the labour shortage in the late 1940s, to the secret government committees reviewing means to limit Common-wealth immigration in the 1950s. In this sense the 1962 Commonwealth Immigrants Act built on past policy rather than breaking with it.

By 1965, however, when Sir Frank Soskice denied that the Labour Party had ever opposed the Act, a further commitment by Labour was enacted which re-established liberal credentials. The first Race Relations Act of 1965 was limited in scope, but the 1968 Act made racial discrimination illegal in the areas of housing, employment, and public services, while the Act of 1976 made indirect discrimination illegal, and established the Commission for Racial Equality. These Acts were introduced by Labour governments, but they were not repealed by Conservatives. The consensus that emerged between the two major political parties—what Shamit Saggar calls the 'liberal race relations settlement'—was thus one which encompassed both the Commonwealth Immigrant Acts and the Race Relations Acts.[38]

An increasing political consensus about this 'settlement' also linked these Acts. Roy Hattersley commented in 1965, the year of the first Race Relations Act: 'without integration limitation is inexcusable, without limitation inte-gration is impossible'. The Race Relations Acts pointed to Britain as a liberal and tolerant nation and gave a public commitment to racial equality. But the Commonwealth Immigrant Acts marked the idea of limitation to tolerance, enshrined racial inequality, and, despite the efforts to demon-strate that they did not operate racial discrimination, were not aimed at white Commonwealth immigrants from Australia, Canada, and New Zealand. Thus the Race Relations Acts made racial discrimination illegal across a range of areas, but preserved the legality of racial discrimination by the government at British borders.

The 'open door' policy of the 1950s was the moment of the Common-wealth. Despite the preference for migrants from continental Europe in recruitment schemes, they were officially aliens, while Commonwealth migrants were British subjects who from the moment of arrival had a range of entitlements, including the right to vote in British elections. This moment, however, proved short-lived and the 1962 Act demonstrated the

[38] S. Saggar, 'Race Relations', in J. Hollowell (ed.), *Britain since 1945* (Oxford, 2003), 318.

fragility of the ideal of a community of equal races and nations. Although proposals to restrict Commonwealth immigration did not originate in the 1962 Commonwealth Immigrants Act, such proposals were made openly as decolonization gathered pace, and concerns about Commonwealth opinion became less significant. This involved a narrowing of British identity from the expansive global Commonwealth of equal nations to a definition of 'our people' that refused entry to many who held British passports.

Commonwealth Migration and European Migrants

There has been considerable debate about the extent to which empire shaped attitudes to race in Britain in the twentieth century. Salman Rushdie sees imperialism as fundamental to an understanding of British racism:

It's impossible even to begin to grasp the nature of the beast [British racism] unless we accept its historical roots. Four hundred years of conquest and looting, four centuries of being told that you are superior to the Fuzzy-Wuzzies and the wogs, leave their stain. This stain has seeped into every part of the culture, the language and daily life; and nothing much has been done to wash it out.[39]

In contrast, Tony Kushner is critical of what he sees as the dominant trend in the historiography: 'that of dealing exclusively with black settlers after 1945 and only referring to the colonial context'. He argues that the importance of empire 'has been overstated in analyses that marginalize other influences and histories'.[40] Many scholars who focus on black and Asian migration, however, give empire limited weight in their analyses, identifying an indigenous racism in which colonial mentalities played a relatively minor role. Bhikhu Parekh, discussing South Asian migrants in Britain in a 1970s BBC broadcast, suggested that because of distinctions between domestic and colonial policy, what he called 'ugly forms of racism' were confined to relations between British rulers and their colonial subjects, while in Britain a 'relatively humane liberalism was maintained and insisted on'.[41] Stuart Hall, speaking in the same series, argued that a 'kind of historical amnesia'

---

[39] S. Rushdie, 'The New Empire Within Britain', in Rushdie, *Imaginary Homelands: Essays and Criticism 1981–1991* (London, 1991), 130.

[40] T. Kushner, *We Europeans? Mass-Observation, 'Race' and British Identity in the Twentieth Century* (Aldershot, 2004), 31–2.

[41] B. Parekh, 'Asians in Britain: Problem or Opportunity?', in *Five Views of Multi-Racial Britain* (London, 1978), 47.

about empire had overtaken the British people since the 1950s, leaving 'an enormous reservoir of guilt and a deep, historical, resentment' which provided a source for the popular appeal of racism. Even so, he suggested that this could not explain 'the growth of a home-grown racism'.[42] Errol Lawrence, commenting on attitudes in the 1970s, similarly argued that the 'imperial past in no way determines the shape of contemporary racism'. Rather, he suggested, 'the attitudes of superior/inferior, responsible/ irresponsible, mother/children, barbarism/civilisation, etc., provide a reserve of images upon which racists and racism can play'.[43]

The twentieth century began in a climate of anti-alienism against migrants and refugees from Europe with the passage of the first of a series of Alien Acts in 1905, prompted by the mass immigration of Jews from Eastern Europe and targeted primarily at limiting the entry of destitute immigrants—in practice predominantly Jews from Eastern Europe fleeing pogroms. This climate meant that in the first half of the twentieth century, many groups of migrants and refugees from Europe were viewed as suspicious, threatening, and criminal foreigners. A belief that British morality was exposed to corrupting foreign influences was particularly apparent in the association of pimping with foreigners, including Eastern European Jews, French, and—in the publicity surrounding the case of the Messina brothers in the 1950s—Maltese.[44]

A First World War postcard depicting Indian troops with the caption: 'Indian gentlemen marching to chastise German hooligans' suggests the instability of racial hierarchies in twentieth-century wars in which imperial forces fought against European enemies.[45] Indian troops were not used in the South African War of 1899–1902, fought against people of European descent in empire, because of fears of undermining white prestige. But they were extensively deployed in the First World War not only in imperial theatres of war but also in France where over 130,000 Indian soldiers served. Indian soldiers who had been wounded in France arrived in Brighton by train to be greeted with cheers, while British buildings converted into

[42] S. Hall, 'Racism and Reaction', in *Five Views*, 25–6.

[43] E. Lawrence, 'Just Plain Common Sense: the "Roots" of Racism', in Centre for Contemporary Cultural Studies, *The Empire Strikes Back: Race and Racism in Seventies Britain* (London, 1982), 68.

[44] A. Bingham, *Family Newspapers: Sex, Private Life and the British Popular Press* (Oxford, 2009), 161–70.

[45] Bodleian Library (ed.), *Postcards from the Trenches* (Oxford, 2008).

military hospitals to care for the Indian wounded included Brighton
Pavilion—a former royal residence.[46] Despite controversy about white
women's employment in these hospitals and strict rules at Kitchener's
Indian Hospital—also in Brighton—to prevent the soldiers mixing with
women of the town, such provision is in strong contrast to the treatment of
Germans in Britain.[47] In the First World War, there were anti-German riots
on a wide scale; the government introduced a policy of mass internment
of Germans in Britain and, by 1919, 28,000 had been deported: one-third
of the pre-war population.[48]

Richard Smith's work demonstrates how black soldiers and war-workers in
Britain in the First World War were initially welcomed for their contribution
to the war effort. But in the aftermath of war, between January and August
1919, there were riots against black communities in several seaports and
cities—the most serious in Liverpool and Cardiff where demobilized soldiers
from the British West Indies Regiment as well as black seamen were attacked.[49] In both Liverpool and Cardiff, relationships between black men
and white women were a trigger for violence in 1919. Lucy Bland's work argues
that even within the history of such violent episodes the racism expressed by
individuals and groups was not homogeneous. Exploring fears of miscegenation and white men's anger at interracial relationships in the 1919 riots, Bland
emphasizes the significance of women actively choosing black men as their
sexual partners and husbands: 'although their choices may also have been
informed by racist ideas, such as the belief that black men had greater
sexual prowess than white men, these women did not seem to have viewed
their trans-racial relationships as "unnatural", or counter-instinctive—the

[46] R. Visram, *Asians in Britain: 400 Years of History* (London, 2001), 181–91; D. Omissi,
'Europe through Indian Eyes: Indian Soldiers Encounter England and France, 1914–1918', *English
Historical Review*, 122 (2007), 371–96.

[47] Omissi, 'Europe through Indian Eyes'.

[48] P. Panayi, *The Enemy in Our Midst: Germans in Britain during the First World War* (Oxford,
1991).

[49] R. Smith, 'The Black Peril: Race, Masculinity and Migration during the First World War',
in Ryan and Webster (eds.), *Gendering Migration*, 19–34; R. May and R. Cohen, 'The Interaction
between Race and Colonialism: A Case Study of the Liverpool Riots of 1919', *Race and Class*, 16/2
(1974), 111–26; N. Evans, 'The South Wales Race Riots of 1919', *Llafur: Journal of Welsh Labour
History*, 3/1 (1980), 5–29; J. Jenkinson, 'The 1919 Race Riots in Britain: A Survey', in R. Lotz and
I. Pegg (eds.), *Under the Imperial Carpet: Essays in Black History 1780–1950* (Crawley, 1986),
182–207.

common terms of press condemnation'.[50] Richard Smith also notes that in the wake of unrest in Canning Town in August 1919, a magistrate described Thomas Pell—a Jamaican who had been attacked in the lodging house he owned—as 'a British subject, entitled to protection as much as any other of His Majesty's subjects. After the gallantry of our subject races during the war it was a very shabby thing for loafers in the docks to turn upon them.'[51]

The pattern whereby black, Indian, and white imperial troops fought alongside the British against European enemies, was repeated in the Second World War, once again involving a considerable traffic from empire to Britain. But in acknowledging the gallantry displayed in the Second World War, references to 'our subject races' were abandoned in an image of a 'people's empire' that emphasized Commonwealth and partnership.[52] After 1941 a similar image was developed of a 'people's resistance' that showed European peoples united in resistance to Nazi Germany. Both images excluded Jews who were also excluded from much war news, especially after 1943 when the BBC, following the advice of a deputation from the British Board of Jewish Deputies, decided to limit coverage of Jews to 'occasional favourable notices' in news bulletins.[53] Given the efforts to produce inclusive imagery of a 'people's war', a 'people's empire' and a 'people's resistance' in Europe, this exclusion is particularly striking, and was made in the context of fears of stimulating anti-Semitism at home.

Although the idea of a 'people's resistance' became a dominant image of Europe in the media after 1941, the early years of the war were a moment of intense anti-alienism against Europeans.[54] A Fifth Column scare intensified in 1940 when, after the fall of France, the invasion of Britain seemed imminent and some 27,000 enemy aliens were interned, many of them German Jews who had only recently escaped to Britain from Nazi persecution. During the

---

[50] L. Bland, 'White Women and Men of Colour: Miscegenation Fears in Britain After the Great War', *Gender and History*, 17/1 (2005), 37.

[51] Smith, 'Black Peril', 31.

[52] Webster, *Englishness and Empire*, ch. 2.

[53] In Apr. 1943 the Director General of the BBC delivered the final word: 'the present time is not opportune for dealing with the Jewish problem in our programmes'. Memorandum from Sir Richard Maconachie, 27 Apr. 1943, WAC, E188/2. For the intervention of the British Board of Jewish Deputies, see record of interview between Sir Richard Maconachie and Commander Oliver Locker-Lampson, 7 June 1943; letter from Sir Richard Maconachie to Lady Violet Bonham-Carter, 27 Oct. 1943, WAC R 34/277.

[54] Wendy Webster, '"Europe Against the Germans": The British Resistance Narrative, 1940–50,' *Journal of British Studies* (*JBS*) 48/4 (2009), 958–82.

height of the scare, all foreigners were regarded as suspicious and threatening. Italy's entry into the war on the side of Germany in June 1940 not only swelled the numbers interned, but also prompted anti-Italian riots in a number of British cities.[55] Mass Observation reported in May 1940 that stories of aliens acting as Fifth Columnists in Holland meant that

> the enemy in our midst is easily visualised. The always latent antagonism to the alien and foreigner began to flare up. Nearly everyone, as previous research has shown, is latently somewhat anti-Semitic and somewhat anti-alien. But ordinarily it is not the done thing to express such sentiments publicly. The news from Holland made it the done thing all of a sudden ... [56]

The treatment of Europeans who were identified as enemy aliens contrasted with the reception of black and Asian imperial troops and war-workers in Britain. In the later stages of the war the majority of black people in Britain were American GIs, and Home Intelligence Reports showed that their courtesy drew much favourable comment in contrast to the behaviour of their white compatriots, and that there was widespread condemnation of the colour bar practised by the American armed forces.[57] However, interracial sex and marriage between black American GIs and white British women were also widely condemned, and there were government attempts to deter such relationships.[58]

In the aftermath of the Second World War, there were riots against black communities in Liverpool and London, but riots in many British cities in 1947 were anti-Jewish following the hanging of two British sergeants in Palestine by the Irgun group.[59] Although attitudes to European groups recruited to the British labour market after 1945 were diverse, they included the view that they were Fascists who had fought for the Germans, 'some of

---

[55] T. Colpi, 'The Impact of the Second World War on the British Italian Community', in David Cesarini and Tony Kushner (eds.), *The Internment of Aliens in Twentieth Century Britain* (London, 1993), 167–87.

[56] Quoted in S. Rose, *Which People's War? National Identity and Citizenship in Wartime Britain 1939–1945* (Oxford, 2003), 94.

[57] D. Reynolds, *Rich Relations: The American Occupation of Britain, 1942–1945* (New York, 1995), ch. 18.

[58] S. Rose, 'Girls and GIs: Race, Sex, and Diplomacy in Second World War Britain', *International History Review*, 19/1 (1997), 152–5.

[59] A. H. Richmond, *Colour Prejudice in Britain: A Study of West Indian Workers in Liverpool, 1941–1951* (London, 1954), 102–8; Tony Kushner, 'Anti-Semitism and Austerity: The August 1947 Riots in Britain', in P. Panayi (ed.), *Racial Violence in Britain in the Nineteenth and Twentieth Century* (Leicester, 1996).

the scum of Europe' and 'the Jews of Europe'.[60] As David Cesarani's work demonstrates, war criminals of a range of nationalities did enter Britain under the European Voluntary Workers (EVW) scheme that recruited people to the British labour market from displaced persons camps in Germany and Austria.[61] However, anti-Semitism in Britain was regarded by the Foreign Office as a reason to exclude Jews from the EVW scheme in a memorandum instructing that 'the situation in Palestine, and anti semitics [sic], clearly prevent the recruitment of Jews'.[62] Very few Jewish survivors of the Holocaust were admitted to Britain—most of them under a scheme allowing 'distressed foreigners' to join relatives in Britain. In this context the Foreign Secretary voiced anxieties about 'the concentration of large numbers of refugees, especially Jewish refugees, in the towns', suggesting that to avoid such concentration, young Jewish men should be encouraged to work in agriculture and Jewish women steered into hospital work.[63]

An identification of EVWs as 'the Jews of Europe', despite their exclusion from the scheme, drew on the history of anti-alienism in Britain in which the term 'immigrant' was widely used to mean Jews in the early part of the century. The late 1940s could be regarded as a transitional period between a focus on an 'immigrant' who continued to be associated with migrants from Europe, particularly with Jews, to an identification of the 'immigrant' as black or Asian in the 1950s. This produced a characteristic opposition between Britishness as white, and 'immigrants' as 'coloured' in which migrants from Europe became increasingly invisible. The process by which European migrants became less visible was uneven, and anti-alienism against them still found a good deal of expression in the 1950s. Advertisements for accommodation that specified 'no coloureds' often also specified 'no Irish'. The children of German war brides playing with British friends, were confronted with anti-German remarks.[64] Poles were called 'bloody

[60] NA, LAB 12/513.

[61] D. Cesarani, Justice Delayed: How Britain Became a Refuge for Nazi War Criminals (London, 2001), ch. 6; D. Cesarani, 'Lacking in Convictions: British War Crimes Policy and National Memory of the Second World War', in M. Evans and K. Lunn (eds.), War and Memory in the Twentieth Century (Oxford, 1997).

[62] Quoted in T. Kushner, The Holocaust and the Liberal Imagination: A Social and Cultural History (Oxford, 1994), 235.

[63] NA, LAB 8/99.

[64] Inge Weber-Newth, 'Bilateral Relations: British Soldiers and German Women', in Ryan and Webster (eds.), Gendering Migration, 65–6.

Poles' and 'bloody foreigners'.[65] After the 1950s, the idea that Europeans were threatening and sinister foreigners recurred as an image of the Irish in the context of IRA bombings in Britain in the 1970s and 1980s. But otherwise it increasingly disappeared.

Post-war European migrants, like EVWs and those who settled in Britain under the Polish Resettlement scheme, shared many circumstances with Commonwealth migrants, particularly location in the labour market in low-paid and low-status work and problems obtaining accommodation. However, the view of black and Asian Commonwealth migrants as a 'colour problem' points up the extent to which, despite many shared circumstances, there was a range of distinctive attitudes to them that did not apply to Europeans. It is interesting that migrants from British colonies in Europe were sometimes incorporated into a 'coloured' category. Although Europeans were generally identified as white, Cypriots were not always seen as uncontestably so: studies of immigration in the 1960s variously defined them as 'white Commonwealth immigrants' and 'coloured Commonwealth citizens'.[66]

Distinctive attitudes to black and South Asian Commonwealth migrants chiefly concerned intimacy and physical contact. Nurses recruited from Africa and the Caribbean record white patients who did not want to be touched.[67] There was a reluctance to employ black women as waitresses, and Sheila Patterson found that fear of possible public reaction meant that firms in London, while employing black people on the food-processing side of the business and some black women behind the scenes in kitchens, did not employ them in jobs which involved 'contact with the public'.[68] A survey by Political and Economic Planning in 1966 found a similar reluctance to employ black women in shops as counter or sales staff, especially in food shops.[69]

Such fears were also apparent in servant-keeping practices. Although there was no image in either metropolitan or imperial contexts comparable to the black Mammy image in the United States, male and female black and

---

[65] Burrell, *Moving Stories*, 168.

[66] W. Webster, *Imagining Home: Gender 'Race' and National Identity 1945–1964* (London, 1998), 102, 123.

[67] Ibid., p. xviii.

[68] S. Patterson, *Dark Strangers: A Sociological Study of the Absorption of a Recent West Indian Migrant Group in Brixton, South London* (London, 1963), 101.

[69] W. W. Daniel, *Racial Discrimination in England, Based on the PEP Report* (Harmondsworth, 1966), 122.

Asian servants were employed in empire, including Aboriginal servants in Australia. After the eighteenth century these practices did not generally extend to the metropolis. Before Indian independence, Indian ayahs were widely employed to care for British children in India and were seen as indispensable to white family life on voyages between Britain and India. But they were dismissed on disembarkation in Britain and left stranded, with no guarantee of a passage home—a history which Rosina Visram has explored through the activities of a home in the East End of London where ayahs stayed, waiting for placements with British families returning to India.[70] In the post-1945 period, despite an acute shortage of servants, the boundaries around white family life in the metropolis were maintained. European migrants and refugees were employed as domestic servants and nannies, but few black and Asian Commonwealth migrants.

A focus on boundary maintenance, characteristic of the colonies, came home to Britain in the 1950s and 1960s in intense concern about sexual boundaries. Miscegenation was identified as a central feature of the 'colour problem' and in strongly gendered terms. In Britain, as in empire, white men's interracial sex was regarded much less seriously with anxieties often framed around the question: 'Would you let your daughter marry a Negro?'[71] White British women were cast as 'our women' whose national role as mothers was important in maintaining the race. Bill Schwarz observes: 'In the England of the 1940s and 1950s the language of miscegenation was the central issue in terms of white perceptions of race, defining the boundaries of England and signifying the inviolate centre which could brook no impurity.'[72] This 'inviolate centre' defining the boundaries of England was a white British woman. Fears of miscegenation were associated with alarms about prostitution and venereal disease which also fore-grounded black men and white women, with black men said to be 'preyed upon by native prostitutes', or alternatively 'living off the bodies of white women'.[73]

---

[70] Vizram, *Asians in Britain*, 51–4.

[71] Webster, *Englishness and Empire*, 53–9.

[72] B. Schwarz, 'Black Metropolis, White England', in Mica Nava and Alan O'Shea (eds.), *Modern Times: Reflections on a Century of English Modernity* (London, 1996), 197.

[73] C. Smart, 'Law and the Control of Women's Sexuality: The Case of the 1950s', in B. Hutter and G. Williams (eds.), *Controlling Women: The Normal and the Deviant* (London, 1981), 50; Lord Elton, *The Unarmed Invasion: A Survey of Afro-Asian Immigration* (London, 1965), 76.

Fears about intimacy, particularly sexual intimacy, with people who were seen as racially different—and inferior—could be attributed to imperial mentalities. Maintaining 'racial purity' reinforced the boundaries of empire. Fears about sexual crossings of racial divides in empire were fuelled by the perception that they would undermine the authority of whites, and particularly the authority of white men. Such fears meant that the British Board of Film Censors banned representations of interracial sex, but only sex between black men and white women, not white men and black women.[74] In some parts of empire interracial sex was made illegal but not in Britain. In contrast, in many states in the USA, laws against interracial marriage had a long history, and were not finally ruled unconstitutional until 1967. Like racial thinking about white superiority, fears about miscegenation were common to many societies where whites held power.

Whatever the influence of empire on British attitudes to Commonwealth migrants, racial thinking in Britain was shaped by the geographical separation between empire and metropolis: one where black and Asian people were seen as belonging in empire, not Britain. In the first half of the twentieth century, despite black communities in seaport towns like Bristol, Cardiff, and Liverpool, a racial separation between metropolis and empire was generally maintained. Coinciding as it did with increasing awareness of loss of imperial power, black and Asian migration to Britain after 1945 was widely perceived as threatening to collapse boundaries between empire and metropolis, black and white. This produced a story, most prominent in the 1950s and 1960s, in which Commonwealth migration was portrayed as a threat to Britishness. Like fears about miscegenation, this story demonstrated distinctive attitudes to black and Asian migrants that did not apply to European migrants or to white migrants from the Commonwealth.

Migration and Decolonization

The story of black and Asian migrants threatening Britishness is notable for the way in which it reversed the authoritarian view of empire. In place of the story of a manly, powerful nation, it portrayed vulnerable, embattled whites under siege from 'blacks next door'. Siege narratives were also characteristic of colonial wars in empire in Malaya and Kenya in the 1950s,

---

[74] J. Robertson, *The British Board of Film Censors: Film Censorship in Britain, 1896–1950* (London, 1985), 60.

and in both contexts England was shown as a domestic sanctuary threatened by violation.[75] While nineteenth-century tales of empire were of an expansive identity, the story of migrants as a threat narrowed to the world of English homes, streets, and neighbourhoods. Indeed the themes developed in this story seemed to exclude the possibility that Britain had ever occupied a position as a colonial power or continued to embrace a global identity through the transition from empire to Commonwealth. Englishness is increasingly invoked as an intimate, private, exclusive identity that is white. The English spend a great deal of their time indoors and their major preoccupation is keeping themselves to themselves.

The narrative of black and Asian migrants threatening Englishness was by no means the only story developed around them. In the 1950s and 1960s attitudes were diverse, and British tolerance was a prominent theme in the media, affirming British difference from the Southern States of America and from South Africa. Even so, anxieties about collapsing boundaries were common to many stories in which boundary-markers made frequent appearances. In keeping with the story of a quiet, private, domestic nation, such boundary-markers were often domestic: windows, doors, letter-boxes, back yards.

Stories which demonstrated anxieties about collapsing boundaries were often told as social exploration, drawing on a nineteenth-century imperial genre, apparent in photography as well as literature, through which the strange customs and people of empire had been portrayed.[76] In the late nineteenth century, such social exploration was quickly adapted to questions of class in the metropolis. In 1890, the year that Henry Stanley published *In Darkest Africa*—his account of his journey into Africa—William Booth published an account of poverty at home entitled *In Darkest England* in which he described the urban poor in London as 'colonies of heathens and savages in the heart of our capital'.[77] In the interwar period, as social exploration was taken up in a range of film documentaries, the separation of questions of race and class continued—race belonging to empire and class to the metropolis. Post-1945 stories of migrants might be regarded as

[75] W. Webster, 'There'll Always Be an England: Representations of Colonial Wars and Immigration, 1948–1968', *JBS* 40/4 (2001), 557–84.

[76] For photography see J. Ryan, *Picturing Empire: Photography and the Visualisation of the British Empire* (London, 1997).

[77] P. Keating (ed.), *Into Unknown England 1866–1913: Selections from the Social Explorers* (Manchester, 1976), 150.

exemplifying boundary collapse, for those that drew on social exploration investigated racial themes at home. Moreover, where the urban crowd had been associated in social exploration literature with fears of unrest and disorder, post-war exploration of black migrants used the working classes to represent order and belonging, making their families and homes into emblems of Englishness.

The relocation of social exploration on questions of race from empire to metropolis is apparent in the BBC documentary *Has Britain a Colour Bar?* (1955). It opens with the narrative voice of Robert Reid telling the audience: 'Not for the first time in our history we have a Colonial problem on our hands, but it's a Colonial problem with a difference. Instead of being thousands of miles away and worrying other people, it's right here, on the spot, worrying us.'[78] Reid quickly hands over the narrative to Renee Cutforth, who exemplifies the shortness of the journeys that social explorers of colonial problems made in post-war Britain by comparison with the 'thousands of miles' involved in imperial exploration: he is shown arriving in Birmingham by train. While the voices of Reid and Cutforth carry the authority of BBC journalists, other white voices are also endowed with authority—those of the working classes who act as informants on the lives of migrants. It became established practice for journalists to use the voices of white working-class informants to support their observations—for example about the domestic lives of Pakistanis in the case of Tom Stacey reporting for the *Sunday Times*, or the domestic lives of 'immigrants' in the case of Elspeth Huxley reporting on Brixton in London in a book that was serialized in *Punch*. Elspeth Huxley chose the 'quiet street' and 'privet hedge' as emblems of Englishness threatened by 'immigrants'. West Indians in particular, she noted, disrupted English quiet and order by playing loud music and keeping late hours at weekends. They also violated domestic boundaries, leaving yards and front steps filthy and windows unwashed, and lying in bed with their feet sticking out of the window.[79]

The white riots in Nottingham and Notting Hill in 1958 produced a rather different image of the white working classes from the order and respectability with which much social exploration endowed them. The shock registered in newspaper accounts was about the alien practices of whites

[78] *Has Britain a Colour Bar?*, BBC TV, 31 Jan. 1955.
[79] E. Huxley, *Back Street New Worlds: A Look at Immigrants in Britain* (London, 1964), 46–7.

in England, as cries of 'lynch the blacks' were heard.[80] Comparisons with the Southern States of America, and especially with events in Little Rock in the previous year, threatened the distinctions made between British liberality and tolerance and practices in America and South Africa. Reaffirming such distinctions, the press made much of the absence of any legal colour bar in Britain, and there was considerable opposition to restrictions on immigration. But there were also those who appropriated libertarian arguments to advocate restriction: mobilizing the idea of a tolerant and decent nation to identify the Britain that was threatened by racial violence, and to legitimate immigration control.[81]

When Enoch Powell delivered his 'rivers of blood' speech in 1968 he made apocalyptic predictions of racial conflict, explicitly warning that, unless Commonwealth immigration was completely halted immediately and 're-emigration' encouraged, Britain would experience the racial conflagration which 'we watch with horror on the other side of the Atlantic'. Powell's speech drew on much of the imagery familiar from social exploration that associated domestic disorder with migrants. In speaking of the English under siege in homes and streets, he made reference to boundary-markers like windows and letter-boxes and the violation of English domestic sanctuaries. Like social explorers he also used white working-class informants to flesh out his picture of the English under siege: the white male constituent he had encountered who told him that in fifteen–twenty years the black man would hold the whip-hand, the white woman who had written to inform him of the excreta pushed through her letter-box.[82]

Powell had disassociated himself from his passionate early engagement with empire long before 1968, and makes no mention of it, nor of the Commonwealth in his speech. Even so, the speech bears traces of loss of imperial power—in the reversal of slavery through which the black man will hold the whip-hand; in the reversal of the manly and powerful authoritarian version of empire through the evocation of a powerless white woman under siege in an English street. Commonwealth migration was rarely portrayed in Robert Reid's terms in *Has Britain a Colour Bar?*—as a colonial problem— but repeatedly as a 'colour problem'. The terms 'immigrant', 'coloured', and

---

[80] See e.g. *Daily Telegraph* (26 Aug. 1958); *Manchester Guardian* (2 Sept. 1958).

[81] Webster, *Englishness and Empire*, 173–4.

[82] J. Enoch Powell, 'Immigration', in John Wood (ed.), *Freedom and Reality* (London, 1969), 213–19.

'problem' were thus closely linked and, through their associations with the Commonwealth, the multiracial community of equal nations of the Commonwealth ideal increasingly came to signify a domestic problem. In 1964, responding to a BBC request for suggestions on radio programmes about the Commonwealth, the Assistant Head of Talks had difficulty in identifying a Commonwealth subject acceptable to the Light Programme audience and wrote: 'The Commonwealth hardly evokes popular passion, except in a form very near the knuckle: coloured immigration.'[83]

Unlike Powell, much social exploration drew on libertarian approaches, seeking to understand the social problem posed by migrants in order to promote greater tolerance, and attributing this problem, at least in part, to what was variously seen as colour prejudice, colour bars, and discrimination rooted in the attitudes of whites. Like Chris Chataway, editorializing on *Panorama* about the colour bar at British Railways in 1956, these accounts condemned such prejudice and sought an educative and campaigning role, engaging their audiences' conscience in the idea that change was needed. In the wake of the Notting Hill riots, the *Observer*, in an editorial, argued that restrictions on Commonwealth immigration 'would be a shameful admission that the problem is too difficult for us to solve and that a multi-racial society is impossible'. Even so, the convergence of these approaches on the idea of a domestic problem suggests how far the demise of the manly, powerful version of empire and an expansive imperial identity was registered through Commonwealth migration.

Migrants' Experiences

The Caribbean speaker in the 1964 BBC documentary *The Colony*, who called expectations about England based on what had been learnt in empire 'false propaganda', went on to say: 'If we had not come we would not be the wiser. We would still have the good image of England, thinking that they are what they are not.' The 'good image of England' recurs in many accounts by Caribbean migrants whose expectations were of a civilized nation commanding loyalty, and drew on a pattern of familial imagery where colonizers and colonized were seen as members of one imperial family. This family was represented particularly through the figure of a Queen or King in celebrations

---

[83] Memorandum from Assistant Head of Talks, 12 Mar. 1964, BBC WAC R 51/783/1, Talks, Commonwealth.

of Empire Day—Queen Victoria's birthday—and the idea of Britain as the motherland. On arrival, often within hours, any sense of Britain as a mother country was usually quickly dispelled as migrants discovered that there were different versions of Britishness in empire and metropolis. Having set out as British subjects they arrived to find that they were 'immigrants', often regarded as dark strangers who did not belong in Britain.

Unbelonging is perhaps the most common theme developed by Caribbean migrants about their loss of 'the good image of England'. Women who migrated from the Caribbean in the 1950s record: 'When we were in school, we were taught that England was the mother country, it supports its own, it looks after us'; 'I felt stronger loyalty towards England. There was more emphasis than loyalty to your own island…It was really the mother country and being away from home wouldn't be that terrible because you would belong'; 'Brought up as we were under a faraway flutter of the Union Jack, I believe that at that time we West Indians did think of ourselves as English'; and 'We really believed that we're going home to a Mother Country, a place that's going to be loving and nice…we were told that the place and everybody in it was nice, virtually angels'.[84] Sam King who served in the RAF in Britain in the Second World War returned to Jamaica when the war was over. He then sailed back to Britain on the *Empire Windrush* and arrived in 1948 thinking that 'You could not be good on your own. Your good was no good. Your good had to be British'.[85]

Travelling with expectations like this, many Caribbean migrants, like Australians, thought of their journey as internal migration within a common British world.[86] Walter Lother from Jamaica records: 'When I came here I didn't have a status as a Jamaican. I was British, and going to the mother country was like going from one parish to another. You had no conception of it being different.'[87] Such a view was disrupted by the discovery that their place within this British world was unknown to most British. Constance Nembhard recalled:

---

[84] Webster, *Imagining Home*, 41–3; Mary Chamberlain, *Narratives of Exile and Return* (Basingstoke, 1997), 71.

[85] Quoted in M. Phillips and T. Phillips, *Windrush: The Irresistible Rise of Multi-Racial Britain* (London, 1998), 17.

[86] W. James, 'The Black Experience in Twentieth-Century Britain', in P. Morgan and S. Hawkins (eds.), *OHBE* Companion Series: *Black Experience and the Empire* (Oxford, 2004), 378.

[87] Quoted in P. Ward, *Britishness since 1870* (London, 2004), 137.

We grew up under the colonial system and we knew everything about England, everything. And we came here, nobody had ever heard of Jamaica. I mean few, few, people. And it was funny, the few who had heard of Jamaica treated you differently. Those who had never heard, they all had the opinion that we lived in trees.[88]

A further discovery was that many British not only knew nothing of their place in the British world, but denied that they had any place in Britain. Sam King noticed a change from wartime attitudes when he returned to Britain with people 'more aggressive' and 'trying to say that you shouldn't be here'.[89] One woman who migrated from British Guiana records:

When we came here we swore we were English because Guyana was British Guiana. We were brought up under the colonial rule. If you don't have a new uniform to go and sing 'God Save the King', you hurt. When you come here, you discovered it's a different thing. If you're English, you have to be white.[90]

The impact of these discoveries was a new identity: West Indian. British racism, Winston James argues, undermined 'island chauvinisms' as well as dismantling hierarchies based on distinctions of skin colour—what he calls 'pigmentocracies'—producing recognition of a pan-Caribbean identity, although one that did not necessarily include Indo-Caribbeans.[91] George Lamming, who migrated from Trinidad to London in 1950, wrote of migrants' shift from island to West Indian identity: 'most West Indians of my generation were born in England.'[92] Thus people who had thought of themselves as British in the Caribbean increasingly came to think of themselves as West Indian in Britain.

Migrants of South Asian descent from the Caribbean often shared this sense of loss of the 'good image' of England—a theme developed in novels and poetry by writers like the Trinidadian Indians V. S. Naipaul and Sam Selvon. But South Asian migrants from the subcontinent, like British people in the metropolis, often knew little of empire as a British world, or of its histories and geographies. Anant Ram whose family came to Britain from the Punjab in 1936 records:

---

[88] Webster, *Imagining Home*, 43–4.

[89] Quoted in Phillips and Phillips, *Windrush*, 82.

[90] Quoted in Webster, *Imagining Home*, 44.

[91] W. James, 'Migration, Racism and Identity Formation: The Caribbean Experience in Britain' in Winston James and Clive Harris (eds.), *Inside Babylon: The Caribbean Diaspora in Britain* (London, 1993), 231–87; S. Vertovec, 'Indo-Caribbean Experience in Britain: Overlooked, Miscategorised, Misunderstood', in James and Harris (eds.), *Inside Babylon*, 165–78.

[92] G. Lamming, *The Pleasures of Exile* (London, 1960), 214.

We had no idea of foreign lands, we were in reality just illiterate villagers. We had only heard of other places, foreign countries. We just knew that the English rule over us, nothing more. We came to know the world after living here. This is a country of good life and I am quite contented with my life.[93]

Like Anant Ram's family, many post-1945 migrants came from the Punjab, a province of British India where the large numbers recruited to the imperial army, particularly Sikhs, fostered a culture of migration through travel in empire on military service. A feature of migration from the subcontinent was the heavy representation of migrants from particular areas—Mirpur and Sylhet as well as the Punjab—in part because of 'chain migration'. Like Anant Ram's family many were also from villages where they had little or no education. Unlike many Caribbean migrants, they had little sense of British culture through language, religion, or literature. While Caribbean migrants included substantial numbers of women who outnumbered men in the early 1960s, initial migration to Britain from the South Asian subcontinent was predominantly male and many expected to return. The Commonwealth Immigrants Act of 1962, putting a brake on primary male migration, began a trend of family reunification and increasing female migration as fiancées, wives, and daughters arrived, prompting an increasing sense of migration as permanent.[94]

As a highly diverse group by, for example, nationality, religion, and language, the self-identification of most first-generation migrants was not as 'Asian'—a term widely used to describe them—but as Bangladeshis, Indians, Pakistanis, Sri Lankans, or by regional identity. This diversity was reinforced by the arrival of many South Asians from East Africa in the late 1960s and early 1970s, after newly independent African states like Kenya and Uganda excluded them from public services and trading licences, and—in the case of Uganda—forcibly expelled them. Most East African Asians were from an urban middle-class milieu in Africa, and had good command of English—77 per cent of men and 57 per cent of women, fluent or fairly fluent.[95] They were particularly likely to distance themselves from an 'Asian' identity that associated them with migrants from the subcontinent. As a man from Kenya commented:

---

[93] D. Singh Tatla, 'This is Our Home Now: Reminiscences of a Panjabi Migrant in Coventry, An Interview with Anant Ram', *Oral History*, 21/1 (1993), 69–70.

[94] H. Ansari, *The Infidel Within: Muslims in Britain since 1800* (London, 2004), 253–4.

[95] J. Brown, *Global South Asians: Introducing the Modern Diaspora* (Cambridge, 2006), 49.

When I came here, I came straight to Leicester and there were a few Asians from East Africa in Leicester, but they were mainly from India and Pakistan you know, they were not with us. Our thinking, our education, our ideas were quite different from them and mainly those from Pakistan and India they used to work in factories, whereas we were looking for good jobs. So there was a barrier there.[96]

Good jobs, however, were hard to come by, and many East African Asians began employment in Britain in jobs that corresponded to South Asian migrants from the subcontinent: manual work in factories and foundries. Such a position in low-pay, low-status work was common to many migrants, including Europeans. Good accommodation was also hard to come by, and many migrants began life in Britain in privately rented rooms in multiple occupation houses—again a circumstance shared by many black, Asian, and European migrants. Like the government in the 1950s, employers and land-lords were often unwilling to discriminate openly, claiming that they held no prejudice, but that British workers, clients, or tenants would be unhappy if they offered jobs or accommodation to migrants.[97] At a time when the labour market position of both working-class and middle-class indigenous women was subordinate to that of men from their own class, migrant women some-times had access to higher status jobs than their male counterparts. This was particularly the case for Caribbean and Irish women recruited as nurses. Downward mobility was nevertheless common to a range of female as well as male migrants.[98] But men felt the decline in their occupational status acutely, experiencing it as much in terms of gender as ethnicity and class, as they felt unable to live up to masculine ideals: material success and provision for their families. Again this applied to European as well as Commonwealth migrants.

Many first-generation migrants developed familial resources to secure emotional as well as physical and economic survival. Mary Chamberlain's work on Barbadian migrants has shown how, in a culture of migration, families played an important role in facilitating migration—through loans to pay passages, or provision of childcare—while migrants reciprocated through contributions from their earnings for the support of family back

---

[96] Quoted in J. Herbert, 'Masculinity and Migration: Life Stories of East African Asian Men' in Ryan and Webster (eds.), *Gendering Migration*, 191.

[97] D. Wilson, 'Gender, Race and the Ideal Labour Force' in Ryan and Webster (eds.), *Gendering Migration*, 96.

[98] McDowell, *Hard Labour*; Burrell, *Moving Stories*.

home.[99] This culture, transferred to Britain, enabled the development of support networks as migrants joined friends, neighbours, and relatives already in Britain. Caribbean women often played an important role in initiating 'pardners' and 'sou sous'—pooling community resources to fund passages to bring children over to Britain or deposits for buying houses in a context where many experienced great difficulty in establishing family life in Britain as a result of racism in the housing market. There was also considerable development of community resources in the foundation of churches and clubs to reaffirm ethnic and religious identities in opposition to exclusions and racisms. Such a strategy was common to the histories of many migrants, including Irish, Caribbean, Polish, and Cypriot groups. The religious diversity of South Asians in Britain is demonstrated by the foundation of places of worship. By the last decade of the twentieth century there were an estimated 1,000 mosques and 200 gurdwaras in Britain, while the Swaminarayan temple in north London, completed in 1995, was the largest Hindu temple outside India.[100]

Commonwealth migrants also engaged in political activism. There were broad coalitions of black and white activists involved in the British Anti-Apartheid Movement, as well as in campaigns against racism in Britain—in the 1970s by the Anti-Nazi League and Rock Against Racism.[101] But much political activity against racism was organized by migrants, from the first Pan-African Conference held in London in 1900 through the League of Coloured Peoples founded by Harold Moody in 1931, to the activities around the *West Indian Gazette*, launched in the spring of 1958 and founded by Claudia Jones, which included the foundation of the Notting Hill Carnival. Anant Ram, whose family 'just knew that the English rule over us, nothing more', became a political activist in the 1960s and 1970s, working in the Indian Association, the Indian League, and the Indian Workers' Association. The 1970s and 1980s were decades of extensive political activism. There was considerable activity in trade unions, with South Asian women playing leading parts in many strikes like those at Imperial Typewriters in Leicester in 1974, and Grunwick photo-processing in London in 1976. By

---

[99] M. Chamberlain, 'Gender and the Narratives of Migration', *History Workshop Journal*, 43 (1997), 87–108.

[100] Brown, *Global South Asians*, 103; Ansari, *Infidel Within*, 11.

[101] R. Fieldhouse, *Anti-Apartheid: A History of the Movement in Britain, 1959–1994* (London, 2004); D. Renton, *When We Touched the Sky: The Anti-Nazi League, 1977–1981* (Cheltenham, 2006).

1992–3 their leading role in the strike at Burnsall metal finishing plant in Birmingham was much less well publicized. There were also a range of campaigns on policing—against the 'Sus' laws, under which disproportionate numbers of black youths were stopped and searched by the police, on deaths in police custody, and on the failure to take racist crimes seriously.

The literature on post-war migration to Britain has little to say about relationships between different migrant groups, particularly between white European and black and Asian Commonwealth migrants. Winston James, commenting in 1993 on 'the boundaries of the imagined black community', looks at the limitations to any sense of solidarity between African-Caribbeans and people of Asian descent in Britain and comments on the considerable mutual antipathy and distrust between them.[102] The focus of much political activism on anti-colonialism as well as anti-racism nevertheless aimed at solidarity with the Fifth Pan-African Congress, meeting in Manchester in 1945, calling for self-determination for all colonized peoples, the *West Indian Gazette* described by Bill Schwarz as 'a medium of uncompromising anti-colonialism', and the Afro-Asian Caribbean Conference opposing the introduction of the Immigration Act of 1962.[103] The term 'Black' with an upper-case 'B', was adopted to signify a shared political identity based on common experiences of colonialism and racism, and often a shared experience of post-war migration. By the 1990s, the idea of political unity between Africans, Caribbeans, and Asians had generally broken down.

Commonwealth migration, however, produced a wide range of new narratives of nation in the literature, films, and music produced by migrants and their descendants. West Indian writers in Britain had produced a substantial literature in the 1950s and 1960s, but their work was largely ignored by white British. In contrast, in the new millennium, novels like Zadie Smith's *White Teeth*, Monica Ali's *Brick Lane*, and Andrea Levy's *Small Island* were highly acclaimed. Black British cinema, a label given to films that drew on the experiences and were mainly made by film-makers from the Asian, African, and Caribbean diasporas, attracted a good deal of attention in the 1980s.[104] Where the narratives produced by whites in the 1950s and 1960s narrowed

---

[102] James, 'Migration, Racism and Identity', 266–74.

[103] Schwarz, 'Claudia Jones', 279.

[104] S. Malik, 'Beyond "The Cinema of Duty"? The Pleasures of Hybridity: Black British Film of the 1980s and 1990s', in A. Higson (ed.), *Dissolving Views: Key Writings on British Cinema* (London, 1996).

THE EMPIRE COMES HOME

definitions of Britishness, the narratives produced by migrants and their descendants often expanded them, putting black and Asian experiences at their centre, and foregrounding these experiences as distinctively British.

The New Millennium

Winston James, reviewing the history of black experience in twentieth-century Britain and assessing the position by the end of the century, writes of the persistence of racism, albeit 'less crudely than previously' and of disadvantage in education and the workplace. But he also reviews a range of positive developments, including the British public gradually reconciling itself to a black presence, the popularity of black music and the Notting Hill Carnival, the more conspicuous black presence in the media, and a remarkable level of intermingling, especially among young people, across racial lines. Juxtaposing the popularity of Zadie Smith's celebration of multiracial London in *White Teeth* with the details of the uglier side of Britain provided in the MacPherson Report on the racist murder of Stephen Lawrence—a black teenager—at a bus stop in south-east London in 1993, he concludes: 'although all was far from well for black people in Britain . . . there has been remarkable progress'.[105]

Findings in surveys, although uneven, support the idea of 'remarkable progress' as well as the persistence of racism. A MORI poll in 2000 found that the distinctive attitudes to black and South Asian migrants about intimacy and physical contact that were so evident in mid-century and which did not apply to Europeans, had been very considerably eroded. Of respondents to the poll, 75 per cent said they would not be upset if a relative married a person of Caribbean or Asian origin. A further 80 per cent said they would not be upset if their neighbour or their boss was black or Asian.[106] Other surveys suggested how far Commonwealth migration changed the meaning of Britishness. Tariq Modood found that 'British' was a common self-identification amongst minority ethnic groups in Britain with a majority, in all groups except the Chinese, agreeing with the

---

[105] James, 'Black Experience', 384–5.

[106] N. Finney and E. Peach, *Attitudes Towards Asylum Seekers, Refugees and Other Immigrants* (Information Centre about Asylum and Refugees in the UK, 2005), 11–12, http://www.icar.org. uk/download.php?id=508/

statement: 'In many ways I think of myself as British', and writes that 'one of the most profound developments has been that "ethnicity" or "blackness" is experienced less as an oppositional identity than as a way of being British'.[107] By the new millennium, terms like 'British Muslims', 'British Asians', and 'black British' had come into common usage, suggesting that these ways of being British enjoyed wide recognition. A survey of British social attitudes in the new millennium found that only a minority agreed with the statement that 'to be truly English you have to be white'—17 per cent of the salariat, 32 per cent of the self-employed, and 31 per cent of the working class.[108]

These findings demonstrate a considerable shift in racial thinking in Britain, but in the late twentieth and early twenty-first century there were a range of other developments which complicate this picture. In mid-century, Commonwealth migrants who thought of Britain as the mother country viewed their journey as internal migration within a common British world, but by the end of the century it was migrants from European Union (EU) member states who had rights of entry and were sometimes viewed as internal migrants within a common European world. The EU's aspirations to abolish internal restrictions on the movement of nationals of member states were gradually realized, particularly through the Single European Act of 1986, which set a date for the abolition of internal frontiers. From 1 January 1993, this meant that nationals could increasingly seek work and take up residence in any other member state. The relative invisibility of European migrants in the second half of the twentieth century is particularly evident in responses to these developments, which aroused little public comment. In strong contrast to European migrants in the first half of the century, and to black and Asian Commonwealth migrants in mid-century, EU migrants in Britain went more or less unremarked until the new millennium when migrants from the new EU accession states, particularly Poles, became highly visible.[109]

---

[107] T. Modood, 'Culture and Identity', in T. Modood and R. Berthoud (eds.), *Ethnic Minorities in Britain: Diversity and Disadvantage* (London: Policy Studies Institute, 1997), 329; T. Modood, 'Defined by Some Distinctly Hyphenated Britishness', *Times Higher Education Supplement* (3 Sept. 2004).

[108] *British Social Attitudes: Focusing on Diversity* (London, 2000), 58.

[109] K. Burrell, 'Migration to the UK from Poland: Continuity and Change in East-West European Mobility', in K. Burrell (ed.), *Polish Migration to the UK in the 'New' European Union* (Aldershot, 2008), 1–19.

Media coverage of the terrorist bombing of London on 7 July 2005 in which fifty-two people died, drew attention to two other late-twentieth-century developments. Before the 1980s, as Humayun Ansari observes, Muslims were generally subsumed within ethnic categories, and ethnic identities—black, Asian, Arab—were seen as the markers of difference rather than religion.[110] The July bombings strengthened a view that had been developed particularly from 1989, when a death sentence by fatwa was imposed on Salman Rushdie after his publication of *The Satanic Verses* and the book was publicly burnt in a Muslim demonstration in Bradford: Muslims in Britain were a threat to Britain and Britishness. Much media coverage was concerned to distinguish between a majority of law-abiding and responsible Muslims and the extremists who had perpetrated the atrocities in London. Even so, many Muslims in Britain reported that they lived in an increasingly hostile climate.

Two bombers who had grown up in Britain attracted particular media coverage in reports of the atrocities in London. Under the headline 'Gratitude!' the *Daily Mail* reported: 'Their families came here seeking asylum and were given homes, schooling and all the benefits of British life. How do they repay us? By trying to blow us up.'[111] Such reporting drew on intense hostility to asylum-seekers apparent from the closing decades of the twentieth century not only in the media but also in the pronouncements of many politicians. As in the case of Muslims, so in the case of asylum-seekers there was concern to distinguish between those who were law-abiding and responsible citizens and those who were fraudulently claiming asylum in Britain, but this was a distinction that assigned 'genuine' and decent refugees mainly to the past.[112]

In 2002, a Report for the Home Office on asylum-seekers found that one of the key factors shaping decisions to come to the UK was 'previous links between their own country and the UK, including colonialism'. It suggested that 'colonial links present powerful connections for many asylum seekers' and that 'asylum seekers in ex-colonies may also view the "mother country" in an idealised way, and consider that it has a duty to accept them when they apply for asylum'.[113] Those seeking asylum, however, included many people who were not from former colonies, and particularly intense hostility was

[110] Ansari, *Infidel Within*, 9.   [111] *Daily Mail* (27 July 2005).
[112] See T. Kushner, *Remembering Refugees: Then and Now* (Manchester, 2006).
[113] V. Robinson and J. Segrott, *Understanding the Decisions of Asylum Seekers* (Home Office Research Study 243, July 2002), pp. viii, 5.

directed at Roma from Europe.[114] Les Back's work shows extensive intermingling among young black and white people in a post-war housing estate
in London in a context where Vietnamese youth who had entered Britain as
refugees were subjected to the worst forms of racial abuse.[115] There was also
some evidence to suggest tension between existing minority ethnic communities and asylum-seekers.[116] In Leeds and Newcastle, refugee agencies
reported that members of established minority ethnic communities were
concerned about perceptions that they were asylum-seekers.[117] A 1991 survey by NOP (National Opinion Polls) found that Asian attitudes towards
refugees and further waves of economic migrants were indistinguishable
from those of whites.[118]

A series of Immigration and Asylum Bills, beginning in 1991, were
designed to deter asylum-seekers from entering Britain. Surveys showed a
widespread belief that asylum-seekers were not genuine and posed a threat
to British culture, and that Britain was a 'soft touch'. 'Refugee' was a term
increasingly associated with dishonesty in the notion of 'bogus' asylum-
seekers, and with criminality through the policy of detention in prisons.
Tony Kushner and Katharine Knox's work shows that it was a term shunned
by those arriving in Britain who might have used this as a self-description,
because it had become a term of abuse in British society.[119] David Feldman,
charting the history of changing entitlements of 'strangers' in successive
welfare systems from the seventeenth century, sees 'the contemporary
assault on the welfare entitlements of asylum seekers' as unprecedented.[120]

Conclusion

Setting the history of Commonwealth migration within the wider history of
migration points to a complex picture in which particular groups—defined

[114] Kushner, *Remembering Refugees*, 188–97.
[115] L. Back, *New Ethnicities and Urban Cultures: Racisms and Multiculture in Young Lives* (London, 1996), 241.
[116] Finney and Peach, *Attitudes Towards Asylum Seekers*, 12–13, 41.
[117] L. D'Onofrio and K. Munk, *Understanding the Stranger* (Information Centre about Asylum and Refugees in the UK, 2004), 29.
[118] S. Saggar, 'Immigration and Public Opinion', *Political Quarterly*, 74/1 (2004), 184.
[119] T. Kushner and K. Knox, *Refugees in an Age of Genocide: Global, National and Local Perspectives during the Twentieth Century* (1999).
[120] D. Feldman, 'Migrants, Immigrants and Welfare from the Old Poor Law to the Welfare State', *Transactions of the Royal Historical Society*, 6th ser., 13 (2003), 104.

sometimes by ethnicity, sometimes by nationality or religion—attained visibility and were the targets of hostility at different moments. White Commonwealth migrants were invisible throughout the century but it was not until after 1945 that migrants from Europe increasingly acquired comparable invisibility. Anti-alienism was a strong thread in attitudes towards Jewish and Irish migrants in the first half of the twentieth century and directed particularly against European enemies in the First and Second World Wars. In the context of these wars, in which imperial forces fought against European enemies, Indians, Caribbeans, and Africans were welcomed in Britain for their contributions to the war effort, but those who stayed on or were demobilized home and then returned, had a more hostile reception when the wars were over.

Before 1945, racial thinking was shaped by the geographical separation between empire and metropolis. Black and Asian people, although British subjects, were seen as belonging in empire, not Britain. In the 1950s and 1960s as the empire came home, migration collapsed this racial separation but produced no vision of a multiracial Britain to match the ideal of a multiracial Commonwealth, exposing the fragility of the Commonwealth ideal. Attitudes in mid-century were diverse but the arrival of black and Asian migrants, coinciding with increasing awareness of loss of imperial power, produced a range of narratives that identified them as a threat to Britishness. They were also widely regarded as people who did not belong in Britain, and one of their key experiences was of unbelonging. By the end of the century, the redrawing of imperial and national boundaries through restrictions on Commonwealth immigration and the abolition of EU internal frontiers, reversed the position at the beginning of the century when migrants from the Commonwealth had unrestricted right of entry, while migrants from Europe were restricted. But Commonwealth migration, as a permanent legacy of empire, had created a multiracial Britain and religious pluralism. The evidence, though uneven, suggested how far Britain, shorn of empire, increasingly embraced a multiracial identity at home: one recognized by many white, black and Asian people. Such a multiracial identity did not extend to Muslims or asylum-seekers, and there was an increasing identification of these groups—both highly diverse by ethnicity and nationality—as a threat to Britishness.

Select Bibliography

H. ANSARI, *The Infidel Within: Muslims in Britain since 1800* (London, 2004).

L. BLAND, 'White Women and Men of Colour: Miscegenation Fears in Britain After the Great War', *Gender and History*, 17 (Apr. 2005), 29–61.

J. BROWN, *Global South Asians: Introducing the Modern Diaspora* (Cambridge, 2006).

R. HANSEN, *Citizenship and Immigration in Post-War Britain* (Oxford, 2000).

C. HOLMES, *John Bull's Island: Immigration and British Society, 1871–1971* (Basingstoke, 1988).

W. JAMES, 'The Black Experience in Twentieth-Century Britain', in P. Morgan and S. Hawkins (eds.), *Black Experience and the Empire* (Oxford, 2004), 347–86.

—— and C. HARRIS (eds.), *Inside Babylon: The Caribbean Diaspora in Britain* (London, 1993).

T. KUSHNER and K. KNOX, *Refugees in an Age of Genocide: Global, National and Local Perspectives During the Twentieth Century* (London, 1999).

S. LAHIRI, 'South Asians in Post-Imperial Britain: Decolonisation and Imperial Legacy', in Stuart Ward (ed.), *British Culture and the End of Empire* (Manchester, 2001), 200–16.

K. PAUL, *Whitewashing Britain: Race and Citizenship in the Postwar Era* (Ithaca, NY, 1997).

M. PHILLIPS and T. PHILLIPS, *Windrush: The Irresistible Rise of Multi-Racial Britain* (London, 1998).

B. SCHWARZ, '"The Only White Man in There": The Re-Racialisation of England, 1956–1968', *Race and Class*, 38 (1996), 65–78.

—— 'Claudia Jones and the *West Indian Gazette*: Reflections on the Emergence of Post-Colonial Britain', *Twentieth Century British History*, 14 (2003), 264–85.

—— (ed.), *West Indian Intellectuals in Britain* (Manchester, 2003).

I. SPENCER, *British Immigration Policy since 1939: The Making of Multiracial Britain* (London, 1997).

L. TABILI, *'We Ask For British Justice': Workers and Racial Difference in Late Imperial Britain* (Ithaca, NY, 1994).

—— 'A Homogeneous Society? Britain's Internal "Others", 1800–Present', in C. Hall and S. Rose (eds.), *At Home With the Empire: Metropolitan Culture and the Imperial World* (Cambridge, 2006).

C. WATERS, '"Dark Strangers" in our Midst: Discourses of Race and Nation in Britain, 1947–1963', *Journal of British Studies*, 36/2 (1997), 207–38.

W. WEBSTER, *Imagining Home: Gender 'Race' and National Identity 1945–1964* (London, 1998).

—— *Englishness and Empire, 1939–1965* (Oxford, 2005).

5

The Empire and British Politics

Richard Whiting

Empire, by its very nature, posed important questions for British politicians about national purpose and political values.[1] The outcome took on a particular quality: that while, from early in the twentieth century, politicians pronounced themselves willing to 'let go' of the empire, the reality was that imperial issues continued to provide moments of real drama for much of the century, and one of the final episodes—the Falklands War—was perhaps the most dramatic of all. It is this coexistence between an area of British politics that had been, in a fundamental sense, settled by the acceptance of ultimate withdrawal, and its regular occurrence on the political agenda, that is the theme of this essay.

The intensity of the imperial factor in British politics was not of the first order. Domestic preoccupations with economic prospects and social stability were naturally a priority. When the wider world came into focus for the British it was essentially in the form of war and international relations. Indeed, one of the reasons for the public tolerance of, or indifference to, the imperial withdrawal has been found in the successful defence and management of Britain's international position, achieved not only through victory in two world wars, but also by a continuing presence in world politics as America's ally.[2]

This superiority of 'international relations' over 'empire' in popular consciousness was also reflected to a degree in political debate and calculation. The clearest indication of the subordinate place of empire in British

---

[1] The author would like to thank Robert Crowcroft and Chris Prior who read earlier versions of this chapter. He is grateful to the executors of the estate of Lord Duncan-Sandys, and to the literary executors of J. P. Mackintosh, for permission to quote from papers in these collections.

[2] See John Darwin, 'Fear of Falling: British Politics and Imperial Decline', *Transactions of the Royal Historical Society*, 5th ser., 36 (1986), 41–2.

politics came in the later 1930s, when, as part of the appeasement strategy, the empire was seen as an acceptable sacrifice for peace in Europe; as Maurice Hankey put it, describing the views of those who wanted to move closer to Germany, 'There are some serious people (even in the FO) who would chuck in a colony or two for Hitler's benefit.'[3] Where strategic questions became intertwined with imperial ones, the latter seemed to act as a drag on the former. Britain's withdrawal of its defence commitment East of Suez in the later 1960s was also snared up with the question of abandoning its Aden colony. Because support for the empire had weakened well before this time, the argument for maintaining a British commitment in such a vital region was perhaps less widely made than it might otherwise have been. As D. C. Watt argued in a controversial contemporary article, 'The case for the British presence has suffered from the fact that it has been defended in the past by the achievements of empire and with the vocabulary of empire. And it has been a victim of the general revulsion against the way in which the costs of empire seem to have grown while the reality has disappeared.'[4]

In view of the apparently greater immediacy of domestic issues on the one hand, and the sharper imperatives of international relations on the other, it was perhaps not surprising that colonial questions were not always of the first importance in parliament: 'colonial debates could clear the House as nothing else could.'[5]

But this is only one side of the story. However much the events of the transfer of power had been anticipated, there was still a sense of shock when the day was not far off. When Cripps announced in 1947 Britain's departure from India, the Conservative MP Cuthbert Headlam felt 'The whole thing to me seems incredible—that we should calmly state our intention to walk out of India in June 1948—whatever the situation in that country may be— is a terrible confession of failure'.[6] Within the parliamentary democracy, key prime ministers of the twentieth century—Baldwin, Attlee, Eden,

[3] Martin Pugh, *State and Society: A Social and Political History of Britain 1870–1997* (London, 1994), 244; Martin Gilbert, *Winston S. Churchill*, v/2. *The Wilderness Years 1929–1935* (London, 1981), 1172, Maurice Hankey to Eric Phipps, 13 May 1935.

[4] D. C. Watt, 'The Decision to Withdraw from the Gulf', *Political Quarterly*, 39 (1968), 321.

[5] David Goldsworthy, *Colonial Issues in British Politics 1945–1961: From 'Colonial Development' to 'Wind of Change'* (Oxford, 1971), 75.

[6] Stuart Ball (ed.), *Parliament and Politics in the Age of Churchill and Attlee: The Headlam Diaries 1935–1951* (Cambridge, 1999), entry for 5 Mar. 1947, p. 492.

Macmillan, Wilson, and Thatcher—all had to grapple with the divisive effects of empire, and for Baldwin and Thatcher, there were moments when their very survival seemed to be at stake. For Eden, Suez and 'empire' was the cause of his downfall. Moreover, even when the die was cast, and decolonization virtually complete, an imperial 'legacy' still made its presence felt in political debate. Politicians grappled with empire in decline still believing that they had a role to play even as power was being transferred. Why were imperial politics so much more fraught than their status as a 'secondary issue' suggests they should have been?

The explanation lies at least in part with the political values within which empire was set, and the complexions of the two major parties. It has often been observed that British life is thoroughly permeated with liberal values that go far beyond the province of the Liberal Party. Such values may be characterized as: a belief in progress; in the potential in people for rational thought and action; in the rights of individuals; and the possibilities of self-determination and self-government to realize these rights.[7] Because these beliefs were taken to be self-evidently right, liberalism had little acceptance of other points of view about life and politics. Desirable political values and behaviour were held to be universal; and it was the responsibility of governments to ensure that they were being aspired to. Liberal views explain why empire was to lead to self-determination; why peoples had to show they were ready for it; why there was a persistent sense of responsibility towards imperial subjects because they had to follow the 'correct' path; and why it was believed that the goal of self-determination was about the convergence of nations towards common values rather than their departure from them.

The willingness to accept that self-determination was the natural outcome for Britain's imperial subjects was crystallized in the political sphere by the Montagu-Chelmsford *Report on Indian Constitutional Reform* published in 1918. Judging that 'we have gone as far as possible along the old lines', it argued that 'Indians must be enabled in so far as they attain responsibility to determine for themselves what they want done'. This was to be viewed from an essentially European perspective: 'The inevitable result of education in the history and thought of Europe is the desire for

---

[7] Elie Kedourie, *England in the Middle East: The Destruction of the Ottoman Empire* (London, 1982 edn.), 14–19. For a perceptive analysis of Kedourie's views on English liberalism and empire, see Maurice Cowling, *Religion and Public Doctrine in Modern England* (Cambridge, 1980), 315–38.

self-determination; and the demand that now meets us from the educated classes of India is no more than the right and natural outcome of the work of the past one hundred years.'[8] The essence of the argument in the Montagu-Chelmsford report was of profound significance: that imperial subjects should henceforth regard their self-determination as an entirely legitimate goal which British governments would welcome rather than resist. The assumptions and expectations that surrounded this declaration were equally important in explaining the way the majority of British politicians thought about empire in the twentieth century.

The Montagu-Chelmsford report was a clear expression of a liberal approach to empire. It did not go unchallenged.[9] There were persistent voices throughout the period questioning the assumptions about the value of self-determination in contrast to the good government which Britain discharged. From this view the recognition of self-determination was a defeatist attitude towards political movements in the empire whose claims to represent their peoples were dubious and whose qualifications to govern were suspect. But the liberal perspective did not imply disengagement. In accepting the right to self-determination as natural, it drew upon a traditional belief in free institutions. But this right, and the politics that went with it, had to be exercised responsibly. People had to be ready for self-government. They might reach such a position through the experience of democracy, but education and social development were crucial too. Thus, even if there was remarkably broad acceptance of the idea that self-determination was a natural and welcome outcome of British rule, there was plenty of scope to argue about 'timing', and when subjects might be ready for independence. This allowed a degree of latitude within the overall 'truth' about self-determination so that sharply different views might coexist within it. The liberal perspective encouraged a continuing sense of responsibility for the empire. It was also assumed that successful self-determination would express, in some essential way, a similarity of outlook and political character between the imperial power and its former subjects; people were, in this respect, the same. Two further consequences flowed

[8] *Report on Indian Constitutional Reform*, Parliamentary Papers (1918), viii, p. 148. Edwin Montagu was at the time Secretary of State for India, and Lord Chelmsford viceroy.

[9] Henry Page Croft believed it was 'an instance of liberalism gone quite mad'. *H C Deb*, 109, 6 Aug. 1918, col. 2396. For Croft, see Andrew S. Thompson, 'Croft, Henry Page, First Baron Croft (1881–1947), Politician', in H. C. G. Matthew and Brian Harrison (eds.), *Oxford Dictionary of National Biography*, online edition.

from these views. First, the belief of those in the early stages of this process, that such self-determination would maintain or even strengthen the empire rather than destroy it. Ramsay MacDonald argued that 'national individuality' was perfectly consistent with an imperial framework.[10] Second, the inevitable disillusionment when, at the point of imperial release, this turned out not to be true; people were not essentially alike in their political character, but often uncomfortably different. The liberal perspective, because of its view about the evolution in a people's character that lay at the heart of their journey to self-determination, believed in a process of convergence; the nationalist outlook, that was the actual force that drove the weakening of empire, assumed and embraced difference.

Indeed, the very notion of trusteeship, which was the way empire was understood, implied a watching brief over territories in the process of becoming themselves. Withdrawal from empire was therefore accompanied by reflections on the extent of British influence and judgements about the character of colonial subjects. While withdrawal from empire was agreed as the eventual outcome, timing was everything. Lord Irwin, Viceroy of India in the 1920s, thought that Birkenhead, his Secretary of State, 'had a rough timescale of 600 years in mind' for when India would be ready for self-government.[11] The liberal views that pervaded British political life embodied a clear idea of progress towards acceptable forms of political behaviour and this informed discussion about whether or not certain parts of the empire were 'fit' for independence.

Such concerns inevitably complicated attitudes towards what was widely accepted as the ineluctable process of the transfer of sovereignty. 'Responsibility' emerged as one of the keywords in political debates during the last days of empire. It certainly struck those on the other side of the imperial relationship, and often as an impediment to progress towards transfer. During the prelude to Indian independence, Sudhir Ghosh, Gandhi's emissary, commented that 'The real obstacle in the way is this extraordinary sense of moral responsibility which our British friends feel for everyone else.'[12] 'Responsibility' assumed that power was there to be exercised as a duty, with discrimination and judgement, so that the course of events might be influenced and manipulated. By the mid-twentieth century these

---

[10] *H C Deb*, 109, 6 Aug. 1918, col. 1158.

[11] Andrew Roberts, *'The Holy Fox': A Life of Lord Halifax* (London, 1991), 19.

[12] P. F. Clarke, *The Cripps Version: The Life of Stafford Cripps* (London, 2002), 457.

assumptions had been overtaken by Britain's declining power. Enoch Powell tried to cut through this deception during a debate on Rhodesia in the 1960s: 'In relation to a Government, whatever may be the case with an individual, there is no meaning in the expression "responsibility" where there is no power.'[13] But a significant number of British politicians refused to follow Powell's logic and still believed that influence and responsibility were in their hands, even if they were unsure about power.

British politicians therefore 'connected' with empire essentially as a process of government; economics, although often seen as the crucial relationship within empire, especially by its critics, played a lesser role. This may seem surprising, since the Ottawa Agreements of 1932 ushered in a set of trading relationships and pricing structures that were to last until entry into the Common Market in 1973.[14] There were, of course, prominent arguments made about the importance of the economic relationship in the empire, from both the Right and the Left. Leo Amery was the principal proponent from the Conservative side of the view that economic relationships produced political cooperation.[15] As long as the economic relationship was strong, then it was possible to be more relaxed about political developments. Full independence within the Commonwealth was acceptable with ties of economic self-interest. The attraction of the economic tie was its relative indifference to political forms and institutions. It sidestepped the awkward questions about whether subject peoples were ready for certain representative institutions that British opinion often thought were necessary for effective self-government. Amery therefore clashed with Churchill over self-government for India, because Churchill saw the connection in essentially political rather than economic terms.

On the Left, Fabians also took a similar view about the economic connection and its value for forging close ties.[16] A long interest in economic development was still evident in a Fabian pamphlet of 1965 which recommended an intensive programme for the African protectorates of Bechuanaland, Basutoland, and Swaziland so that 'we can look one another in the eyes and take hands and really be friends'.[17] Joseph Chamberlain's vision of

---

[13] H C Deb, 788, 16 Nov. 1969, col. 639.

[14] Anthony Howe, Free Trade and Liberal England, 1846–1946 (Oxford, 1997), 295.

[15] W. R. Louis, In the Name of God, Go! Leo Amery and the British Empire in the Age of Churchill (London and New York, 1992), esp. 65.

[16] Ibid. 34.

[17] Unprotected Protectorates (Fabian Research Series, 250; London, 1965), 18.

economic links being at the heart of empire lived on well into the twentieth century. Economic progress for the Africans was also a card played by defenders of the Central African Federation in the 1950s and 1960s. But, however attractive in theory, there were obvious drawbacks to economics playing a key role in the relationship between Britain and its empire. A version rooted in production of goods was discredited by some well-publicized failures, such as the groundnuts scheme attempted by Attlee's post-1945 Labour government. Trade, too, was an uncertain basis for political connections. Amery's vision was of the colonies supplying raw materials and acting as markets for British goods. However, countries traded most intensively where they linked on the basis of similarity in their levels of development, rather than dissimilarity; Amery's model did not accord with the realities of convergence. Even within the structure for trade developed by the Ottawa Agreements, Britain took very few manufactured goods from its empire.[18] Trading patterns on this model were therefore no route for the prosperity of the dependent territory, and likely to stimulate rather than remove the sources of nationalist politics. Trade, too, tended to adapt to political change rather than determine it. Traders were inclined to accept political realities as the price of entry to a market. Free trade, embedded in the nation's consciousness, also worked against political manipulation of economic relationships.

The linkage formed through 'government' was therefore the dominant connection with empire, and certainly a complex one. It was not always forged through the transfer of institutions, that is, the imposition of a 'Westminster model' upon dependent territories as fundamental to their passage to independence.[19] Nationalist politicians too often showed little interest in pursuing political acclimatization to a unified state through the mechanisms of local government.[20] The question embedded within the 'government' connection was perhaps a more general and fundamental

---

[18] I. M. Drummond, 'Britain and the World Economy', in R. C. Floud and D. McCloskey (eds.), *The Economic History of Britain since 1700*, ii. *1860 to 1970* (Cambridge, 1981), 303.

[19] A. F. Madden has pointed out that it is an 'over-simplification to allege, in the context of hurried transfers of power in the mid-twentieth century, that the British have sought consistently to spawn a brood of little Westminsters'. See 'Origins and Purposes of British Colonial Government', in Kenneth Robinson and Frederick Madden (eds.), *Essays in Imperial Government Presented to Margery Perham* (Oxford, 1963), 21.

[20] B. Keith Lucas, 'The Dilemma of Local Government in Africa', in Robinson and Madden (eds.), *Imperial Government*, 205.

one, and it was whether, what politicians often assumed to be universal principles of political organization and behaviour, could ever be so. This was powerfully intertwined with the issue of race that lay at the core of the imperial relationship, and which was brought into play by questions about government. It was this dimension that gave the issue of fitness to govern its special intensity. It arose most sharply in eastern and central Africa. Was the imperial relationship founded on a unified British interest forged between the government at Westminster and white settlers, or was it rooted in a sense of universal brotherhood which transcended racial divisions? It was therefore the relationship through government that ensured the imperial connection still remained 'in play' in British politics even during its decline.

The assumptions which, if not universally held, nonetheless guided the attitudes of many parliamentarians towards empire, that liquidation of British rule was the accepted end point, and that their subjects had to be treated in accord with British standards of justice and administration, always had the potential to run into conflict with some of the realities of British rule. That rule rested on two main pillars: the commitment of colonial administrators to devote themselves to a region and its people for much of their careers, and the willingness to repress disorder vigorously. The contrast between those priorities and the assumptions of domestic political discussions was brought out in episodes such as the Amritsar massacre of 1919, in which General Dyer's troops opened fire without warning on an unarmed crowd, killing 379 and wounding 1,200, according to the British account. This was a clearly pathological occurrence, one which Winston Churchill described as a 'monstrous event in singular and sinister isolation', and he went on to assert that 'British power in India does not stand on such foundations'.[21] Those who saw British rule as resting on goodwill which would put 'the coping stone on the glorious work which England has accomplished' announced their horror at the episode, and even those who doubted India's capacity for self-government, such as Birkenhead, still believed in their right to equality before the law.[22] At the heart of the controversy lay the question of what was appropriate force for ruling the empire.[23] Those opposed to Dyer

---

[21] *H C Deb*, 131, 8 July 1920, cols 1725 and 1730.

[22] *H C Deb*, 131, col. 1708, E. S. Montagu; and John Campbell, *F. E. Smith: First Earl of Birkenhead* (London, 1983), 515–16.

[23] There is a useful analysis by Derek Sayer in 'British Reaction to the Amritsar Massacre', *Past & Present (P&P)*, 131 (1991), 130–64.

essentially articulated the common law rule that the State's use of force must be commensurate with the threat it faced. That threat was of an illegal assembly within a general context of subject peoples who were to be treated with goodwill consistent with the fact that they would at some point in the future be a self-governing nation within the empire. The Indian population had to be treated as British subjects. Churchill made much of the fact that the crowd was unarmed.

Dyer's opinion that he would have used heavier firepower had that been at his disposal flatly challenged this view. Dispersal of the crowds at Amritsar was not just a local matter, but about sending a message to the rest of the Punjab that the disorder that had preceded it would not be tolerated. It was about having a 'moral effect' on the Punjab. It was not about treating Indians on equal terms with the British but about disciplining inferior subjects prone to the appeals of agitators. Such a notion of exemplary force was rejected by the Commons in its debate about Amritsar, but, as Sayer has commented, Dyer's defence 'was rooted in widely held norms' and supported by the Lords.[24] It pointed to the reality of empire as based on power and coercion, that did not always sit happily with the belief that it could not be run on different standards from those prevailing within Britain. It was this point that was made much later by Enoch Powell in the Commons debate over the Hola Camp scandal in 1959, when eleven Mau Mau detainees were beaten to death; Britain could not behave differently in its government of colonial subjects from the way it administered those at home.[25]

The tension between British politics and the attitudes of colonial administrators was significantly less striking, but it was there. For the colonial administrators, the tradition of lengthy service among a population with whom they tried to build an understanding and whose language they learned did not always sit easily with the publicly proclaimed commitment to the handover of government.[26] In the Commons, when Baldwin defended the Irwin Declaration of 1929 that the British government's goal

[24] Ibid. 160.

[25] H C Deb, 610, 16 June 1959, cols. 235–7. The argument that this is precisely what the colonial situation often required is made by Susan Carruthers, 'Being Beastly to the Mau Mau', Twentieth Century British History (TCBH), 16 (2005), 489–96.

[26] See the interesting comparison between the 19th-century colonial administrators and those who have set about the reform of modern day societies in Rory Stewart, The Places In Between (London, 2004), 272 n. 59. Stewart was deputy governor of Southern Iraq, 2003–4.

was dominion status for India, he remarked that this did not mean that imperial service had been diminished: 'There is work for the best we have got.'[27] But there remained a significant gap between the aspirations of those who became administrators and the realities of their roles, which required some creativity if it was to be bridged. One administrator who was to play a central role in the Punjab, Penderel Moon, explained his decision to join the Indian civil service by the fact that he was 'the victim of propaganda' when a recruiter came to Winchester 'and painted a very idealistic picture of the work to be done'.[28] The effect did not last long and perspectives were adjusted; on the boat out he and his fellow recruits believed that British rule had about twenty-five years to run. There was a difference of perspective between, on the one hand, the majority assumptions of British political debate about the path to self-government and the equality with which imperial subjects were to be treated en route, and, on the other, the guiding principles of those who actually ran the empire, namely a lifetime commitment blended with vigorous policing. However, the political effects of this contrast were distinctly limited. Although there were plenty of disgruntled ex-colonial administrators frustrated by the cession of imperial power, they were not able to muster enough political force to hold up the process, and the non-political traditions of British military life ensured that the same was true of those who policed and disciplined the empire.

In terms of the impact of empire on British politics, it was the Conservatives' response that was the most important. Moderate Conservatism was the key to British political stability in the twentieth century. It was the instrument for the destruction of the Liberal Party and encouraged a constitutionalist and moderate Labour Party. It was not, of course, without its critics. It could, on occasions be too accepting of 'social forces', too tender, for some, towards the trade unions, for example. But it did encourage an appreciation of British politics as essentially stable. The triumph of moderate Conservatism was Baldwin's achievement. It combined an acceptance of democracy with a reticence about power and aggression, and aligned itself with the more modest aspirations of interwar Britain compared to ambitions of the Edwardian era. It was distrustful of 'dynamism'

---

[27] H C Deb, 231, 7 Nov. 1929, col. 1311.

[28] Mark Tully, 'Introduction', in Penderel Moon, *Divide and Quit: An Eyewitness Account of the Partition of India* (4th edn., Oxford, 1998), p. xii. Moon joined the Indian Civil Service in 1929.

and had made this a point of difference with Lloyd George. In this low key way it was quite optimistic about the relevance of Conservatism for an urban and democratic Britain. The Montagu-Chelmsford 'line' on empire was entirely consistent with this view of the world. What it had defeated was a rather different outlook and temperament, characterized by Churchill and his close friend F. E. Smith, Lord Birkenhead. This was, especially in Churchill's case, a more restless, aggressive, and, at root, pessimistic relationship with the world after 1918.[29] The success of Baldwin's version of Conservatism was crucial to the muted impact of 'empire' on British politics in the interwar period.

The prevalence of the view that within empire there was an irresistible trend towards self-government marginalized a 'diehard' defence of British identity which, had it been more widespread, would have required a strenuous and aggressive assertion of its position against an influential anti-colonialism. Politics would have undoubtedly become more bitter as a result. There was much to swallow in the acceptance of such moderation: that national self-determination was somehow an authentic (and hence unstoppable) expression of a population's aspirations and history, when it could be more accurately understood as a political strategy for interested parties; that the twin supports of imperial government, commitment of administration and firmness of policing, might be somehow at odds with the essential nature of the British state. But, by and large, such truths were accepted.

For Labour such judgements were more readily embraced, and the Party had an easier pathway through the imperial politics of the twentieth century. It was on the winning side, even if not a cause of that victory.[30] The liberal progressivism within which Labour's politics was cast complicated the anti-colonial position with expectations that independence politics would fit the patterns they themselves believed in; that nationalism was necessarily a vehicle for trustworthy and honest political behaviour, consistent with its notion of the universality of what was a desirable political ethic.

---

[29] For a succinct delineation of these differences, see J. P. Parry, 'High and Low Politics in Modern Britain', *Historical Journal* (*HJ*), 29/3 (1986), 753–70, esp. 768–9. For Churchill's pessimism, see Cowling, *Religion and Public Doctrine*, 283–312.

[30] Nicholas Owen, 'Critics of Empire in Britain', in Judith Brown and Wm. Roger Louis (eds.), *The Oxford History of the British Empire* (*OHBE*), iv. *The Twentieth Century* (Oxford, 1999), 208–10.

If these values were part of the liberal outlook, and if this outlook was broadly spread across much of the political spectrum, then there was also scope for disappointment in the imperial relationship. The assumption that core values were shared, and that essentially common standards of behaviour implanted through Western influence would survive the transfer of power, was often painfully exposed for its falsity, even for those with long experience. Lord Carrington, who engineered the final resolution of the Rhodesian crisis in 1980 through elections in which Robert Mugabe's Patriotic Front was the key participant, has made plain in his memoirs his dismay for the views of other participants, including the representatives of Julius Nyrere of Tanzania:

A great preacher of democracy to the Commonwealth community, Nyrere sent his foreign minister to the ultimate act of Rhodesian independence months later. The Foreign Minister approached me.

'Lord Carrington., I knew all along you were going to fix it so that Mugabe won!'

I looked at him without warmth.

He continued, 'But why by so much? Why did you make him win by so much?'[31]

From the other end of political spectrum, the Labour MP John Mackintosh was a committed anti-colonialist who had taught at Ibadan University in Nigeria, and written about its politics. He was critical of those who assumed that all Africa needed was time for the 'Westminster' model of democratic representation to work effectively, that is, for the habits and conventions to be established that would support those particular kind of institutions. Mackintosh thought this was fantastical. Western democratic forms had flourished where the range of disagreement, and the scale of issues to be arbitrated, was relatively small. Given the major issues that had to be confronted in Nigeria about the status of tribal and regional authorities, the parallel was more accurately with times in Britain when fundamental issues had pulled at the heart of the constitution, as in the case of Home Rule on the eve of the First World War.[32]

What his analysis showed was Nigerian politicians believed that once power was to be won, it was to be used to its utmost to entrench support,

[31] Lord Carrington, *Reflect on Things Past: The Memoirs of Lord Carrington* (London, 1988), 294.
[32] John Mackintosh, *Nigerian Government and Politics* (London, 1966), ch. 7, 'Nigerian Democracy'.

and that reasoned argument and electoral organization were inadequate tools for defending a party's position. These points were well made in academic analysis, but when Mackintosh considered relations from the socialist perspective the judgement was rather different. For a socialist believes there are some values that are applicable to all societies irrespective of 'context', and this made what went on in post-independence periods the cause of some anguish. What caused particular upset was the indulgence and outward display amongst African politicians. A particular British ethic praised self-restraint and austerity, to show that power had to be discharged according to rules and because it was held in trust for the people. It was hard to see this in West Africa. As he wrote 'in countries as poor as those in West Africa, extreme luxury, huge cars, houses with fountains and seven bath-rooms, loans to build more houses which are rented back to the government and so on, become very offensive and all this was a blow and brought disillusionment to the nationalists' recent allies'.[33]

Such disappointments, and the painful awareness that the assumptions of liberal politics were not shared by the nationalists whose cause had been often recognized, and, from some quarters, applauded, were perhaps inevitable. Nationalist leaders saw their strength coming from the mass mobilization of the peoples to confront their sense of inferiority before the colonial power, and to challenge the 'inevitability of gradualness' on which the Western view of their path to independence was predicated.[34] The friendships which many British politicians believed were part of the justification of the imperial relationship therefore, at least in the arena of public politics, were accompanied by evidence of difference in values that in turn point to the element of fracture that often came with imperial withdrawal.

Political values which accepted eventual decolonization and imperial decline were powerfully implanted across the political spectrum, but led on occasion to disillusionment. They were also open to challenge from within both parties. Amongst Conservatives there was a view that, instead of the acceptance of self-government there was a legitimate claim to the exercise of authority by the imperial government. On the left, while one passage through imperial decline was through the anti-colonial struggle,

[33] National Library of Scotland, Mackintosh papers, 195, 'A Socialist Attitude to Africa', unpublished lecture notes, n.d.
[34] Tom Mboya, 'The Mass Movement', in E. Kedourie (ed.), *Nationalism in Africa and Asia* (New York, 1970), 479–80.

and therefore an engagement with empire, there was another which wanted to focus on the social democratic state shorn of its imperial encumbrance. The changing balance of these perspectives was played out over the century.

India had a profound effect on the paths both parties took through imperial politics. As the core element in the empire, and the one that most comprehensively embodied its key characteristics—administrative, economic, and military—its experience was a powerful test of the assessments that politicians made about the purposes of imperial rule. The question of what to do about India helped define and ultimately reinforce Baldwin's moderation, while however undignified the exit under Labour in 1947, it was taken within the Party as a sign of Attlee's sureness of touch and the rightness of his convictions. But while the influence of India may have been profound, it was not necessarily taken to be decisive. That is, even though India might be 'lost' this did not mean the die was cast everywhere else. While Enoch Powell famously decided that once India had gone there was little point in maintaining the imperial identity, this was a far from universal reaction.

Part of the reason for this was the exceptional character of India and British rule there. At a simple level, there was the sheer size and complexity of India and its society. It had a population of over 300 million in 1921, and was divided by religion, language, and regional identities. However, urbanization, and the possibilities this created for new forms of politics, was increasing. The government of India was divided between the one-third of India that remained under the control of the princes, themselves a group of varied power and status, and the rest that was directly administered by the Secretary of State for India in London and the Viceroy in Delhi. This was administration heavily dependent upon the collaboration and participation of Indians in both law and order and government. In the interwar period a new element was the increasing level of political participation especially at provincial level but also in central government. So the British governed an increasingly dynamic polity. India was therefore, in its size and complexity, not always easy to grasp or comprehend as a country that Britain might govern in an actively interventionist way.[35] Other areas of British influence were different in being smaller, more coherent, and therefore presenting the

---

[35] This section draws heavily on Judith Brown, 'India', in *OHBE* iv. 423–7. The journalist Ryszard Kupuscinski recalls turning away from the vastness of India and Asia to the 'more graspable, approachable' Africa; *Travels with Herodotus* (Harmondsworth, 2008), 100.

possibility of more active rule. Therefore the 'lesson of India' was not necessarily one that was automatically extended to the rest of the empire, despite Powell's own conclusions.

The condition and status of India account in part for the nature of the political debate about its future in the interwar period. It generated an intense, if incoherent, political conflict. The issues in the debate were clear enough, but their prosecution was heavily influenced by the vagaries of a mercurial personality, namely Winston Churchill's. The pledge that India would move to dominion status, made in the Montagu-Chelmsford reforms of 1917–19 and renewed in the Irwin declaration of 1929, rested on the view that self-government would be a political mechanism within the larger unit of the empire which in its essence would remain intact; indeed, might even be strengthened by this expression of a liberal commitment to self-realization. In December 1934, at a speech to his party, Baldwin set out the argument:

Remember: what have we taught India for a century? We have preached English institutions and democracy, and all the rest of it. We have taught her the lesson and she wants us to pay the bill. There is a wind of nationalism and freedom blowing round the world and blowing as strongly in Asia as anywhere in the world. And are we less true Conservatives because we say 'the time has now come'? Are those who say 'the time may come–some day', are they truer Conservatives?[36]

For Churchill, railing against the passing of a resolute pre-1914 political generation, and its replacement by an apparently judicious and therefore spineless interwar successor, self-government was at the heart of the question.[37] His core point was that good government was far more important than self-government. As he put it, 'the present infatuation of the Liberal mind, and, I must say, the more intellectual part of the Socialist mind, is at the moment very serious. Their error is the undue exultation of self-government.' This was being pressed to the extinction of all other principles.[38] A greater good, by contrast, could come from the protective force offered by the British presence: 'beneficial aid from an external source for a virtuous object'. The particular claim for this good government lay with the

[36] Cited in Keith Middlemas and John Barnes, *Baldwin: A Biography* (London, 1969), 713.
[37] For a useful discussion of Churchill's stand on India, see Geoffrey Best, *Churchill: A Study in Greatness* (London and New York, 2001), 134–40.
[38] *H C Deb*, 297, 11 Feb. 1935, col. 1654.

masses of Indian society, for whom, argued Churchill, nationalist movements had little to offer. Apart from what Churchill called the 'Depressed
classes', the 'original stock', the British 'have as good a right to be in India as
anyone else'.[39] As he put it in a broadcast of 30 January 1935, the chief shame
of the India Bill of 1935 was that 'we finally withdraw our guardianship from
this teeming myriad population of Indian toilers. We withdraw our protection from their daily lives,' and this was a 'solemn abdication and repudiation of duty'.[40] Lest there be any doubt about the pessimistic assessment of
Indian capacities that was the counterpart of such an argument, Churchill
had made dismissive and insulting comments about Gandhi that caused
long-lasting offence in India.[41]

Such arguments were bound to have some support from those in the
army and administration whose chief justification was the long-term commitment they had provided to India. As Archibald Boyd-Carpenter lament-
ed, 'Is there nothing left to us, who have borne the burden and the heat of
the day in the administration of India, in creating its wealth, in giving it its
justice, and assuring its unity and security?'[42] It also resonated within the
Conservative Party. As opposition to Baldwin emerged over India, this
became in one contemporary's view the greatest threat to the unity of the
Conservatives since tariff reform.[43] Baldwin himself had a serious wobble
when the anti-reform group of parliamentarians was energized by news in
March 1931 that Irwin was having discussions with Gandhi about constitutional reform. Baldwin seemed to waver in his support for the reform
process, and there was talk of his possible replacement by Neville Chamberlain. The situation was retrieved when Baldwin reaffirmed his support both
inside and outside the House for the pledge that had been given over
dominion status, but it had indicated the way in which India could galva-
nize emotions in day-to-day politics.[44]

The Lancashire cotton interest provided an additional theme in the India
controversy, alongside the more specifically constitutional one. The price of
India's advance towards self-government seemed to be discrimination

[39] *H C Deb*, 297, 11 Feb. 1935, col. 1651.
[40] Gilbert, *Churchill*, 1060.
[41] Best, *Churchill*, 135.
[42] *H C Deb*, 297, col. 1331.
[43] Earl Winterton, *Orders of the Day* (London, 1953), 188.
[44] Philip Williamson and Edward Baldwin (eds.), *The Baldwin Papers: A Conservative Statesman 1908–1947* (Cambridge, 2004), 253–9.

through duties on imports from Britain. Some blamed the ineffective mobilization of the Lancashire cotton interest for its plight in the 1930s.[45] Oswald Mosley found in the industry's condition a particular example of the listlessness of a parliamentary democracy towards the problems of unemployment and depression, and was able to exploit anxieties for which the Government of India Bill had no answer. The British Union of Fascists was added to the India Defence League as a group to make trouble over the path to self-government, and Mosley toured the Lancashire cotton towns in the 1930s with his plans for a protected Indian market for their output.[46]

In addition to 'pressure from without' there were opportunities to exploit connections with India over some of the more difficult aspects of the 1935 Bill. The princes who controlled one-third of India had agreed to participate in a federal system in 1931, but then changed their minds, influenced by Congress's opposition to the Bill. Their resistance was exploited by the Churchill group in Britain whose contacts with some of the princes seemed to give them the upper hand over the government. As Samuel Hoare complained, 'Rothermere and they [Churchill and John Courtauld, Conservative MP for Chichester] are spending large sums of money upon a daily correspondence with their friends and it is evident that they are obtaining much earlier information as to what is happening behind the scenes than am I ... The House was not unnaturally astonished that while he [Churchill] seemed to know everything that was happening, I seemed to know nothing.'[47] There were fears, briefly, that the Bill might be lost, but in the event, even though the cooperation of the princes was unforthcoming and the reforms at the level of central government remained inoperative, the Act was passed and India was, for the time being, off the agenda of British politics.[48]

In the end, the row over India strengthened Baldwin's position rather than weakened it.[49] The multi-stranded nature of resistance over India

[45] *H C Deb*, 297, col. 1257 (Stewart Sandeman).

[46] Martin Pugh, 'Lancashire, Cotton, and Indian Reform: Conservative Controversies in the 1930s', *TCBH* 15/2 (2004), 143–51, esp. 147.

[47] Gilbert, *Churchill*, 1092, Samuel Hoare, Secretary of State for India, to Lord Willingdon, then Viceroy of India, 1 Mar. 1935.

[48] Brown, 'India', 430.

[49] Robert Rhodes James, *Memoirs of a Conservative: J. C. C. Davidson's Memoirs and Papers 1910–1937* (London, 1969), 385.

revealed its shortcomings rather than its assets. The specific economic interest of Lancashire cotton was never an unambiguous ally of the imperial connection. While Mosley had treated it as an issue about industry and production, it was more accurately seen as one about trade, which in turn depended upon Indian goodwill, and therefore the cotton interest was nervous about endangering this by standing out against self-government.[50] Churchill had never made Lancashire cotton the centre of his argument; it was essentially about the claims of the British to provide good government. However, the nature of British rule in India, with its dependence upon collaboration and Indian recruitment to the bureaucracy, made such a case hard to argue, and one that received less support from within the administrative classes than might have been envisaged. Moreover, the British presence was a layer over the top of a society recognized to be complex and different from that of the imperial power. For India to advance required the reform of economic and social issues that British rule could not touch; as Baldwin argued, these were 'matters with which only Indians can deal'.[51] Therefore the path to self-government was one which could easily be presented as an ineluctable process whose obstruction would show a betrayal of trust.

Against the case even a united opposition group would have had an uphill struggle. But the campaign against Indian self-government suffered disunity at its heart. J. C. C. Davidson, Conservative insider and Baldwin's confidant, in his reflections on the Indian question, noted that the diehard group who opposed the government never regarded Churchill as a proper Conservative but as an ex-Liberal. Moreover, his reputation for unstable judgement was not an asset: 'Thus, although the Tory opponents of the Government's Indian policies welcomed Winston's support, they always rather apologized for the fact that Winston was in their camp.'[52] John Charmley has observed that the tenor of Churchill's speeches was unsuited to a sceptical age, and that 'Churchill had been speaking in the House for a very long time and if his listeners were not exactly bored, they had the feeling that they had heard

[50] Winterton, *Orders of the Day*, 191. For a full analysis, see also Andrew Muldoon '"An Unholy Row in Lancashire": The Textile Lobby, Conservative Politics, and Indian Policy, 1931–1935', *TCBH* 14 (2003), 93–111.
[51] *H C Deb*, 297, col. 1716.
[52] Rhodes James, *Memoirs of a Conservative*, 384.

it all before'.[53] In the process of attrition that the passage of the Bill became, these were formidable difficulties, let alone the sense amongst many MPs that there were matters at home that were more compelling for their constituents.

While Conservative opposition to the Government of India Bill had been defeated, the failure to bring in the princes meant the reform process had stalled. This uncertain and incomplete path to self-government still carried the possibility of an enduring connection with Britain, despite the fact that by the end of the 1930s imperial control had grown weaker.[54] The Second World War dashed this expectation. Cripps's promise made in 1942 of Indian independence after the war cut the links with the 1935 Act, while the burdens of war—financial and human—seemed to have crushed British resources for further imperial influence in India. As the then Viceroy, Lord Wavell, commented in 1946, 'we are running on the momentum of previous prestige'.[55]

These realities suggested little alternative to the rapid retreat in 1947 that left a divided India that was also in turmoil. From this perspective, the parliamentary defence of withdrawal practically wrote itself. But the argument still had to be made, and when Attlee provided it he exposed the flawed model of the transfer of power which the British had resorted to for much of the pre-1939 period. It did not have to be made against the Conservatives, from whom little by way of concerted opposition was heard.[56]

The most significant critical voice was that of Sir John Anderson, independent MP for the Scottish Universities. Anderson had a double strand to his authority. He had been a conspicuously successful Governor of a turbulent Bengal 1932–7, and had supervised the granting of self-government within the province under the provisions of the 1935 Act. He had managed the home front during the Second World War.[57] He was the wartime Chancellor of the Exchequer from 1943 onwards. His unusual status had

---

[53] John Charmley, *Churchill: The End of Glory, A Political Biography* (2nd edn., London, 1995), 281.

[54] John Darwin, 'A Third British Empire? The Dominion Idea in Imperial Politics', in *OHBE* iv. 82.

[55] Brown, 'India', iv. 442; Darwin, 'Third British Empire?', 85.

[56] For a precise and exhaustive analysis of why this was the case—including the liability of Churchill, see Nicholas Owen, 'The Conservative Party and Indian Independence, 1945–1947', *HJ* 46/2 (2003), 403–36.

[57] G. C. Peden, 'Anderson, John, First Viscount Waverley (1882–1958), Civil Service Administrator', in *Oxford Dictionary of National Biography*, online edition.

derived from his role in the war, as someone with an unrivalled reputation as an administrator who also thereby acquired political weight, and was still intact in the post-war transition. His criticisms were threefold: the government should not have set a specific date for the handover of power; it was wrong to allow Indian politicians to form a government without a constitutional settlement; it had failed to take measures to improve the efficiency of the administration and the police. It would therefore be impossible for the British to leave India in an orderly fashion.[58] All these were perfectly intelligible within the conventional framework that had been applied to Indian development: the stress on the handover of power only when conditions were right; the assumption that the British still had influence over events; and that transfer was a sequential and not a discontinuous process.

Attlee's reply was not based only on the grim acceptance of existing conditions; it demolished the pretences that had been woven through parliamentary debates about India. First, the capacity of the imperial parliament to understand developments in India was very limited: Attlee commented on 'how little we know about India and how soon what knowledge we have gets out of date'. Second, the capability of the British to stiffen the administrative machine and strengthen the police was exhausted. Third, and perhaps most tellingly, the notion of orderly transfer rested upon an apprenticeship in responsibility, and this had been flawed. Reserving to the imperial government what were regarded as the really vital functions, such as finance and law and order, also meant excusing Indian politicians from some of the most awkward decisions of government. As he put it, 'of the reforms we have carried out over these years we have taught irresponsibility not responsibility'.[59] All the props of the argument over India that the Conservatives had deployed against their diehards, that functions would only be passed on when it was timely to do so, that the British would be in control of the process leading to self-government within the empire, and that these were realistic alternatives to the determined exercise of authority, had been removed. What was left was the continuity of representative institutions.

Attlee's reputation survived intact, and was even enhanced. Certainly, Labour was able to draw upon it in later years to reassure themselves that

---

[58] *H C Deb*, 434, 6 Mar. 1947, col. 526. For the Headlam's confirmation of the effectiveness of Anderson in the India debates, see Ball (ed.), *Headlam Diaries*, 491.

[59] *H C Deb*, 434, cols. 768–9.

withdrawal from empire could provide the opportunity for great acts of leadership.[60] That credit could be drawn from a hurried departure, from 'scuttle' in Churchill's description, seemed to underline the difficulties that lay with the defence of empire. For Conservatives, the speed of events that led to Indian independence had also been one of the factors that frustrated the organization of significant opposition.[61] Because India exposed so powerfully how the economic, military, and strategic assets of empire were in decline, and also how far those who had invested their careers in imperial service—whether administrative or military—were reconciled to their demise, it was a major stage in the debates over empire in British politics. There was more to come: the Suez Crisis of 1956 demonstrated the weakness of influence where it depended on the exercise of military strength within an international relations context. Britain was no superpower. Moreover, within domestic politics, Suez seemed to divide the generations and the classes, which suggested that imperial defence was a declining asset.

Suez was a genuine crisis: that is, its outcome was to be a fundamental statement about Britain's position in the Middle East and the world, and things were never to be the same in its aftermath. It is this that explains both its intensity and the apparent brevity of its impact. In the autumn and winter of 1956 it dominated Eden's life and Westminster politics. Within the Conservative Party, it generated two opposing viewpoints of roughly equal intensity. When British forces bombed Egyptian air bases and invaded the Canal zone, public opinion was also bitterly divided. On Sunday 4 November, Edward Heath witnessed 'a terrifying scene' as demonstrators against the invasion tried to force their way into Downing Street: 'This was not a demonstration organized by a few left-wing extremists. It was supported by thousands of people who genuinely believed that what was happening was politically, militarily and morally wrong.'[62] As Chief Whip, Heath had to face in both directions as he tried to reassure the Suez group of MPs who wanted to topple Nasser and reassert British power in the Middle East that the diplomatic negotiations over the status of the canal did not rule out military action, and attempted to have the same effect on those opposed to

---

[60] People's History Museum, Manchester, Labour Party Archive (LPA), PLP minutes, Harold Wilson's address to the Parliamentary Labour Party, 15 June 1966.

[61] Owen, 'Conservative Party and Indian Independence', 427.

[62] Edward Heath, *The Course of My Life: My Autobiography* (paperback edn., London, 1999), 173.

intervention by arguing that the diplomatic efforts were not simply a cover for eventual invasion. It is a measure of the strains within the Party that Heath's success in protecting the government's majority was regarded as a major achievement: in the words of his biographer, 'Suez made Ted Heath.'[63] Edward Boyle experienced perhaps more sharply than most the differing opinions over Suez after he resigned as a Treasury minister at the beginning of November. He received many letters from academics, especially from Oxford, praising his action, yet much hostility from his constituents, the strength of whose views led him briefly to consider departing from British politics.[64]

The Suez group of Conservative MPs, whose principal spokesmen were Charles Waterhouse and Julian Amery, vigorously opposed their government's policy in the Middle East, which aimed to maintain British informal influence by agreeing to removal of sources of irritation to the Egyptians, especially in the form of the British base in the Suez Canal zone. Their origins lay in opposition to the Anglo-Egyptian agreement of 1954 that allowed for the withdrawal of British troops, and their impact intensified when, after troops had departed, Nasser nationalized the Suez Canal. During the debates over the 1954 Agreement, Waterhouse complained that 'we are really losing our will to rule', and Amery believed that it represented 'a certain moral collapse'.[65] They had some influence over the government, in that Churchill, in his last days as prime minister, sympathized with their concerns about evacuating the Suez base and tried to use their views to persuade Eden to take a tougher line than he otherwise might have done in the negotiations. By the time of the crisis itself, it required a bellicose speech at the Llandudno party conference to secure the position of the government.[66]

[63] John Campbell, *Edward Heath: A Biography* (paperback edn., London, 1994), 97.

[64] For the letters, see Special Collections, Brotherton Library, University of Leeds, the papers of Edward Boyle, deposit 660, items 3499–948. For problems with his constituents, see Tony Benn, *Years of Hope: Diaries, Letters and Papers 1940–1962* (London, 1994), 233, entry for 9 Apr. 1957.

[65] For the Suez group see Sue Onslow, 'Suez Group (act. 1953–1957)', in *Oxford Dictionary of National Biography*, online edition, and also *Backbench Debate within the Conservative Party and Its Influence on British Foreign Policy, 1948–1957* (Basingstoke, 1997), chs. 6–10. H C Deb, 531, 29 July 1954, col. 742 (Waterhouse), col. 776 (Amery).

[66] Anthony Nutting, *No End of a Lesson: The Story of Suez* (London, 1967), 82. Nutting, who was subsequently to resign over the invasion of the Canal Zone, had to read the speech in the absence of its author, Lord Salisbury.

Eden's stance in the autumn of 1956 reflected the views of the Suez group, namely that military force should be used to reassert the British position in the Canal zone, and, by extension, restore its standing in the Middle East. But it was a position that proved impossible to sustain. The abrupt cessation of the military operation and subsequent withdrawal was met with a demand by the group that Britain should retain a military presence in the zone, but in the end only 15 MPs abstained from supporting their government during the debate of 6 December.[67] A crisis that made painfully explicit the limitations on British power, that had divided both the nation and the Conservative Party, and had turned parliamentary politics into a cauldron, in the end had a modest impact on party politics. In the 1959 election, Suez was hardly mentioned.[68] Why so? Part of the reason was the way the Suez group understood the evolution of government policy in the Middle East. For them, the 1954 Agreement that led to the evacuation of the Suez base was crucial, because it removed the ability to act swiftly against Nasser; 1956 was the inevitable outcome of a fundamental weakening in military capability and a naïve faith that a concession to Nasser would be met by cooperation and friendship in the future. The game was up, as it were, before the invasion in 1956. The emergence of Macmillan as prime minister in the aftermath was vital too, despite his flexible attitude during the crisis. The Suez MPs blamed R. A. Butler, rather than Macmillan or Eden for the debacle, since Butler had given the order to withdraw and had been perceived as opposed to the invasion from the outset; those on the left of the Party were able to tolerate Macmillan because he had been the first to advocate withdrawal.[69] With Macmillan as the choice for prime minister of most Conservative MPs, a generous budget in 1957, and rapprochement with the Americans under way, the route away from Suez, although fraught with difficulty, was laid out.[70] Of those who had resigned in outrage at events, only Nutting suffered significantly, as burdened by his knowledge of collusion, he stood down as an MP. Boyle, by contrast, was welcomed back to the front bench as a junior minister for education early in 1957. Labour's support embraced both progressive opinion that had been so vehement in

[67] Onslow, 'Suez Group'.

[68] D. E. Butler and Richard Rose, *The British General Election of 1959* (Basingstoke, 1960), 64.

[69] Nutting, *Lesson*,158; Heath, *Course of My Life*, 178.

[70] For an acute analysis of this period, see Simon Ball, *The Guardsmen: Harold Macmillan, Three Friends, and the World They Made* (London, 2004), ch. 9.

its opposition to the invasion, and the working-class voters who had generally regarded any such opposition as unpatriotic, which limited its ability to exploit Suez. For neither party then, was there much incentive to linger over the issue. The crisis itself was a painful verdict on the reality of British power, but its outcome was also a confirmation of much that had happened since the Second World War.

While such major landmarks pointed to the decline of imperial influence, empire issues still arose with episodic intensity in British politics. This was thanks to Africa. Africa was, of course, the colonial empire; it was not the empire of international relations or strategic significance. It did not, therefore, impose sharp imperatives about what could be afforded or what was vital for security. While Suez sapped the confidence of the British that it had the 'ability to deal with situations', on the smaller scale of colonial insurgency it could still respond with resolution and determination, as in the case of the Mau Mau in Kenya.[71] While the international context had an important, even crucial bearing upon British policy in Africa—witness the significance of events in the Belgian Congo—it was less easy to argue that the sadly inevitable decline in British power reduced the options available within particular African nations. What took the place of the strategic or economic arguments that might have driven an acceptance of decolonization was the strength of African nationalism. While the political reality of this was undeniable, its nature was a matter for debate. Nationalism for some was assumed to mean the freely developed consciousness of a people; for others, it covered a good deal of coercion and violence. George Cunningham, a Labour Party official, reporting on a visit to Rhodesia in 1965, was sceptical about the claims by nationalist leaders of mass discontent:

If this was ever the case, their enthusiasm has been weakened by the division between of ZAPU and ZANU and the bitter and foolish jealousies between them. There is little doubt that most of the African population of the Highfield and Harare townships were glad when Smith sent troops into those areas earlier this year. ZAPU and ZANU members had not only been beating each other up but had been threatening and attacking others to support one or other party.[72]

---

[71] Wm. Roger Louis, 'The Dissolution of the British Empire', in *OHBE* iv. 343. The quotation is from Sir Charles Johnston, the Governor of Aden, in 1961.

[72] LPA, Judith Hart papers, 2/45, 'Rhodesia', 7 Oct. 1965.

Nationalism often carried weight because it seemed to stand for the authentic views of the 'people', and by this very fact, to be a progressive movement. To lift the veil and expose some of the realities of such political movements did not diminish the necessity of coming to terms with their force, but it did make contestable its moral superiority. Hence one Conservative response to Macmillan's 'Wind of Change' speech to the South African parliament, in which the pivotal moment was his reference to the spread of African nationalism, was the formation of the Monday Club. Its broader aim was to halt the left-wing trend in Conservative policy; its immediate inspiration was to fight to against the 'Wind of Change' in Africa to which their leaders had appeared to capitulate.[73] The thread of a Conservative resentment at the loss of authority and status that their own governments had presided over was therefore picked up over Africa.

Doubts about what kind of politics constituted black African nationalism were a further variant upon the imperial theme of the readiness of colonial subjects to govern themselves, to which tribalism provided a particular dimension. What gave the particular intensity to African politics was race. Colonial issues were most difficult where the British had to meet the claims of white settlers and black Africans. Parallels were drawn between the condition of the blacks in America and in Africa, to make the point that, since the latter were not represented in the imperial parliament, the British had a particular responsibility to guard their interests.[74] But for many on the Conservative side, white settlers also had special claims on the loyalty of the British government, whatever their differences in outlook and culture.[75] Within the Conservative Party there was the continuing importance of guardianship, fuelled by resentment at the cool political calculation which so easily downgraded the empire. Yet again, the defining component of Britain's political identity was being sacrificed to the generalities borrowed from a different, liberal, political culture. Labour, too, had a great deal invested in Africa. For some, the ability to solve its problems would be proof of the fact that Britain still had a role to play on the world stage. For

---

[73] Patrick Seyd, 'Factionalism within the Conservative Party: The Monday Club', *Government and Opposition*, 7/4 (1972), 418.

[74] W. Arthur Lewis, Michael Scott, Martin Wight, Colin Legum, *Attitude to Africa* (Harmondsworth, 1951), 7.

[75] See S. J. Ball, 'Banquo's Ghost: Lord Salisbury, Harold Macmillan, and the High Politics of Decolonization, 1957–1963', *TCBH* 16/1 (2005), 74–102, esp. 83 for a portrait of Salisbury's ties and affections with Rhodesia.

those on the left, anti-colonialism, far from being an irrelevance compared to the continuing development of a social democratic Britain, was evidence that the Party was the voice of humanitarianism. Africa would demonstrate its capacity for enduring brotherhood with the oppressed, and for the universality of its political values.

For both parties, then, Africa fuelled domestic argument between some of their more vocal elements, even if their leaderships trod essentially similar paths. But the line of moderation was not an easy one. Macmillan was severely tried by the conflicts over Africa in the later 1950s and early 1960s, while Wilson devoted prolonged efforts to try and solve the Rhodesian crisis throughout 1964–70.[76] Anyone trying to deal with African politics found the conventional liberal approach—that reasonable men can sit around a table and reach agreement, and that 'moderate' influences, once identified, are the key to eventual settlements—severely tested. White settlers had much to lose by any compromise; their minority status brooked no erosion. Often they had useful connections with MPs in London, through such bodies as the Conservatives' Commonwealth Parliamentary Association. These were to be exploited, alongside the simple but effective tactic of saying 'no'. As with Northern Ireland, the British found themselves dealing with politicians with whom they had little in common by temperament or outlook. On the other side, African nationalism was powerful and also supported by 'world opinion' as the legitimate expression of the African majority. Its threat was validated by the experience and responses of France and Belgium. Britain wanted neither an Algeria nor a Congo on its hands. In the grip of such fierce forces, 'reason' and 'moderation' were hard to find.

These pressures gave an urgency to resolving Britain's position in Africa, which lay in the much more rapid move to black majority rule and independence in the early 1960s than had been anticipated in, say, 1958. Rhodesia was the exception to this liquidation of formal commitment, because of its powerfully entrenched white settler interest which had a significant presence in both urban and rural society.[77] From the Unilateral

---

[76] S. J. Ball, 'Banquo's Ghost: Lord Salisbury, Harold Macmillan, and the High Politics of Decolonization, 1957–1963', *TCBH* 16/1 (2005), 74–102, esp. 83, for an incisive analysis of his relationship with Salisbury, who was not only firmly on the pro-empire side of the party, but also a friend from schooldays. Douglas Hurd, *An End to Promises: Sketch of a Government 1970–1974* (London, 1979), 40.

[77] John Darwin, *Britain and Decolonisation: The Retreat from Empire in the Post-War World* (Basingstoke, 1988), 194–7, 314.

Declaration of Independence in 1965 to the eventual victory of Robert Mugabe in elections in 1980, the Rhodesian question provided the most difficult aspect of the 'imperial legacy', and one which still had some life in it as Zimbabwe seemed to be headed for ruin in the first decade of the twenty-first century.[78] This caused frustration on both sides of the political divide in Britain. For some Conservatives it was a further instalment in the betrayal of Britain's imperial identity, this time for a failure to support the white settlers (or, eventually, moderate African leaders); for the left, it was frustration that good intentions could not prevent the British being put on the defensive against the demands of black nationalism and world opinion.

A good indication of the contrast between what happened in Rhodesia after 1965 compared to the experience in the rest of central and eastern Africa is provided by the role of Iain Macleod, colonial secretary from 1959 to 1961. A vital force for decolonization in central Africa, he was to adopt a more measured voice over Smith's Rhodesia. William Roger Louis has commented that 'In speed and decisiveness, he was to Africa what Mountbatten had been to India'.[79] Although only in office for two years, he set in motion Tanganyika's independence in 1961, Uganda's in 1962, and Kenya's in 1963. A measure of the transformation this embodied can be gained from the estimate of his predecessor, Alan Lennox-Boyd, that Kenya might have been independent in 1975.[80] Macleod was crucial for the implementation of Macmillan's view that the colonial empire could not be sustained. If resolute defence of empire had been incompatible with moderate Conservatism in Baldwin's day, the late 1950s provided fresh underpinning for this position. The long economic boom from the end of the second world war was providing support for loosening some of the constraints of convention which had been in place for the first half of the century. Macmillan used the growing affluence of British society to his electoral advantage, even as he admitted its fragility. The emphasis upon personal needs and the legitimacy of their fulfilment weakened the significance of imperial values of authority and example. As early as 1957, Macmillan was anticipating the legalization of homosexuality between consenting adults and permitting the establishment

[78] Peter Carrington, 'Did We Put a Tyrant in Power?', *The Times*, online edition (5 Apr. 2008). Lord Carrington was Foreign Secretary at the time of the Lancaster House conference which led to Mugabe's election victory in March 1980.

[79] Louis, 'Dissolution', 351.

[80] Ibid.

of betting shops.[81] There was a convergence between what a progressive Conservatism would have to support domestically, and the judgement that to defend the colonial empire would be to take on not only specific conditions within British territories but also a broad swathe of international opinion that empire was out of date.[82]

Macleod's approach of accepting black majority rule and independence proved successful in the case of Kenya for which a conference in early 1960 reached agreement between moderate Europeans and African delegates for an eventual black majority in the legislature. Much more difficult was the question posed by the Central African Federation of Nyasaland, Northern and Southern Rhodesia which had been put together between 1951 and 1953 as a way of preserving British influence in central Africa. Plans for the Federation had been developed under the Labour government, and Patrick Gordon Walker, the Commonwealth Secretary, had supported the scheme as a way of strengthening ties with Britain and preventing the encroachment of South Africa on the central region. However, James Griffiths, the Colonial Secretary, developed reservations because of the hostility of African opinion; as he put it 'the Africans are growing up'. It was Labour's duty to act as their representatives, and in the Commons they would be voting not only for their constituencies 'but for millions of Africans whose voices we are'.[83] For 'pro-Empire' Conservatives the value of the Federation lay in bringing home the unity between the British and white settlers in Africa. Frederick Bennett rebutted criticism of their fellow countrymen in Rhodesia, because 'fellow countrymen who live in Central Africa do not have less integrity and moral values than us'. It followed from this that justifying the Federation through agreement was futile; the responsibility of parliament was to impose an arrangement which could provide for economic and subsequently political development.[84]

White settlers in the federation wanted to be free of British involvement in order to maintain the colour bar that protected their jobs. While from this perspective, Federation was a disappointment, it also frustrated African ambitions for a fuller political role. This basic tension had been tilted

[81] Ball, *Guardsmen*, 340.
[82] For Macmillan's awareness that empire did not sit well with 'middle opinion', see Ritchie Ovendale, 'Macmillan and the Wind of Change in Africa, 1957–1960', *HJ* 38/2 (1995), 472, 474.
[83] *H C Deb*, 497, 4 Mar. 1952, col. 216; *H C Deb*, 513, 24 Mar. 1953, col. 676.
[84] *H C Deb*, 497, 4 Mar. 1952, col. 295, Julian Amery.

heavily in favour of black interests by the suppression of Hasting Banda's movement in Nyasaland in 1959 and the deaths at the Hola camp in Kenya, in the same year. These events put the Macmillan government firmly on the defensive against a vigorous Labour opposition and criticism from within their own ranks. Macleod had to push the Federation towards black majority rule while at the same time avoiding a coup by white settlers, much more numerically and politically powerful than in Kenya. This was a much faster and more abrupt change than had been anticipated before the upheavals of 1958–9. Then the future seemed to be of a federation which secured the representation of white interests but which over time would be blended with African representation based on property and literacy qualifications; that is, not universal suffrage.[85]

The avenue of response for the Macmillan government in this dynamic situation was the review of the Central African Federation which had been promised at its inception and which was established at the end of 1959 as the Monckton Commission. This recommended that faster progress be made towards African majority rule in Northern Rhodesia following its concession in Nyasaland, and also that the Federation itself could only survive with consent, and therefore the possibility of secession had to be accepted.[86] For Roy Welensky, the Federation's president, this was betrayal of assurances that he believed had been given that the Commission's remit did not include the question of secession.

The constitutional review was particularly acrimonious and difficult over Northern Rhodesia. Welensky warned that if black majority rule came to Northern Rhodesia, Southern Rhodesia would secede. He also lobbied Conservative MPs and had some sympathy from the Commonwealth Secretary, Duncan Sandys, whose relations with Macleod deteriorated rapidly.[87] Lord Salisbury, an ally of Welensky, formed a Watching Committee to press the argument against Macmillan and Macleod. Such a device had as its antecedents the anti-appeasement movement against Chamberlain and the opposition to the India Bill of the mid-1930s.[88] Macleod's tactic involved seeking parity between whites and blacks in the North Rhodesian legislature

[85] Darwin, *Decolonisation*, 269.

[86] Philip Murphy, 'Introduction', *Central Africa. Part 1: Closer Association 1945–1958*, ed. Murphy, in S. R. Ashton (ed.), *British Documents on the End of Empire*, Series B, vol. ix (2005), pp. lxxvi–lxxix.

[87] Robert Shepherd, *Iain Macleod: A Biography* (2nd edn., London, 1995), 219–24.

[88] Ball, 'Banquo's Ghost', 88.

with the expectation that this would lead to a black majority through what Murphy has described as a 'hugely complicated system of cross-racial voting'.[89] White Rhodesians had to be convinced that this did not fundamentally weaken their position. This was the inspiration behind Salisbury's famous charge against Macleod in the House of Lords in March 1961 that he had been 'too clever by half' in his dealings with the whites in Northern Rhodesia. The way that the constitutional talks turned upon detailed allocations of seats within the legislature had apparently favoured Macleod's well known skills as a bridge player.[90]

The lines of division within the Conservatives were very clear. For Bennett, one of the diehards, the idea of an unstoppable force of popular feeling in Africa was suspect: 'people talk too much about there being a "wind of change" in Africa without realising that that wind of change is being formented by agitators and taken advantage of by the Communist Party.' For those who supported Macleod, the picture was very different. It was important that political structures emerged from the popular will rather than being imposed from above, and while the Central African Federation made some economic sense, 'in a conflict between economics and politics, politics is apt to win'. Moreover, the ties between Britain and the white settlers were not to be exaggerated: 'They are not English, they are Rhodesians; or they may be pre-war farmers in the White Highlands of Kenya or post-war artisans in the Copper Belt in Northern Rhodesia.'[91]

The drama of Salisbury's speech in the Lords should not conceal the fact that Conservative opinion in the Commons had begun to swing back in favour of Macleod.[92] Because Macleod's strategy was a balancing act between white and black turning on intricate details of representation, the dispute revived in June 1961 over fresh initiatives by Macmillan to appease Welensky. While he was successful in this aspect, they aroused fierce opposition amongst African nationalists. In October Macleod was replaced by Reginald Maudling. Maudling was, like Macleod, of a liberal outlook, but of a different and more pragmatic temperament.[93] His determination to push

---

[89] Murphy, 'Introduction', *Central Africa*, p. lxviii.

[90] Ball, 'Banquo's Ghost', 90; Shepherd, *Macleod*, 225.

[91] *H C Deb*, 645, 25 July 1961, cols. 279 (Bennett) and 303, 307 (Nigel Fisher).

[92] Shepherd, *Macleod*, 225; Philip Murphy, *Party Politics and Decolonization: The Conservative Party and British Colonial Policy in Tropical Africa, 1951–1964* (Oxford, 1995), 187.

[93] For Maudling's sceptical view of his predecessor's invocation of 'the brotherhood of man' to support decolonization, see Shepherd, *Macleod*, 255.

forward with a settlement that pointed more decisively towards majority African rule surprised his predecessor, Macleod. Whatever the reason— anxiety about the erosion of law and order in Africa, a response to failure over the bid to join the EEC—Maudling was determined to press his case to the point of resignation.[94] As he explained to Macmillan, his proposals for the qualifications for representation in the legislative council were 'of fundamental importance to me'. Anything less than these he thought would lead to more bloodshed and disorder, and in such an event he told Macmillan 'you will see how I should regard my own responsibility'.[95] Macleod had played his own card by suggesting that if Maudling and his under-secretaries at the Colonial Office resigned, he would also go.[96] The pressure from the other side was that Welensky was outraged that what had appeared to have been agreed in June 1961 was being revised and that this transmitted itself to parliament through the opposition of many Conserva- tive backbenchers. All this was happening at a time when the Conservatives' standing with the public was dire and, as R. A. Butler put it, 'it needed every man at his post to win back the situation by the next election'.[97] Macmillan was clearly reluctant to reopen the settlement, but even though Maudling had to compromise over some of its components, the outcome went in his favour.[98]

What is important about the whole episode of the Central African Federation, is the political wear and tear it caused. Macleod had threatened to resign in February 1961 when his efforts in favour of parity for Africans looked like being stalled; Macmillan moved Macleod on from the Colonial Office in October 1961, wearied by the conflicts the policy had caused and the fact that what had been intended as a balancing act of putting Sandys in charge of Commonwealth relations had merely brought a further element of strain within the government. What is particularly striking is that Macleod's successor, Maudling, with less invested in the politics of Africa, followed the same path as his predecessor over the distribution of representation within the Northern Rhodesian legislature—in tilting it more decisively towards

[94] The National Archive, Kew (NA), Prime Minister's Office Papers (PREM), R. A. Butler to Macmillan 18 Jan. 1962, and Martin Redmayne to Macmillan, 9 Jan. 1962, both in PREM 11/3942.

[95] NA, PREM 11/3942, Maudling to Macmillan, 12 Jan. 1962.

[96] NA, PREM 11/3942, Martin Redmayne to Macmillan, reporting a conversation with Macleod, 9 Jan. 1962.

[97] PREM 11/3942, R. A. Butler to Macmillan, 18 Jan. 1962.

[98] Murphy, 'Introduction', Central Africa, p. lxxxv.

black majority rule—and had shown little inclination to bend to domestic political pressures.[99]

The rapid move to decolonization in Africa initiated by Macmillan and Macleod was supported by a powerful constellation of forces: the dangers of Britain being left in isolation to fend off an apparently overwhelming black nationalism, and the compatibility between their strategy and the tenor of Conservatism in affluent Britain. What had been surprising was the intense political conflict it had caused within the Conservative Party even to cabinet level. Disengagement from Africa had been a painful process whatever the rationale for doing so. Harold Wilson once remarked that what he most admired about Macmillan was the way he talked about empire but led the Tories away from it. This continued the approach taken over India under Baldwin and during the post-war Independence crisis.[100] However, while the debates over India had been protracted and at times the most serious issue for the Conservatives, the divisions of opinion had not reached so closely into the heart of the government. Butler, who had acquired sole responsibility for Central African Affairs in 1962, reckoned that the move to stronger representation of African interests against the views of Welensky and his allies in the Conservative Party was a 'struggle far bigger than the India Bill'.[101] The argument that those who opposed the liberal line over Africa resorted to, as their fundamental point—that the British were abandoning their own people—pointed to an interest more firmly embedded than had been the case in India. Macleod had gained far less political benefit from his decisive African policy than Attlee had extracted from the 'scuttle' from India. Claims that Africa might have destroyed his chances of being party leader probably made more of that possibility than was realistic, but both he and Maudling earned the persistent hostility of those on the right of the party.[102] So while the arguments about the trend of events, or the overwhelming pressures of the international situation could be easily artic-

---

[99] David Goldsworthy, 'Maudling, Reginald 1917–1979, Politician', in *Oxford Dictionary of National Biography*, online edition.

[100] John Mackintosh, 'Has Social Democracy Failed?', *Political Quarterly* (July–Sept. 1978), p. 262.

[101] That is, the India Bill of 1935, when Butler was parliamentary Under Secretary of State at the India Office. 'Minute by Mr Butler on the nature of the Central African problem' 6 Mar. 1963, in Murphy, *Central Africa Part II, Crisis and Dissolution 1959–1965*, in Ashton (ed.), *British Documents on the End of Empire*, 362.

[102] John Ramsden, *The Winds of Change: Macmillan to Heath, 1957–1975* (London, 1996), 150.

ulated, the political brokerage associated with them had been demanding
and costly.

Wilson had his own opportunity to leave his mark on British imperial
politics when Southern Rhodesia landed in Labour's lap. Duncan Sandys, as
Commonwealth Secretary, had managed to get a settlement in 1961 that had
held out some possibility of a larger African role in the legislature, and this
had been ratified by a referendum despite Nkomo's opposition. However,
subsequent events pointed towards a more assertive white position. In 1962
Edgar Whitehead, who had been a supporter of the Central African Federation, was displaced in favour of Winston Field and the Rhodesia Front, who
suffered the same fate in 1964 for his refusal to support a declaration of
independence. He was succeeded by Ian Smith, who did. In November 1965
Smith announced the Unilateral Declaration of Independence (UDI), after
both the Conservatives and then Wilson's Labour government had tried to
reach agreement on greater African participation in the legislature. The
white settler interest in Rhodesia was powerfully established, being numerically strong, and with footholds in both rural and urban society. Since 1923
they had enjoyed a good deal of internal self-government; there was no British
involvement in either administration or internal security. As Smith showed
with the suppression of black political parties in 1964, his government was
confident of being able to contain nationalist pressure for majority rule.

Wilson entered the crisis with firm beliefs in a Britain that had extensive
interests and involvement in the wider world. His attachment to the Commonwealth had been forged in his youth by a visit to Australia; he was also
deeply opposed to racial discrimination. Africa was also important for the
Party, perhaps more so than India had been. Labour MPs had opposed the
lack of progress for blacks under the Central African Federation, and as
Callaghan told the parliamentary party, 'we were pledged to the full advancement of the African people and we must regard that as a sacred
pledge'.[103] Close personal links were forged with young nationalist leaders
such as Hastings Banda, Julius Nyrere, Kenneth Kaunda, Tom Mboya, and
Joshua Nkomo. In Morgan's view the Party had become 'the natural voice of
colonial liberation movements everywhere'.[104] Brockway exploited the use

---

[103] *H C Deb*, 609, col. 1334, 22 July 1959, LPA PLP minutes, 19 Nov. 1958 for Callaghan's
comments.
[104] Kenneth O. Morgan, 'Imperialists at Bay: British Labour and Decolonization', *Journal of
Imperial and Commonwealth History*, 27/2 (1999), 233–54, at 239–41.

of parliamentary questions on colonial affairs as a way of giving some representation of African interests in the imperial parliament. Barbara Castle had made one of the major speeches in the Commons debate on the inquiry into the deaths of Kenyan detainees at the Hola Camp which had been one of the most difficult moments for the Conservative government.[105]

The Labour Party therefore had a powerful connection with African affairs, through which it was able to give a practical expression of its views on what Britain stood for in the world. The fact the recent history of white self-government in Rhodesia made this a particularly difficult nut to crack did not stop some Labour MPs asserting where British responsibilities lay: 'It is our responsibility. It is the British government and the British people who are basically responsible and who must take decisive action to bring this matter to a conclusion at the earliest possible moment.'[106] This was, in formal terms, correct. The Southern Rhodesia Act of 1965, passed in response to UDI, declared that 'Southern Rhodesia continues to be part of Her Majesty's Dominions and that the Government and Parliament of the United Kingdom have responsibility and jurisdiction as heretofore and in respect of it'.[107] Yet this remained an empty assertion once Wilson had decided, in line with previous governments, that armed intervention against white Rhodesia was out of the question. Many Labour MPs had clear expectations that its own government ought to be able to bring white Rhodesians to heel and deliver the country to African rule; the very limited power that its government had over Rhodesia suggested they were going to be disappointed. For Wilson, the challenge was how to manage what was, in the short term, an intractable problem yet deal with the expectations of his own Party for a morally acceptable solution.

In the early stages Wilson tried to extract as much ethical significance as possible from measures designed to bring Rhodesia into line which, as he had determined from the outset, would stop short of military force. Wilson's approach was not only to break off connections with an illegal regime but also to implement sanctions against Rhodesia which would have mandatory force through the support of the United Nations (UN). Conservatives were opposed to bringing in the UN for fear of losing the option of

[105] She called it 'one of the greatest miscarriages of justice in colonial history', *HC Deb*, 610, 27 July 1959, col. 222.

[106] Eric Heffer, *HC Deb*, 722, 7 Dec. 1965, col. 315.

[107] *The Public General Acts and Church Assembly Measures 1965 Part 2* (1965), ch. 76, p. 1762.

negotiations with the Smith regime and also for unleashing hostility towards South Africa.[108] Wilson was able to create a good deal of synthetic fervour on his own side by emphasizing the moral dimension of the Rhodesia problem and claiming that Conservatives accepted the Smith regime. He called the decision on mandatory sanctions the 'greatest moral issue Britain has had to face in the post-war world'.[109] Edward Heath was furious with Wilson for taking this line, and for Labour to claim moral superiority over the Rhodesian question when Wilson was unwilling to direct sanctions against South Africa. Labour's policy was as much shaped by compromise and calculation as moral principle: it was 'sheer hypocrisy of the basest kind' to suggest otherwise.[110]

The only strategy open to Wilson was the 'long haul' and to demonstrate to the wider British public that he had made every reasonable effort to negotiate with Smith to end the illegal regime, which was the benefit of their two meetings on HMS *Tiger* in December 1966 and HMS *Fearless* in October 1968. These broke down in the first case over the provisions for an interim government before the implementation of a new constitution, and in the second, over the provision that Britain wanted built into the constitution appeal to the judicial committee of the Privy Council. Both were particular aspects of the stumbling block that Britain wanted the Rhodesian population as a whole to approve the new measures, and could not afford to be seen to be capitulating to the perpetuation of white rule. Even if these meetings served to underline the irreconcilable differences between the Wilson and Smith governments, they aroused suspicions within the Labour Party that Wilson might be giving too much away in the desire to bring the Smith regime back into legality. In the *Fearless* talks there was to be an interim period when the people of Rhodesia were to be consulted through a Royal Commission about the acceptability of the new constitution. The conditions governing the four-month period were what caused most concern to Labour's pro-African group. Smith was not to step down, but to lead a broad-based interim government including some new Europeans and two Africans. Smith was to consult with Britain's governor, but the latter had restricted executive capacity. Some release of political detainees was

[108] *HC Deb*, 737, 7 Dec. 1966 cols. 1393–8 (Maudling).

[109] *HC Deb*, 737, 8 Dec. 1966, col. 1630.

[110] *HC Deb*, 737, 8 Dec. 1966, cols. 1698–9. For Heath's lasting anger at Wilson over this episode, see Campbell, *Edward Heath*, 205.

expected to take place, and censorship lifted. But Smith's overall charge was to remain intact; the role of the British government was likely to be marginal and there was to be no military presence. These proposals appeared to be too trusting. Judith Hart, minister of state at the Commonwealth Office, thought a military presence to be vital.[111] John Mackintosh believed the approach of the British government underestimated the determination and self-confidence of the whites but also ignored the ease with which constitutional guarantees could be subverted or set aside.[112] There was relief amongst pro-Africanists that Smith rejected the terms on offer on HMS *Tiger*, and some surprise that he had.[113]

The same fears arose over the second set of talks, on HMS *Fearless* in October 1968, that Smith was going to get too easy a ride back to legality with the prospect of his repudiating any promise to move to black majority rule.[114] In the debate on the terms, 49 Labour MPs voted against their government and a further 100 abstained. The main aim of the government became to dampen down the expectations of those of its MPs who became agitated about Rhodesia and raised the possibility of some kind of armed intervention. George Thomson, the Commonwealth Secretary, in the debate over the *Fearless* negotiations, had pointed out that Britain had responsibility for Rhodesia but no effective power within the country, and in the previous year had also tried to defuse the issue:

Because the Party felt so deeply about the matter, it did not follow that the problem admitted of any immediate solution. We must be careful not to fall into the same trap that had engulfed the Americans in Vietnam. We had to face up to the long-term perspective, the long haul: but his did not mean that the Government yielded one particle of its principles on this issue.[115]

One of the 'particles' of principle had, in fact, been yielded pretty much from the outset. Wilson had argued in the Commons in December 1965 that majority rule was some way off:

---

[111] LPA, Hart Papers, 2/46, draft letter to Harold Wilson, 29 Nov. 1966.

[112] National Library of Scotland, Mackintosh papers, typescript, 'Where now in Rhodesia?', n.d.

[113] LPA, Hart papers, 2/46, letter of Head of UK mission to the UN, Hugh Foot to Judith Hart, 27 Dec. 1966.

[114] *HC Deb*, 770, cols. 1139–40, 22 Oct. 1968, Alex Lyon.

[115] LPA, PLP minutes, 13 Dec. 1967.

I said that time would have to be measured not by the clock or by the calendar, not by weeks or months or years, but by achievement, and the real test of achievement—I said this very, very bluntly to Mr Nkomo and Mr Sithole—would be the willingness of the African nationalists to work within parliamentary conditions and to work within the existing constitution, to get themselves elected to the House under the B roll and the A roll, and one hopes—I pressed this on Mr Smith—to get themselves accepted as members of the Government as Parliamentary Secretaries and Junior Ministers so as to gain experience not only in multi-racial parliamentary activities but in multi-racial government activities.[116]

This interpretation of the route to African rule did not cut much ice with African nationalists, anxious to break the tutelage of whites over their political progress, and keen to reject any suggestion that they were 'not ready' for self-rule.[117] The British insistence that any proposal for legally approved independence had to be satisfactory to the Rhodesian people was meant to be a feasible alternative to NIBMR (No Independence Before Majority Rule). One justification for it was the fear that NIBMR would consolidate moderate white opinion behind Smith. When Barbara Castle met the Kenyan politician Tom Mboya, she was rapidly disabused of the assumption that Africans might see it the same way. As he explained to her: 'The fact is that the only way to force the moderates to take a stand is to do what Macleod did in Kenya as Colonial Secretary: tell them there is going to be an African government.' For Castle this was 'wise realism' and 'all Harold's clever tactics looked like a cheap and tawdry trick'.[118]

However, the view that Macleod had set a standard of how to respond to African nationalism that could be applied to the Rhodesian case was not shared by its originator. Macleod argued that the approach pursued over Kenya could not be transferred to either Northern or Southern Rhodesia because of the stronger positions of the white settler populations. As the Southern Rhodesian crisis developed his main contribution was to stress the difficulty of the issue, to hope that moderate Rhodesian opinion might save the day, and to put forward the suggestion that a small Commonwealth mission might visit the country. One of the lines of division was over the question of 'punitive' sanctions. While some Conservative MPs supported

---

[116] *HC Deb*, 722, 10 Dec. 1965, col. 786.

[117] See Tom Mboya, 'Mass Movement', 479–87.

[118] Barbara Castle, *The Castle Diaries 1964–1970* (London, 1984), entry for 13 Sept. 1966, p. 168.

the cutting off of certain connections with Rhodesia as an illegal regime, they stopped short of sanctions intended to impose economic damage on the country and therefore to coerce it. Macleod was part of this group, to the disappointment of Conservatives who had liberal views on imperial issues and who, in the words of Nigel Fisher, 'looked to Macleod as our natural leader'. In order to probe further Macleod's opposition to economic sanctions Fisher invited him to meet with a group of Conservative MPs who were in favour of them:

We were all friends and admirers of Iain's but it was a painful evening. He dealt patiently, but to most of us unconvincingly, with every point we made. But we could not change his mind any more than he could change ours and I wished afterwards that I had not arranged the meeting. It did not alter our affection and admiration for him, but it shook temporarily our sense of sympathy and identity with his views.[119]

It is possible Macleod felt that pushing ahead so fast and decisively over Kenya had drawn heavily on his credit with the mainstream of the Party, not because it was mistaken but because of the turmoil it had caused, and that a more subdued approach over Rhodesia would provide some reassurance that he would not continue to run ahead of majority opinion. Whatever the reason, it meant that Wilson was not troubled by a liberal Toryism outflanking his moral stance and exploiting the ebbing away of Labour's 'African' credibility.

Wilson's policy of trying to reach some agreement with Smith also served the needs of the Conservative leadership. Although the white settler interest was much stronger in Rhodesia than it had been in East Africa there was little to be gained by aggressive support for it. It would not have sat happily with the moderate Conservatism towards empire that had been established by Baldwin and Macmillan, nor with Heath's own dislike for racial discrimination. However, opinion within the Party, not only in parliament but in the country, had as one of its strands the view that the whites in Rhodesia were being abandoned to majority rule before it was safe and sensible to

---

[119] Nigel Fisher, *Iain Macleod* (London, 1973), 275. See also the verdict of Bill Kirkman, a journalist and an admirer of Macleod, who wrote of the way his reputation was tarnished 'by his weak and equivocal attitude in the autumn of 1965 to the illegal declaration of independence by the Smith regime in Southern Rhodesia'. W. P. Kirkman, *Unscrambling an Empire: A Critique of British Colonial Policy 1956–1966* (London, 1966), 51.

do so, and that this all smacked of the appeasement of African-Asian opinion.[120] Had Wilson adopted a tougher line towards the Smith regime, including military intervention, then the question of whether or not to support white Rhodesia would have been posed more awkwardly. As it was, the Conservative shadow cabinet recognized that differences between their and Wilson's approach before UDI were negligible, and even when oil sanctions had been introduced the fact that without the backing of military force they were unlikely to be successful meant that outright opposition to them was not worth its costs.[121] But even if the differences between the two front benches were hardly substantial, the issue itself was a divisive one within the Party. The Conservative leadership did not want discussion and debate on Rhodesia if they could avoid it, and Labour's policy of seeking negotiations largely helped them towards this aim.[122]

Proof of its success in this regard is the experience of those who tried to press the case for a settlement with Smith further than the Wilson government was prepared to go. Sandys, as Secretary of State for Commonwealth Relations, had opposed the speed with which Macleod had tackled African majority rule in the Central African Federation, and was not instinctively progressive as Maudling was to be, but had nonetheless accepted the case for rapid decolonization.[123] Sandys was less constrained by broader party loyalties after the 1966 general election when he was not reappointed to the shadow cabinet. Over Rhodesia he kept up an energetic public campaign to urge the case for negotiations with Smith. As *The Times* commented in 1967, 'Mr Sandys has shown himself determined that the government should not be allowed to forget Rhodesia.'[124] Sandys's line was that negotiations should be encouraged by not requiring as a prerequisite that Smith renounce UDI. It was not easy for Sandys to achieve much momentum for his campaign in 1967 because Smith seemed to want to go back on some elements in the

[120] Bodleian Library, Conservative Party Archive, CCO 4/9/87, for correspondence between Michael Fraser of the Central Office to J. L. Wooding of the Knutsford Conservative Association, 8 Dec. 1965.

[121] CPA, Leader's Consultative Committee, 1/2/1, meeting of 28 Oct. 1964, and 1/2/7, meeting of 20 Dec. 1965.

[122] CPA, LCC 1/2/11, meeting of 13 Dec. 1967.

[123] Rhodes House Library (RHL), British Empire collection, interview with Nigel Fisher, S.452.

[124] *The Times* (8 May 1967).

Tiger constitution and was unwilling to accept the right of appeal to the Privy Council which was a crucial safeguard within the British proposals.[125]

More relevant for domestic politics was the position Sandys occupied as a result of his campaign for negotiations to be resumed with Smith. Sandys was formally committed to uninterrupted progress to majority rule, but was equally critical of its capacity to deliver representative government in the near future. There was also a link with domestic issues. He was clearly happy amongst those sceptical about recent liberal legislation in areas outside colonial politics, who were also hostile to the 'Wind of Change'. He was involved in the campaign to restore capital punishment, and many of those Conservatives who had voted against sanctions on Rhodesia in 1965 when their front bench had abstained had also opposed the private member's bill abolishing the death penalty. However, when two ardent defenders of white interests in Rhodesia, Patrick Wall and John Biggs-Davidson, shared the platform with him at a rally in Trafalgar Square in January 1967, he recommended removal of some of the more provocative sections from their speeches about the double standards evident in the toleration shown to violence carried out by black African politicians, about the dangers of black majority rule, and the benefits which white settlers had brought to Africa.[126] But however much Sandys wanted to finesse his message, he was drifting closer to some of the fringe groups on the Right and away from his connections forged when he had been involved in African affairs as a minister. Fisher, who had observed him at work when parliamentary under-secretary at the Colonial Office, and subsequently when this was amalgamated with the Commonwealth Relations Office in 1963, was surprised at the direction he followed over Rhodesia and race later in the 1960s. Their connection was enough to get Fisher on the platform at the Trafalgar Square rally, but, as *The Times* noted, 'he looked slightly surprised to be there at all'.[127] Further afield, Sandys found that because of the line he had taken on Rhodesia, 'I may be losing the sympathy of my African friends.'[128] Sandys's career showed both the scope for serious disagreement with the

---

[125] Churchill Archives Centre, the papers of Lord Duncan-Sandys, DSND 14/25, Sandys to Ian Smith, 30 Apr., 13 Dec. 1967.

[126] DSND 14/25, Box 2, pt. 2, drafts of speeches, 9 Jan. 1967.

[127] *The Times* (16 Jan. 1967).

[128] DSND 14/14, Sandys to Malcolm Macdonald, 9 Jan. 1967.

'liberal' line over black rule in Africa, but also the peripheral and isolated role that awaited those who wished to exploit it outside the Commons.

Labour MPs who had been frustrated by the lack of progress against Smith also had to recognize the helplessness of their position. By the end of the 1960s the choice seemed to be between supporting 'freedom fighters' or accepting the exclusion of blacks from the political process for the medium-term future. However, some of those on the anti-colonial side wanted to preserve influence even as the logic of events was shifting away from the British. In 1970, the African Manifesto Group published its *African Manifesto: An Appeal to Labour Party Members.* The Group contained those who had taken the lead in pressing the claims of African nationalism against their party leadership, and their allies from the respectable liberal circles of the day—John Hatch, Lord Soper, the Revd Mervyn Stockwood, for example. While regretting the dissipation of good feeling that they felt had previously existed between the Labour Party and the leaders of African nationalism, they saw a way out: 'if our Party is to participate fully in the international socialist community, the end of the British empire cannot be made an excuse to abandon our responsibilities to our African comrades. For this would lead to our isolation from their battles, to a weakening of international solidarity.'[129] Instead of the link forged through the instrument of parliamentary democracy, as it had been in the 1950s when Labour MPs used parliament to 'represent' African interests, it was now being reformulated through 'international socialism' that legitimated support for the 'freedom fighters'. But there was a distinctive responsibility for Britain, to atone for its links with the apartheid regime in South Africa. It therefore had to re-establish 'fraternal links' with African nationalists: 'The Party must be seen to be involved, attending conferences, inviting them to ours, seeking to provide practical assistance, encouraging its own young members to offer their time and knowledge in service to these budding socialist societies.' Even if the relationship was now recast within the more amorphous world of international socialism, there was still the assumption that African societies were on a journey to which the values of Western ones might make a contribution. Political character and experience was transferable across national boundaries. Even if the Manifesto Group left few traces, this was a coherent statement by leading Labour MPs about how they conceived

---

[129] African Manifesto Group, *African Manifesto: An Appeal to Labour Party Members* (n.d., 1970), p. 3 (n.p.), copy in LPA, Hart papers, 2/47.

some of the enduring features of their relationship with black Africa in the
new disposition of forces that had emerged at the beginning of the 1970s.

Africa clearly exercised a powerful attraction across the political spectrum, even if it assumed a much greater power on Britain's side than actually
existed. Over the fate of the Aden Colony, there was little such sentiment.
Part of the reason was that Aden was also a base, so its future was tied to the
fierce debates about defence spending at a time of relentless pressure on
government finances.[130] The British forces in Aden faced growing opposition and violence from Marxist groups who had been unappeased by the
Conservatives' announcement in 1964 that independence would be granted
in 1968 because Britain still intended to retain a base there, and Aden would
still be part of the Federation of South Arabia which could conveniently be
portrayed by its opponents as an unsatisfactory alliance between the progressive, urban population of the port and the semi-feudal character of the
local rulers in its hinterland. The position was made more difficult by
Labour's decision to withdraw from the base in January 1968, at the time
of the granting of independence, which became public with the 1966
Defence Review. At this point, the Labour leadership faced criticism that
any presence East of Suez came at the cost of Labour's programme for social
democracy at home. When Joel Barnett, then a Treasury minister, pointed
out that the East of Suez policy jeopardized the government's economic
targets of reducing expenditure, and Frank Allaun argued that social problems at home could only be solved by cuts in expenditure abroad, Michael
Stewart, the Foreign Secretary, countered with the assertion that there was a
'need to help these small states enter the 20th century. Withdrawal led to
risks and has to be carefully phased; it should not jeopardize the security of
the area; and must not leave a power vacuum, the result of which would
disrupt the whole life of the area.' Denis Healey had to reassure his party
that Britain was not being 'Kiplingesque' East of Suez: 'one could not simply
walk out and ignore the consequences. We need time to phase our withdrawal without causing chaos.'[131]

George Brown, the Foreign Secretary, had come to accept the argument
for withdrawal, but urged the need to leave the Colony 'in good order',

---

[130] There is a good treatment in John W. Young, *The Labour Governments 1964–1970*, ii.
International Policy (Manchester, 2003), 89–98.
[131] LPA, PLP minutes, 25 May 1966.

rather than as a 'Congo' for Britain.[132] However, this was impossible to fulfil, and, in conditions of mounting disorder in Aden, but little public disquiet at home, in September withdrawal was brought forward to November from its original January 1968 date. However inevitable, this was 'scuttle' in conditions of chaos.

Aden's colonial status had been caught up in a major change in British defence policy 'East of Suez'. As Darwin has suggested, that decision, although taken in conditions of financial stringency, was essentially a political one.[133] Shifts in outlook of such a fundamental character often occur not because of any one particular factor, but of a conjunction of conditions all pointing in the same direction. Even those who had argued for a more hard-headed approach to British responsibilities, and had been critical of 'great-power posturing', recognized the significance of what had happened.[134] Labour MPs had argued during the height of the conflicts over Britain's role in 1966–8 that there was a domestic project of social welfare at home that was more worthy of attention than commitments overseas. By the 1970s, the chance for what was essentially a 'decolonized' state to turn inwards upon its own concerns, was fulfilled. That decade was, of course, an atrocious one, as troubling for the sense of internal order and stability as any in the twentieth century. Margaret Thatcher's premiership from 1979 offered the possibility of some redemption as she began redirecting the state's activities and reaffirming the importance of personal responsibility. Her tone and beliefs broke decisively with those of her predecessors. However, the resolution of the Rhodesian crisis seemed to belong to an earlier era, in its acknowledgement of the primacy of international politics and its acceptance of a one party Marxist state as the outcome.

Wilson's meetings with Smith on HMS *Tiger* and HMS *Fearless* in the 1960s had created the picture of a conflict that was essentially between the British government and white Rhodesians. In the 1970s this was increasingly displaced by one in which the outcome was to be determined by groups outside Britain. The Portuguese revolution of 1974 led to the removal in 1975

[132] LPA, PLP minutes, 28 June 1967. In his memoirs, Brown commented that while accepting withdrawal from East of Suez and the removal of land troops, 'I did not agree with my colleagues on the speed and the timetable to which we subsequently decided to adhere.' George A. Brown, *In My Way: The Political Memoirs of Lord George-Brown* (London, 1971), 141.

[133] Darwin, *Decolonisation*, 294.

[134] Richard Crossman, *The Diaries of a Cabinet Minister*, ii. *Lord President of the Council and Leader of the House of Commons, 1966–1968* (London, 1976), 639.

of a powerful support for Smith in Angola and Mozambique, and the onset of guerrilla warfare waged by the Patriotic Front parties of Nkomo and Mugabe. Lord Carrington, the Conservatives' shadow foreign secretary, had become convinced that international recognition of any settlement was crucial. That, in turn, meant acceptance of participation of the Patriotic Front in any test of Rhodesian opinion. However, this had become complicated by the internal settlement Smith had reached in May 1978 with the black nationalist leaders Muzorewa and Sithole. Rhodesia now had a multiracial political settlement that was headed towards black majority rule.[135] Why not recognize the Muzorewa government and forestall the intrusion of the Patriotic Front? During a debate on South Africa in July 1979, Julian Amery spotted that Thatcher was holding back from such recognition, and urged her to take the opportunity it presented: 'you have the chance—you may never have it again!'[136]

The pro-Rhodesian group of Conservative MPs could now argue that the annual renewal of sanctions—against which they regularly voted in the House—was even more prejudicial to an effective solution of the Rhodesian problem than it had been in the past. Moreover, there was real doubt that any elections in which the Patriotic Front participated would be fair. The sanctions issue was not only a problem for the Conservative leadership in the Commons, as the number who voted against renewal grew from 27 MPs in 1977 to 111 in 1978, but more especially at the Party conference, where in 1978 it was anticipated as the major source of division between the leadership and the Party in the country.[137] Any resolution to abandon sanctions would have caused a major complication to the leadership because they had been imposed through the UN.

Carrington had to convince Thatcher that the internal settlement achieved with Muzorewa could not provide a lasting resolution of differences within Rhodesia-Zimbabwe. Once this was achieved, and the conference on the future of Rhodesia was underway at Lancaster House, Carrington had to negotiate the 1979 Party conference. Before he took office he had acknowledged that he was out of step with some influential opinion

---

[135] Darwin, *Decolonisation*, 319.

[136] *H C Deb*, 971, 25 July 1979, col. 653.

[137] *H C Deb*, 957, 8 Nov. 1978 cols 1144–5; URL: <http://www.margaretthatcher.org/>, 'Archive', minutes of Conservatives Leaders' Consultative Committee, 220th meeting, 4 Oct. 1978, accessed 14 Feb. 2009.

within the Party on Rhodesia such that his position could not be assured: 'I gave myself about six months.'[138] Negotiations were to secure a ceasefire, interim rule by a British governor, and then elections in which the Patriotic Front were to participate. Breaking off from the Lancaster House proceedings he devoted effort to his party conference speech: 'I have seldom taken more trouble with any speech's composition.'[139] It had the desired effect; Carrington managed to deflect the argument that his strategy would lead to the replacement of a multiracial constitution by a one-party Marxist state. While the *Daily Telegraph* commented that there was a 'nip of Munich in the air' it conceded the effectiveness of Carrington's speech, which managed 'to convince the conference that the sole object of the government's complex diplomacy was to benefit Bishop Muzorewa's administration by inducing the Popular Front to lay down its arms'.[140] It was successful, and carried the conference overwhelmingly.

While Carrington had brought a particularly long-running problem to a close, the imperial dimension was still a factor for the Thatcher government, thanks to the drama of the Falklands War of 1982. This was an unusual component of Britain's imperial saga in the sense that it involved the challenge of another nation, Argentina, to a British colony, rather than an essentially internal transfer of power. It might have gone the same way as other examples in Britain's colonial experience, since it involved a distant territory of limited value. The difficulty of reconciling the islanders' wish to remain ruled from Britain with the persistent claims from nearby Argentina was heading to resolution by means of an arrangement whereby the sovereignty of Argentina would be recognized, but with the Falklands 'leased back' to British administration for a significant period. This was derailed by the Argentinian invasion of 2 April 1982. This occasioned an emergency debate in the Commons on Saturday 3 April. There could be no question after this debate of the government doing anything other than retaking the Falklands. Speaker after speaker from the Conservative benches spoke of the 'humiliation' of their government; Powell asked that Thatcher live up to her billing as the 'Iron Lady'.[141] Labour too, asserted the necessity of standing up

---

[138] Lord Carrington, *Reflect on Things Past: The Memoirs of Lord Carrington* (London, 1988), 286.

[139] Ibid. 299.

[140] *Daily Telegraph* (11 Oct. 1979).

[141] *H C Deb*, 6th series, 21, 3 Apr. 1982.

to Argentina. Although a perilous mission, without the air mastery that had been regarded as essential, it ended in success.

How far did this 'round off' the colonial experience in a more satisfactory manner than it might otherwise have been left? It was not a characteristic type of colonial relationship or colonial challenge. It restored confidence as a military, rather than a political event. What it did do was arrest the sense that Britain had lost the capacity to solve the problems facing it, which the imperial retreat, and the disgrace of Suez, had inculcated. It gave to the state an external, non-European, dimension that had largely been abandoned without, prior to the Falklands, being replaced by an effective 'decolonized' one. But was it a successful stand against the tide of imperial retreat that some Conservatives had demanded for so long? It might have been: after all, Thatcher was not Baldwin, and was no supporter of the moderate conservatism that had negotiated withdrawal from empire. There was also a colonial aspect to the Falklands War. What the Argentinians threatened was a colonial possession. When the invasion occurred, Sir Nigel Fisher pointed out that this was a failure to protect a colony: 'We have failed—and failed lamentably—to defend the integrity of one of Britain's few remaining colonies.'[142] But the Falklands War was no atonement for past weakness. Thatcher's was a post-imperial conservatism.[143] What was at stake, according to a succession of speakers in the Commons debate, was the right of self-determination for the islanders. Michael Foot argued that it was about the Falkland islanders' right of association with Britain and there was 'no question in the Falkland Islands of any colonial dependence or anything of the sort'.[144] But 'self-determination' as a principle was corrosive of imperial authority. Sovereignty was about territory as much as people.[145] Thus, the way that the case was made for recapturing the Falklands—self-determination for the islanders—showed just how irreversible was the detachment from empire that had been at the heart of mainstream British politics for so long.

Thatcher's willingness to challenge the notion of British decline, to rail against the orthodoxies that had dominated British politics for so long and

---

[142] H C Deb, 6th series, 21, 3 Apr. 1982, col. 649.

[143] Shirley Robin Letwin, The Anatomy of Thatcherism (London, 1992), 37.

[144] H C Deb, 6th series, 21, col. 638.

[145] Thus Enoch Powell: 'I do not think we should be too nice about saying that we defend our territory as well as our people.' H C Deb, 6th series, 21, col. 1159. See also E. Kedourie, The Crossman Confessions and Other Essays in Politics, History and Religion (London, 1984), 82.

which had found a home in her own party, and to search for a purposeful national identity while at the same time embracing the market economy, make her own experience of 'empire' all the more instructive. Her lack of enthusiasm for the Commonwealth is well known, and another contrast with some of the prevailing attitudes in post-1945 Britain.[146] The Commonwealth had carried the hopes of those who believed that the empire might live on in a grouping of progressive, independent nations held together by common values. This was true for Harold Wilson, for whom the value of support to developing countries was an added dimension.[147] But this was to end in disappointment, as Wilson had to endure a 'nightmare' Commonwealth conference in September 1966 where, at the height of the Rhodesian crisis, he was accused of racism.[148] Thatcher did not start out with much enthusiasm for the Commonwealth, and the experience of trying to withstand the pressure for economic sanctions against South Africa in the 1980s only confirmed that. In her view, they threatened to destroy the South African economy without being the most effective way of bringing apartheid to an end. As Geoffrey Howe has recalled, in arguing the case at the Nassau meeting in 1985 that sanctions were not the way to promote change in South Africa, 'we were effectively alone'.[149] The consequence was that at a special Commonwealth conference held in London in August 1986, Britain was for the first time overruled and sanctions went ahead. Nor was there much consolation in the final victory as white South Africa accepted the need for change, since there were other more powerful influences at play besides Thatcher's, especially those within the international business community.[150]

Thatcher's anxieties were particularly strong over the reversion of Hong Kong to China in 1997. She was concerned about its future in the hands of a nation whose leaders she distrusted. The main question was how far its status could be protected when China's position was unassailable. Hong Kong had been accepted for many years after 1949 by the People' Republic of China because Britain had shown little interest in introducing constitutional

[146] John Campbell, *Margaret Thatcher*, ii. *The Iron Lady* (2nd edn., London, 2003), 139.
[147] Ben Pimlott, *Harold Wilson* (London, 1992), 433–4.
[148] Brian Harrison, *Seeking a Role: The United Kingdom 1951–1970* (Oxford, 2009), 113.
[149] Geoffrey Howe, *Conflict of Loyalty* (London, 1994), 481.
[150] Campbell, *Margaret Thatcher*, 328, 334.

reforms in the event of eventual decolonization.[151] The Joint Agreement of 1984 which guaranteed Hong Kong's special status within China for fifty years after 1997 was accepted within British diplomatic circles as the most that could be achieved, but Thatcher subsequently supported the efforts by Chris Patten, governor from 1992, to develop democracy in the colony before the handover which dismayed those who had developed the 1984 agreement and angered the Chinese.

Where Thatcher had clearer links with traditional views of the empire was over her expressed sense of greater affinity with the white dominions than with the rest of the Commonwealth. Baldwin had identified empire especially with the white dominions.[152] Precisely because these had acquired greater self-government than the colonies, their status might have been expected to continue more or less unchanged through the imperial turbulence of the 1950s and beyond. However, there is a powerful argument that their own experience was part of the larger process of decolonization, as they adopted the symbols of nationhood that signalled a weakened element of 'Britishness' in their cultures and also pursued foreign policies which addressed their own rather than British interests.[153]

Thatcher's premiership is therefore an interesting commentary on the place of empire in British politics in the last quarter of the twentieth century. Her instincts had been to challenge the strategy of compromise and negotiation that had characterized the transfer of power. She stood against the prevailing political culture. She had to be convinced of the wisdom of acknowledging Mugabe's role in any settlement of the Rhodesian impasse, and the handover of Hong Kong had been hard to swallow. In these she had been forced to accept the logic of British policy along traditional lines. Where she had been able to insist on her views to the point of successful resolution, namely in the Falklands War, the achievement of a national purpose had been shorn of imperial significance. Even in her contrary stance, Thatcher confirmed the reality of a post-imperial British politics.

---

[151] Brian Hook, 'National and International Interests in the Decolonisation of Hong Kong, 1946–1997', in Judith M. Brown and Rosemary Foot (eds.), *Hong Kong's Transitions, 1842–1997* (Basingstoke, 1997), 85, 89.

[152] Philip Williamson, *Stanley Baldwin: Conservative Leadership and National Values* (Cambridge, 1999), 260–1.

[153] A. G. Hopkins, 'Rethinking Decolonization', *P&P* 20/1 (2008), 211–47. Harrison, *Seeking a Role*, 103.

For the whole of the twentieth century, the majority of politicians debated the issue of where Britain belonged in the wider world. For a minority of these, empire provided an enduringly satisfactory answer. For the majority, the dominant strand in the political outlook recognized some kind of path to self-government, preferably within the empire or Commonwealth, as an ideal outcome, but accepted that empire was increasingly at odds with other opinions that gathered force in international politics. However, this same way of thinking about the world also instilled a sense of responsibility—however burdensome—that meant the legacy of empire had a significant impact on British politics.

Select Bibliography

S. J. BALL, 'Banquo's Ghost: Lord Salisbury, Harold Macmillan, and the High Politics of Decolonization, 1957–1963', *Twentieth Century British History*, 16/1 (2005), 74–102.

G. BEST, *Churchill: A Study in Greatness* (London and New York, 2001).

J. BROWN, *Modern India* (Oxford, 1994).

—— and Wm.R. Louis (eds.), *The Oxford History of the British Empire*, iv. *The Twentieth Century* (Oxford, 1999).

J. CAMPBELL, *Margaret Thatcher*, ii. *The Iron Lady* (2nd edn., London, 2003).

LORD CARRINGTON, *Reflect on Things Past: The Memoirs of Lord Carrington* (London, 1988).

M. COWLING, *Religion and Public Doctrine in Modern England* (Cambridge, 1980).

J. DARWIN, *Britain and Decolonisation: The Retreat from Empire in the Post-War World* (Basingstoke, 1988).

N. FISHER, *Iain Macleod* (London, 1973).

M. GILBERT, *Winston S. Churchill*, v/2. *Documents, The Wilderness Years 1929–1935* (London, 1981).

D. GOLDSWORTHY, *Colonial Issues in British Politics 1945–1961: From 'Colonial Development' to 'Wind of Change'* (Oxford, 1971).

B. HARRISON, *Seeking a Role: The United Kingdom 1951–1970* (Oxford, 2009).

A. G. HOPKINS, 'Rethinking Decolonization', *Past & Present*, 20/1 (2008), 211–47.

E. KEDOURIE, *England in the Middle East: The Destruction of the Ottoman Empire* (London, 1982 edn.).

S. R. LETWIN, *The Anatomy of Thatcherism* (London, 1992).

W. R. LOUIS, *In the Name of God, Go! Leo Amery and the British Empire in the Age of Churchill* (London and New York, 1992).

P. MURPHY, *Party Politics and Decolonization: The Conservative Party and British Colonial Policy in Tropical Africa, 1951–1964* (Oxford, 1995).

N. OWEN, 'The Conservative Party and Indian Independence, 1945–1947', *Historical Journal*, 46/2 (2003), 403–36.

B. PIMLOTT, *Harold Wilson* (London, 1992).

R. SHEPHERD, *Iain Macleod: A Biography* (2nd edn., London, 1995).

P. WILLIAMSON, *Stanley Baldwin: Conservative Leadership and National Values* (Cambridge, 1999).

—— and E. BALDWIN (eds.), *The Baldwin Papers: A Conservative Statesman 1908–1947* (Cambridge, 2004).

6

The Empire/Commonwealth in British Economic Thinking and Policy

Jim Tomlinson

I

In 1903 the industrialist Sir Vincent Caillard spoke of his conviction 'that the welfare and prosperity of the United Kingdom, and of almost all, if not of all, the British colonies, must depend to an immense extent upon the maintenance of the Empire'.[1] Forty years later, Ernest Bevin, the Foreign Secretary told parliament: 'I know if the British empire fell . . . it would mean that the standard of life of our constituents would fall considerably.'[2] By the end of the twentieth century such views would have been unthinkable. The name 'empire' had of course been abandoned, but even if we substitute 'Commonwealth', it is plain that no serious commentator could have seen the prosperity of Britain in the late twentieth century in this light; overwhelmingly, economic discussion proceeded as if the Commonwealth was of no account.

This chapter charts the career of metropolitan beliefs about the economic meaning and importance of empire such as those espoused by Caillard and Bevin, the context in which they arose, and the challenges they faced. It analyses the waxing and waning of such sentiments, and how they related to the broad context of shifting approaches to the British economy. But an aggregate chronological picture of 'waxing and waning', while important and accurate in the round, obscures some of the cross-cutting patterns which emphasize that there was never one 'thing' called the empire, but

[1] V. Caillard, *Imperial Fiscal Reform* (London, 1903), 31.
[2] House of Commons 21 Feb. 1946, cited by C. Feinstein, 'The End of Empire and the Golden Age', in P. Clarke and C. Trebilcock (eds.), *Understanding Decline: Perceptions and Realities of British Economic Performance* (Cambridge, 1997), 217.

different empires according to the understandings brought to bear by a range of analysts and policy-makers. Equally, within Britain, empire had greatly varying significance for different regions; for some parts of the country the direct economic connections were small, for others absolutely crucial to their welfare.

In sum, the chapter seeks to explain how the empire/Commonwealth figured in the complex evolution of Britain's understanding of, and policy responses to, its economic problems through the turbulent passage of the twentieth century. The key questions will be: How did the empire come to be seen as a privileged economic space? How did policy-makers, major political parties, interest groups, and opinion-formers understand the ways in which the empire fitted into Britain's economic life? How and why did this change in the course of the century?

II

Caillard's statement was made in the course of the tariff reform controversy that reached its crescendo in the years between 1903 and 1910. That debate was not just about the empire. As recent scholarship has emphasized, neither was it a narrow contest of *economic* ideas, free trade versus protectionism and tariffs, but a much broader contest between two world views, in which economic arguments were embedded in deep structures of political and cultural perception. Free trade was part of a popular, liberal, cosmopolitan discourse, which while undoubtedly appealing to the immediate material interests of consumers—'the cheap loaf'—resonated much more deeply with how many Edwardian Britons of all classes saw the world.[3] More directly relevant here is our understanding of the significance of the movement for tariff reform, which was the product of a Conservative politics which sought to unite two key themes—the defence of property and the encouragement of empire.[4] The second of these can be traced back to the foundation of the Imperial Federation League in 1884, which sought to encourage closer Imperial unity whilst sidestepping the free trade versus

---

[3] F. Trentmann, *Free Trade Nation* (Oxford, 2007); A. Howe, *Free Trade and Liberal England 1846–1946* (Oxford, 1997), 230–73.

[4] E. Green, *The Crisis of Conservatism: The Politics, Economics and Ideology of the British Conservative Party, 1880–1914* (London, 1995), 11–23.

protection argument, the latter, also from the 1880s, being advocated by the National Fair Trade League.[5]

The link between such desires for unity and tariffs was made explicitly by Chamberlain in 1895, when he became Colonial Secretary, with his call for empire free trade, but while this notion had a short life in the face of opposition from the white empire (and destroyed the Imperial Federation League), it cemented the link between imperial enthusiasm and economic policy that came to the fore in the debates after 1903 when Chamberlain launched his tariff reform campaign.[6] Chamberlain, and other key figures in the attempt to make the empire a privileged economic space, saw material interests as the surest foundation for strengthening imperial bonds. This, notably, was the basis of Leo Amery's proposals for a self-sufficient common market embracing the empire, within which the interdependence would be based on the exchange of British manufactures for colonial food and raw materials.[7] However, we should not exaggerate the homogeneity of imperial advocacy at this time. Alfred Milner, regarded by many as the key figure in such imperial thinking, and the *Round Table* movement he founded, put less emphasis on the economic basis of imperial settlement than many of his followers.[8]

Conservative enthusiasm for empire was, of course, of long standing but what brought it to the centre of their politics at the beginning of the twentieth century was the Boer War, and its exposure of imperial weakness. This weakness was interpreted in the light of contemporary social Darwinist thought, which saw Britain as losing out in the global struggle for survival against the rising power, especially the USA and Germany. This notion of responding to perceived weakness underpinned tariff reform, because reform was intended to simultaneously correct British economic 'decline' and to strengthen the empire by deepening its economic interconnections, creating a market to rival those of the size of Germany and the USA.[9] Thus Chamberlain became the first in a line of Conservative politicians who put 'reversing decline' at the centre of their politics, and in his case saw

[5] Ibid. 30–41.

[6] Ibid. 39–41.

[7] W. R. Louis, *In the Name of God, Go! Leo Amery and the British Empire in the Age of Churchill* (New York, 1992), 17–27.

[8] J. Thompson, *A Wider Patriotism: Alfred Milner and the British Empire* (London, 2007), esp. 205–6.

[9] A. Friedberg, *The Weary Titan: Britain and the Experience of Relative Decline, 1895–1905* (Princeton, 1988).

the empire as central to that reversal.[10] However, it must be stressed that general support for protectionism was not mainly driven by imperial enthusiasm. As one of the main 'imperial visionaries' of the period realistically noted: 'In Great Britain, no less that in the Dominions, this hard core of interest was not really imperial at all. It was the national system of political economy seeking to protect itself outwards into a nicely balanced structure of bartered shelter.'[11]

Empire free trade was never a plausible option because the white empire was not willing to allow British manufactures free access to their home markets; they wanted to develop their own industries, and to this end some had introduced preferential tariffs in the 1890s.[12] Imperial preference addressed this issue, but only at the fatal cost of threatening the availability of cheap food, the main proximate cause of rising working-class living standards in Britain in the last quarter of the nineteenth century.[13] For the Conservatives tariff reform proved electorally disastrous in 1906. But it was not a policy that could be readily jettisoned, precisely because it was so interwoven with the Party's whole outlook, including especially its enthusiasm for empire, though it is important to note that there was a minority of free trade Conservatives who regarded the fiscal controversy as damagingly dividing pro-imperialists by attaching the empire to protectionism.[14] The Liberals had diverse views on the empire, but mainstream liberalism argued that imperial unity would be harmed by bargaining over tariffs; preference would be a 'solvent, not cement, of imperial ties'.[15]

Between 1910 and the First World War the Conservative party was 'in a mess' following the failure of the 1910 elections to show that tariff reform could form the basis of a viable anti-progressive politics.[16] The party response was to back away from a full-blooded commitment to tariffs, especially on food, but this partial retreat left the Party in poor ideological

---

[10] D. Cannadine, 'Apocalypse When? British Politicians and British "Decline" in the Twentieth Century', in Clarke and Trebilcock (eds.), *Understanding Decline*, 261–84.

[11] W. Hewins, cited in W. Hancock, *Survey of British Commonwealth Affairs*, ii. *Problems of Economic Policy 1918–1939*, pt 1 (Oxford, 1940), 191–2.

[12] Green, *Crisis*, 196–7.

[13] C. Feinstein, 'What Really Happened to Real Wages? Trends in Wages, Prices and Productivity in the UK, 1880–1913', *Economic History Review* (*EcHR*), 43/3 (1990), 329–55.

[14] S. Drage, *The Imperial Organization of Trade* (London, 1911).

[15] Howe, *Free Trade*, 290.

[16] Green, *Crisis*, 304.

and electoral shape on the eve of the war. But the war marked a decisive reversal of fortune, not least because ultimately it destroyed many of the underpinnings of the 'Free Trade Nation', and opened the way to protectionism.[17]

In the great debates of the Edwardian period the Liberals were able to formulate tax policies, directed especially at landowners, which enabled them to finance social reform without recourse to tariffs. In this way they successfully countered the Conservative attempt to link social reform with tariffs and empire. But in the war the need for revenue and the need to save shipping space led to a break in free trade with the McKenna Duties of 1915. Though quantitatively insignificant, these duties breached the free trade wall, and were followed by other protective policies in the war and early post-war period—the defence of 'key industries' and the Dyestuffs Act of 1920.

The relationship between these measures and the empire was complex. On the one hand, to many, tariffs were now thought of much more as 'industrial policy' than had been the case before the war, given that the war had exposed shortcomings in British industry generally, and in some cases dangerous reliance on German imports. Many industrialists saw this as an opportunity to free advocacy of protection from the incubus of debate about empire.[18] On the other hand, once protectionism became more generally acceptable the possibility of successfully linking it to empire was reopened. Also, there is no doubt that the imperial contribution to the war effort reinforced the view that as a unit it would be stronger if bound together more strongly by economic, as well as diplomatic and military, links.[19]

This kind of argument featured prominently in the Report of the Balfour of Burleigh Committee on post-war industry, which came out in favour of imperial preference, albeit coupled with a rejection of taxes on food.[20] This Report registered a major wartime protectionist shift in business opinion, clearly articulated by the newly formed Federation of British Industry. But while some industrialists clearly linked protectionism to empire

---

[17] Trentmann, *Free Trade Nation*, 285–330; Howe, *Free Trade*, 280–2.

[18] Trentmann, *Free Trade Nation*, 305–6.

[19] A. S. Thompson, *Imperial Britain: The Empire in British Politics, c.1880–1932* (Harlow, 2000), 157–85.

[20] *Final Report of the Committee on Commercial and Industrial Policy after the War*, Cd. 9035, BPP 1918, vol. xiii; Trentmann, *Free Trade Nation*, 289–92.

enthusiasm, most did not: businessmen could accept giving preferences on existing duties, but, with the exception of old tariff reformers like Hewins, a tariff on food and imperial economic union attracted little support.[21] In the event, this protectionist business sentiment was to yield little policy success in the short run, with only minor deviations from free trade implemented in the 1920s, and these accompanied by even more minor imperial preferences. On the other hand, there had been a major shift in business opinion in a protectionist direction; many industrialists were biding their time, awaiting an opportunity to pursue that agenda.[22]

In the short run, as Drummond has persuasively argued, it was the unemployment of the 1920s that created a political space within which the 'imperial visionaries' could somewhat more effectively pursue their objectives. Men such as Milner and Hewins built upon the pre-1914 experience of growing economic interconnections between Britain and the white empire to suggest a 'developmental' model in which the British state would encourage emigration and capital outflows, and in return give preferential entry to the expanded dominion export production.[23] These ideas were pursued especially by Leo Amery as a junior minister from 1917 and as Colonial Secretary from 1924 to 1929 (and Dominion Affairs, 1925-9). This vision never fully captured British (or dominion) governments in the 1920s, but some elements found support. Within Whitehall the vision was largely disparaged by the Treasury, not least because of its potential for 'extravagant' public spending; Amery's ideas were a version of the 'proto-Keynesianism' which the 1920s Treasury so firmly set itself against.[24] Political support for trade preferences diminished after Baldwin's loss of the 1923 election, and under Labour in 1924, and then with Churchill as Chancellor from 1924 to 1929, free traders were predominant. But unemployment drove a major departure in policy—empire settlement.

The idea that the government should actively encourage and subsidize emigration from Britain emerged in wartime discussions, largely in the context of fears about the post-war fate of ex-servicemen. Some of these, it was believed, could be employed in an expanded British agriculture, but

---

[21] Trentmann, Free Trade Nation, 292.

[22] F. Capie, Depression and Protectionism: Britain between the Wars (London, 1983); A. Marrison, British Business and Protection 1903–1932 (Oxford, 1996), 430–5.

[23] I. Drummond, Imperial Economic Policy 1917–1939: Studies in Expansion and Protection (London, 1974), 32–40.

[24] Ibid. 127–32.

many more were expected to find rural occupations overseas.[25] Initially support for such ideas was limited, in part because of differing views on the likely state of the post-war labour market, but the collapse of the post-war boom from 1920 changed many minds. Combined with pressure from Amery, and from Australia, the desire to reduce mass unemployment led to the Empire Settlement Act of 1922.[26]

By far the most important outcome of this Act was financial support for British emigrants to Australia, partly by direct payment of transport costs, partly by subsidized 'development loans' to Australian public authorities. The other dominions were largely uninterested—in Canada, for example, only a tiny scheme was ever implemented, not least because part of the 'vision' of this policy was to settle the unemployed on the land, but in Canada problems of agricultural over-production and falling prices were already evident in the 1920s.[27] A similar idea of rural settlement was evident in the approach to emigration to Australia, but in the event, and unsurprisingly, most of those who gained assisted passages in the 1920s ended up in urban areas. The money spent on agricultural expansion (much less than the scheme allowed) largely went into high cost, protected sectors which added to the problems of agricultural collapse in the 1930s.[28] In South Africa Afrikaner opposition to British immigration blocked any substantial influx, while New Zealand was in principle more welcoming, but gave priority to its own substantial ex-servicemen problem.[29]

Overall, the British state assisted the emigration of 345,400 people between 1922 and 1931, almost exactly half of total outflow.[30] This total was considerably below the pre-war level, and the contribution to relieving unemployment limited. While unemployment in Britain was high, by international standards support for the unemployed was quite good, so the economic benefits of emigration to the individual were not obviously large. While not all the money allocated to support emigration was spent, some that was spent was probably wasted, in the sense that many emigrants

---

[25] K. Fedorowich, *Unfit for Heroes: Reconstruction and Soldier Settlement in the Empire between the Wars* (Manchester, 1995).

[26] Drummond, *Imperial Economic Policy*, chs. 2 and 3; id., *British Economic Policy and the Empire 1919–1939* (London, 1972), 70–88, 143–6.

[27] Fedorowich, *Unfit for Heroes*, ch. 4.

[28] Drummond, *British Economic Policy*, 118, 141–2.

[29] Fedorowich, *Unfit for Heroes*, 129–30, 179–81.

[30] Drummond, *British Economic Policy*, 140.

would have likely gone in any event; the subsidy involved a 'deadweight' expenditure. On the other hand, the 1920s was undoubtedly the decade in which British state-funding had most significance for inter-imperial migration.[31] Crucially, the policy rested upon a domestic, non-imperial problem—unemployment—but as a solution to that problem it gained from the widespread sharing of at least a watered-down version of the 'vision' across much of the political spectrum, including Labour politicians, most notably J. H. Thomas.[32] It should also be noted that unemployment at home was the major stimulus to the Colonial Development Act of 1929, which followed on from previous initiatives whose focus had been on the exploitation of the physical resources of the empire, rather than 'development' in the sense which emerged from the 1940s of raising incomes in the colonies.[33]

If state-supported emigration in the 1920s can be seen as the major politically-viable component of the 'imperial vision', 'empire marketing' can be seen as an alternative to the politically impossible route of significant imperial preference. This policy gave state support, amounting to $3.7 million between 1926 and 1933, to an Empire Marketing Board (EMB) which encouraged the people of Britain to 'Buy Empire Goods from Home and Overseas'. (The inclusion of domestically produced goods in the campaign followed pressure from farmers.)[34] This, too, found sufficient bipartisan support to overcome Treasury scepticism, though it never received the full £1 million a year funding that was in principle available to it.[35] Building on a tradition of commercial advertising which emphasized the 'Imperial exotic', but also ideas of cooperation and interdependence, the EMB survived until Ottawa, though it is impossible to say with how much effect.[36]

---

[31] For perspectives on this from sending and receiving countries respectively, see M. Harper, *Emigration from Scotland between the Wars: Opportunity or Exile?* (Manchester, 1998); E. Richards, *Destination Australia: Migration to Australia since 1901* (Sydney, 2008).

[32] P. Gupta, *Imperialism and the British Labour Movement, 1914–1964* (London, 1975), 134–61.

[33] D. Morgan, *The Official History of Colonial Development*, iv. *Changes in British Aid Policy* (London, 1980); *Colonial Development and Welfare Acts, 1929–1970: A Brief Review*, Cmnd. 4677, BPP 1970/71, vol. 8; A. Porter and A. Stockwell (eds.), *British Imperial Policy and Decolonization*, i., *1938–1951* (London, 1987), ch. 3.

[34] S. Constantine, *Buy and Build: The Advertising Posters of the Empire Marketing Board* (London, 1980).

[35] Drummond, *Imperial Economic Policy*, 29.

[36] Constantine, *Buy and Build*, 15–17.

The story of British imperial economic policy in the 1920s was one of a battle between imperial visionaries and (qualified) free traders, in which the latter largely won the big battle, but the former won some ground mainly because of the impact of unemployment.[37] But unemployment also raised fears about public spending, and this mitigated against big, developmental expenditure in the 1920s, however much its supporters sought to justify it as employment creation. In other respects the empire mattered little to British policy, though South Africa and Australia had some influence on the decision about the return to gold in 1925, especially the all-important issue of timing.[38]

The departure from gold and the imposition of a tariff in 1931 opened up a new era in British economic policy, with the old liberal shibboleths of free trade, the gold standard and a balanced budget either abandoned or subject to unprecedented peacetime challenge. The move to protection had the most obvious implications for policy on the empire; it meant that the principle of free trade no longer acted as the key barrier to exploring the possibility of some kind of imperial preference system. This was the background against which the Ottawa conference of 1932 was held. It followed previous imperial conferences, dating back to 1902, in which Britain sought to reduce dominion tariffs, while the dominions sought free entry for their products into the British market. But whereas at previous conferences there was no direct bargaining, Ottawa was characterized by intensive, often bad-tempered bilateral deal-making, in a fashion quite at odds with rhetoric about an underlying commonality of interests.[39]

The toughness of the bargaining was in large part the consequence of the economic environment of slump and unemployment. From the British point of view the key issue throughout was how far any agreement would expand employment.[40] Britain believed that maximizing the employment opportunities meant moving as far as possible towards imperial free trade. But the objections to this on the dominion side were as strong as ever; enhanced British competition would threaten domestic industrial employment. In Britain the cry for cheap food no longer had the same force as

[37] Drummond, *Imperial Economic Policy*, 422–6.
[38] L. Pressnell, '1925: The Burden of Sterling', *EcHR* 31/1 (1978), 67–88; K. Tsokhas, 'The Australian Role in Britain's Return to the Gold Standard', *EcHR* 47/1 (1994), 129–46.
[39] Drummond, *Imperial Economic Policy*, 170–4, 219–21.
[40] Ibid. 235, 296.

before 1914, but now protection of British agriculture was a growing potential barrier to dominion food exports.[41] As a result of these forces, what
emerged from Ottawa was a set of agreements which did increase imperial
preferences, but on a scale which fell far short of the hopes entertained in
London. Ottawa did divert trade into empire channels, though this trend
was also affected by sterling's departure from gold, which both increased the
competitiveness of sterling goods, as opposed to those of gold countries,
and also allowed more expansionary domestic monetary policies in sterling
countries. Overall, the effect of Ottawa was not entirely trivial, but fell far
short of any idea of seeing inter-imperial trade as the sovereign remedy for
slump and unemployment.[42] The major beneficiaries were the dominions,
not Britain, as British policy was more willing to divert imports from
foreign to imperial sources than the dominions were willing to reduce
protection of their home industries.[43] Detailed studies of major dominion
products underpin the generalization that British government enthusiasm
for imperial trade acted as a powerful bargaining counter for the suppliers
of such products.[44]

By the mid-1930s the empire was more of an economic bloc than ever
before. A combination of trade and monetary policies underpinned this, as
noted above. The latter led to the development of what came to be called the
sterling area, as dominions (other than Canada) sought monetary stability
(and easier access to the London capital market) by fixing their exchange
rate to a floating pound, and holding their exchange reserves in sterling.[45]
This created a whole new dynamic in British policy, though it was the
Second World War that was to turn this area into a key part of the 'imperial
system' in British eyes.

The Second World War, like the First, encouraged Commonwealth sentiment, as the members participated together in the Allied war effort. Across
the political spectrum there were assertions of the importance of the
Commonwealth to Britain's post-war future. For example, the left-wing
Labour MP Shinwell asserted in 1944 that 'the UK should do its utmost by

---

[41] Trentmann, *Free Trade Nation.*

[42] Drummond, *Imperial Economic Policy*, 286–9.

[43] T. Rooth, *British Protectionism and the International Economy: Overseas Commercial Policy
in the 1930s* (Cambridge, 1993).

[44] K. Tsokhas, *Markets, Money and Empire: The Political Economy of the Australian Wool
Trade* (Melbourne, 1990), esp. 1–15, 196–209.

[45] I. Drummond, *The Floating Pound and the Sterling Area, 1931–1939* (Cambridge, 1992).

close co-operation and regard for the different points of view of he nations of the Commonwealth to preserve in the peace the unity of purpose and sentiment which has held them together in time of war'.[46] Notions of the empire as a privileged economic space were strengthened, with the sterling area and imperial preference seen as underpinning close economic links. The sterling area increased in importance because it provided a mechanism to fight the war while economizing on dollar spending, the latter a key issue as the ability to obtain American goods became crucial to the war effort. Britain's wartime needs for imports were paid for by a combination of overseas asset sales, accumulation of 'sterling balances' (essentially unpaid for imports), especially from India and Egypt, and by Mutual Aid from the USA. But the underlying balance of payments deterioration, just about sustainable in wartime, required radical adjustment once the war was over. It was above all in the context of this payments problem that British attitudes to the Commonwealth took shape in the 1940s.

American support for the British balance of payments in the war led to American questioning of the imperial preference system, because of the emerging American view on the desirability of a non-discriminatory international trade regime in the post-war period. This American view led the Mutual Aid agreement of 1941 to include Article VII, committing Britain to eliminating 'all forms of discriminator treatment in international commerce'.[47] The precise significance of this for imperial preference was for years after disputed by the American and British, in part because this preference came to have a political significance clearly outweighing its economic importance. For America it came to be seen as symbolic of the old, discriminatory policies which Britain needed to abandon if she was truly embracing a multilateral trading world—and also a necessary step if the American Congress were to support post-war aid for Britain. On the British side, hanging on to some vestige of imperial preference became a sign of continuing policy autonomy in the face of America pressure, important even to those who saw little long-run economic benefit from the policy.[48]

---

[46] Cited in R. Gardner, *Sterling-Dollar Diplomacy* (New York, 1969), 154–5.

[47] R. Sayers, *Financial Policy 1939–1945* (London, 1956), 405–13; L. Pressnell, *External Economic Policy since the War*, iii. *The Post-War Financial Settlement* (London, 1986), ch. 4.

[48] F. Mackenzie, *Redefining the Bonds of Commonwealth, 1939–1948* (Basingstoke, 2002), 199–209.

While there were 'visionaries' such as Beaverbrook who had some influence in policy-making circles in the 1940s, and who saw imperial preference
as the core of a future strengthened Commonwealth, in the main the British
approach was informed by a combination of the political symbolism noted
above, and a pragmatic recognition of the potential for such preference to
aid the payments position. In a world of 'dollar shortage', such preferences
offered discrimination against dollar goods, to be given up only as that
shortage diminished. Thus they could be seen as an important part of the
British 'make me good Lord, but not yet' strategy, in which in principle
commitment to non-discrimination was combined with short-run expedi-
ents to protect the balance of payments.[49] This strategy was at the core of
Anglo-American economic relations in the 1940s. But in negotiating these
relations the issue of imperial preference was bound to raise profound issues
about how far the white Commonwealth would allow decisions to be made
solely by Britain. Mackenzie has argued that in fact the discussions of these
preferences revealed how far Britain was not allowed that role by increasingly assertive dominion governments.[50]

From a British point of view the discussion of imperial preference was
complicated by the divergent views and interests of the dominion governments. Canada, with its close US ties, was least concerned with the loss of
preferences, and South Africa's gold reserves reduced their sensitivity. New
Zealand gained most from quantitative restrictions on non-empire imports,
but Australia was heavily dependent upon preferences to protect its new
industries as well as markets in Britain.[51] The practical outcome of all the
debate of the late 1940s was that imperial preferences were, for the time
being, maintained on only a slightly reduced level. But the discussions on
this issue revealed how far Britain could no longer assume that it could
speak for a unified Commonwealth on trade matters, and how far the
dominions were determined to stand up for their divergent interests.[52]

As the narrative so far has made clear, up until the 1940s it was almost
entirely the dominions that played a significant role in British economic

---

[49] R. Toye, 'The Attlee Government, the Imperial Preference System and the Creation of the
GATT', *English Historical Review* (*EHR*), 108 (2003), 912–39.

[50] Mackenzie, *Redefining the Bonds*, 260–8.

[51] Ibid. 146.

[52] For an incisive discussion of the post-war relationship between Britain and the dominions,
which sees an economic and cultural 'decolonization' culminating in the 1960s, A. Hopkins,
'Rethinking Decolonization', *Past & Present* (*P&P*), 200/1 (2008), 211–47.

policy debate. With the partial exception of India (returned to below), the dependent empire figured very little. But the need to save dollars impacted not only on relations with the dominions, but also very substantially on British policy on other parts of the empire. Above all, the Attlee government pursued policies to maximize dollar exports from colonies like Malaya and the Gold Coast (and minimize imports into these places), which have been seen as leading to a period of striking imperial exploitation.[53] For the colonies as a whole in the period 1945–51, inflows were about $40 million, while sterling balances grew by about $160 million.[54]

How far this outcome was the result of any direct intention to exploit the colonies can be disputed. From a British perspective it followed from the long-standing notion that the economic development of Britain and her colonies was interdependent and complementary, and from the assumption that what was good for Britain was good for the colonies. This implied a division of labour between manufacturing activity in the UK, and food and raw material production in the colonies, a doctrine, it should be noted, which found little opposition in the Colonial Office, which saw colonial industrialization as likely to be socially and politically disruptive.[55] Paradoxically, this was the same period in which notions of colonial development were getting a major new impetus, after their limited beginnings in the interwar period.[56]

More controversial at the time was the way in which Britain turned the imperial terms of trade in its favour and directly squeezed the incomes of colonial producers by bulk purchasing of colonial products at below world prices. This had begun during the war, but continued into the peace. It led Creech Jones, the Colonial Secretary, to tell cabinet colleagues in early 1947: 'I know full well how important it is that our overseas payments should be kept as low as the possibly can be, but I cannot believe that this justifies a course which is contrary to our declared policy in regard to both Colonial and to commercial matters and contrary also to the policy which has long

[53] A. Hinds, 'Sterling and Imperial Policy, 1945–1951' *Journal of Imperial and Commonwealth History* (*JICH*), 15/2 (1987), 148–69. J. Tomlinson, *Democratic Socialism and Economic Policy: The Attlee Years, 1945–1951* (Cambridge, 1997), 61–7.

[54] D. Morgan, *The Official History of Colonial Development*, ii. *Developing Colonial Resources, 1945–1951* (London, 1980), ch. 1.

[55] A. Porter and A. Stockwell (eds.), *British Imperial Policy and Decolonisation 1938–1964*, ii. *1938–1951* (London, 1987), document 44.

[56] Morgan, *Official History*, vol. iv.

been pursued by the Labour Party.'[57] But nothing came of this protest, and indeed policy on colonial trade was tightened over the next three years.[58] This pursuit of dollars famously led to some particularly ill-conceived schemes to develop African primary products, most famously the ground-nuts scheme. This economically driven project was linked to a broader 'vision' of Africa as a bastion of British colonialism, untainted by the nationalism of Asia, a vision which was integral to at least some Labour ministers' views of the future of the Commonwealth.[59]

While the traditional issue of imperial trade and preference was import-ant in the 1940s, it was accompanied by another issue which was also largely 'imperial' in character, that of the sterling area. (The area was largely coterminous with the empire except for the exclusion of Canada.) The foundations of the area were laid in the 1930s with the break-up of the gold standard, and the tying of most empire currencies to the pound. But it became much more significant after 1940 with the introduction of tight, area-wide, exchange control. This meant that access to non-sterling curren-cies, especially dollars, could be used for trade discrimination, and indeed this became more important than imperial preference in encouraging inter-imperial trade and discriminating against the dollar.

The issue which emerged in the late 1940s was how far this area should be seen as a key component of a long-run British strategy of fostering a strong pound as an integral part of a more unified empire. This was known as the 'two world' option in the 1940s, the idea of sustaining two currency blocs in the West built around the dollar and the pound. This option was supported by some empire enthusiasts and some economists, but it never predomi-nated in British thinking.[60] It was strongly argued against by Keynes in 1945, when he stressed that the area was hungry for dollar goods, and could not be plausibly built up into a self-sufficient entity.[61] It was also rejected by Cripps, the Labour Chancellor in the late 1940s, partly for the same eco-nomic reasons, but also because a long-term separate bloc would threaten political relations and economic support from the USA. He wrote: 'I do not

[57] Porter and Stockwell (eds.), *British Imperial Policy*, document 42.

[58] Tomlinson, *Democratic Socialism*, 63.

[59] Feinstein, 'End of Empire', 222–3; J. Kent, 'Bevin's Imperialism and the Idea of Euro-Africa, 1945–1949', in M. Dockrill and J. Young (eds.), *British Foreign Policy, 1945–1956* (London, 1989), 47–75; Gupta, *Imperialism*, 303–48.

[60] Tomlinson, *Democratic Socialism*, 28, 41.

[61] D. Moggridge, *Maynard Keynes: An Economist's Biography* (London, 1992), 817.

believe that we have at present the resources or reserves to forge a third independent economic area, let alone any strategic area between the Russians and the Americans.' Therefore Britain should commit to 'one world', whilst guarding against the dangers of too close association with the capitalist USA.[62]

But while a highly discriminatory sterling area was dismissed as a long-term strategic choice, in the short run it certainly functioned that way in the 1940s. A corollary of this was an absence of control over British foreign investment within the area, so that the Attlee period saw an extraordinary outflow of capital. This outflow was *not* to the dependent colonies—as noted above they suffered net disinvestment in this period. Some of it took the form of a rundown of India's sterling balances, though this was accompanied by complex and controversial negotiations with India.[63] Most of the outflow was to South Africa and Australia, though the precise figures remain in doubt.[64] In relation to contemporary macroeconomic policy this outflow was a problem, because there was considerable 'leakage' in the exchange controls in the dominions, so these capital outflows indirectly hit the dollar position. For the British economy in the 1940s the scale of these outflows are striking and paradoxical. As Cairncross observed:

Given the straits to which the British economy was reduced in 1947, when it was necessary to ration even bread and potatoes, an outflow of capital equal to about 8 per cent of national income and nearly equal to total net domestic capital formation . . . is a very extraordinary event. It was certainly not the purpose or which the American and Canadian loans were procured.[65]

This capital outflow was an unintended consequence of the sterling area system, and one which allowed the London financial markets to rebuild their traditional role as suppliers of capital to the 'white Commonwealth'. There was a convergence of interest between capital-hungry dominions and the desire of the City of London to reverse wartime losses in holdings of

[62] PRO CAB134/222, S. Cripps, 'The Dollar Situation', 4 July 1949.

[63] B. R. Tomlinson, 'Indo-British Relations in the Post-colonial Era: The Sterling Balances Negotiations, 1946–1949', *JICH* 13/3 (1985), 142–62.

[64] Compare A. Conan, *Sterling in the Post-War World* (Oxford, 1956), 125–6, which suggests Australia was the biggest recipient, with A. Cairncross, *Years of Recovery* (London, 1986), 158, which calculates that South Africa predominated; but the dominance of these two together is clear.

[65] Cairncross, *Years of Recovery*, 153.

overseas assets. But this aspect of British empire relations was little commented upon at the time—the political debate was focused more upon imperial preference on the one hand, and the viability of the sterling area on the other, with its implications for British foreign investment little discussed, though the government certainly believed that in principle London's role as a financial centre should be revived, especially given the loss of foreign earnings resulting from the war.[66]

Later critics of policy in the early post-war years have seen adherence to the sterling area as part of an imperial *folie de grandeur*, in which national economic interests were sacrificed to desires for acting as a great power.[67] This became a key component of 'declinist' writings of the 1950s and 1960s. But while its relevance to those decades is returned to below, it is worth noting that this characterization seems unhelpful in understanding the 1940s. While such *folies* may well be perceived in the 1940s, adherence to the sterling area in this period was plausibly defended at the time as a *transitional* policy, encouraging the growth of international trade whilst the dollar shortage was corrected.[68] As Harold Wilson bluntly put it at the time, while the imbalance of trade with the US continued 'non-discrimination is nonsense', but once that imbalance reduced exchange controls were relaxed, and so the area stopped being a major obstacle to the 'one world' vision.[69]

Into the early 1950s imperial visionaries could take some comfort from British economic policy; their wider views may have gained only limited support, but the post-war economic situation meant the pursuit of trade and currency policies which reinforced the economic significance of empire. For a period there was a 'Commonwealth economic system', particularly focused on the multiple economic links between Britain, Australia, and New Zealand.[70] But as emphasized above, this system was highly contingent on passing economic circumstances and contemporary understandings, and both of these shifted in a manner highly disadvantageous to imperial economic links in the 1950s.

---

[66] R. Rowthorn and J. Wells, *Deindustrialization and Foreign Trade* (Cambridge, 1987).

[67] C. Barnett, *Lost Victory: British Dreams, British Realities, 1945–1950* (London, 1995), 369.

[68] C. Newton, 'Britain, the Sterling Area and European Integration, 1945–1950', *JICH* 14 (1985), 163–82.

[69] PRO CAB 129/36, H. Wilson, 'The Future of Multinational Economic Co-operation', 12 Sept. 1949.

[70] J. Singleton and J. Robertson, *Economic Relations between Britain and Australasia 1945–1970* (Basingstoke, 2002), 1–4.

III

Under the Conservatives in the early 1950s the imperial visionaries fought a 'last stand' against the international economic liberalism embodied in the International Monetary Fund (IMF) and General Agreement on Tariffs and Trade (GATT) set up in the 1940s. While the pace of liberalization in Britain was slow, the direction was unambiguous. At successive Conservative conferences in the mid-1950s Amery led the forces critical of this trajectory, but to no avail. This failure partly reflected the commitment of the party leadership to the principles of international economic liberalism, as the best underpinning for the full employment and economic prosperity they were promising to the electorate. Especially after 1953, with the threat of a major US slump passed, liberalization looked to be compatible with domestic buoyancy.

Underpinning this belief was a growing recognition that the pattern of trade which would best support the fully employed economy was one inimical to Commonwealth trade. The traditional pattern of such trade was the swapping of British manufactured goods for food and raw materials from the empire. Even for the dominions, who had sought to diversify their economies, the dominance of their exports to Britain by primary products was pronounced. But in the 1950s it became increasingly clear that the growth in British imports was in manufactured goods, which rose from 17 per cent of total imports in 1946–9 to 41 per cent in 1960–9.[71] Very few of these were bought from Commonwealth countries, who, in so far as they produced manufactured goods, were not usually competitive with North American, West European, or Japanese suppliers. Hence the change in commodity composition of British imports, consequent in turn on rising incomes, was also a change in geographical patterns, away from the Commonwealth.

The biggest gainers were Western European. As Table 6.1 shows, these countries grew not only as the source of imports but also as a market for British exports, as their fast growth and appetite for manufactured goods led to an increasing role for 'intra-industry' exchanges amongst the populous rich counties as the main motor of world trade. Hence the driver of trade growth in the 'long-boom' was much more the exchange of consumer durables for consumer durables, than the exchange of manufactures for raw

[71] R. Rowthorn and J. Wells, *De-industrialization and Foreign Trade* (Cambridge, 1987), 173.

Table 6.1 Direction of UK Exports 1935–1973 (percentages)

	Western Europe	Dominions	Former Colonies
1935–8	27	29	19
1950–4	26	30	23
1955–9	27	26	23
1960–4	35	22	17
1965–9	39	20	12
1970–3	43	17	10

Source: C. Feinstein, 'End of Empire', 229.

materials which had so long been at the centre of the imperial visionaries' notions of imperial trade.

Geographical Pattern of British Trade

This pattern, it should be emphasized, was neither planned nor foreseen. It was the result of market forces operating in an increasingly liberalized environment. Its effect was the economic marginalization of the empire in British trade—the white Commonwealth countries were too small as markets and uncompetitive as producers, the dependent Commonwealth too poor to function as major contributors to this kind of trade expansion. These truths were clear to the major leaders of business in Britain. Having committed themselves and their organizations to the broad policy of trade liberalization, they also protested little against the erosion of Commonwealth preferences, especially once it became clear that retaining these in combination with a European Free Trade Area was not a viable option, and that membership of the EEC was the route to market expansion.[72] While long-standing connections with imperial markets were not severed overnight, and remained important for some British producers, sustained in part by such bodies as the Crown Agents, the overall trend was unmistakable.[73]

---

[72] N. Rollings, *British Business in the Formative Years of European Integration, 1945–1973* (Cambridge, 2007), 40–1, 120–42. Rollings also stresses the shift in British foreign direct investment towards Europe from the 1950s as reinforcing this European orientation, pp. 43–70.

[73] On the role of the Crown Agents, see D. Sunderland, *Managing British Colonial and Post-Colonial Development* (Woodbridge, 2007). This body, amongst other roles, purchased goods on behalf of colonial governments and other public authorities. It mainly brought British, though this was not a legal requirement. Founded in 1833, it collapsed during the banking crisis of the early 1970s.

The battles over imperial preference had clear winners and losers in the mid-1950s. The arguments over the sterling area were, however, only just beginning in these years. Under the Attlee governments, and into the early 1950s, belief that the area was a 'good thing' for Britain was almost universal.[74] But from the mid-1950s this started to change, as criticisms were made and increasingly taken up in policy-making circles. An important early source of criticism was Alan Day, who argued that the strength of the US economy, coupled to the adverse movement in Britain's terms of trade meant the future of sterling as a major currency was bleak, though he did not link the problem to 'overstretch' or the empire. Nevertheless, his arguments opened up the future of sterling to sceptical scrutiny, right up to cabinet level.[75] Within a few years such scepticism about sterling became linked to a major shift in metropolitan perceptions of the economic significance of empire. This followed from the embedding of criticism of approaches to sterling to a much broader critique of British policy—a critique which has come to be called 'declinist'.

Key initial texts in publicizing declinist ideas include Shanks, Sampson, and Macrae, though eventually the literature was enormous.[76] But one of the most prominent books, and the one of most significance in linking economic decline to empire, was Shonfield's *British Economic Policy since the War*.[77] This argued that the (alleged) poor performance of the British economy was due primarily to errors of economic policy. These errors were fundamentally ones of 'overstretch', of excessive overseas, and especially imperial commitments, that the economy could not afford. Hence the balance of payments was burdened with too high a level of military spending, excessive foreign investment, and, above all, the costs of the sterling area. For Shonfield, these burdens were the direct and dominant cause of slow economic growth through the creation of a constantly vulnerable balance of payments position, which led successive British governments into growth-reducing deflationary policies. Such arguments have been

---

[74] H. Gaitskell, 'The Sterling Area', *International Affairs*, 28 (1952), 170–6.

[75] A. Day, *The Future of Sterling* (Oxford, 1954), 6–8; PRO CAB 134/1675 'Problems of the Sterling Area', 25 June 1956; CAB 134/1674 Economic Policy Committee Minutes, 20 Feb. 1957.

[76] M. Shanks, *The Stagnant Society* (Harmondsworth, 1961); A. Sampson, *Anatomy of Britain* (London, 1962); D. Macrae (ed.), *Sunshades in October* (London, 1963).

[77] A. Shonfield, *British Economic Policy since the War* (London, 1956).

very effectively criticized by Catherine Schenk.[78] But what matters here is not the validity of Shonfield's arguments, but the way in which they established a declinist theme which reverberated powerfully in discussions of the 1950s and 1960s, and indeed continue to be reflected in analyses down to the present.[79]

Strictly speaking, the sterling area was not an imperial entity, but in discussions of the time 'although there was a clear formal distinction between the sterling area and the Commonwealth, there was no such distinction politically. Britain's leadership of the economic grouping helped to reinforce its traditional leadership of the political grouping'.[80] But, as the desirability of that economic grouping from a British perspective was challenged, so the desirability of the political connection was also increasingly questioned. Thus, declinism fed into increasingly negative assessments of the economic consequences of empire. But the story was more complicated, because the waning of empire enthusiasm (and the process of decolonization), was in turn part of the declinist mindset—even those who welcomed decolonization saw it as a sign of loss of British energy, purpose, and resolve.[81] The important point here is that a lot of the virulence of economic declinism in Britain can be explained by it being part of a wider 'culture of decline', a culture very much underpinned by a sense of loss of great-power and imperial status.[82]

In their discussion of this period, Cain and Hopkins argue that the drive for decolonization which emerged in the late 1950s had a close relationship to the waning appeal of the sterling area to what they perceive as the dominant force in British policy-making, 'gentlemanly capitalism'.[83] Certainly, the assessment that what mattered economically was not colonial status, but

---

[78] C. Schenk, *Britain and the Sterling Area: From Devaluation to Convertibility in the 1950s* (London, 1994); J. Tomlinson, 'Balanced Accounts? The British Balance of Payments Problem in the 1950s and 1960s', *EHR* 124 (2009), 863–84.

[79] S. Pollard, *The Wasting of the British Economy* (London, 1984), 22–70; W. Hutton, *The State We're In* (London, 1995).

[80] J. Miller, *Survey of Commonwealth Affairs: Problems of Expansion and Contraction, 1953–1969* (Oxford, 1974), 271.

[81] Feinstein, 'End of Empire', 215; J. Tomlinson, 'The Decline of Empire and the Economic "Decline" of Britain', *Twentieth Century British History*, 14/3 (2003), 203–4.

[82] S. Ward (ed.), *British Culture and the End of Empire* (Manchester, 2001), 8–11.

[83] P. Cain and T. Hopkins, *British Imperialism: Crisis and Deconstruction 1914–1990* (London, 1993), 265–6, 283. See also D. Kroweski, *Money and the End of Empire: Britain's International Economic Policy and the Colonies, 1947–1958* (Basingstoke, 2001).

how far newly independent countries would remain friendly towards Britain seems to have been central to Macmillan's audit of 1957.[84] How far economic issues were the key driver in British policy may nevertheless be disputed; Hopkins's own analysis stresses that the overall aim of British policy in the wake of the audit was sustaining great-power status.[85] Analysis of the British business response to decolonization suggests it was often a case of the British government imposing a political deal against the wishes of corporate leaders, partly because the latter were so often seriously divided in their approach to African and Asian independence.[86] Therefore, it can be contended, that while the condition that the process would not necessarily be harmful had to be satisfied, the prime driver of decolonization was political: 'just as economic considerations had once facilitated the acquisition of territory, so now they operated in reverse. Territories could be given up when nothing essential seemed to be lost by transfer of political power.'[87] But too sharp a dichotomy between 'economic' and 'political' reasons is unhelpful; perceptions of low benefits and high economic costs associated with empire could make the political decisions much easier.

If calculating the balance sheet of empire contributed to the hugely important shift to a process of decolonization in the late 1950s, the linkage made between commitment to empire and economic decline also contributed to another major shift in British policy at this time—the application to join the EEC. Declinism associated the empire and Commonwealth with outdatedness, nostalgia, and lack of purpose. The answer for many was to embrace the European Community as a symbol of forward-lookingness and modernization.[88]

It was the Conservative leadership who first enthusiastically embraced the Common Market as a superior economic arena to the Commonwealth. The debate about the economic importance of empire was joined very publicly

---

[84] T. Hopkins, 'Macmillan's Audit of Empire', in Clarke and Trebilcock (eds.), *Understanding Decline*, 234–60.

[85] Ibid. 260.

[86] N. White, 'The Business and Politics of Decolonization: The British Experience in the Twentieth Century', *EcHR* 53/3 (2000), 544–64.

[87] R. Hyam, 'The Primacy of Geo-politics: The Dynamics of British Imperial Policy 1763–1963', *JICH* 27/2 (1999), 50.

[88] This theme is very evident in recent historical accounts: R. Denman, *Missed Chances: Britain and Europe in the Twentieth Century* (London, 1996); R. Broad, *Labour's European Dilemmas from Bevin to Blair* (London, 2001).

at the Conservative Party's annual conferences in 1952, 1953, and 1954 in the context of a debate about how far adherence to the GATT should be allowed to constrain imperial preference. These conferences pitched the leadership against forces led by Leo Amery, perhaps the last of the 'imperial visionaries'. The leadership was on the defensive on this issue, initially held out the prospect of a reform of the GATT, but nevertheless played down the possibilities of imperial preference. The leadership won an overwhelming victory at the 1954 conference, and the preference issue was now effectively off the agenda.[89] But disagreements about the economic importance of the Commonwealth did not fade away entirely in Conservative circles. In 1956, for example, the Foreign Secretary called for a policy of 'UK producer first, Commonwealth producer second and foreigner last'.[90] But as notions of British economic weakness gained ground, and the EEC appeared to be working, the 'Europeans' in the party came to dominate policy, leading to the decision to make the first EEC application in 1961, an application that was rejected in 1963.[91]

In the Labour Party, pro-EEC sentiment remained in the minority until the mid-1960s. Labour demonstrated strikingly pro-Commonwealth views in the early 1960s, in part a result of short-term political calculation. The Conservative application to the EEC of 1961 aroused a great deal of opposition, in Britain and in the Commonwealth, and the failure of the application reinforced those who believed the Conservatives had made a huge political error. But Labour's opposition was heartfelt. Gaitskell's speech of 1962 summed up a common Labour view when he spoke of joining the EEC as abandoning '1000 years of history'.[92] There were those who supported the Conservative application: characteristically, Roy Jenkins was dismissive of the idea of the Commonwealth as a 'tight economic unit', clearly incapable of matching Europe's benefits of a 'large, unified, dynamic and highly competitive market', as part of his argument for entering the Common Market.[93]

The majority of the Labour Party supported the Commonwealth for a variety of reasons. At the grandest level, many saw it as the underpinning for

---

[89] NUCUA *Conference Reports*, 1952, 51–5; 1953, 59–66; 1954, 37–44.

[90] PRO PREM 11/2136, Selwyn Lloyd to Macmillan 3 Sept. 1956.

[91] J. Young, *Britain and European Unity, 1945–1992* (London, 1993), chs. 2 and 3.

[92] P. Williams, *Hugh Gaitskell* (Oxford, 1982), ch. 23.

[93] R. Jenkins in Fabian International Bureau, *The Common Market Debate* (London, 1962), 11; id., *Essays and Speeches* (London, 1967), 119.

Britain's continuing great-power status, especially as now the process of independence made it possible to overcome past associations with colonial subordination and exploitation. In economic terms, this benignity could be extended to seeing the Commonwealth as not only the major target of British development aid, but also an arena in which mutually beneficial trade could be further developed. This latter notion sat somewhat uneasily with the recognition that cheap food from the Commonwealth continued to provide significant benefits to British working-class consumers.[94]

In the run-up to the 1964 election the Labour Party converted these perspectives into a detailed policy agenda for strengthening Commonwealth economic links. Attacking Conservative 'defeatism' on the issue of Commonwealth trade, Harold Wilson, Labour's leader, put forward proposals including preferences in capital contracts, guaranteed markets for Commonwealth products in British markets, development of industries in Britain to supply Commonwealth investment needs, and worldwide commodity agreements to stabilize primary product prices. Labour's 1964 election manifesto asserted that the party 'is convinced that the first responsibility of a British Government is still to the Commonwealth'.[95]

But while Labour's enthusiasm for the Commonwealth was neither opportunistic nor wholly rhetorical, it did not translate into successful policy once the party gained office. Partly this was because of rapid disillusionment with the Commonwealth over such political issues as Biafra, South Africa, and Rhodesia. The idea that the Commonwealth would act as a powerful, united, British-led force in world affairs soon faded. But the economic prospects were also quickly reassessed. Partly this was a matter of Labour rediscovering some old truths: the Commonwealth was not the basis for a closely knit trading area, and this idea was become increasingly unrealistic in the face of the shifts in commodity and geographical composition of British trade identified above, and well understood in policy-making circles by the mid-1960s. The message was clear: 'Commonwealth trade has to be considered in the context of world trade and a closed

---

[94] Gupta, *Imperialism*, 349–96; K. Morgan, 'Imperialists at Bay: British Labour and Decolonization' *JICH* 27/2 (1999), 233–54. For a discussion of Labour's attitudes to the Commonwealth in the context of broader argument's about Britain's world role, see B. Harrison, *Seeking a Role: The United Kingdom 1951–1970* (Oxford, 2009), 101–14.

[95] J. Tomlinson, *The Wilson Governments 1964–1970*, iii. *Economic Policy* (Manchester, 2004), 22–4.

Commonwealth trading system would be neither feasible nor desirable.'[96] Other aspects of Labour's plans also proved either unworkable or very limited in significance. By 1966 Labour was making its own application to join the EEC, signalling its disillusionment with both the economic and political benefits of the Commonwealth.[97]

Some in Labour's ranks, notably Douglas Jay, hung on to the Commonwealth idea in the debates surrounding Britain and Europe, in part because of the continuing if limited salience of arguments about cheap food, but more because it seemed the only alternative to the EEC. Labour's application, like the Conservatives, was also rejected, but the third, in 1971, took Britain in in January 1973. The negotiations around that accession showed how narrow the concern with the economic significance of the Commonwealth had become, with New Zealand butter and Caribbean sugar the only serious issues, and ones which were never likely to be decisive in the discussions. From the 1970s the Commonwealth was no longer seen as a significant element in debates about the British economy.

In the long view the decline of importance of the Commonwealth in British economic debate can be seen as simply a 'recognition of reality'; from the 1950s the pattern of trade was shifting, and political recognition of that fact followed.[98] Of course that 'reality' was itself a consequence of a political (if bipartisan) decision: to pursue a policy of liberalizing Britain's international economic relations. Freer trade and the reduction in exchange control meant that the market forces of increased trading between rich countries on the one side, and the relative weakness of the pound on the other, were allowed to exert themselves. The result was the decline in the significance on inter-Commonwealth trade, and the decline in the importance of sterling (and the sterling area) in financial markets. Of course, these policies could have been reversed or at least qualified by efforts to maintain stronger inter-commonwealth connections. The idea that swapping raw materials for cars within the Commonwealth was more advantageous than swapping Morris Minors for Renault Dauphines appealed to long-standing notions of the gains from trade.[99] But Labour's experience after 1964 suggest

[96] J. Tomlinson, *The Wilson Governments 1964–1970*, iii. *Economic Policy* (Manchester, 2004), 25.

[97] D. Seers and P. Streeten, 'Overseas Development Policies', in W. Beckerman (ed.), *The Labour Governments' Economic Record, 1964–1970* (London, 1972), 118–56.

[98] C. Schenk, 'Decolonization and European Economic Integration: the Free Trade Area Negotiations, 1956–1958', *JICH* 24/3 (1996), 444–63.

[99] P. Streeten and H. Corbet (eds.), *Commonwealth Policy in a Global Context* (London, 1973).

how difficult it would have been to resist the pressures to allow Britain's newly affluent consumers to spend their discretionary income on European and American manufactured goods. The problem of the Commonwealth was that it contained too few of the rich of the world to form a large enough market for the new types of trade—especially intra-industry trade in sophisticated manufactured goods.

From the 1970s there was a continuing dwindling in the importance of Commonwealth trade. There was a parallel decline in the importance of sterling. As early as the beginning of the 1960s doubts were growing in the City about links between the perceived economic benefits of expanding City earnings from overseas transactions and the strength of sterling. Following the growth of Euro-dollars, London increasingly became an 'offshore' financial centre, its business increasingly conducted in dollars, its prosperity increasingly decoupled from the fate of sterling. The working out of this new factor took time, but the trauma of the 1967 devaluation effectively put paid to the sterling area.[100] The demise of sterling both stimulated and was reinforced by Commonwealth countries diversifying their international exchange reserves out of sterling, but there were also long-term attractions to holding reserves in dollars.[101]

While significant trade continued amongst Commonwealth members, and sterling continued to be held as a component of most Commonwealth countries' international reserves, these links largely reflected normal economic decisions, owing very little to Commonwealth status. Hence in the final decades of the twentieth century the most significant direct economic effect of the Commonwealth was in aid policy. Aid now played a central role in official discussions at Commonwealth meetings.[102]

While between the wars colonial development policy was largely an adjunct of British unemployment concerns, from the 1940s it developed as a largely separate sphere of policy. After the widening of the scope of the Colonial Development and Welfare (CDW) Act of 1940, about £324 million was spent under its auspices between 1946 and 1970, though the sums spent

---

[100] W. Clarke, *The City in the World Economy* (Harmondsworth, 1967), 245; B. Tew, 'Policies Aimed at Improving the Balance of Payments' in F. Blackaby (ed.), *British Economic Policy 1960–1974* (Cambridge, 1978), 335–6.

[101] Tew, 'Policies', 336–7.

[102] e.g. Central Office of Information, *Britain and the Commonwealth* (London, 1992), 22–33.

fell sharply from the 1960s as decolonization gathered pace.[103] Apart from
the CDW channel, aid was given to South Asian members of the Commonwealth through the Colombo Plan of 1950.[104] Down to 1958 aid policy was
closely interwoven with the maximization of sterling export receipts, and a
1957 White Paper stressed Britain's limited role in the long-run development
of former colonies.[105] But the following year Britain announced a more
ambitious policy, partly due to Cold War considerations, partly due to
pressure from within the Commonwealth, and partly due to domestic
opinion, where concern with Third World poverty was becoming evident.
While the role of Britain as private investor and banker to Commonwealth
countries was still emphasized, a new era of official development aid began
in 1958, with the Commonwealth as the major recipient.[106] In 1964 an
Overseas Development Ministry was created, but the volume of aid under
the 1964 Labour government was held back by balance of payments considerations.[107] A renewed expansion began at the end of the 1960s, partly in
the wake of the influential report of a committee chaired by the former
Canadian Prime Minister, Lester Pearson, which called for an aid target of
1 per cent of GDP, and which found strong support in Britain.[108]

In the 1950s and 1960s, as the significance of the Dominion economic
connection declined, poor countries became a much more significant part
of the Commonwealth. For its enthusiasts, the Commonwealth could now
be seen as a benign arena, within which economic development could be
supported and encouraged. In trading relationships what mattered for those
poor countries was their access to the markets of the rich, and in that debate
Commonwealth preferences were of little significance, though Britain, partly prodded by the Commonwealth, did play a role in the drive to generalized

---

[103] Morgan, *Official History*, iv. 8–11, though note that Morgan's claim that this spending
amounted to around 1 % of British GDP in the 1950s and 1960s is a considerable exaggeration.

[104] Much of this 'aid' was in the form of running down of sterling balances, which unsurprisingly the Asian countries did not regard as aid at all. See A. Hinds, *Britain's Sterling Colonial
Policy and Decolonization, 1939–1958* (Westport, Conn., 2001), ch. 7.

[105] *The UK's Role in Commonwealth Development*, Cmnd. 237, BPP 1956/7, vol. 26.

[106] J. Tomlinson, 'The Commonwealth, the Balance of Payments and the Politics of International Policy: British Aid Policy, 1958–1971', *Contemporary European History*, 12/3 (2003), 417–22.

[107] There was much debate about the effects of aid on the balance of payments, linked to the
highly contentious issue of how far such aid should be tied to purchases from Britain. PRO T317/
1524 Treasury, 'Select Committee on Aid', 20 May 1970.

[108] *Report of the Select Committee on Overseas Aid*, House of Commons Papers 299, BPP 1969/
70, vol. 23.

preferences in the 1960s.[109] But in shaping flows of aid, the Commonwealth connection remained extremely important, dominating British bilateral aid-giving.[110]

In the last few decades of the twentieth century the most obvious evidence of Britain's Commonwealth connection was the presence of large numbers of ethnic minorities in Britain, most of whose ancestors originally came from Commonwealth countries. This issue is dealt with elsewhere in this volume, but in the context of Britain's economic policies it is worth noting that the initial inflows of these migrants in the 1940s and 1950s was encouraged by the British as a way of addressing labour shortages. When the influx started to be controversial, it was initially the economic ministries who resisted controls, as economically damaging.[111] When controls did come in 1962 they were designed to maximize Britain's economic advantage from immigration, by effectively only allowing in those with substantial human capital. This policy was clearly at odds with the aims of Britain's aid policy, which sought to transfer resources from Britain to poor Commonwealth countries. For example, in the 1960s about 1,000 doctors from Commonwealth LDCs were entering Britain every year, but there was little comment on the economic damage this exerted on the sending countries.[112]

IV

Defending his focus on the dominions in his history of British imperial relations, Drummond notes that this focus fairly reflects the concerns of British policy-makers in the 1920s and 1930s—and we might say, the pre-1914 and post-1945 periods also, with only the minor qualification of the short-lived attention to dollar-earning colonies in the 1940s.[113] In this overall perspective what is perhaps most striking is the lack of concern with Indian issues in discussions of British economic policy. India may have been the jewel in the imperial crown, but seems to always have been marginal for

[109] Miller, *Survey: Problems of Expansion and Attrition*, 288–9.

[110] Bilateral aid is that given directly rather than channelled through multilateral agencies like the World Bank.

[111] K. Paul, *Whitewashing Britain: Race and Citizenship in the Post-War Era* (Ithaca, NY, 1997), 121–7, 140–1.

[112] Labour Party Archives, *Study Group on Immigration*, 1969–71.

[113] Drummond, *British Economic Policy*, 121. Also, Thompson, *Imperial Britain*, 188: 'It was the self-governing Dominions which were regarded as the bedrock of empire, and the basis of its strength and prosperity'.

those concerned with national economic issues. This was not the result of India's insignificance for the national economy. In 1913 she was Britain's largest single export market, and those exports crucially underpinned the multilateral system of international payments which underpinned contemporary globalization.[114] She was also a major recipient of British investment, and therefore a big source of income for British investors. Why was India so neglected in British economic discussions before the First World War?

The key point was that those who sought to encourage imperial economic links—the tariff reformers—saw the empire in terms of the settler colonies, with their populations of 'kith and kin'. For tariff reformers, therefore, India was an 'afterthought... it was not central to their strategy for promoting economic competitiveness and growth'.[115] India was, of course, different from the dominions, not only in not being peopled by British stock, but also by its dependent status. This meant that Britain had the constitutional capacity to impose its policies on India. But such imposition had to be tempered by political realities—the realities both of raising revenue in India so that its government was not reliant on the London exchequer, and, in the longer run, of not arousing Indian nationalist sentiment.[116] In economic terms India was also distinct from the dominions—distinctive in its poverty, but also in the effect that poverty had in making possible low-wage competition against British goods. For British advocates of close ties with the dominions it was assumed that the economies were complementary; Britain would supply the manufactured goods, the dominions the primary products.[117] But India did not fit this notion, and so again raised different issues for British policy in comparison with the dominions.

In looking at these issues two industries are focused upon as examples—cotton and jute. In both cases the empire in the form of India loomed large in the industry's prosperity, and led to political action to try and affect imperial policy. Cotton is a well-known case, jute much less so, and their similarities and differences together bring out most of the dilemmas in British economic policy in dealing with this crucial imperial possession. These examples also clearly illustrate another important theme of this

---

[114] S. Saul, *Studies in Overseas Trade* (Liverpool, 1960).

[115] Thompson, *Imperial Britain*, 103.

[116] B. R. Tomlinson, *The Political Economy of the Raj 1914–1947* (Cambridge, 1979), 27–9.

[117] Drummond, *British Economic Policy*, 31. This view was not, of course, universally shared in the dominions.

chapter: the limitations of focusing on Britain as a whole when talking about the economic significance of empire. Both cotton and jute were highly regionalized products, creating intense *localized* interconnections with the empire, which made the empire matter much more to those involved in those industries than to the generality of Britons.

Cotton goods were Britain's single largest export from the Napoleonic period almost to the Second World War, and by 1913 India was easily the biggest market. India's own factory industry producing cotton goods also expanded rapidly before the First World War, but it did so without protection. In 1894, when a small tariff was put on British imports for revenue purposes, this was offset by an excise duty on Indian factory products in order to maintain a 'level playing field'.[118] In the First World War the Indian government raised extra revenue by increasing the tariff, without increasing the excise duty, and thereafter effective tariff autonomy was granted, as politically the British felt it impossible to stimulate nationalist feeling by preventing Indian protection of key industries.[119]

Lancashire protested bitterly against the erosion of their access to Indian markets. But these protests were of no avail, because of the British government's desire to sustain the Indian government's tax revenues, as well as to assuage nationalist opinion. By the time of Ottawa in 1932, India was treated on a par with the dominions in respect of tariff policy.[120] Led by Raymond Streat, secretary of the Manchester Chamber of Commerce, Lancashire did manage to negotiate minor tariff concessions in the mid-1930s, but these were marginal to the overall decline of the industry.[121] Lancashire's position was also hit by the rise of Japanese cotton imports into India, which proved largely unaffected by tariff discrimination against them.

On independence India and Pakistan raised tariffs further, largely eliminating the British product from their markets. The Indian industry now expanded into export markets, and in the early 1950s overtook Japan as a

---

[118] P. Harnetty, 'The Indian Cotton Duties Controversy, 1894–1896', *EHR* 77 (1962), 684–702. But see Tomlinson, *Political Economy*, 15–16, for the argument that cotton was a special case. Non-factory cotton goods were not subject to this duty, but largely sold in different segments of the market than Lancashire goods.

[119] Drummond, *British Economic Policy*, 123–4.

[120] B. R. Tomlinson, 'India and the British Empire 1880–1935', *Indian Economic and Social History Review*, 12/4 (1975), 339–80.

[121] M. Dupree 'Fighting against Fate: The Cotton Industry and the Government during the 1930s', *Textile History*, 21/1 (1990), 93–112.

supplier to Britain.[122] Lancashire's protests at this result of empire free trade were ineffectual, as the British government believed there were larger off-setting benefits from Indian preferences for other British goods. Voluntary export restraints were introduced in 1959 (stimulated mainly by imports from Hong Kong, which rose very sharply in the 1950s), but these were not very restrictive, and by the mid-1960s the Lancashire industry had more or less ceased to exist.[123]

Throughout the twentieth century Lancashire was faced with competition in the Indian market for Indian produced goods, and after 1917 this competition was more damaging because it was aided by protection. Historically Lancashire had been the heartland of free trade, and one of the biggest gainers from a free trade empire. Nevertheless, there was a distinct shift amongst cotton employers towards tariff reform in the early 1900s, and the trend of opinion was further reinforced in the First World War. This, it should be noted had little to do with views on the empire, and seems mainly to have been linked to allegiance to the Conservative Party.[124]

Jute was distinctive from cotton in drawing all of its raw material from Bengal, while its products faced competition from India not only in the subcontinent but across the world, where jute sacks were a staple item in late nineteenth-century international trade. Calcutta's jute industry grew to equal Dundee's in scale of output by the 1890s, and thereafter followed an expansionary trend until the 1970s.[125] By contrast, the Dundee industry reached its apogee in the Edwardian period, and thereafter became a pioneer declining staple industry, collapsing in the 1930s, reviving in the 1940s and 1950s, but declining again sharply from the beginning of the 1970s. It ceased to exist in 1999.

On the protection issue, jute shows evidence of the nationwide pattern, as the turn of the century saw the conversion of many of Britain's capitalists to

---

[122] J. Singleton, 'Lancashire's Last Stand: Declining Employment in the British Cotton Industry, 1950–1970' *EcHR* 39/1 (1986), 100.

[123] J. Singleton, *Lancashire on the Scrapheap* (Oxford, 1991).

[124] P. Clarke, 'The End of Laissez-faire and the Politics of Cotton', *Historical Journal*, 15/3 (1972), 493–512; Marrison, *British Business*, 172–92.

[125] Gordon T. Stewart, *Jute and Empire: The Calcutta Jute Wallahs and the Landscapes of Empire* (Manchester, 1998), pp. ix, 15. Indian output equalled Dundee's by about 1890, was four times as much by 1913, and ten times by the 1950s. Pakistan also emerged as significant producer after Partition.

protectionism.[126] In Dundee there had been such calls as far back as the 1870s, and there was strong support by the time of the Tariff Commission in the early 1900s.[127] But the jute employers were far from unanimous on the issue, certainly before the 1930s. While Sir George Baxter, a linen and jute owner, stood on a protectionist platform in the landmark by-election of 1908, James Caird, another important local jute proprietor, was a key financial backer of free trade propaganda.[128]

Baxter, who lost to Churchill, at that time a Liberal, perhaps wisely focused his protectionist demands on Germany, rather than India, an empire country upon which it would be politically very difficult to impose protection.[129] An alternative strategy to protection against Indian jute manufactures was to seek a duty on Indian exports of raw jute going to non-empire countries, but this too ran up against the complexities of Britain's 'imperial mission' in India.[130] The deterioration of the 1930s, which gave Dundee probably the heaviest unemployment of any city in Britain, led to renewed pressures for protection. Britain remained largely free trade until 1931, and even after tariffs were put on non-empire products in 1932, free entry for jute products from India continued. In 1929 a leading figure in the industry, George Bonar, had argued for a 'deal' with government by which the increase in European competition of the 1920s would be halted by protection, and in return the industry would put its house in order.[131] Protection against Europe came in 1932, but while the European producers had expanded in the 1920s, they largely served their home markets, so protection against them made little difference in Scotland.

[126] Marrison, *British Business.*

[127] London School of Economics, Archives: Tariff Commission papers TC1 2/7 *Report of the Tariff Commission,* ii. *The Textile Trades,* pt. 7, *Evidence on the Flax, Hemp and Jute Industries* (London, 1906). There was a crucial local debate in the Dundee Chamber of Commerce in Jan. 1904, when a majority supported the idea of a 'bargaining' tariff: Dundee City Archives (DCA), Dundee Chamber of Commerce Minute Book 15 Jan. 1904; *Dundee Advertiser* (16 Jan. 1904).

[128] Trentmann, *Free Trade Nation,* 105–19.

[129] Dundee City Library, Local History Collection, '1908 Election'. One Unionist leaflet distributed in the 1908 election itemized the tariffs in European countries, calling for Britain to 'resume our power of fiscal negotiation with the view of trying to have such tariffs reduced'. Another called for imperial preference on jute goods in Canadian and Australian markets.

[130] Despite Dundee hostility, an export levy without any imperial preference was introduced to raise revenue in 1916. See Stewart, *Jute,* 77–86.

[131] G. Bonar, *The Industrial Outlook,* Lecture by George Bonar, 19 Jan. 1929 (Dundee, 1929).

There were protests in Dundee about the continuing free access of Indian goods, and debates in the House of Commons, but nothing was done to protect the home industry from empire imports.[132] Part of the problem from a Dundee point of view was the failure to form a protectionist alliance in the industry; Labour (and Communist) policy continued to be opposed to import controls as striking at the interests of Indian workers. The Left put its faith in improving labour conditions in India creating a 'level playing field'.[133] But beyond that was the British government's political sensitivity in the face of rising nationalist support, and this underpinned the trade agreements of 1938 which cemented free entry for Indian goods into the British market.

Protection came to Dundee jute as a consequence of its perceived strategic importance in war, and the creation of the Jute Control in 1939 which sold imported products at Dundee prices.[134] Despite post-war governments enthusiasm for liberalization the Jute Control lasted until the late 1960s, when it was replaced by much less restrictive quotas. Prior to that abolition, the protection afforded by the Control had already been reduced, partly due to low-key but persistent pressure from India.[135] Resistance in Dundee on the basis of the effects on unemployment of higher level of imports slowed reductions in protection. But after 1969 the pace of liberalization was speeded up, and a crucial blow was dealt when the Thatcher government, which had reduced overseas aid to India and Bangladesh, cut jute quotas to help restore relations with those countries.[136]

In comparison with cotton, protection in jute was much more significant through most of the golden age. Cotton had no protection from

---

[132] Stewart, *Jute*, 122–37; *Hansard* (Commons) vol. 331, 2 Feb. 1938, cols. 239–306; for examples of Dundee's arguments, Dundee Chamber of Commerce, *The Jute Industry and India* (Dundee, 1937); id. *Critical Position of the Jute Industry* Address by the President, 2 Sept. 1937 (Dundee, 1937).

[133] A. S. Thompson, *The Empire Strikes Back: The Impact of Imperialism on Britain from the Mid-Nineteenth Century* (Harlow, 2005), 78–82; John Sime, leader of the jute union, visited India in the 1920s with Tom Johnston MP, and focused much attention on Indian unions: Johnston, *Memories* (London, 1952), 50–84; G. Doud, 'Tom Johnston in India', *Scottish Labour History Journal*, 19 (1984), 6–21.

[134] Thus Stewart (*Jute*, 139) is mistaken in saying that Dundee had to wait for Indian independence to gain protection.

[135] PRO CAB 129/114 Board of Trade 'Import Policy for Jute Goods', 30 July 1963.

[136] PRO BT 303/726, N. Marten, Overseas Development Administration, to Lord Trenchard, Department of Trade and Industry, 21 Sept. 1979.

Commonwealth imports between 1932 and 1958, and even after that date much less than jute had under the Jute Control of 1939–69.[137] In both cotton and jute the pressure for protection of the domestic industry had to contend with the fact that the major competitors were poor Commonwealth countries. British governments faced significant pressure from India against protectionism, and they listened both because of fears about the potential loss of tariff preferences for British goods in India, and because of an increasing focus on facilitating development in poor countries, and Britain's belief that this meant especially aiding the development of poor Commonwealth countries.[138]

On the other hand, both cotton (after 1958) and jute did have some protection, the latter down to the 1980s, attracting sympathetic attention as low-wage, labour-intensive industries suffering unusually acute competitive pressures. The 'big picture' of the post-war textile trade is the sustaining of trade restrictions in that sector longer than most other parts of manufacturing. The reason these restrictions were so long-lived was primarily because of the employment issue. As the Dundee jute story illustrates, post-war governments down to 1979 were extremely sensitive to the employment consequences of decline, and sought to balance the pace of contraction against the creation of other employment opportunities. And this was not just rhetorical—for example, there seems little doubt that the delay of the review due in 1967, and the freezing of quotas from 1969 to 1973, is in large part explained by the surge in unemployment in Dundee in those years.

For Lancashire and Dundee, empire trade meant fierce competition for their staple product, and it was difficult for the industries to persuade government to consistently aid them in their fight with Indian producers. Cotton had some success between the 1890s and the First World War, jute between 1939 and 1969. The first of these was aided by the exceptional political significance of Lancashire's mass of marginal parliamentary seats, the second by the needs of war. In the twentieth century, in both places,

---

[137] M. Rose, *Firms, Networks and Business Values: The British and American Cotton Industries since 1750* (Cambridge, 2000), 273.

[138] Ead. 'The Politics of Protection: An Institutional Approach to Government Industry Relations in the British and United States Cotton Industries, 1945–1973' *Business History*, 34/4 (1997), 144–5. Note, however, that in the jute case the link with Hong Kong, and sensitivity about that countries potential for responding to British protectionism by running down sterling balances and disrupting the sterling system did not apply.

employers moved into the protectionist camp in line with their broadly
Conservative allegiances, while finding that their concern with India
meshed poorly with the overwhelming focus on the dominions in national
trade discussions. From their perspective, empire trade was always as much
a problem as a solution to competitive pressures.

V

This chapter has focused upon contemporary British beliefs and understandings about the economic role of empire. This is clearly distinct from
retrospective judgements about the costs and benefits of empire, a substantial number of which have been produced in recent years. Most of these
focus on the pre-1914 period, and the balance of their judgement is that in a
context of a free trade empire, which was in turn only a relatively limited
part of Britain's total global economic connections, the aggregate benefits
for the British economy were small. However, there have been dissentients,
especially arising from an emphasis on the benefits which accrued in the
First World War from the pre-war expenditure on imperial defence.[139]

Reflecting on the balance of these arguments, Feinstein emphasized three
points. First, that damage done to colonial economic development by
imperial subordination does not necessarily accrue equivalent advantage
to the colonizer.[140] Long-lasting damage could be done to the economic
interests of the colonized without a corresponding advantage to Britain.
Second, that the economic consequences for the national economy are a
very different matter to the economic impact on individuals or corporations. Undoubtedly, the empire enabled many Britons and many British
companies owned by them to gain great personal benefits in employment
and profits, without these registering in a significant way in the prosperity of
the national economy.[141] Third, Feinstein argues, assessment of the costs
and benefits of empire has conflated discussion of dominions and colonies.

---

[139] A. Offer, 'The British Empire: A Waste of Money?' *EcHR* 46/2 (1993), 215–38.

[140] Feinstein, 'End of Empire', 232–3.

[141] For two very different discussions of British companies and the empire, see D. Fieldhouse,
Unilever Overseas (London, 1978), esp. 565–76, and B. Tomlinson, 'Continuities and Disconti-
nuities in Indo-British Economic Relations: British Multinational Corporations in India,
1920–1970', in W. Mommsen and J. Osterhammel (eds.), *Imperialism and After* (London,
1986), 154–66.

Here, he stresses, 'the connections which really counted were those with the dominions, with their relatively high per capita incomes'.[142]

The last of these is not just a retrospective judgement. As this chapter has outlined, for most of the twentieth century, insofar as the empire was deemed economically important to government and national interest groups, it was the dominions that were being focused upon. The only exception was the concern with colonies in the 1940s and early 1950s, when real benefits accrued from obtaining their products cheaply in war-time, and subsequently exploiting their dollar-earning ability. But though at this time all sorts of fantasies were entertained about the potential for colonial economies to permanently underpin British prosperity, in the event this was a passing phase—and soon recognized to be such. Macmillan's audit drove home the economic insignificance of colonies.

How far did Britain gain from the dominion (as opposed to the overall empire) connection? In the pre-1914 period it is difficult to see enormous benefits—cheap imports, outlets for migrants, expanding markets, and profitable investments all existed in the dominions, but these opportunities owed little directly to the political leverage given by empire. After all, exactly the same type of benefits, but on own even larger scale, accrued from the connection with the USA. These benefits are best seen as part of the gains from the 'first great age of globalization' accruing to the dominant industrial, commercial, and financial power of the age, rather than mainly accruing as a result of the exercise of imperial power.[143] On the other hand, the demographic connection that bound Britain to the dominions cannot be dismissed as of no account. Amery's notion of a 'Southern British World' may always have been overly roseate, but it did reflect a linkage which only declined fast in the late twentieth century when Britain and the dominions, with varying levels of enthusiasm, embraced a multi-ethnic future.[144]

Attempts to recreate these mutual benefits between Britain and the dominions in the 1920s were constrained by changed circumstances. In Britain population growth was slowing and the willingness to sacrifice domestic agriculture to imports diminished; the frontier of settlement in

[142] Feinstein, 'End of Empire', 233.

[143] M. Daunton, 'Britain and Globalization since 1850: I. Creating a Global Order, 1850–1914', *Transactions of the Royal Historical Society*, 16 (2006), 12–27.

[144] For an interesting perspective on this, S. Constantine, 'British Emigration to the Empire-Commonwealth since 1880: From Overseas Settlement to Diaspora?', *JICH* 31/2 (2003), 16–35.

the dominions was being reached, and diminishing returns setting in. British labour and capital continued to flow into the dominions, but the declining buoyancy of primary product markets was eroding the basis for the huge mutual gains of the pre-1914 years.[145] In the 1930s there was a further coming together, but this time on a defensive rather than expansionary basis. There may have been mutual benefits, though probably the balance of advantage lay with the dominions. In the war the dominions once more aided the British war effort, and interconnections were further strengthened. For a period after the war the dominions (and the colonies) formed a close trading and currency unit, but this proved transient. New trade patterns in a dollar-dominated world eventually meant disintegration, though this was not fully and publicly recognized until Britain's application for EEC membership in the early 1960s.[146] By the 1970s only the economic welfare of New Zealand was at all closely tied to the British economy; from a British point of view the dominions were now economically marginal.[147]

Britain's economic relationship to the empire, like so much twentieth-century British history, has commonly been viewed through the lens of declinism, though that perspective may now be in retreat.[148] In this narrative, Britain retreated into empire markets in the late nineteenth century in the face of growing competition elsewhere in the world, especially from Germany and the USA. Reinforced by the Ottawa Agreements, this defensive and restrictive posture, encouraging cosy collusion and inefficiency, endured into the 1970s, when, at last the cold shower of European

---

[145] Drummond, *British Economic Policy*, 27–9.

[146] S. Ward, 'A Matter of Preference: The EEC and the Erosion of the Old Commonwealth Relationship' in A. May (ed.), *Britain, the Commonwealth and Europe* (Basingstoke, 2001), 156–80.

[147] Even in the case of butter, New Zealand's most important export to Britain, trade was declining as British consumption fell and home production increased: B. Brown, 'From Bulk Purchase to Butter Disputes: NZ Trading Relations with Britain', in R. Patnam (ed.), *New Zealand and Britain: A Special Relationship in Transition* (Palmerston North, 1997), 46–7. This imperial relationship was the subject of highly-charged debate in New Zealand: for one perspective on this, see R. McLuskie, *The Great Debate: New Zealand, Britain and the EEC: The Shaping of Attitudes* (Wellington, 1986).

[148] J. Tomlinson, 'Thrice Denied: Declinism and the Narrative of British History in the Long Twentieth Century', *Twentieth Century British History*, 20/2 (2009), 227–51; A. S. Thompson and G. Magee, 'A Soft Touch? British Industry, Empire Markets and the Self-Governing Dominions, c.1970–1914', *EcHR* 56/4 (2003), 690–1.

competition was unleashed, and in combination with Thatcherite reforms, once again made British industry internationally competitive.[149]

This narrative has little to be said for it. The British economy did not suffer from 'decline' before 1914; its interwar performance was good by the (low) standards of the day; its slow growth in the post-war golden age relative to Western Europe was mainly due to other countries catching up with Britain's high GDP/head in 1950.[150] Above all, the narrative relies on the undoubted economic problems of the 1970s being seen as a culmination of long-run and deep-seated 'decline', rather than the result of highly specific and contingent events of the early and mid years of that decade. After the 1970s productivity growth returned to a level almost exactly the same as that of the 1950s and 1960s.[151]

If this declinist narrative is set aside, it follows that the role of empire in British economic 'decline' needs re-evaluation. Such a re-evaluation would stress, as above, that the movement into empire markets before 1914 was not in search of security but in search of profits, made in most cases with little 'artificial' protection from imperial preference or other devices. The rapid growth of inter-imperial trade before the First World War largely reflected the growth of the dominion economies, and Britain's continuing competitive strength.[152] Clearly in the 1930s empire markets were protected—but the key driver for higher British reliance on the dominion buyer was the macroeconomic buoyancy of sterling countries. Similarly in the 1940s; British exports did well in the dominions largely due to exchange controls on dollar purchases, and some lessening of European competition due to the destruction and disruption of war. Crucially, as these conditions changed, British market share in empire markets fell exactly the same as

---

[149] G. Owen, *From Empire to Europe: The Decline and Revival of British Industry since the Second World War* (London, 1999); S. Broadberry, *The Productivity Race: British Manufacturing in International Perspective, 1850–1990* (Cambridge, 1997) is more nuanced.

[150] S. Pollard, *Britain's Prime and Britain's Decline: The British Economy 1870–1914* (1989), 260–71; Patrick O'Brien, 'Britain's Economy between the Wars: A Survey of a Counter-Revolution in Economic History', *P&P* 115 (1987), 107–30; N. Crafts, 'The Golden Age of Economic Growth in Western Europe, 1950–1973' *EcHR* 48/3 (1995), 429–47.

[151] S. Broadberry and N. Crafts, 'UK Productivity Performance from 1950 to 1979: A Restatement of the Broadberry-Crafts View', *EcHR* 56/4 (2003), 723.

[152] G. Magee, 'The Importance of Being British? Imperial Factors and the Growth of British Imports, 1870–1960', *Journal of Interdisciplinary History*, 37/3 (2007), 341–69; Thompson and Magee, 'Soft Touch?'.

in non-empire markets. There was no 'shelter' in the dominions.[153] India does seem to be different, with changes in GDP and relative prices not explaining Britain's dominance of this market, but even here how far this rested on imperial 'favouritism' and how much on the sophistication of Britain's merchanting and commercial organization remains unclear.[154]

The idea of British producers entrenching their inefficiency behind protective walls created by governments commonly goes along with the idea that those governments had a nostalgic view of empire, which led to continuing embrace for that body rather than an early embrace of the benefits of the European Union. This, as we have seen, was a trope of 1950s and 1960s declinist literature, and it also feeds into the 'missed opportunity' view of Britain's early relations with the European Union.[155] But this is unhelpful. In the 1940s into the early 1950s the prospects of an economically successful EEC looked highly remote.[156] Conversely, the empire was booming, with fast growth in the dominions and some of the colonies. British policy-makers of the time need to be rescued from the condescension of posterity; they made a sensible choice to see European unity as an attractive but highly risky option, and Commonwealth ties as more beneficial as long as the dollar shortage lasted. Once that shortage eased, the pattern of trade started to shift, and the benefits of the sterling area become less clear, British policy-makers showed little hesitation in abandoning 'a thousand years of history'. The discussions of 1961 to 1963 around Britain's EEC application show it was some dominion rather British politicians who hung on to the illusions of 'race patriotism'—but not for long.[157]

Finally, alongside the declining economic importance of the dominions, the political retreat from colonial Empire was also strikingly rapid from the late 1950s. There was little inclination to hang on, as long as the overarching

---

[153] Schenk, *From Devaluation to Convertibility*, 78–87.

[154] Magee, 'Importance', 355–6; B. R. Tomlinson, *The Economy of Modern India 1860–1970* (Cambridge, 1996), 105–12; Thompson, *Empire Strikes Back*, 171–5. Compare Broadberry, *The Productivity Race*, 94–7, who sees British firms before 1914 forced into Empire markets by protectionism elsewhere, with this pattern fragmenting their output and therefore the realization of economies of scale.

[155] Rollings, *British Business*, 7–9; e.g. Denman, *Missed Chances*; Broad, *Labour's European Dilemmas*.

[156] A. Milward, *The United Kingdom and the European Community*, i. *The Rise and Fall of a National Strategy, 1945–1963* (London, 2003), ch. 1.

[157] Ward, 'Matter of Preference'; Hopkins 'Rethinking'.

aim of establishing a stable and hopefully friendly post-independence government seemed to have been secured. The success of this strategy was, of course, mixed. But, by and large, it was successful enough that giving up formal imperial control did not lead to significant losses of economic benefit to British companies and British individuals; but equally the patterns of British trade and investment were such that by the end of the 1960s, ex-colonies, like most of the third world, were of marginal significance to the British national economy.

Select Bibliography

P. CAIN and T. HOPKINS, *British Imperialism: Crisis and Deconstruction 1914–1990* (London, 1993).

P. CLARKE and C. TREBILCOCK (eds.), *Understanding Decline: Perceptions and Realities of British Economic Performance* (Cambridge, 1997).

S. CONSTANTINE, 'British Emigration to the Empire-Commonwealth since 1880: From Overseas Settlement to Diaspora?', *Journal of Imperial and Commonwealth History*, 31 (2003), 16–35.

I. DRUMMOND, *Imperial Economic Policy 1917–1939: Studies in Expansion and Protection* (London, 1974).

K. FEDOROWICH, *Unfit for Heroes: Reconstruction and Soldier Settlement in the Empire between the Wars* (Manchester, 1995).

W. HANCOCK, *Survey of British Commonwealth Affairs*, ii. *Problems of Economic Policy 1918–1939*, pt. 1 (Oxford, 1940).

A. HOWE, *Free Trade and Liberal England 1846–1946* (Oxford, 1997).

W. R. LOUIS, *In the Name of God, Go! Leo Amery and the British Empire in the Age of Churchill* (New York, 1992).

G. MAGEE, 'The Importance of Being British? Imperial Factors and the Growth of British Imports, 1870–1960', *Journal of Interdisciplinary History*, 37 (2007), 341–69.

A. MARRISON, *British Business and Protection 1903–1932* (Oxford, 1996).

D. MORGAN, *The Official History of Colonial Development*, iv. *Changes in British Aid Policy* (London, 1980).

A. OFFER, 'The British Empire: A Waste of Money?', *Economic History Review*, 46 (1993), 215–38.

A. PORTER and A. STOCKWELL (eds.), *British Imperial Policy and Decolonisation 1938–1964*, ii. *1938–1951* (London, 1987).

T. ROOTH, *British Protectionism and the International Economy: Overseas Commercial Policy in the 1930s* (Cambridge, 1993).

C. SCHENK, *Britain and the Sterling Area: From Devaluation to Convertibility in the 1950s* (London, 1994).

G. STEWART, *Jute and Empire: The Calcutta Jute Wallahs and the Landscapes of Empire* (Manchester, 1998).

P. Streeten and H. Corbet (eds.), *Commonwealth Policy in a Global Context* (London, 1973).

A. Thompson, *Imperial Britain: The Empire in British Politics, c.1880–1932* (Harlow, 2000).

B. R. Tomlinson, *The Political Economy of the Raj 1914–1947* (Cambridge, 1979).

J. Tomlinson, 'The Commonwealth, the Balance of Payments and the Politics of International Poverty: British Aid Policy, 1958–1971', *Contemporary European History*, 12 (2004), 417–22.

F. Trentmann, *Free Trade Nation* (Oxford, 2007).

S. Ward (ed.), *British Culture and the End of Empire* (Manchester, 2001).

7

Social Life and Cultural Representation: Empire in the Public Imagination

Andrew Thompson with Meaghan Kowalsky

Introduction

In the mid-1970s, the historian of political ideas and expatriate New Zealander, J. G. A. Pocock, called for a rewriting of the history of the British peoples in terms of 'an inter-cultural story' concerned with 'the conflict and cross-breeding between societies differently based'.[1] Because of an eagerness to emphasize their European credentials, Pocock argued, the English had effectively annihilated the idea of the Commonwealth. To revive the term 'British' history, he went on to suggest, it was vital to take more seriously its imperial dimensions, especially the great transatlantic expansion that had established the colonies of settlement. As Pocock recognized, however, the post-war study of the history of the British Isles had 'balkanized' into its different nations, while largely insular dominion histories rarely referred to the internal development of other 'British' societies. The circumstances were hardly favourable, therefore, for the more expansive, integrated histories of a wider British world that he envisaged.[2]

Pocock's plea fell largely on deaf ears. The following decade, the leading British historian, David Cannadine, could still lament the introversion of his colleagues. Singling out for particular criticism the proliferation of academic specialisms across the profession, Cannadine spoke powerfully

---

[1] J. G. A. Pocock, 'British History: A Plea for a New Subject', *Journal of Modern History* (*JMH*), 47/4 (1975), 601–21. See also id. 'History and Sovereignty: The Historiographical Response to Europeanization in Two British Cultures', *Journal of British Studies* (*JBS*), 31 (1992), 358–89; 'The New British History in Atlantic Perspective', *American Historical Review*, 104/2 (1999), 490–500; and *Political Thought and History* (Cambridge, 2009).

[2] S. Ward, 'Imperial Identities Abroad', in S. Stockwell (ed.), *The British Empire: Themes and Perspectives* (Oxford, 2008), 220.

of a failure to provide any 'agreed themes' around which the writing and teaching of Bи th history could cohere. A generation of scholars, he alleged, had 'cut themselves off... from the general national culture which they existed to enhance'; their discipline had thus become increasingly irrelevant to the public at large.[3] The Indian-born novelist Salman Rushdie summed up the situation more pithily—if provocatively—in *The Satanic Verses* (1988) when he declared that the problem for the 'English' (interestingly, not 'British') was that their history had essentially taken place overseas and so they could not understand its importance.[4]

Whatever their purchase in the past, these claims no longer resonate today. For the last two decades historians have been busy reassessing the place of empire in Britain's domestic history by exploring the range of attitudes people held towards it, the multiple meanings they ascribed to it, and the variety of experiences they derived from it.[5] Such is their success that the study of the relationship between Britain's domestic history and its imperial history has rapidly established itself as one of the most vibrant fields of scholarship. It is nonetheless a field beset by an array of methodological and conceptual difficulties. An expanding secondary literature, unearthing ever more examples of the ways in which British society was 'imperialized', has provoked several scholars to ask whether there may not now be a risk of 'empire reductionism' whereby imperialist attitudes are read into a whole range of phenomena only tangentially connected to overseas rule, if at all.[6]

---

[3] D. Cannadine, 'British History: Past, Present and Future?', *Past & Present* (*P&P*), 116/1 (1997), 178.

[4] S. Rushdie, *The Satanic Verses* (New York, 1988), 343.

[5] For two pioneering studies, see J. M. MacKenzie, *Propaganda and Empire: The Manipulation of Public Opinion, 1890–1960* (Manchester, 1984) and id. (ed.), *Imperialism and Popular Culture* (Manchester, 1986); subsequently, A. M. Burton, *After the Imperial Turn: Thinking With and Through the Nation* (Durham, NC, 2003); C. Hall, *Civilising Subjects: Colony and Metropole in the English Imagination, 1830–1867* (Chicago, 2002); C. Hall and S. O. Rose (eds.), *At Home with the Empire: Metropolitan Culture and the Imperial World* (Cambridge, 2006); B. Porter, *Absent-Minded Imperialists: Empire, Society and Culture in Britain* (Oxford, 2004); A. S. Thompson, *The Empire Strikes Back?: The Impact of Imperialism on Britain From the Mid-Nineteenth Century* (Harlow, 2005).

[6] See esp. Porter, *Absent-Minded Imperialists*. For a shrewd assessment of the terms of the debate see S. Ward, 'Echoes of Empire', *History Workshop Journal*, 62/1 (2006), 264–77 and R. Price, 'One Big Thing: Britain, Its Empire, and Their Imperial Culture', *JBS* 45 (2006), 602–27.

If we are to break out of this impasse it is vital to step back from the specific points of contention to try to lay bare the underlying forces in British society that shaped its responses to empire. First and foremost, we need to understand the implications of the increasing pluralism of modern British society.[7] In the twentieth century, just like the nineteenth, metropolitan responses to the colonies were divided along the lines of class, religion, region, and gender, as a diverse array of people sought to conscript the empire (or opposition to it) to their cause. If attitudes towards the empire often appear inconsistent, even contradictory, it is precisely because people were more likely to embrace that empire when they felt that it could be adapted to their own wants and needs. Second, we need to recognize the 'untidiness of empire', and the very different types of 'British connection' that developed across its constituent parts.[8] Not everywhere was like India or tropical Africa, and many people were influenced by one aspect of Britain's imperial experience without necessarily being aware of or affected by others. Third, the ways in which the colonies were represented in British culture reflected, to a considerable extent, the calls upon that culture to justify British rule. In this regard, what wasn't said could be just as important as what was: well into the twentieth century silence and denial helped to hide the more egregious and embarrassing aspects of British overseas rule, just as they had done so before.[9] Fourth, the historian of the twentieth century is confronted by the complicating fact that much 'British' history continued to be one of connections across the world and not just the empire; phenomena that clearly derived from abroad did not do so exclusively from the colonies. For these reasons (and others) the impact of imperialism on Britain was much more uneven and unpredictable than is sometimes imagined.

Yet to emphasize the diversity of metropolitan responses to empire is not to deny the existence of a later Victorian *mentalité* from which the central components of an 'imperial mindset' that persisted into the twentieth

---

[7] For the 20th century, see esp. R. McKibbin, *Classes and Cultures: England 1918–1951* (Oxford, 1998).

[8] J. Darwin, 'Britain's Empires', in Stockwell (ed.), *British Empire*, 3.

[9] For the general point, see R. Price, *Making Empire: Colonial Encounters and the Creation of Imperial Rule in Nineteenth Century Africa* (Cambridge, 2008). For its application to one of the major colonial counter-insurgency campaigns of the 20th century, see C. Elkins, *Britain's Gulag: The Brutal End of Empire in Kenya* (London, 2005) and D. Anderson, *Histories of the Hanged: Britain's Dirty War in Kenya and the End of Empire* (London, 2005).

century were assembled. These components include the vision of a 'Greater Britain'; the India-direct rule complex; informal influence in South America and the Middle East; and the idea of Britain's centrality in a 'global' world whose resources were there to be exploited for Britain's economic and military advantage. Indeed, the 'big' story of this chapter is in many ways the slow demolition of this *mentalité*, albeit with several significant discursive shifts along the way. While not necessarily apparent at the time, the real substance of empire was lost soon after the Second World War. When India gained its independence, and the white dominions ceased to be thought of as part of the 'empire', what remained were in many ways its least appealing parts—a handful of troublesome dependencies and marginal settler colonies, whose highly privileged European populations enjoyed lifestyles apparently far removed from a Britain still in the grip of post-war austerity. It was at precisely this moment, moreover, as colonial rule came to be defended more as a temporary expedient than as long-term commitment, that belief in 'empire' shaded into a belief in 'great powerdom'—a belief that proved stubbornly persistent in the post-war period. Only in the face of successive economic crises, which exposed the absurd pretensions of maintaining such a world role for what they really were, could the process of post-imperial readjustment truly begin.

This chapter begins chronologically, therefore. It sketches this twentieth-century trajectory, uncertain as it was, of metropolitan experiences of empire, and explores how people's understandings and perceptions of the colonies changed over the course of the twentieth century as the world surrounding them changed too. The focus is primarily on the period from the First World War through to the 1970s, although, as we shall see, it will also be necessary to refer back to the Edwardian era and forward to more recent times.

Shifting Experiences over Time

The two world wars transformed the meaning as much as the physical reality of empire. Other chapters in this volume explore the effects of the First and Second World Wars upon debates about the strategic significance, economic value, and political viability of the colonies. This chapter shows how these global conflicts, requiring as they did an unprecedented mobilization of colonial manpower and resource, thereby exposed a greater proportion of the British population to the empire and accentuated its *military* aspects in the public imagination.

At the outset of the twentieth century British society experienced a quickening of the imperial pulse as a result of the South African War (1899–1902). The biggest armed conflict in which the country was engaged between the Napoleonic and First World Wars was the occasion for a sudden intensification of imperial propaganda, a hardening of racial discourses, and an underlying shift in the ways in which empire and society now related to and needed each other.[10] A 'home' front also emerged, partly to bolster the morale of a nation at war, partly to provide for the disabled soldiers as well as the dependent relatives of those who lost their lives.[11] That said, the 'empire at war' in 1899 was conceived largely as a white affair: the troops that fought alongside Britain were from the newly emerging dominions, not the dependent colonies, and the conflict's consequences for South Africa's black and coloured communities received scant attention and little public sympathy.

In 1914, by contrast, the entire British empire took up arms against Germany. Whereas Indian troops had not been deployed in large numbers on the South African veldt, they saw extensive action overseas after 1914.[12] Mass-circulation newspapers carried pictures of both white and coloured colonial soldiers before they embarked to the front, and later during the victory parades, while Caribbean and Indian soldiers were billeted and hospitalized in Britain, the former returning to repatriation camps after the war ended. The machinery of wartime propaganda, moreover, projected images of a multiracial empire united in a common crusade against Prussian militarism.[13]

The empire also loomed large in the post-war period of reconstruction. Demobilized British soldiers were resettled in the colonies.[14] Military expenditure in the Middle East became caught up in an 'anti-waste'

---

[10] D. E. Omissi and A. S. Thompson, 'Introduction: Investigating the Impact of the War', in Omissi and Thompson (eds.), *The Impact of the South African War* (Basingstoke, 2002), 1–20.

[11] A. S. Thompson, 'Publicity, Philanthropy and Commemoration: British Society and the War', in Omissi and Thompson (eds.), *Impact of the South African War*, 99–123.

[12] D. E. Omissi, 'Europe through Indian Eyes: Indian Soldiers Encounter England and France, 1914–1918', *English Historical Review* (*EHR*), 122 (2007), 371–96 and id., *Indian Voices of the Great War: Soldiers' Letters, 1914–1918* (New York, 1999). See also id., 'India: Some Perceptions of Race and Empire', in Omissi and Thompson (eds.), *Impact of the South African War*, 215–33.

[13] M. L. Sanders and P. M. Taylor, *British Propaganda during the First World War, 1914–1918* (London, 1982), 50, 152.

[14] K. Fedorowich, *Unfit for Heroes?: Reconstruction and Soldier Settlement in the Empire between the Wars* (Manchester, 1995).

campaign conducted through the pages of the popular press. A series of seaport riots—targeting minority ethnic groups working in the merchant marine—provoked questions about the identity and status of colonial peoples in Britain.[15] And a battery of nationalist revolts in Ireland, Egypt, Iraq, and India ushered in new anxieties about Britain's imperial future.[16] By the 1920s, therefore, several of the assumptions that had hitherto under-pinned British rule—allowing it to be tacitly supported or even taken for granted—were more widely questioned, as moments of controversy in the colonies multiplied, and then reverberated at home.[17] Far from simply being a period of popular disillusionment with empire, however, the inter-war years saw a renewed effort by imperialists to propagate their ideals, including a drive towards protectionism.[18] The dizzy heights of 'war impe-rialism' now gave way to an emphasis on the empire as a bulwark of liberal, democratic values—whether in the form of the League of Nations' man-dates, or the Balfour Declaration (1926) on Anglo-Dominion relations.[19] As the empire emerged from the Paris Peace Conferences not only intact but greatly extended, as international crises multiplied, and as the USA and USSR retreated further into isolation, the view that Britain had a distinct role to play in the world continued to command widespread support.[20]

Britain's experience of the Second World War and its aftermath saw a similar effort to reinvigorate the concept of imperialism. The public was

[15] J. Jenkinson, *Black 1919: Riots, Racism and Resistance in Imperial Britain* (Liverpool, 2009); 'Black Sailors on Red Clydeside: Rioting, Reactionary Trade Unionism and Conflicting Notions of "Britishness" Following the First World War', *Twentieth Century British History* (*TCBH*), 19 (2008), 29–60 and 'The Glasgow Race Disturbances of 1919', in K. Lunn (ed.), *Race and Labour in Twentieth Century Britain* (London, 1985), 43–67.

[16] J. Darwin, *Britain, Egypt and the Middle East: Imperial Policy in the Aftermath of War, 1918–1922* (London, 1981); J. Gallagher, 'Nationalisms and the Crisis of Empire, 1919–1922', *Modern Asian Studies*, 15/3 (1981), 355–68; K. Jeffrey, *The British Army and the Crisis of Empire, 1918–1922* (Manchester, 1984).

[17] See e.g. W. K. Hancock's *Survey of Commonwealth Affairs*, i. *Problems of Nationality, 1918–1936* (Oxford, 1937), which picked up on many of these anxieties and berated imperial historians for being far too complacent. I am grateful to Saul Dubow for this reference.

[18] J. M. MacKenzie, 'The Popular Culture of Empire in Britain', in J. M. Brown and Wm. R. Louis (eds.), *The Oxford History of the British Empire* (*OHBE*), iv. *The Twentieth Century* (Oxford, 1999), 212–32.

[19] S. Constantine, *Emigrants and Empire: British Settlement in the Dominions between the Wars* (Manchester, 1990) and *Buy and Build: The Advertising Posters of the Empire Marketing Board* (London, 1990).

[20] B. Harrison, *Seeking a Role: The United Kingdom, 1951–1970* (Oxford, 2009), 535.

presented with a variety of images of a rejuvenated 'people's empire',[21] an empire pulling together 'across differences of race and ethnicity', promoting the economic, social, and technical uplift of its dependent peoples, and capitalizing on the possibilities that such development projects presented for job creation in Britain. Furthermore, this was an empire that also continued to cherish its kith and kin ties with the 'old' dominions, not least Australia, which, despite the shock of the fall of Singapore in 1942, established itself as the principal recipient of post-war migrants from Britain, and London's key partner in its nuclear programme. In view of the colonies' contribution to the defeat of Nazi Germany, the 'uncertain and distant' prospects of a devastated Europe,[22] and the scope for African and Asian dependencies to earn scarce dollars for Britain and to provide vital raw materials, sticking with the empire still seemed to make sense.[23]

The Left's commitment to the colonies as a progressive force in the world did, however, have to jostle with growing concerns about both the costs and consequences of colonial rule.[24] During the war there had been considerable pressures to distance Britain from 'the stigma of heavy-handed empire building',[25] partly to secure American support. After 1945, in the face of growing colonial unrest, Britain was forced to adopt counter-insurgency strategies, and to export them from one military hot spot to another. The partitions of India and Palestine, the Suez Crisis, and violent episodes of decolonization in Malaya, Kenya, and Cyprus all cast doubt on the extent of Britain's capacity to play a leading and independent role on the world stage. The rhetoric of Britain's 'moral authority' to rule was increasingly undercut by the grim realities—however selectively they were reported—of what was actually happening in the colonies.

---

[21] W. Webster, *Englishness and Empire, 1939–1965* (Oxford, 2005), 7–8.

[22] A. G. Hopkins, 'Rethinking Decolonization', *P&P* 200/1 (2008), 216–18.

[23] Darwin, 'Britain's Empires', 18.

[24] As memories of the Depression lingered, and wartime austerity continued, the economic appeal of empire temporarily revived after 1945. Cut off from continental markets and sources of supply, during the Second World War Britain had necessarily traded with countries that could be relied upon and reached—the dominions, the colonies, and the United States. The years 1945–52 saw Commonwealth exports supply scarce dollars to the Sterling Area, the survival of imperial preferences, and a further redirection of exports from Britain to empire markets. Significantly, multilateral patterns of trade, and a more open international economy, did not reassert themselves until the latter part of the 1950s. See also Jim Tomlinson, Ch. 6 in this volume.

[25] Ward, 'Echoes of Empire', 274.

Mindful of the dangers of metropolitan opinion growing weary of the colonial responsibilities, Kenya's white population launched a vigorous public relations campaign which repackaged concepts of character, vigour, and virtue in a language of partnership and development.[26] Yet, as we shall see, sympathy for Kenyan settlers was dwindling by the 1950s, as the liberal theory of empire was more widely denounced as a cover for white privilege, endemic racism, and systematized violence.[27] It is at this juncture that one can begin to detect a gradual shift away from more established patterns of thinking about the colonies towards a fundamental reappraisal of how the very concept of empire stood in relation to the kind of country that Britain aspired to be.

By the later 1950s and early 1960s the empire no longer seemed to be entirely in step with a 'modern' Britain. In fact, these years were as much or more about comprehending the actual and impending loss of empire as they were about responses to particular episodes of decolonization. There were myriad ways in which this loss was comprehended, and one has to be careful about attributing to a complex process more coherence than it actually had. The empire's appeal as a foil against which to define the national character is, however, a recurring theme. Having ceased to be regarded as a source of strength, the colonies began to be imagined and depicted as a thing of the past, even before the process of formal decolonization had completely come to an end.[28]

The social and cultural 'crisis' of the 1960s might be regarded as one of the first by-products of the end of empire. The values and beliefs of those who had championed colonial rule were increasingly portrayed as being out of kilter with British society at this time. Concepts of 'duty', 'loyalty', 'hierarchy', and 'self-sacrifice'—hitherto regarded as the social bedrock of British power—were now irreverently challenged through the medium of satire.[29]

---

[26] S. Ball (ed.), *Parliament and Politics in the Age of Churchill and Attlee: The Headlam Diaries, 1935–1951* (Cambridge, 1999), 159 (12 Sept. 1939). For a discussion on attitudes towards British planters in Malaya see diary entries 7–8 Jan. 1942 and 8 Feb. 1942.

[27] Harrison, *Seeking a Role*, 535; Thompson, *The Empire Strikes Back?*, 212. See also Richard Whiting, Ch. 5 in this volume.

[28] S. Howe, *Anti-Colonialism in British Politics: The Left and the End of Empire, 1918–1964* (Oxford, 1993); P. Keleman, 'Modernising Colonialism: The British Labour Movement and Africa', *Journal of Imperial and Commonwealth History (JICH)*, 34/2 (2006), 223–44.

[29] For contemporary understandings of the empire as a 'training ground' for developing these virtues as well as demonstrating them, see P. J. Cain, 'Empire and the Languages of Character and Virtue in Later Victorian and Edwardian Britain', *Modern Intellectual History*, 4/2 (2007), 249–73.

To be sure, the questioning of these values was not confined to Britain; they were also contested across several fronts—religious, familial, and commercial, as well as military and imperial. But the way in which these values were called into question was inseparable from Britain's emotional retreat from empire.

As an imperial mindset was at first derided and then steadily eroded, a path was paved during the 1960s and 1970s for new, and more negative, narratives of British state formation to take hold. Among academics, journalists, and policy-makers, the discourse of 'decline'—for some a by-product of the dissolution of empire, for others an inevitable consequence of holding on to it for so long—moved to the heart of debates about the modernization of Britain.[30] Yet beyond the political classes, amongst a wider public, the empire appears to have become less and less relevant. It was a dwindling dimension of the British people's past, as they ceased to relate to or even perhaps to reflect on it.

And then, unexpectedly, the empire struck back. For the last two decades the British have, however inadequately and incompletely, begun the process of trying to come to terms with their imperial past. In this last phase, still very much with us, the question of whether Britain should have an empire and, if so, how it should run it, has reconfigured itself into one of how it should package and manage its memory. The visible empire of colonies has almost disappeared, yet it has been replaced by various competing and conflicting ideas, or public memories, of empire. The presence in Britain of not just first-, but second- and third-generation immigrants from the 'new' Commonwealth, has meant that some younger people in minority ethnic communities have been keen to discover more about the life histories of their parents, and to rework British identities around their own culture and beliefs.

Meanwhile, amongst the population at large, or particular parts of it, attitudes to the imperial past have ranged from the temptation to nostalgia (typically involving forms of idealized remembrance that tacitly refuse to engage with the more controversial aspects of Britain's colonial record), to

---

[30] J. Tomlinson, 'The Decline of Empire and the Economic "Decline" of Britain', *TCBH* 14/3 (2003), 201–21; id. 'Managing the Economy, Managing the People: Britain circa 1931–1970', *EHR* 58/3 (2005), 555–85; G. Ortolano, 'Decline as a Weapon in Cultural Politics', in W. R. Louis (ed.), *Penultimate Adventures with Britannia: Personalities, Politics and Culture in Britain* (London, 2008), 201–14.

heritage excursions (in which people seek to recover the colonial careering of their ancestors), and to roots-tourism (in which they trace their ancestor's migratory patterns). There have also been various efforts to make reparation or restitution, symbolic and material, for cross-generational colonial 'wrongs'. These have raised difficult questions in the news media and parliament about how far back we should travel to right these 'wrongs', what happens when the demands for reparation from injured parties (for example, for land restitution) conflict with the security and well-being of others, and whether we are not in danger of furthering a grievance-driven political culture in which enmity and resentment are more likely to be accentuated than alleviated. Behind all of these developments lurks a sense in which, for whatever reasons, the events of Britain's imperial past seem, to a remarkable extent, to be shaping the British people's ideas of themselves into the twentieth-first century.

Having put in place this broad chronological framework, we now need to explore more thematically the various ways in which the empire entered into the everyday lives of the British peoples. We will do this under four headings: the migration of men and women to and from the colonies; the representations of the colonies in the media and the realm of recreation; moments of public controversy surrounding the colonies; and the psychological and emotional consequences of decolonization.

Migration

Migration was arguably the aspect of empire that touched most British people most profoundly.[31] It played a tremendous social and imaginative role in British society, expanding people's horizons and instilling a powerful sense of belonging to a wider British world, the building blocks of which included the global spread of English-speaking culture, via journalism,

---

[31] For empire migration and its repercussions for Britain, see Constantine, *Emigrants and Empire*; Fedorowich, *Unfit for Heroes*; M. Harper, *Emigration from North-East Scotland* (Aberdeen, 1988); id., *Adventurers and Exiles: The Great Scottish Exodus* (London, 2003); id., *Emigrant Homecomings: The Return Movement of Emigrants, 1600–2000* (Manchester, 2005); and id. with M. E. Vance (eds.), *Myth, Migration and the Making of Memory: Scotia and Nova Scotia, c.1700–1990* (Halifax, Nova Scotia, 1999); E. Richards, *Britannia's Children: Emigration from England, Scotland, Wales and Ireland since 1600* (London, 2004); and M. Harper and S. Constantine (eds.), *OHBE Companion Series, Migration and Empire* (Oxford, 2010).

publishing, higher education;[32] the solidarity (and shared racial ideology) among skilled workers in the metropole and (settler) colonies;[33] and the growth of significant overseas colonial memberships among several of Britain's leading professions.[34] Even those parts of British society that were largely indifferent to other aspects of Britain's colonial 'mission' might have deep-rooted family connections to the colonies—personal contact rather than government policy embedded this aspect of imperialism in people's lives.

For many Britons, therefore, emigration was the essence of empire. Whereas for much of the nineteenth century America was the favoured destination for settlers, by the early twentieth century Canada had displaced it. Opportunities for British labour in the United States diminished considerably from this time, as the unskilled faced severe competition from migrant workers from southern and eastern Europe, while the demand for skilled work was increasingly met domestically. By contrast, the flow of migrants from Britain to the colonies held up well in the first decades of the twentieth century. Encouraged by the Empire Settlement Act of 1922, and facing strict US immigration quotas, 55 per cent of the 1.8 million Britons who emigrated during the 1920s went to the dominions. The following decade, the proportion of people emigrating to the empire peaked at 80 per cent, although the total number of emigrants was much reduced. Just over a hundred thousand people left Britain for the colonies from 1935 to 1939, a figure equivalent to only three-quarters of those who had departed for Canada alone in the year 1913.

[32] C. Hilliard, 'The Provincial Press and the Imperial Traffic in Fiction, 1870s–1930s', JBS 48 (2009), 653–73; K. Pickles, 'Exhibiting Canada: Empire, Migration and the 1928 English Schoolgirl Tour', Gender, Place and Culture, 7/1 (2000), 81–96; S. J. Potter, News and the British World: The Emergence of an Imperial Press System 1876–1922 (Oxford, 2003); id., Newspapers and Empire in Ireland and Britain c. 1857–1921 (Dublin, 2004); T. Pietsch, 'A Commonwealth of Learning? Academic Networks and the British World, 1890–1940' (DPhil Thesis, University of Oxford, 2008).

[33] J. Hyslop, '"The Imperial Working Class Makes Itself "White": White Labourism in Britain, Australia and South Africa before the First World War', Journal of Historical Sociology, 12/4 (1999), 398–424; id., The Notorious Syndicalist: J. T. Bain, a Scottish Rebel in Colonial South Africa, (Johannesburg, 2004); N. Kirk, Comrades and Cousins: Globalization, Workers and Labour Movements in Britain, the USA and Australia from the 1880s to 1914 (London, 2002).

[34] Thompson, Empire Strikes Back?, 17–29.

After the Second World War, despite a tight labour market at home and growing debate over the merits of continued emigration,[35] the number of people leaving Britain temporarily surged. From 1946 to 1949, over half a million departed, mostly for the empire, many travelling on the assisted passage schemes introduced by Australia and New Zealand in 1947. Emigrant numbers then declined, albeit just over 1 million people still left Britain for the dominions from 1946 to 1957, encouraged by the repeated renewal of the Empire (later Commonwealth) Settlement Act, which did not finally lapse until 1972. Polls conducted by the British Institute of Public Opinion during this decade showed that between 28 and 42 per cent of people answered 'yes' when asked 'if you were free to do so, would you settle in another country?' This is a striking statistic. It points to a great deal of latent interest in the prospect of bettering oneself through emigration, even after the Second World War. It is also more broadly indicative of the way in which the world of the imagination had been shaped by the material experience of empire.[36]

The Post Office archives provide a fascinating insight into the density and intricacy of the kith-and-kin networks that connected British society at home to the overseas British societies of the empire.[37] Regular flows of information (and money) reveal how empire migration was deeply woven into the fabric of British family life. At the start of the twentieth century, the volume of letters despatched to the colonies grew by a third, and the volume of parcels by a quarter, in barely five years, with 5 million pounds of mail and 314,731 parcels sent from Britain to Canada in 1909, and 1.3 million pounds of mail and 124,671 parcels flowing in the opposite direction.[38]

After the First World War, the volume of letters sent to and from Britain and her colonies increased dramatically. Innovations in transport

---

[35] S. Constantine, 'Waving Goodbye? Australia, Assisted Passages, and the Empire and Commonwealth Settlement Acts, 1945–1972', *JICH* 26/2 (1998); A. J. Hammerton and A. Thomson, *Ten Pound Poms: Australia's Invisible Migrants* (Manchester, 2005).

[36] M. Hutching, *Long Journey for Sevenpence: An Oral History of Assisted Immigration to New Zealand* (Victoria, 2007), 75–6.

[37] G. B. Magee and A. S. Thompson, 'Lines of Credit, Debts of Obligation: Migrant Remittances to Britain, c.1875–1913', *EHR* 59/3 (2006), 539–77 and 'The Global and the Local: Explaining Migrant Remittance Flows in the English-speaking World, 1880–1914', *Journal of Economic History*, 66 (2006), 177–202.

[38] Thompson, *The Empire Strikes Back?*, 59–60.

technology, in particular the Empire Air Mail Scheme, inaugurated in 1934, greatly facilitated the conveyance of first class mail. Whereas previous surcharge costs had served as a disincentive to the sending of letters overseas by air mail, the removal of that surcharge allowed correspondents to send and receive letters at no additional cost. The results were impressive. In 1934, a little less than 175,000 pounds of letters was sent from Britain to extra-European destinations; in less than two years that figure had more than doubled to 363,400 pounds.[39] By 1939, over 40,000 pounds of post was being conveyed through the Empire Air Mail Scheme in a single week alone, and by the outbreak of the Second World War, Imperial Airway's ton-mileage figure (calculated by multiplying the weight of the commercial load by the distance over which it travelled) was over twenty times greater than what it was in 1924.[40] Most illuminating is what this meant for families wishing to keep in touch with loved ones overseas: in the run-up to Christmas, for example, the volume of parcels and post sent from Britain to the empire swelled dramatically. In 1936, 27 tons of mail was successfully despatched in a frantic six-week period. Twelve months later, the figure had reached 81 tons, and, in 1938, the seven-week total was a striking 222 tons.[41]

While the Second World War disrupted the international exchange of letters and parcels, it is clear that the development of air transport had altered radically the nature of Britain's relationship with her overseas empire. In the aftermath of war, the Conservative leader, Anthony Eden, could still speculate that 90 per cent of Britain's mail from abroad came from outside Europe.[42] Nor was it only mail that was moving around the British world: money too was on the move. Over £3 million of remittances were sent by overseas settlers to family and friends back in Britain in 1909, with as much as £1 million flowing in the opposite direction—a considerable flow of private capital which would be equivalent to over £200 million in today's money.[43] Fifty years later, over £12 million—almost £1 billion today—was

[39] Post Office Archives: Imperial and Foreign Letter Mails, Summary 1936. Post 43/20.

[40] Post Office Archives: Empire Air Mail Inauguration Brochure, 1938, Post 50/15; United Kingdom Empire Air Mail Traffic: Average Weekly Traffic. Post 50/14.

[41] Robin Higham, *Britain's Imperial Air Routes, 1918 to 1939: The Story of Britain's Overseas Airlines* (London, 1960), 223.

[42] Harrison, *Seeking a Role*, 80.

[43] URL: <http://www.nationalarchives.gov.uk/currency/results.asp#mid>, accessed 22 Nov. 2009.

remitted to and from Britons overseas: the empire was disbanding but its financial ties were not.[44]

What we know about return migration similarly suggests a strong sense of connection between Britain and its settler colonies. It is estimated that as many as 40 per cent of all emigrants may have returned—if true, this would amount to some 2 million people, each with first-hand knowledge of the colonies.[45] Some came back for good, others temporarily—to marry someone from their former place of settlement, to attend the funeral of loved ones, or simply to see family and old friends. Not all of these colonists came back with favourable impressions, of course. Homesickness, destitution, and disillusion, as much as success, could motivate return; such people would hardly have been a positive advert for the colonies. At the other end of the spectrum, however, there would have been plenty of enthusiasts who had made good by emigrating, and who sought to profit from their experience and to preach the virtues of empire migration.

Migrants, moreover, were drawn from all echelons of British society. Skilled labourers left the country in sizeable numbers to work on the railways, in the building trades, or the mining sector. From the beginning of the twentieth century, Britain's colonies also provided a widening field of employment for an expanding and diversifying professional population—accountants, engineers, doctors, nurses, teachers, municipal planners, policemen, scientists, and journalists all moved back and forth between metropole and colony with surprising ease. At a time when there were fewer job prospects in many professions in Britain, and an oversupply of trained people, some of those who lacked the resources to establish themselves in their chosen career at home sought to do so in a colony first. Other migrant professionals were lured overseas by the prospect of greater responsibility, better pay, or more varied and interesting work.

The medical profession provides an interesting example. Serving as a doctor in the armed forces in India made it possible to accumulate the funds to buy a practice at home. Many doctors admitted to having an 'indescribable fascination' with the Indian subcontinent, as an adventurous life in the Raj was felt to offer more than 'the comparative mundanity of practice back home'.[46]

---

[44] Post Office Archives, Remittances from Abroad, Post 33/4034B.

[45] Richards, *Britannia's Children*, 214; Harper, *Emigrant Homecomings*, 106.

[46] A. Crozier, 'Sensationalising Africa: British Medical Impressions of Sub-Saharan Africa, 1890–1939', *JICH* 35/3 (2007), 398.

The proportion of the British Medical Association's membership from India and the colonies thus grew from 18 per cent in the early 1900s, to 26 per cent in the 1920s, to 30 per cent in the 1940s. By 1939, the BMA had some sixty-seven branches in India and the colonies, and was regularly lobbying the India and Colonial Offices on their members' behalf. Moreover, throughout these years, research into the effects of, and cures for, several diseases was conducted not just in India but on an empire-wide basis, with the expenditure and effort involved being justified as much in terms of imperial 'efficiency' as humanitarian concern. The names of key medical institutions are instructive here: the Imperial Cancer Research Fund (f. 1902), the British Empire Cancer Campaign (BECC) (f. 1923), the Empire Rheumatism Council (ERC) (f. 1936), and the British Empire Society for the Blind (f. 1950). A leading role in the campaigns of the BECC and ERC was played by the Australian-born Frank Fox (1874–1960), a journalist on the *Morning Post*, an ardent tariff reformer, and secretary of the Fellowship of the British Empire Exhibition. The efforts of Fox and others to create an imperial medical and scientific community were, however, directed more toward the dominions than the colonial empire in Africa and Asia.[47]

To fully grasp the implications of these trans-imperial family ties we need to drill down into local and regional history. Take, for example, the Cornish migrant experience.[48] The migration of skilled miners from Cornwall to the goldfields of South Africa had major social consequences, in particular for the family economy of the region and for the lives of many Cornish women. Early marriage, coupled with migration, resulted in wives and mothers staying behind in Cornwall with full responsibility for maintaining the family home, while their husbands spent several years abroad working in South Africa in order to boost household income. Migration was a deliberate economic strategy, as a result of which the well-being of many Cornish families hinged on the prosperity of the gold mines of Johannesburg. With

[47] D. Cantor, 'Cortisone and the Politics of Empire: Imperialism and British Medicine, 1918–1955', *Bulletin of the History of Medicine*, 67/3 (1993), 463–93; J. Hill, 'Globe-Trotting Medicine Chests: Tracing Geographies of Pharmaceuticals', *Social and Cultural Geography*, 7/3 (2006), 1470–97.

[48] Magee and Thompson, 'Lines of Credit, Debts of Obligation'; P. J. Payton, *The Cornish Overseas* (Fowey, 1999); S. P. Schwartz, 'Cornish Migration Studies: An Epistemological and Paradigmatic Critique', in P. Payton (ed.), *Cornish Studies*, vol. 10 (Exeter, 2002), 136–65; B. Deacon and S. Schwartz, 'Cornish Identities and Migration: A Multi-Scalar Approach', *Global Networks*, 7/3 (2007), 289–306.

the constant flow of remittances, these colonies were a lifeline for Cornwall for the first two decades of the twentieth century, a state of 'dependency' neatly captured by the Cornish historian A. L. Rowse. His memoirs record how, during childhood, individual families and the wider community had felt strong ties not only to their home in St Austell, but to the various mining towns along the Witwatersrand. More specifically, Rowse recalled the constant comings and goings of migrants, the receipt of letters, post-cards and gifts, as well as the importance of remittances, and the exchange of journals.[49]

Two decades later, a Mass Observation survey of 1948 revealed that about a quarter of the population of Britain continued to have close contact with friends or relatives living in the empire, overwhelmingly in Canada, Aus-tralia, and New Zealand—the places most people knew best.[50] How far these ties of sentiment and culture were sustained beyond this moment is an open question. A case study of the Leicester press highlights the importance of emigration during the 1950s in terms of 'the continuing consciousness of empire among the British people'.[51] Leicester, of course, was a city that notably experienced considerable inward migration, especially from South Asia, in the years after the Second World War. Yet during the 1950s the city's local newspapers were also peppered with stories of ordinary people who had settled in the dominions in search of a better life. Emigration was invariably treated positively: those who left Britain for the colonies belonged to 'us', to be contrasted with the growing number of coloured immigrants settling in the city who were initially perceived as 'them'. On 17 February 1959, the *Leicester Mercury*, with a readership of well over a hundred thousand people, went so far as to run a full-page of letters from emigrants to Australia under the banner 'The Good Life Down Under'. The regular reporting of emigration through the 1950s and into the early 1960s suggests that the editors of Leicester's press deemed the subject to be of considerable interest to their readers, as does their promotion of the idea of a Common-wealth Festival: 'Many Leicester people have emigrated to Commonwealth countries and these countries would make an interesting display.' As the

---

[49] As reprod. in Payton, *Cornish Overseas*, 43.

[50] G. K. Evans, *Public Opinion on Colonial Affairs* (London, 1948). See also *A Report on Feelings about the British Empire* (Mass Observation Archives, University of Sussex, 1948).

[51] L. Chessum, 'Race and Immigration in the Leicester Local Press: 1945–1962', *Immigrants and Minorities*, 17/2 (1998), 36–56.

author of this case study concludes: 'These tales of emigration and home-coming emphasised the links between Leicester whites and Commonwealth whites in other parts of the world.'[52]

By the early 1960s, however, scholars have detected a 'shrivelling of the concept, and the reality, of the British World'.[53] Its 'ethnic basis' was clearly disintegrating—Britain's falling birth rate, coupled with the recovery of its economy and commitment to making full use of available manpower meant that the dominions were now looking elsewhere for their labour needs.[54] The shift of metropolitan opinion toward emigration at this time is further reflected in public attitudes to child migration. In the summer of 1942 a vastly over-subscribed and government-subsidized scheme of overseas evac-uation, which had been confidently promoted by the language of 'imperial unity' and 'patriotic duty',[55] successfully relocated 2,644 British children from grant-aided schools to the colonies. After 1945, several major British charities continued to promote juvenile migration schemes, yet by the late 1950s and early 1960s they were fast running out of children to send.[56] Although these charities liked to congratulate themselves on populating the empire with 'good white British stock', their optimism in poor children's adaptability and malleability was waning. Moreover, the reality (albeit slow to fully emerge)[57] of what awaited these children was sometimes far removed from their rhetoric, as vulnerable youngsters were placed in institutions that subjected them to years of abuse.[58] More generally, as the

---

[52] L. Chessum, 'Race and Immigration in the Leicester Local Press: 1945–1962', 40.

[53] Hopkins, 'Rethinking Decolonisation', 228–31.

[54] Ibid. 231.

[55] P. Lin, 'National Identity and Social Mobility: Class, Empire and the British Government Overseas Evacuation of Children during the Second World War', TCBH 7/3 (1996), 310–44.

[56] S. Constantine, 'The British Government, Child Welfare, and Child Migration to Australia after 1945', JICH 30/1 (2002), 99–132.

[57] As early as 1924, serious concerns about the treatment of child migrants in Canada prompted the Labour government to despatch a committee of investigation, chaired by Margaret Bondfield, parliamentary secretary at the Ministry of Labour, which resulted in the cessation of funding for unaccompanied children under the age of 14. ibid. 101.

[58] See, E. Boucher, 'The Limits of Potential: Race, Welfare and the Interwar Extension of Child Emigration to Southern Rhodesia', JBS 48 (2009), 914–34; J. Grier, 'Voluntary Rights and Statutory Wrongs: The Case of Child Migration, 1948–1967', History of Education (HofE), 31/3 (2002), 263–80; G. Sherington, '"Suffer the Little Children": British Child Migration as a Study of Journeying between Centre and Periphery', HofE, 32/5 (2003), 461–76; M. Langfield, 'Volun-tarism, Salvation and Rescue: British Juvenile Migration to Australia and Canada, 1890–1939',

'new' Commonwealth vied with the 'old', constitutional changes in the dominions eroded formal ties,[59] and Britain's future relationship to Europe was more widely debated, so the appeal of a 'kith and kin' empire was gradually being undermined.

Representations

People in Britain encountered the empire in myriad ways. Those who worked or fought or travelled in the colonies, and directly experienced British rule, were always a minority of the population. Many more, however, experienced the empire imaginatively through the realms of recreation and religion.[60] Much has been written about the manifestations of empire in popular culture.[61] Culture could operate variously as a form of camouflage to disguise what was really happening in the colonies; or as a way of registering underlying, discursive shifts in metropolitan ways of thinking about empire; or as an arena in which conflicting perspectives on British rule confronted each other. In the twentieth century it did all three. Here the focus will be on education, popular fiction, and the cinema. What type of imperial imagery did these media present to the public? And how far did they succeed in embedding the rituals and traditions of empire into the lifestyles of the working or middle classes?

In the first half of the twentieth century, generations of schoolchildren encountered the empire through a growing body of publicity and propaganda, among which Empire Day is probably the best known. Celebrated on Queen Victoria's birthday (24 May), the occasion was promoted by Reginald Brabazon, the 12th Earl of Meath (1841–1929).[62] A philanthropist before he became an imperialist, Meath's hope was to use Empire Day to educate

---

JICH 32/2 (2004), 86–114 and R. A. Voeltz, 'The British Boy Scout Migration Plan, 1922–1932', Social Science Journal, 40/1 (2003), 143–51.

[59] Hopkins, 'Rethinking Decolonisation', 229.

[60] For the importance of religion in the representation of empire, see Jeffrey Cox, Chapter 3 in this volume. The missionary ideal remained important as late as the 1950s; only with the accelerated secularization of the 1960s did this aspect of the imperial 'project' weaken.

[61] See esp. many of the seventy-plus volumes published by Manchester University Press as part of the 'Studies in Imperialism' series', edited by J. M. MacKenzie, and inaugurated in 1985 and 1986 with Propaganda and Empire and Imperialism and Popular Culture.

[62] J. English, 'Empire Day in Britain, 1904–1958', Historical Journal, 44/1 (2006), 247–76; I. Grosvenor, '"There's No Place like Home": Education and the Making of National Identity', HofE, 28/3 (1999), 235–50; Thompson, Empire Strikes Back?, 120–2.

schoolchildren about the importance of the colonies and their responsibilities toward them. Until 1913, Meath bankrolled the movement to the tune of £5,000 per annum, before handing over responsibility to the Royal Colonial Institute in the early 1920s. The British government did not officially endorse the event until 1916, in the midst of an army recruitment crisis. Oral testimony suggests that Empire Day remained a firm fixture in the school calendar until at least the mid-1940s. After 1947, the movement experienced a rapid decline in funds and membership and received much less coverage in the press. By the time its name was changed to Commonwealth Day in 1958 it was already widely perceived as a relic of a bygone era.

For almost half a century, however, the excitement and spectacle of Empire Day had held the public's attention. In schools there were pageants in which children dressed up to represent the colonies; marching, parading, and flag waving; patriotic singing and musical programmes—activities representing a welcome departure from the regular and the routine. Empire Day, moreover, was marked by large-scale community events, extensively reported by local and national newspapers, while a range of extra-parliamentary organizations rallied behind the movement, some overtly imperialist (the National Service League and the British Empire Union), but many not—the Salvation Army, the Women's Institute, the Co-operative Movement, as well as countless local churches, all lent their active support.

Between the wars, Empire Day, previously largely consensual, was increasingly a cause of dispute.[63] Even some imperialists appear to have eschewed its more militaristic aspects, preferring instead to emphasize the ideals of imperial cooperation and international friendship.[64] There were also teachers whose political convictions sat uncomfortably with the type of jingoistic sentiment that could be expressed on these occasions, and who broke ranks and refused to participate. On the Left, Empire Day was attacked by the Communist-inspired Teacher Labour League, the League Against Imperialism, the *Educational Worker*, and the *Daily Worker*. The Labour Party's annual conference passed an anti-Empire Day resolution in

---

[63] English, 'Empire Day in Britain', 258–63. Although, in the Edwardian years, Empire Day had been vigorously opposed by progressives on the London County Council, and by socialist and feminist teachers: see e.g. D. Copelman, *London's Women Teachers: Gender Class and Feminism, 1870–1930* (London; New York, 1996), 119–20, 220–6.

[64] To this end, Major Fred Ney, founder of the Overseas Education League, promoted Empire Youth Sunday from 1937: see T. G. August, *The Selling of the Empire: British and French Imperialist Propaganda, 1890–1940* (Ann Arbor, 1985), 108.

1926, though the leadership, when again in power, chose studiously to ignore it. Conservatives seized upon these left-wing attacks on Empire Day as an opportunity to denounce 'seditious groups'. In some parts of the country, intense local feuding resulted. In Blaydon in County Durham, for example, tensions between supporters and critics of Empire Day escalated to the point where the police had to intervene to preserve law and order.[65]

During these decades, the whole idea of Empire Day was reconceived. In Labour circles, especially, the rhetoric of imperial supremacy was downplayed in favour of an image of the empire as a co-operative association of nations. Meanwhile there was a wider move to link Empire Day more closely to remembrance of the dead. War memorials became the centrepiece of many celebrations, as the movement's promoters sought to adapt the event to the new mood of 'peaceableness' that had swept over British public life after 1918.[66]

Like Empire Day, imaginative literature presented the public with many of its more vivid depictions of empire. The power of popular fiction lay exactly 'in its capacity to intensify and distil the essence of experience by particularising a general process and rendering it in personal terms' which could be 'immediately apprehended by ordinary people'.[67] Admittedly, there was much literature in which the empire did not loom large, partly reflecting the way in which interwar culture was noticeably more insular (and indeed feminized) than its Edwardian counterpart.[68] Furthermore, consumers of popular forms of fiction who did encounter the wider world in their reading were just as likely to read about the Holy Land and America as Britain's colonies, perhaps more so.[69] What is of interest for our purposes, therefore, is popular fiction that engaged directly with the empire. Here the

---

[65] English, 'Empire Day in Britain', 267.

[66] J. Lawrence, 'The Transformation of British Public Politics After the First World War', *P&P* 190/1 (2006), 185–216; 'Forging a Peaceable Kingdom: War, Violence and the Fear of Brutalisation in Post-First World War Britain', *JMH* 75/3 (2003), 557–89.

[67] D. Lammers, '"Who will do the Work?" The Loss of Empire in British Popular Fiction after the Second World War', *Centennial Review*, 23 (1978), 255.

[68] On this point, see esp. A. Light, *Forever England: Femininity, Literature and Conservatism between the Wars* (London, 1991).

[69] J. Rose, *The Intellectual Life of the British Working Classes* (New Haven, 2001). See also M. Green, *Dreams of Adventure, Deeds of Empire* (London, 1980). See also Hilliard's study of syndicated fiction, 'The Provincial Press and the Imperial Traffic in Fiction', which shrewdly observes that 'As historians of modern Britain, we sometimes attribute more weight to an activity involving the colonies than we do to the same activity when it involves other countries...

works of 'light fiction', or romantic novels, merit more attention. It is worth emphasising that it was through these long-forgotten novels that many readers 'discovered' the colonies, even if we now tend to remember the more 'highbrow' works, such as those by E. M. Forster and George Orwell. Significantly, while masculine imperial adventure stories have been well covered by historians, their feminine romantic counterparts have not.[70]

Romantic fiction was mostly written by women, for women. The biographies of its most celebrated and widely read authors are instructive here. Gertrude Page (1873–1922) emigrated to Rhodesia with her husband in 1900 and stayed there for the rest of her life. Her twenty-three romantic novels, published from 1902 to 1923, provided detailed descriptions of Rhodesian life and landscapes, and revered the European men and women who had settled there.[71] Kathlyn Rhodes (1877–1962) travelled in Egypt after its occupation by the British: her fifty-plus volumes of fiction, produced from 1899 to 1954, included many romances in African desert settings.[72] Among Cecil Adair's (1856–1932) three hundred novels, published from 1910 to 1932, were her popular stories of the Second Boer War. Dolf Wyllarde, the nom de plume of Dorothy Lowndes (1871–1950), who wrote prolifically from 1897 to 1939, portrayed settler life in Jamaica, South Africa and India, in particular the consequences of families split between Britain and its colonies. Mary Gaunt (1861–1942) moved to London from Australia after her husband's death in 1900. Her twenty-plus love and adventure novels idealized an array of British missionaries, officials, and scientists, all bent on regenerating the colonies.[73]

The genre of romantic fiction, therefore, attracted some of the most successful female novelists of the day, many of whom had a direct connection to the colonies. Meanwhile India under the Raj provided them with one of their most popular settings. Anglo-Indian love stories were a genre of light fiction that flourished from the 1890s to the 1930s. Well acquainted

---

we need to take care that we do not reflexively privilege imperial investments over other ones' (673).

[70] Albeit the 19th century is better served than the 20th: see e.g. J. Tosh, *Manliness and Masculinities in Nineteenth Century Britain: Essays on Gender, Family and Empire* (Harlow, 2005).

[71] e.g. *The Rhodesian* (1912).

[72] R. Anderson, *The Purple Heart Throbs: The Sub-Literature of Love* (London, 1974), 181–94.

[73] P. Romero (ed.), *Women Voices on Africa: A Century of Travel Writings* (Princeton, 1992), 91–104.

with Anglo-Indian life and the opportunities it presented to middle-class women for travel, adventure, and social mobility, the authors of these novels used to be household names, even if they have long since been forgotten.[74] Fanny Penny (1847–1939), the wife of a Madras chaplain, wrote some forty-five novels. Bithia Croker (1849–1920), married to a lieutenant-colonel in the Royal Scots Fusiliers, spent fourteen years in India and Burma, and set twenty of her books there. Maud Diver (1867–1954) was the daughter of an Indian army officer; after returning to England in 1896, she wrote many accounts of British heroism in the subcontinent.[75] Margaret Peterson (1833–1933), daughter of a professor of Sanskrit at Elphinstone College in Bombay, and married to an Indian civil servant, took the subject of inter-racial attraction as the plot for many of her works. Perhaps best known of all was the reclusive Ethel Dell (1881–1939). Many of her thirty-three novels were set in India, a place she had never visited, but read about obsessively. Despite her avoidance of the press, Dell had a devoted public. The actor Sir John Gielgud later recalled 'the Ethel Dell craze' of the 1920s,[76] while the missionary Edward Thompson (father of the Marxist historian E. P. Thompson) felt that the tensions existing in interwar India had been exacerbated by the conception of Indian life in her novels.[77]

Although these novelists sought to educate their audience about 'real Anglo-Indian life', the India they portrayed was predictably largely a romanticized one.[78] Exotic backdrops, tales of love and improbable adventures, handsome and chivalrous heroes, beautiful heroines—all were staple fare.[79] In so far as Indians themselves featured in these stories, they were invariably heavily typecast characters: cardboard figures condemned for their superstition, barbarity, fanaticism, and cruelty, or partners in

[74] M. Stieg, 'Indian Romances: Tracts for the Times', *Journal of Popular Culture*, 18/4 (1985), 2–15.

[75] B. Parry, *Delusions and Discoveries: India in the British Imagination, 1880–1930* (London, 1998), 71–99; S. Lahiri, *Indians in Britain: Anglo-Indian Encounters, Race and Identity 1880–1930* (London, 2000), 91–3.

[76] P. Dell, *Nettie and Sissie: The Biography of Ethel M. Dell and Her Sister* (London, 1977), 100.

[77] E. Thompson, *The Other Side of the Medal* (London, 1925), 114.

[78] H.-M. Teo, 'Romancing the Raj: Interracial Relations in Anglo-Indian Romance Novels', *History of Intellectual Culture*, 9/1 (2004); Stieg, 'Indian Romances', 2–15.

[79] Lahiri, *Indians in Britain*, 91; Parry, *Delusions and Discoveries*, 70, 87. For a further examination of the representation of Africans in fiction see: G. D. Killam, 'The "Educated African" Theme in English Fiction about Africa, 1884–1939', *Phylon*, 27/2 (1966), 155–64 and *Africa in English Fiction, 1874–1939* (Ibadan, 1968).

disastrous interracial unions. The British were consistently presented as the superior race, and the virtues of their rule—social, economic, and political—loudly proclaimed. Thus if these novelists played a part in shaping, as well as reflecting, popular impressions of India, they did so in such a way as to underscore the legitimacy and necessity of British rule, and to marginalize the role of Indians in their own history.[80]

Even such a stylized form of fiction as this could not, however, divorce itself from a rapidly changing external environment. By the later 1930s, the world these novels portrayed was ceasing to be credible. Indian people did not know, nor wish to keep, their 'place'. Nor were the benefits of British rule beyond question. Fewer and fewer writers were moved to pen the kind of heroic romances of empire that had previously been so popular.[81] Those that did found that their sales began to tail off and that their books had shorter print runs.

One of the few novelists whose writing repeatedly brought her back to India, and whose popularity did not diminish after 1945, is the neglected Margaret Rumer Godden (1907–98).[82] After growing up near Dacca, where her father worked as a shipping agent for the Brahmaputra Steam Navigation Company, Godden returned to Britain to publish what is perhaps her best book, *The River* (1946), later turned into a film. Set in a big house beside the banks of a river in Bengal, the novel's central character, and author's alter ego, Harriet, is caught between the two worlds of her comfortable Anglo-Indian childhood, and the growing doubts cast over Britain's ongoing presence in India—during filming students from Calcutta University had actually gathered to set fire to the set while chanting 'foreigners out'.[83] Described by one scholar as a 'critical insider', Godden and her fiction were highly independent.[84] When opening a dance school in Calcutta in 1930, she unconventionally accepted Indian and Eurasian pupils, while her best-seller *Black Narcissus* (1939), which remained in print for nearly sixty years, is

---

[80] Stieg, 'Indian Romances', 3.

[81] Although the appeal of empire (of all kinds) may have lasted into the 1950s in other genre, such as juvenile fiction. Many of G. A. Henty's novels, for example, were reissued during this decade, while comics like the *Eagle* presented imperial stereotypes (Sergeant Luck of the Legion, Livingstone) as to the manner born.

[82] A. Chisholm, *Rumer Godden: A Storyteller's Life* (London, 1999).

[83] P. Lassner, *Colonial Strangers: Women Writing the End of the British Empire* (New Brunswick, NJ, 2004), 99.

[84] Ibid. 71.

notable for its acute reflections on a group of Anglican nuns struggling to set up a convent in the Himalayan foothills and the ultimate failure of their 'civilising mission'.[85] It was, as her biographer describes it, a novel about 'why the British had to leave India, and why much of what they had tried to do there was bound to fail'.[86] It, too, was turned into a film, produced in 1946, and released in 1947, as a newly independent India was engulfed in civil war and partitioned. More than anything else, Godden's novels evoked the fragility and ultimate futility of colonial rule. They sent out the message that it was ultimately self-deluding for the British to expect to secure the support and respect of those whom they had colonized.[87]

After the First World War, new technologies presented new opportunities to sell the empire to the British public (and, later, to mediate popular perceptions of decolonization).[88] Cinema attendance surged in the interwar years. With the development of 'talkies' and colour, regular visits to the movies became the norm, even for the urban poor.[89] Imperial adventure films proved very popular at the box office during the 1930s. Hollywood, as much as the British film industry, was quick to grasp that lavishly shot productions about the empire could make money. Whether produced and directed by the Hungarian-born, Anglophile Korda brothers, or by the Americans Henry Hathaway and George Stevens, this genre of film either actively championed British rule, or alternatively subsumed it within a

---

[85] W. Webster, 'Reconstructing Boundaries: Gender, War and Empire in British Cinema, 1945–1950', *Historical Journal of Film, Radio and Television* (*HJFRT*), 23/1 (2003), 53–5.

[86] Chisholm, *Rumer Godden*, 92.

[87] Other genres of popular Indian fiction also had to adapt to survive. Take the historical works of John Masters (1914–83). Born in Calcutta, Masters' family's connection with India went back five generations. He served as an officer in the Indian Army during the 1930s and 1940s, later tried (and failed) to create Himalayan adventure holidays, and then turned to writing. His first book, *Nightrunners of Bengal* (New York, 1951), was a story of the Indian Mutiny, which sold 300,000 copies in the first six months. Meanwhile, *Bhowani Junction* (New York, 1954), a thinly disguised autobiographical novel about independence, later made into a successful film, was among the few books to deal compassionately with the fate of people of British and Indian parentage who were accepted by neither community, and to expose the painful dilemmas of identity and allegiance they faced. Here Masters was writing from experience: the family had Indian ancestry through his great-grandfather's marriage.

[88] For the latter, see B. Schwartz, 'Afterward: "Ways of Seeing"', in S. Faulkner and A. Ramurthy (eds.), *Visual Culture and Decolonisation in Britain* (Aldershot, 2006). See also: J. Richards, 'Imperial Heroes for a Post-Imperial Age: Films at the End of Empire', in S. Ward (ed.), *British Culture and the End of Empire* (Manchester, 2001), 128–45.

[89] A. August, *The British Working Class, 1832–1940* (Harlow, 2007), 212.

Hollywood vision of a benign American internationalism. These films, however, can also be read as a response to the social and economic conditions of the 1930s:[90] at a time when the male breadwinner was often out of work, they frequently sought to reaffirm an injured masculinity, while as class divisions became more pronounced 'many negative images of the upper class surfaced to reflect this tension, even in films set in Africa'.[91] In the circumstances of the Depression, moreover, the escapist elements of such films were all the more attractive as people flocked to the cinema to forget their troubles.

The outbreak of the Second World War drew this cycle of imperial epics to a close. In fighting fascism, British wartime propaganda contrasted the tyrannies and cruelties of Nazi Germany, Fascist Italy, and Imperial Japan with the principles of democracy and freedom espoused by the Western Allies and embodied in the August 1941 Atlantic Charter. The paternalistic imperialism and racial stereotyping of imperial adventure films became embarrassing to officials in the Ministry of Information, and was known to cause offence within the colonies. During the war a few films such as the *49th Parallel* (1941) and *West Indies Calling* (1943) actually gestured towards a greater racial tolerance and understanding—reflecting the perceived need to counter American anti-imperialism and to propagate the idea of a 'people's Empire' as a counterpart to the 'people's war'.[92] Once the war was over, however, this inclusive racial imagery subsided, while the superficially attractive idea of welfare imperialism was soon to be confronted by the realities of the ill-fated Tanganyika groundnuts scheme (see below, p.287).

---

[90] K. Dunn, 'Lights...Camera...Africa: Images of Africa and Africans in Western Popular Films of the 1930s', *African Studies Review*, 29/1 (1996), 149–75.

[91] Ibid. 151. For further representations of Africa on film see, M. Paris, 'Africa in Post-1945 British Cinema', *South African Historical Journal* (*SAHJ*), 48/1 (2003), 61–70, and D. M. Anderson, 'Mau Mau at the Movies: Contemporary Representations of an Anti-Colonial W', *SAHJ* 48/1 (2003), 71–90.

[92] BBC radio broadcasters, meanwhile, focused their attention on working-class opinion. Fearing that workers believed the empire was run by the ruling classes to their own detriment, their programmes sought to show how colonial rule could be accommodated to the desire for social improvement at home. See T. Hajkowski, 'The BBC, the Empire, and the Second World War, 1939–45', *HJFRT* 22/2 (2002), 135–55; W. Webster, 'The Empire Answers: Imperial Identity on Radio and Film, 1939–1945', in P. Buckner and R. D. Francis (eds.), *Rediscovering the British World* (Calgary, 2005), 321–39; S. Nicholas, '"Brushing up Your Empire": Dominion and Colonial Propaganda on the BBC's Home Services, 1939–1945', *JICH* 32/2 (2003), 207–30.

The introduction of the 'emancipated woman' was one way in which producers tried to modernize the imperial film genre during the 1950s.[93] To some extent, this development was prefigured in the women's literature of the interwar era, when the serialized 'emigrant story', of which the Amalgamated Press was a leading publisher, allowed women a new, adventurous way of life in Australian sheep stations, Canadian forests, and South African mining camps. The women in these stories were outdoor characters who could shoot, hunt, and ride.[94] By contrast, in post-war films the emphasis was upon an empire of development and welfare, which in turn led to a greater emphasis on the feminine qualities of the emancipated woman. The heroines of *Men of Two Worlds* (1946) and *North West Frontier* (1959), played by Phyllis Calvert and Lauren Bacall respectively, were intrepid and independent, yet also liberal, feminine, and caring.

By the 1960s, Hollywood had largely ceased producing such films. The core cinema-going audience was now under 30 and perceived as anti-establishment. During this decade one witnesses a gradual move in cinema away from empire and its ideals. As Pathé productions about Kenya (1961), Uganda (1961), and Rhodesia (1964) continued to 'justify the right of Britain to hold on to her colonies through images of development' and to 'applaud trusteeship',[95] other films began to grapple with more problematic aspects of the nation's relationship to its imperial past. *Born Free* (1962) shifted attention away from the subject of hunting and towards conservation of the natural environment. The film was set in Kenya, a favoured site for the filming of African wildlife, where the settler population had drastically reduced the game population during the interwar years,[96] and where, after 1945, the development of national parks and new wildlife protection acts

[93] W. Webster, 'Domesticating the Frontier: Gender, Empire and Adventure Landscapes in British Cinema, 1945–1959', *Gender & History*, 15/1 (2003), 85–107.

[94] B. Melman, *Women and the Popular Imagination in the Twenties: Flappers and Nymphs* (Basingstoke, 1986), 134–45.

[95] A. Ramamurthy, 'Images of Industrialisation in Empire and Commonwealth during the Shift to Neo-Colonialism', in S. Faulkner and A. Ramamurthy (eds.), *Visual Culture and Decolonisation in Britain: British Art and Visual Cultures since 1750: New Readings* (Aldershot, 2006), 43–71.

[96] E. I. Steinhart, 'Hunters, Poachers and Gamekeepers: Towards a Social History of Hunting in Kenya', *Journal of African History* (*JAH*), 30/2 (1989), 252–55 and *Black Poachers, White Hunters: A History of Hunting in Colonial Kenya* (Oxford, 2006). See also W. K. Storey, 'Big Cats and Imperialism: Lion and Tiger Hunting in Kenya and Northern India, 1898–1930', *Journal of World History*, 2/2 (1991), 135–73.

went hand–in hand with the growth of middle-class tourism.[97] Based on a best-selling book by the German-born Joy Adamson, a prizewinning artist and conservationist, married to George Adamson, an assistant warden with the Kenya Game Department,[98] the film was a box office success. It told the story of a motherless lion cub, Elsa, brought up by the Adamsons and then released back into the wild. Although it may have reinforced the message that 'the primary responsibility for protecting African wildlife' continued to rest with Western society, the film did at least include African and Indian actors—the Adamsons were among the voices arguing at this time for greater African involvement in wildlife management.[99] *Born Free* also contributed to a growing public awareness of environmental issues in Britain.[100]

Guns at Batasi (1964), set in a fictional newly-independent African state, depicted the British as they attempted to come to terms with the loss of empire. In particular, it explored the impact of that loss on the British army, and, by implication, British masculinity. The film asserted the racial superiority of the British, by contrasting African mayhem with British order. Yet it did so in such a way as to painfully expose how that superiority was in itself no longer sufficient to sustain colonial rule.[101] The story revolves around the British character Sergeant-Major Lauderdale, played brilliantly by Richard Attenborough. Lauderdale commands a battalion of the new state's army until African officers are ready to take over. An internal coup leads to the demand that the senior 'native' officers in the camp are handed over to supporters of the new regime. Lauderdale refuses, thereby putting British control of 'Afro-Britannia Mines' in jeopardy, and is posted home in disgrace as a result. Anachronisms abound in this film, not least Lauderdale himself, who is portrayed sympathetically, yet as a man whose attitudes are of the past and whose life is now without purpose. As one historian acutely observes of British cinema at this juncture, 'the loss of a comfortable

[97] J. M. MacKenzie, *The Empire of Nature: Hunting, Conservation and British Imperialism* (Manchester, 1988).

[98] Established at the turn of the century, the Department initially sought to license and regulate sport hunters, later to preserve game and oversee a conservation programme.

[99] R. Matheka, 'Decolonisation and Wildlife Conservation in Kenya, 1958–1968', *JICH* 36/4 (2008), 624.

[100] W. Beinart and L. Hughes, *Environment and Empire* (Oxford, 2007), 230–1.

[101] Webster, *Englishness and Empire*, 207–10.

continuity with the nation's past was [now] coupled with the necessity to comprehend that loss'.[102]

Controversy

The two world wars, growing nationalist resistance, and emerging pressures for decolonization meant that after 1914 colonial peoples were more likely to challenge the benefits of British rule, and to imagine for themselves alternative futures. They also meant that during the twentieth century the realities of colonial power and coercion were to be less easily concealed from a domestic audience. Across the century several factors raised public anxieties about the empire. Chief among these were the presence of coloured people in Britain who came from the colonies; the use of armed force to uphold coercive labour practices in the colonies; and military action to crush or contain popular dissent.

Although far less traumatic than that of France, Britain's retreat from empire still had the potential therefore to cause controversy at home. Moments of heightened public debate about British rule were more frequent after 1918, as the purpose of empire was questioned, and people's willingness to bear its burdens tested.[103] Of course, the critics of empire did not have it all their own way, and we must also be alert to the ways in which British society's views of the challenges of colonial nationalism were coloured by a determined propaganda effort on the part of government departments, newspaper editors, film-makers, novelists, and settlers to rally the British public behind their vision of a rejuvenated empire by defending white rule and denigrating subject peoples.[104]

India's involvement in the First World War brought tens of thousands of coloured soldiers to Europe to fight on the battlefields of Belgium and France—a 'warrior peasantry' drawn mainly from the provinces of northern India. Letters home, preserved by military censorship, reveal how these soldiers

---

[102] P. Jaikumar, *Cinema at the End of Empire: A Politics of Transition in Britain and India* (Oxford, 2006), 191.

[103] See S. Kent, *Aftershock: Politics and Trauma in Britain, 1918–1931* (Basingstoke, 2009), 10–35.

[104] S. Carruthers, 'A Red Under Every Bed? Anti-Communist Propaganda and Britain's Response to Colonial Insurgency', *Contemporary Record*, 9/2 (1995), 294–318 and 'Two Faces of 1950s Terrorism: the Film Presentation of Mau Mau and the Malayan Emergency', in J. D. Slocum (ed.), *Terrorism, Media, Liberation* (New Brunswick, 2005), 70–93.

felt a deep sense of personal loyalty to the King-Emperor George V.[105] Some 14,514 wounded Indian men were taken to hospitals set aside for them in Southampton, Bournemouth, and Brighton where, as well as meeting medical staff on the wards, they also mixed less formally with the men and women of the town. Some aspects of the Indian soldiers' experience of Britain appear to have been positive. They were warmly received by the crowds that gathered on their arrival, while hospitals took particular care over religious provision. There were, nonetheless, several points of contention including hospital regulations—often found too strict—and the difficulty of finding British medical staff to care for them.[106]

Contact between British female nurses and Indian soldiers proved particularly sensitive. In India intimacy between white women and Indian men was frowned upon. When white nurses were employed in the Pavilion and York hospitals in Brighton it was therefore on the understanding that their duties were supervisory rather than medical. No women were employed in Kitchener's Indian Hospital (KIH), where the first patients arrived in 1915. The KIH, moreover, initially sought to confine wounded Indian soldiers to hospital grounds to prevent them from mixing with women of the town. This led to protests from the soldiers and rules were later relaxed, but only on the condition that they visited the town in pairs, accompanied by a British soldier. Another flashpoint resulted from the policy of returning lightly wounded Indian troops to the trenches after they had recovered from their injuries, a policy the soldiers felt to be grossly unfair.[107]

Such racial anxieties intensified in the years after the First World War. The reaction of the British press and public to the massacre of an unarmed Indian crowd gathered in the Punjab city of Amritsar on 13 April 1919 was predictably polarized.[108] The British government moved quickly to disavow the actions of the officer who ordered his troops to fire, the irascible General Reginald Dyer, and he was forced to resign. Anglo-Indian opinion and sections of the London press rallied to Dyer's side, as 'Defender of Empire'. Yet working-class opinion was hostile to Dyer, whose use of 'overwhelming force' to maintain colonial rule raised the prospect of such tactics spreading

[105] Omissi, 'Europe through Indian Eyes', 371–96 and Omissi (ed.), *Indian Voices of the Great War*.

[106] R. Visram, *Asians in Britain: 400 Years of History* (London, 2002), 176–89, at 187.

[107] Omissi, 'Europe through Indian Eyes', 376–79.

[108] D. Sayer, 'The British Reaction to the Armristsar Massacre, 1919–1920', *P&P* 131 (1991), 130–64; N. Collett, *Butcher of Amristsar: General Reginald Dyer* (London, 2005).

back to Britain, for example to deal with labour unrest. Delegates at the Labour Party conference in Scarborough in 1920 resolutely denounced the actions of the British in the Punjab. As the *Manchester Guardian* was quick to comment, 'General Dyer's more thorough supporters by no means intend to stop at India... After India, Ireland. After Ireland, British workmen on strike.'[109]

In 1919 racial tensions erupted during a series of seaport riots in Glasgow, South Shields, Hull, Liverpool, Cardiff, and Barry. These disturbances show just how varied, inconsistent and context-specific the labour movement's responses to the colonies tended to be. They also gave what contemporaries had begun to call the 'colour problem' (or 'black peril') much greater prominence.[110] 'Five people were killed, dozens were injured, and at least 250 arrested in this major episode of twentieth-century British rioting.'[111] All of these towns and cities had settled populations of African, West Indian, South Asian, and Chinese workers, many of whom had filled jobs recently vacated by British merchant sailors on war service—the National Sailors' and Fireman's Union had actually targeted West Indians in their recruitment campaigns, preferring them to 'cheap' Chinese labour.[112]

Although representing only a fraction of the total overseas labour force in Britain's mercantile marine, it was coloured colonial seamen who were singled out by white crowds. Increased competition for peacetime jobs, coupled with a fear of the shipping industry using foreign labour to reduce wages, led British sailors to revive a long-standing campaign for restrictive employment practices and the so-called 'colour bar'. Another important feature of local protests was the jealousy and antipathy expressed toward relationships between black men and white women. Such relationships raised the spectre of miscegenation—the half-caste child—and were thus considered a threat to the fabric of metropolitan society.[113] During the riots

---

[109] 'Unionist Revolt', *Manchester Guardian* (9 July 1920), 6–7.

[110] Jenkinson, *Black 1919*. The latter term referred specifically to the assault or rape of white females by black males.

[111] Ibid. 1.

[112] L. Tabili, *'We Ask for British Justice': Workers and Racial Difference in Late Imperial Britain* (Chicago, 1994) and 'The Construction of Racial Difference in Twentieth Century Britain: The Special Restriction (Coloured Alien Seamen) Order, 1925', *JBS* 31/1 (1994), 54–98.

[113] R. Smith, 'The Black Peril: Race, Masculinity and Migration during the First World War', in L. Ryan and W. Webster (eds.), *Gendering Migration: Masculinity, Femininity and Ethnicity in Post-War Britain* (Ashgate, 2008); L. Bland, 'White Women and Men of Colour: Miscegenation Fears in Britain after the Great War', *Gender & History*, 17/1 (2005), 29–61.

many coloured people had to be removed from their homes and placed in protective custody. Government then offered repatriation, on a voluntary basis, to all those colonial sailors who had come to work in Britain during the war. By the end of 1921, as many as twelve hundred may have left Britain this way. Repatriation, however, divided opinion. Concern was expressed in government quarters about the effects of disaffected veterans, especially from the Caribbean, returning home with stories of the racial prejudice they had experienced in British seaports and stoking up anti-British feeling.

Violent labour unrest would indeed engulf the Caribbean archipelago, though not for another two decades.[114] Of more immediate concern was the prospect of colonial production undercutting British export markets, especially for Lancashire cotton textiles. By the time Mahatma Gandhi, leader of India's most successful trade union in Ahmedabad, visited London in 1931 to discuss India's constitution,[115] the Lancashire mills were experiencing mass unemployment 'with only half of all available spindles in the cotton mills still in use'.[116] Gandhi had instigated a boycott of British exports. Yet he still visited Lancashire (albeit with a police escort) to meet textile workers in Bolton, Springvale, Darwen, and Blackburn. He listened to their concerns, and tried to explain his principles of Indian self-sufficiency. The workers' reaction was not as negative as one might have expected. Several of the cotton unions were in fact supportive of Indian constitutional change, and while eager to tell Gandhi of the suffering caused by the determination to stop Indians from buying Lancashire cloth, they nonetheless greeted him warmly. The real restiveness over the tariff question and the nationalist boycott was among manufacturers' and employers' associations, and local chambers of commerce; and it was from these quarters that the greatest hostility to Gandhi was expressed.

In was in the later 1930s that the West Indies briefly recaptured the attention of the British labour movement.[117] Political awareness and trade unionization had grown across Barbados, Jamaica, and Trinidad, amidst an

---

[114] See e.g. O. N. Bolland, *On the March: Labour Rebellions in the British Caribbean, 1934–1939* (London and Kingston, Jamaica, 1995).

[115] Thompson, *Empire Strikes Back?*, 76–8.

[116] A. Muldoon, '"An Unholy Row in Lancashire": The Textile Lobby, Conservative Politics, and Indian Policy, 1931–1935', *TCBH* 14/2 (2003), 93. See also M. Pugh, 'Lancashire, Cotton, and Indian Reform: Conservative Controversies in the 1930s', *TCBH* 15/2 (2004), 143–51.

[117] S. Howe, *Anti-Colonialism in British Politics: The Left and the End of Empire, 1918–1964* (Oxford, 1993), 90; M. Nicholson, *The TUC Overseas: The Roots of Policy* (London, 1986).

international collapse in the price of sugar. There were several strikes and riots, culminating in disturbances in Jamaica in 1938, when forty-seven people were killed, and many more injured and arrested. This situation prompted the Trade Union Congress (TUC) to form a Colonial Advisory Committee (CAC). Alongside the *Daily Herald, Reynolds' News,* and the *Tribune,* the CAC pressured the Colonial Office to speed up the pace of economic and constitutional reform. So shocked was Walter Citrine, the TUC's General Secretary, by conditions in the colony that he expressed shame to be British: 'the white people', he wrote, 'treat the natives like dirt'.[118]

None of the controversies discussed thus far had the potential to reverberate across the whole nation. The closest Britain came to a French-type 'Algerian situation' after 1945 was during the Kenyan Emergency. Described by one scholar as the 'horror story' of the British Empire, the Emergency was part of the now largely 'forgotten wars' of decolonization.[119] The metropolitan response to Mau Mau—a secret society that grew into a violent insurrectionary movement in Kenya during the late 1940s—was complex, combining as it did elements of cover-up and denial, a powerful settler propaganda campaign aimed at discrediting its leaders, and, simultaneously, growing public misgivings about the intransigence of these settlers and their readiness to resort to violence.

Kenya's settlers (and career expatriates)[120] owned more land per capita than any other British colonists in Africa.[121] For the Kikuyu people, especially, white settlement had proved 'a complete disaster'.[122] Restricted to 2,000 square miles of tribal reserve, their landholdings were a mere fraction

---

[118] Cited in Paul Weiler, 'Forming Responsible Trade Unions: The Colonial Office, Colonial Labour and the Trades Union Congress', *Radical History Review,* 28–30 (1984), 367–92.

[119] Quotation taken from J. Lonsdale, 'Constructing Mau Mau', *TRHS* 40 (1990), 239–60. See also Lonsdale, 'Mau Maus of the Mind: Making Mau Mau and Remaking Kenya', *JAH* 31/3 (1990), 393–421; and D. Kennedy, 'Constructing the Colonial Myth of Mau Mau', *International Journal of African Historical Studies,* 25/2 (1992), 241–60.

[120] The term 'settlers', while a convenient shorthand, is potentially misleading. In Kenya the actual number of 'real' settlers, i.e. those farming the land, was relatively small; many of the remaining British people living in the colony Kenya are better described as career expatriates.

[121] Anderson, *Histories of the Hanged,* 22. Kenya's white settler population grew from 3,175 in 1911 to 12,529 in 1926. By 1952 there were 42,000 white Europeans living in the country. See B. Berman, *Control and Crisis in Colonial Kenya: The Dialectic of Domination* (Athens, Ohio, 1996), 130.

[122] J. Newsinger, *The Blood Never Dried: A People's History of the British Empire* (London, 2006), 185.

of what the settlers held, yet they numbered approximately a quarter of a million, compared to Kenya's sixty thousand or so white settlers. Leading critics of the settlers' fervent racism included Dr Norman Leys, a medical officer in the colony (1905–13); W. McGregor Ross, Director of Public Health (1900–22); and J. H. Oldham, Secretary of the International Missionary Council. Each of these men had questioned whether 'white civilization' was in fact Africa's best hope.

Prior to the Hola camp massacre of 3 March 1959, however, much of the violence against Mau Mau was ignored by the news media at home. While the British public would have been conscious of deaths on the British side—a dozen European soldiers, fifty European police, and thirty or so settlers—it is not at all clear that they would have had much comprehension of the thousand Kikuyu hanged, and tens of thousands of Kikuyu either killed in action or interned. Why, then, were people in Britain so blind to what was happening in Kenya until the end of the decade?

Long before Mau Mau, Kenya's settlers, a mixture of urban-based businessmen, professionals and government employees, as well as landholding farmers, had launched a highly effective public relations campaign.[123] Working with the colonial government, their main goal was to propagate more widely in Britain the view that European leadership was vital to African progress.[124] With anti-colonial agitation mounting across the Gold Coast, Nigeria, and the West Indies, Kenya's settlers were acutely aware that they were living in a changing world. The Kenya Association, founded in 1932, advertised the attractions of Kenya to prospective settlers, and lobbied for their interests at home. It distributed thousands of pamphlets, guidebooks, and postcards, with titles such as 'Kenya: the Land Where Life is Still Worth Living' and 'Kenya: Britain's Fairest Colony'. The Association's work was ably supported by Elspeth Huxley. After growing up on her parents' coffee farm near Nairobi, she left Kenya at the age of 18 to forge a career writing about Africa.[125] Author of a celebratory two-volume

---

[123] The following two paragraphs are partly based on Will Jackson's path-breaking study into mental illness and social marginality amongst Kenya's settler population: 'White Man's Country? Kenya Colony and the Making of a Myth', *Journal of East African Studies*, 5/2 (2001), 344–68.

[124] C. J. Morris, 'The Projection of Britain's New Empire in Africa, 1939–1948' (University of Leeds, PhD Thesis, 1995); R. Smyth, 'The Genesis of Public Relations in British Colonial Practice', *Public Relations Review*, 27 (2001), 149–61.

[125] C. S. Nicholls, *Elspeth Huxley: A Biography* (London, 2002), 93–4 and Lassner, *Colonial Strangers*, 118–60.

biography of Hugh Cholmondeley, third Baron Delamere,[126] the 'founding father' of colonial Kenya, she stated their case forcefully and sympathetically, a passionate advocate of greater powers for Europeans, especially over matters concerning Africans.[127]

Accompanying this public relations campaign was a drive to promote Kenya as a tourist destination.[128] By 1950 about a million Britons were travelling abroad each year, and there was much money to be made from foreign travel, both for tourist agencies at home and for favoured destinations overseas. Tourist brochures, guides and handbooks were issued by the East African Tourist Travel Association, as well as by an array of Kenya publicity associations based in Nairobi and London.[129] Targeting British and other anglophone tourists, these agencies promoted particular, idealized visions of Africa and of the Europeans who lived and worked there. Thomas Cook, which had previously enjoyed a flourishing business in Egypt, opened a branch in Nairobi in 1932. Its monthly magazine, *The Traveller's Gazette*, ran features on hunting, railway journeys, wildlife, travel routes, scenery, and landscape. In addition to a wealth of 'factual' information on living costs, climate, and clothing, such material often contained potted, sanitized histories of Kenya, while invoking the freedom African travel offered from the routines and restrictions of metropolitan life. During the 1950s, the annual number of tourist arrivals in Kenya almost doubled from 24,000 to 45,000 people, and continued to climb steeply the following decade.[130]

It was in this context that the European Elected Members Organization (EEMO) appeared in October 1952. In conjunction with the Kenya Association, EEMO raised over £20,000 for a 'Truth for Kenya' campaign, involving press releases, lectures, media interviews, and parliamentary lobbying, all of which 'underscored the danger of Mau Mau to white civilised society in Kenya'.[131]

---

[126] The title summed up Huxley's views: *White Man's Country* (1935). See also *Settlers of Kenya* (1948). Later publications, such as *Red Strangers* (1939), arguably took greater account of African perspectives.

[127] K. Tidrick, *Empire and the English Character* (London, 1990), 143.

[128] See esp. J. Ouma, *The Evolution of Tourism in East Africa* (Nairobi, 1970).

[129] The Kenya and Uganda railways; the East African Publicity Association (f. 1938); the Kenya Information Office (f. 1939); the East Africa Tourist Travel Association (f. 1947); the Joint East Africa Board; and the Nairobi City Council—in addition to the aforementioned, Kenya Association and Electors' Union, individual hotels and lodges, and private firms. See Jackson, 'White Man's Country?', 59–66.

[130] Ouma, *Evolution of Tourism*, 27.

[131] Kennedy, 'Constructing the Colonial Myth of Mau Mau', 256–7.

During the Emergency, much of the British press appears to have taken its cue from these settler organizations and their metropolitan sympathizers.[132] Papers of all political shades were filled with atrocity stories of the terrible brutality of Mau Mau. Oath taking was among the most popular topics. On 8 October 1952, under the headline 'Death for Disobedience', *The Times* told its readers about the multiple oaths a Kikuyu youth had been forced to swear: 'If I am asked to bring the head of a European and I refuse, this oath will kill me. If I am called at any time during the night and do not go, this oath will kill me. If I reveal any secrets of Africans who are Mau Mau members, this oath will kill me ... If I see anyone stealing European property I will not tell about it; instead I will assist him to hide it; if I refuse, this oath will kill me.'[133] Nor was such reporting confined to the right-wing press. Two months later the *Guardian* ran a story of a Kikuyu police reservist who told a court trying Jomo Kenyatta how he had been dragged into a room of a house, then had blood smeared on his forehead and hips in the form of a cross seven times, as he was circled by Mau Mau initiators and forced to take the oath.[134]

Officials and settlers did not have everything their own way, however. As they knew only too well, public sympathy for Kenya's highly privileged European community could not be taken for granted. The Kenya novel, the 'pulp fiction of its day', probably did little to help their cause.[135] Tales of 'straying husbands, illicit liaisons and frustrated passions' may have put Kenya on the map of middlebrow culture. Yet such sensationalism was hardly appreciated by the settlers themselves.[136] Indeed, when the novelist

---

[132] *The Times*, for example, ran 433 news items on Mau Mau from 1952 to 1960, including 20 editorials.

[133] 'Mau Mau Youth's Seven Oaths. Death for Disobedience', *The Times* (8 Oct. 1952), 5.

[134] 'Mau Mau Ritual Described', *The Guardian* (12 Dec. 1952), 7. See also H. Adi and A. Ramamurthy, 'Fragments in the History of the Visual Culture of Anti-Colonial Struggle', in Faulkner and Ramamurthy (eds.), *Visual Culture and Decolonisation in Britain*, 245; Lonsdale, 'Mau Maus of the Mind', 399; and J. Lewis, '"Daddy Wouldn't Buy me a Mau Mau", The British Popular Press and the Demoralisation of Empire', in J. Lonsdale (ed.), *Mau Mau and Nationhood: Arms, Authority and Narration* (Oxford, 2003), 227–49. The fictional treatment of Mau Mau from metropolitan writers further reinforced these images and messages. See D. Maughan-Brown, *Land, Freedom and Fiction: History and Ideology in Kenya* (London, 1985), 49–179 and 'Myths on the March: The Kenyan and Zimbabwean Liberation Struggles in Colonial Fiction', *JSAS* 9/1 (1982), 93–117.

[135] J. Lonsdale, 'Kenya: Home County and African Frontier' in R. Bickers (ed.), *OHBE Companion Series: Settlers and Expatriates: Britons over the Seas* (Oxford, 2010).

[136] See C. J. D. Duder, 'Love and the Lions: The Image of White Settlement in Kenya in Popular Fiction, 1919–1939', *African Affairs*, 90 (1991), 427–38 and T. R. Knipp, 'Kenya's Literary Ladies and the Mythologizing of the White Highlands', *South Atlantic Review*, 55/1 (1990), 1–16.

Nora Strange toured the colony in 1932 she was held partly responsible for Kenya's reputation as 'a place in the sun for shady people'.[137]

Nor were initial British press reports about Mau Mau unequivocal in their support for the settlers. Criticism from leftist periodicals was predictable, but 'much of the mainstream press also viewed settler calls for law and order with suspicion'.[138] Popular right-wing newspapers, in particular the *Daily Mail*, used lurid photographs to depict the barbarity and primitiveness of Mau Mau. Yet, at the same time, the *Daily Mirror*'s leading investigative journalist, James Cameron, was at pains to distance his paper's readers from the 'racial arrogance' of Kenya's Europeans, and the brute force they used to suppress any form of opposition. Cameron's articles were increasingly critical of the foundations of British policy in Africa which, he argued, was failing to address the Emergency's political and economic causes.

Coverage of Kenya in the British press waxed and waned during the 1950s. It was not until March 1959 that the 'moment of imperial implosion' finally came.[139] The exposure of brutality at the Hola detention camp led to a public outcry. Detainees refusing to undertake forced labour were attacked by guards, and eleven of them beaten to death. How far the critics were encouraged by the knowledge that incoming Colonial Secretary Iain Macleod, who took up office in October, was intent upon accommodating moderate African nationalists, and hence willing for his opponents in the colonial administration and settler society to be compromised by the Hola camp revelations, is a moot point.[140] What is not in doubt is that, by the end of the 1950s, Macmillan could be heard criticizing the settlers for their decadence. They were the butt of contemporary satire (for example, in Vicky's cartoons in the *Evening Standard*); the Gallup polls were registering less and less enthusiasm for their cause; and a new group of younger, professional middle-class Tory MPs, for whom Hola had been 'characteristic of a muddled reactionary approach to colonial affairs',[141] appeared much

---

[137] N. Strange, *Kenya Today* (London, 1934). See also E. Waugh, *Remote People* (London, 1931) for a discussion of both the indigenous and settler populations in Africa.

[138] Kennedy, 'Constructing the Colonial Myth of Mau Mau'.

[139] S. Carruthers, 'Being Beastly to the Mau Mau', *TCBH* 16/4 (2005), 495.

[140] Newsinger, *Blood Never Dried*, 193. See also P. Murphy, *Party Politics and Decolonisation: The Conservative Party and British Colonial policy in Tropical Africa, 1951–1964* (Oxford, 1995), 58–85.

[141] D. Sandbrook, *Never Had It So Good: A History of Britain from Suez to the Beatles* (2006), 290.

less susceptible to 'kith and kin' sentiment in Africa from which they were increasingly to disengage.[142]

Nor was the value of Britain's other African colonies still self-evident either. In this regard, it is worth recalling the work of the Colonial Development Commission. Traditionally expected to pay their own way, the colonies' demands on the British taxpayer amounted to no more than £3 million in 1930. By 1950, the figure had risen to £40 million, as a greatly expanded cadre of specialists and technicians sought to provide the colonies with the necessary public infrastructure for economic growth. However, in the pursuit of a new note of partnership and development, there were serious miscalculations in colonial policy, the best known of which is the costly groundnuts scheme in Tanganyika. The scheme was supposed to transform Tanganyika's economy by turning 3 million acres of land into a vast peanut farm, thereby demonstrating the continuing ambitions of the colonial state in tropical Africa. £36 million was spent before the experts departed, defeated by the soil and the pests, with nothing having been done to ease Britain's vegetable oil and fat shortages. It was not only the Conservative Party that jumped on the episode, as a handy stick with which to beat Attlee's government: music and variety hall artists and performers on the radio used it as fodder for their comedy too. The whole affair did much to discredit Labour's post-war vision for the Commonwealth, especially in Africa, as an engine of economic development.[143] As Evelyn Waugh was later moved to remark of the scheme, 'the fault was pride; the hubris which leads elected persons to believe that a majority at the polls endows them with inordinate abilities'.[144]

Legacies

The longer-term effects of the retreat from empire upon the British people, emotionally, temperamentally, and psychologically, have yet to be adequately

---

[142] Thompson, *The Empire Strikes Back?*, 213. For the 'hard-nosed pragmatism' that led the centre-right of the Tory party to disengage from kith and kin in Africa, see J. Lewis and P. Murphy, '"The Old Pals Protection Society?" The Colonial Office and the British Press in the Eve of Decolonisation', in C. Kaul (ed.), *Media and the British Empire* (London, 2006), 60–1.

[143] J. S. Hogendorn and K. M. Scott, 'The East African Groundnut Scheme: Lessons of a Large-Scale Agricultural Failure', *African Economic History*, 10 (1981), 81–115.

[144] E. Waugh, *A Tourist in Africa*, in N. Shakespeare (ed.), *Waugh Abroad: Collected Travel Writing* (New York, 2003), 1007.

addressed in the historiography, even if several social and political commentators have freely expressed opinions on the matter. Reflecting on the 'national condition' during the 1980s, the journalist Peter Scott described Britain as 'an imperial but provincial nation'.[145] He ventured that Britain was struggling to come to terms with the loss of its empire, and that Britain's persistent need for the 'clouds of imperial glory' reflected the artificiality of its national identity, which, unlike the ethnic identities of the English, Welsh, or Scots, lacked deep roots in its lands or histories. In a similar vein, the former cabinet minister, Tony Benn, boldly proclaimed Britain to be the 'last colony' of the empire, and the British people the last to await liberation. Benn was convinced that the development of a truly democratic culture had been stifled by Britain's mistaken belief that it could continue to be a global power.[146]

One section of society that had to negotiate the winding down of British rule was the civil servants responsible previously for administering it.[147] How effectively did post-war British society reabsorb these people? Between 1947 and 1997, approximately 25,000 officials returned to Britain, the vast majority arriving before the end of the 1960s—compared to France the numbers were fairly small, there being no significant 'pied-noir' community.[148] Returning British officials faced the challenge of finding suitable alternative employment. 'Hard-headed realism rather than misty-eyed nostalgia' perhaps best describes the response of British society to their plight.[149] This was partly a matter of their qualifications (which were not always recognized back home), and partly of what they were seen to represent. The very label 'ex-' colonial civil servants, widely used at the time, seemed to signify they were of the past. Thought to have dealt only with 'backward' or uneducated peoples, to be accustomed to lives of luxury, and to be prejudiced against commerce and industry, they were seemingly out of step with 'modern' Britain.

---

[145] P. Scott, *Knowledge and Nation* (Edinburgh, 1990), 171.

[146] T. Benn, 'Britain as a Colony', in T. Mullin (ed.), *Arguments for Democracy* (London, 1981), 3–17.

[147] S. Stockwell, 'The Reception of Returning Colonial Service Personnel in Britain at the end of Empire', paper presented at a British history conference at the University of Lille, 2005.

[148] Many of these officials had also, of course, been 'out there' for relatively short periods of time because the British colonial service had expanded so rapidly in the late 1940s.

[149] Ibid.; E. Buettner, *Empire Families: Britons and Late Imperial India* (Oxford, 2005), 188–96.

Indeed, one does not have to search very far for some rather unflattering literary portrayals of colonial administrators at this time. Several of W. Somerset Maugham's short stories, for example, spoke in salacious detail of the moral failures of Europeans in Malaya; unsurprisingly, he won few friends among the colony's civil servants and planters as a result.[150] The sense among some of these returning service families that British society was at best indifferent, and at worst hostile, towards them was thus keenly felt, which may go some way to explain why so many 'ex-colonials' preferred to mix socially with others of their kind when back in Britain.[151] Nor was this sense of dislocation experienced only by the men: for the wives of colonial officials, reintegration into British society often entailed an unwelcome increase in routine domestic responsibilities. The experiences of colonial children are less well documented, yet memoirs of those who grew up in the colonies recall returning to lives of 'genteel poverty' in suburban semis, and a feeling of being different from other children at school.

It is, however, easy to fall into the trap of being overly negative and pessimistic about the fate of colonial returnees. In general officials coming back to Britain were relatively easily absorbed into a rapidly expanding managerial and professional class in the 1960s—an era of full employment. Indeed, as one study reminds us, many of these individuals went on to enjoy considerable success in domestic public service, diplomacy, academia, and business, the versatility and service ethic they had displayed in the colonies now helping them to launch second careers back home.[152]

The later 1950s and early 1960s are best viewed as twilight years during which the word empire gradually lost much of its resonance. As international liberalism, under the umbrella of the IMF (International Monetary Fund) and GATT (General Agreement on Tariffs and Trade), undermined the notion of empire as 'privileged economic space', so too in the cultural sphere there were significant discursive shifts in metropolitan thinking about the empire. Anthony Burgess's trio of novels—*Time for a Tiger* (1956), *The Enemy in the Blanket* (1958), and *Beds in the East* (1959)—was a harbinger of what was to come: namely, a growing sense of the largely

---

[150] A. Curtis, *The Pattern of Maugham: A Critical Portrait* (London, 1974), 154–75.

[151] See e.g. the memoir of C. Baker, who served in Kenya, the Gold Coast, Cyprus, and Nyasaland, returning to Britain in 1961: *Retreat from Empire: Sir Robert Armitage in Africa and Cyprus* (London, 1998).

[152] A. Kirk-Greene, 'Decolonisation: The Ultimate Diaspora', *JCH* 36/1 (2001), 133–51.

superficial and transient impact of British rule, especially when it came to imparting the kind of values that the 'civilizing mission' had professed. As colonial dependencies won their independence, frequently after intense internal struggles, and British newspapers reported coups, one-party rule and corruption in one newly independent state after another, it is perhaps hardly surprising the imperial ideal lost much of its allure and that the British public began to disengage from empire. When asked their opinion on aspects of overseas rule by Gallup, for example, many people simply felt unable or unwilling to respond.[153]

In other quarters too, change was in the air. National service, which lasted from 1945 to 1963, exposed a generation of young men to the empire who would not otherwise have known it in 'peacetime'. In Egypt, Malaya, Kenya, and Cyprus national servicemen formed part of British military contingents. As a result of terrorist attacks and counter-insurgency operations in these regions, almost four hundred men were killed in action. Although it is clear that national service was frequently a life-changing experience, the impact of a posting to the colonies upon those conscripted would repay further study.[154] There appears to have been little public outcry when these 'civilian soldiers' were sent into action in the far reaches of Britain's shrinking empire.[155] Rather, surviving memoirs suggest that, whatever their political disposition, many national servicemen found themselves adopting a 'typical white settler mentality', which not only denigrated the 'enemy' but precluded any questioning of the rights and wrongs of the colonial situation.[156]

[153] J. D. B. Miller, 'The End of Bombast and Pessimism', *JCH* 15/1 (1980), 53–65, at 60; G. Woodcock, *Who Killed the British Empire?: An Inquest* (London, 1974), 313.

[154] D. French, *Army, Empire and Cold War: British Military Policy, c 1945–1970* (forthcoming).

[155] Sandbrook, *Never Had It So Good: A History of Britain from Suez to the Beatles, 1956–63*, 150, 154. Although the execution of two regular British soldiers by the militant Zionist group, Irgun, in the British mandate of Palestine on 29 July 1947 did produce a public outcry in Britain: it was widely covered and roundly condemned by the press, and led to attacks on synagogues and recognizable Jewish properties in urban centres. See B. Bowyer, *Terror out of Zion: Irgun Zvai Leumi, LEHI, and the Palestine Underground, 1929–1949* (New York, 1977); S. Zadka, *Blood in Zion: How the Jewish Guerrillas Drove the British out of Palestine* (London, 1995). For the 'soul-tearing fury' towards the Jewish people in Palestine that the hangings produced in fellow British soldiers, see the memoir of Trevor Hall (Royal Artillery, 1945–8), *Enduring the Hour: a British Soldier in Palestine, 1946–1947* (Lincolnshire, 2005), 44.

[156] Recollections of Peter Burns in B. S. Johnson (ed.), *All Bull: the National Servicemen* (London, 1973), 88–9; recollections of Gerry Lynch in G. Forty (ed.), *Called Up: A National Service Scrapbook* (London, 1955), 263–71. See also J. Newsinger, 'The Military Memoir in British Imperial Culture: The Case of Malaya', *Race & Class*, 35/3 (1994), 47–62.

Certainly such an outlook seems to have been commonplace in the years immediately after the Second World War. By the time of the Suez Crisis, however, there is evidence to suggest that such attitudes were changing. Soldiers sent to occupy the canal later recalled questioning why they were there, and how they had felt the pointlessness and absurdity of it all.[157] In Egypt, and elsewhere, their confusion was compounded by officers in the Regular Army, who rarely took it upon themselves to explain to the troops the exact reasons for their presence or why they were involved in the fighting.[158]

What, then, happened to those values, such as 'duty', 'loyalty', 'hierarchy', and 'authority', previously considered to be the social bedrock of empire, yet now increasingly called into question? It is tempting to link the erosion of these values to the process of decolonization. After all, 'within scarcely a generation' the 'whole hierarchical embrace of empire' had been dismantled,[159] such that the British aristocracy could no longer credibly claim 'to be the national and imperial ruling class by hereditary right'.[160] In similar vein, a recent study of the post-war British cinema argues that Suez was crucial in changing people's attitude toward military authority, and in ushering in a new willingness to challenge old, deferential values.[161]

Yet the decline of deference was clearly experienced elsewhere in Europe at this time. Rather than posit a causal relationship with decolonization, therefore, it may be more instructive to ask what it was about the retreat from empire that made the process distinctive in Britain's case. The aftermath of the Suez Crisis, discussed in more detail elsewhere in this volume, sheds some light on this question. Among those who felt that Suez epitomized what was wrong with post-war Britain were the 'Angry Young Men' of the post-war era. Most famously, John Osborne and Alan Sillitoe captured the pessimism and disillusionment of the late 1950s and early 1960s, and especially the lack of opportunities for the working class.[162] For both men,

---

[157] See e.g. D. McCullin, *Unreasonable Behaviour: An Autobiography* (London, 1990), esp. ch. 6; Thompson, *The Empire Strikes Back?*, 210; T. R. Royle, *National Service: The Best Years of Their Lives* (London, 2002), 150, 154.

[158] Royle, *National Service*, 156, 172.

[159] Sandbrook, *Never Had It So Good*.

[160] D. Cannadine, *Ornamentalism: How the British Saw Their Empire* (Oxford, 2001), 5–6, 154, 166–7, 172–3 at 173.

[161] S. Harper and V. Porter, *British Cinema of the 1950s: The Decline of Deference* (Oxford, 2007), 243–65.

[162] See e.g. A. Sillitoe, *Key to the Door* (London, 1961).

Suez provided a licence to rail against the arrogance and ineptitude of Britain's ruling class.[163]

Osborne (1929–94) was born into genteel poverty in South Wales. A jobbing actor who wrote his first play in 1949, he was one of the most important talents to emerge in British theatre in the fifties.[164] His chief subject was England and the English, and he was not afraid to challenge established attitudes and beliefs—he was among the first playwrights to question the point of the monarchy on a prominent public stage. *Look Back in Anger* (1956) was a hit in the bookshops (hundreds of thousands of copies were sold) as well as an acclaimed play. It told the story of Jimmy Porter, under siege in an attic flat with his wife Alison, mistress Helena, and chum Cliff, on a series of provincial Sundays. Jimmy's hatred for the middle-class establishment and its values is palpable, and his targets include the Sunday papers, the social system, Conservative MPs, phoney politeness, and nostalgia for the imperial past.[165] Interestingly, this anger was pitched oddly against his respect for his wife's father, Colonel Redfern, who had returned from India after 1947 and is one of the few figures for whom Jimmy shows any affection—a representative of a time when there were still causes to fight for. Following the smash hit of *Look Back in Anger*, Osborne's next play, *The Entertainer* (1957), used the decline of the music hall as a metaphor for the dwindling of Britain's power and its transient grip on empire.[166] The play was another great success, given added political bite when Laurence Olivier, leading member of the theatrical establishment, took the key role of the charismatic yet disreputable music hall star, Archie Rice. The humiliating military fiasco of Suez was very much the backdrop to the performance, the Board of the Royal Court only agreeing to it being staged after considerable debate.

Sillitoe (1928–2010) was born in Nottingham of working-class parents. From 1946 to 1949 he did national service as an RAF wireless operator in Malaya, called upon to direct Lincoln bombers towards Communist guerrillas and their transmitters. He later recalled how the war against the MRLA (Malayan Races Liberation Army) 'had nothing to do with us', and how he

---

[163] M. Donnelly, *Sixties Britain: Culture, Society and Politics* (Harlow, 2005), 25.
[164] Alongside Harold Pinter, Samuel Beckett, and John Arden.
[165] R. Hayman, *John Osborne* (London, 1968), 4.
[166] See D. Shellard, *The Golden Generation: New Light on Post-War British Theatre* (London and New Haven, 2008), 79–80 and *British Theatre Since the War* (London, 1999), 28, 82.

had deliberately provided less than accurate bearings so that the bombs missed their targets.[167] After demobilization, Sillitoe was hospitalized for eighteen months with tuberculosis: it was then that he began to write. His first novel, *Saturday Night and Sunday Morning*, published in 1958, provided a vivid portrait of masculinity and Nottinghamshire working-class life. Awarded the Authors' Club First Novel Award, it was made into a film starring Albert Finney, and then adapted as a stage play in 1964. Arthur Seaton, a young factory worker, faced with the end of his youthful philandering, is the anti-hero of the novel. Yet Arthur's opposition to authority is explained by a hatred of the government, and law and order, generally; notwithstanding the author's time in Malaya, Sillitoe explored social values as much through his sense of family and region as through the empire.[168]

The failings of the British governing elite that animated these 'Angry Young Men' further fuelled the television satire boom of the early sixties.[169] In *Beyond the Fringe* and *That Was The Week That Was* (*TW3*), David Frost, Peter Cook, Jonathan Miller, Dudley Moore, and Alan Bennett deployed the weapons of comedy to demolish the deference they so despised. Themselves part of a generation raised on notions of duty and service,[170] they nonetheless held up to scrutiny the props of British power—the monarchy, military, and empire—as well as the social structure they felt to have sustained it. Britain was viewed 'as a stifling, moribund place, held back by class prejudice and nostalgic complacency about its imperial past'.[171] In some of their sketches about Britain's pretensions to greatness a note of ambivalence underpins the exuberant and irreverent humour. Peter Cook's grandfather had worked for the Federated Malay States Railway, and his father as a District Officer in Nigeria; the ridicule he poured on the idea that African independence was the culmination of Britain's imperial mission was counterbalanced by his cynicism towards the legitimacy and motivations of colonial nationalist leaders.[172] But what helped to give their satire its edge was the way in which these comics confronted the decline in Britain's international status—the realization that Britain could no longer perform the role it once had, and that by trying to do so it was inevitably entering troubled waters. *TW3*'s parody of events that led up to emergency rule in Nyasaland is a case in point. It mercilessly derided the Macmillan

[167] Johnson (ed.), *All Bull*, 224–9.
[168] Sillitoe, *Key to the Door*, 352–446.
[169] Donnelly, *Sixties Britain*, 50.
[170] Ward, 'Echoes of Empire', 92.
[171] Donnelly, *Sixties Britain*, 69.
[172] Ward, 'Echoes of Empire', 97, 104–7.

government for its ready resort to imprisonment without trial, as well as for ignoring the findings of the Devlin Report and the Monckton Commission regarding African representation and Federation.[173]

Critical reflection on the state of the nation was not confined to the world of comedy. Cultural anxieties about Britain's economic performance and international status spread through the media and academia, as a range of analysts and commentators, each wedded to their own diagnoses and solutions, debated 'What's wrong with Britain?' Several new narratives of British state formation emerged at this time, all of which were integrally linked to perceptions of British power. Chief among these was the 'culture of decline'. As argued elsewhere in this volume, both the loss of empire, and Britain's previous reluctance to let go of it, could in theory be blamed for the sluggishness of its economy and its apparent lack of enterprise. However, it was the idea of 'overstretch'—of excessive overseas responsibilities and commitments—that came to dominate debate, and that drew commentators to the conclusion that imperial balance sheets were now badly overdrawn.[174] The waning of empire enthusiasm and the 'declinist' mindset of these decades were in fact inseparable, as the European Economic Community (EEC) and the so-called 'special relationship' with the United States gradually displaced the 'new' Commonwealth as symbols of modernity and progress.

In 1962, the Commonwealth also acquired its own institute. Opened by Queen Elizabeth II, in Holland Park, it was a successor to the Imperial Institute, which had struggled along for forty years as a scientific and propaganda outfit while failing to attract sufficient funding or visitors.[175] The Commonwealth Institute did not fare any better. Across Western Europe, the 1960s and 1970s were decades in which colonial museums were 'evacuating colonialism from their galleries' in search of 'new missions'.[176] For the Commonwealth Institute this meant, first and foremost, celebrating the cultural diversity of this new consortium of nations, and promoting greater knowledge of the newly independent states over which

---

[173] 'The Devlin Report: A Grimm Fairy Tale', in D. Frost and N. Sherrin, *That Was The Week That Was* (BBC Publications, 1963), 34–41.

[174] J. Tomlinson, 'The Decline of the Empire', *TCBH* 14/3 (2003), 201–21.

[175] M. Crinson, 'Imperial Story-Lands: Architecture and Display at the Imperial and Commonwealth Institutes', *Art History*, 22/1 (1999), 99–123; W. Golant, *Image of Empire: The Early History of the Imperial Institute, 1887–1925* (Exeter, 1984).

[176] R. Aldrich, 'Colonial Museums in a Post-Colonial Europe', *African and Black Diaspora*, 2/2 (2009), 137–56.

the Queen remained head. In reality, however, the Institute struggled from the start. There was limited support from the Commonwealth itself, and, as Britain edged towards accession to the EEC, its galleries seemed less and less relevant—many of the objects on display were actually returned to member states.

Since the early 1960s, a variety of post-imperial 'troubles' (several of which are considered elsewhere in this volume) have been intermittently salient in British public life. They include: the arrival of Asian refugees from Kenya, Uganda, and Malawi; the Rhodesia settler issue, and the fallout from the 1965 Unilateral Declaration of Independence; the 1973 oil 'crisis' and the ongoing legacy of the partition of Palestine; the 1982 Falklands War; and the anti-apartheid movement. By comparison, the twenty-first century's interest in the *history* of empire and Britain's imperial heritage has been less episodic, and as much evident in the cultural as the political sphere.

Above all, disentangling the multiple legacies of empire for a contemporary, postcolonial, and globalized world is a task that several national museums have taken up with alacrity. In 2002, the British Empire and Commonwealth Museum opened in Isambard Kingdom Brunel's railway building at Temple Meads in Bristol.[177] Like several other institutions, including the British Library, the National Maritime Museum, the National Portrait Gallery, and the Merseyside Maritime Museum, its galleries have sought to grapple with different aspects of Britain's imperial past, and, in so doing, to confront the thorny question of how we as a society reappraise and relate to it. When trying to present the colonial record, in all its variety and complexity, to a diverse and demanding public, all of these museums have been forced to recognize that the empire is still very much wrapped in feelings of pride, shame, anger, and guilt. With varying degrees of success, they have sought to reclaim the histories of minorities and their struggles against imperialism, to show how ethnic and racial identities have been inherited from the empire, and, above all, to catalogue the contribution of immigrants to British society. Curators and their advisory boards have, however, adopted different approaches. The Merseyside Maritime Museum, for example, was opened in 2007, the year marking the bicentenary of the abolition of the slave trade. Extensive consultation with local community groups brought out the sharply conflicting perceptions of what the slave trade

---

[177] Although the museum's main galleries are now closed, pending a planned relocation to London.

meant to Liverpudlians. Many white people in the city tended to see slavery's evils as having been overshadowed by the role played by abolitionists, whereas for black people slavery continued to evoke 'poignant and immediate memories of suffering, brutalisation and terror'. The director, David Fleming, thus shunned the idea of the museum as a 'neutral space', and openly declared that its mission was 'to help counter the disease of racism'.[178]

Meanwhile, over the last decade, other institutions have been charged with serving up positive, nostalgic portrayals of imperialism, and of a wilful amnesia towards the more egregious and embarrassing aspects of colonial rule. Some critics see this attitude as deeply ingrained in the British psyche. According to the media commentator Yasmin Alibhai-Brown, for example, 'what holds us back from confronting the truths about the Empire is not censorship or self-censorship, but an entire historical legacy which dwells on the good that the Empire spread, and which is still sustained by traditionalists'.[179] Clearly, as far as empire is concerned, the past persists. Half a century on from the major episodes of decolonization, the British people still have a living relationship to their imperial past, coupled with a new-found curiosity about the world that the British helped to create. This should not surprise us. For so long as 'new' empires and imperialisms are seen to be part of the current international order, exploring historical experiences of colonialism, and their continuing effects on former colonizers (as well as the colonized), will continue to be as much an ethical and emotional, as an academic and professional process, informed by injustices, ideologies, and interests that, for better or worse, are perceived to be shaping today's world.

---

[178] A. S. Thompson, *Living the Past: Public Memories of Empire in the 21st Century*, Trevor Reese Memorial Lecture 2007 (London, 2008). See also A. Woollacott, 'Making Empire Visible or Making Colonialism Visible?: The Struggle for the British Imperial Past', *British Scholar*, 1/2 (2009), 160–2, comparing the Merseyside Maritime Museum with Bristol's Empire and Commonwealth Museum's 'Breaking the Chains' exhibition, the author claims the latter gave greater emphasis to the more positive aspects of imperial history. The premise of the comparison is questioned by Stephen Howe, 'Making Colonialisms Visible—Or, the Evidence of Things Not Seen', *British Scholar*, 1/2 (2009), 4–11. See also D. Paton and J. Webster, 'Remembering Slave Trade Abolitions: Reflections on 2007 in International Perspective', *Slavery and Abolition*, 30 (2009), 164, which suggests that the vast majority of institutions have been responsive to recent scholarly work, for example in 'foregrounding the paternalist and racist overtones of abolitionist propaganda'.

[179] Y. Alibhai-Brown, 'Personally, I'm all for a Museum of the Empire', *Independent* (17 June 2002), 15.

Select Bibliography

J. M. Brown and Wm. R. Louis (eds.), *The Oxford History of the British Empire*, iv. *The Twentieth Century* (Oxford, 1999).

S. Constantine, *Emigrants and Empire: British Settlement in the Dominions between the Wars* (Manchester, 1990).

S. Faulkner and A. Ramurthy (eds.), *Visual Culture and Decolonisation in Britain* (Aldershot, 2006).

C. Hall and S. Rose (eds.), *At Home with the Empire: Metropolitan Culture and the Imperial World* (Cambridge, 2006).

B. Harrison, *Seeking a Role: The United Kingdom, 1951–1970* (Oxford, 2009).

A. G. Hopkins, 'Rethinking Decolonisation', *Past & Present*, 200/1 (2008), 211–47.

S. Howe, *Anti-Colonialism in British Politics: The Left and the End of Empire, 1918–1964* (Oxford, 1993).

P. Lassner, *Colonial Strangers: Women Writing the End of the British Empire* (New Brunswick, NJ, 2004).

J. M. MacKenzie, *Propaganda and Empire: The Manipulation of British Public Opinion 1880–1960* (Manchester, 1984).

B. Porter, *Absent-Minded Imperialists: Empire, Society and Culture in Britain* (Oxford, 2004).

D. Sandbrook, *Never Had It So Good: A History of Britain from Suez to the Beatles* (London, 2005).

A. S. Thompson, *The Empire Strikes Back?: The Impact of Imperialism on Britain from the Mid Nineteenth Century* (Harlow, 2005).

R. Visram, *Asians in Britain: 400 Years of History* (London, 2002).

S. Ward (ed.), *British Culture and the End of Empire* (Manchester, 2001).

W. Webster, *Englishness and Empire, 1939–1965* (Oxford, 2005).

8

Empire, Nation, and National Identities

Krishan Kumar

Banal Nationalism, Banal Imperialism

Surveying the treatment of empire—specifically the British empire—in films and on television in Britain since the 1960s, Jeffrey Richards notes that it was almost wholly critical and hostile.[1] This was against a background of more or less general ignorance, among the British population at large, of what the British empire was or had been. At the same time the 1997 poll revealing that ignorance recorded a surprising degree of pride—more than 70 per cent of respondents—in the fact that Britain had had an empire. Sixty per cent also regretted the loss of empire, and an almost equally large percentage—58 per cent—believed that the empire had done 'more good than harm' in her colonies. 'How is it', asks Richards, 'that after thirty years of exposure to largely hostile depictions of the Empire and in the light of demonstrated and colossal factual ignorance about it, the public are still proud of their vanished Empire?' He attributes this to a largely English 'crisis of national identity'—the Scots, Welsh, and Irish are, he thinks, more sure of themselves—and comments that 'the English retreat into a nostalgia for an empire which they barely remember and of which they know almost nothing.'[2]

It is interesting that some famous polls conducted by the Colonial Office in 1947 and 1948, when the British empire was still more or less intact, revealed an almost equal degree of popular ignorance of the empire—for

[1] I should like to thank Andrew Thompson for his very helpful remarks on an earlier draft. Thanks too to John Darwin for his stimulating contribution to the Nuffield College seminar in April 2008 when the individual chapters to this volume were discussed.

[2] J. Richards, 'Imperial Heroes for a Post-Imperial Age: Films and the End of Empire', in Stuart Ward (ed.), *British Culture and the End of Empire* (Manchester, 2001), 143. The poll Richards refers to was conducted by Gallup for the *Daily Telegraph*; see the *Daily Telegraph* (26 Aug. 1997).

instance, few people could name a single colony (one man suggested Lincolnshire), and some people thought that the United States was still part of the empire. Again, though, this was combined with a general sense of the importance of empire and the special responsibilities it placed upon Britain.[3] Evidently consciously held knowledge of empire, as tapped by opinion polls and the like, may be only one way of understanding the influence of empire on the general population of a society. It may even be the least important way.

All this indicates the difficulty and complexity of assessing the impact of empire—especially, in this case, the impact on the home society. On the one hand there are those—largely but not only of the 'postcolonial' school—who are inclined to see empire everywhere, suffusing the consciousness of the population in a multitude of significant ways.[4] On the other hand—partly in reaction to what they see as unexamined and largely ideological assertions on the part of the postcolonialists— are the sceptics who think that the impact of empire has been vastly exaggerated, and that its long-term influence has been slight.[5]

---

[3] See J. M. MacKenzie, 'The Persistence of Empire in Metropolitan Culture', in S. Ward (ed.), *British Culture and the End of Empire* (Manchester, 2001), 28. For a critical discussion of this poll and other surveys of the time, see A. S. Thompson, *The Empire Strikes Back? The Impact of Imperialism on Britain from the Mid-Nineteenth Century* (Harlow, 2005), 207–9. As Thompson remarks, 'people did not need to know a lot about [the empire] in order to have an opinion on it'.

[4] See e.g. J. M. MacKenzie, *Propaganda and Empire: The Manipulation of British Public Opinion 1880–1960* (Manchester, 1984); C. Hall, *Civilising Subjects: Metropole and Colony in the English Imagination 1830–1867* (Chicago, 2002); A. Burton (ed.), *After the Imperial Turn: Thinking with and through the Nation* (Durham, NC, 2003); K. Wilson (ed.), *A New Imperial History: Culture, Identity and Modernity in Britain and the Empire 1660–1840* (Cambridge, 2004); P. Gilroy, *After Empire: Melancholia or Convivial Culture?* (Abingdon, 2004); C. Hall and S. O. Rose (eds.), *At Home with the Empire: Metropolitan Culture and the Imperial World* (Cambridge, 2006). Bernard Porter—following MacKenzie—provocatively calls this group the 'Saidists', as followers of the postcolonial theorist Edward Said, particularly his influential *Culture and Imperialism* (New York, 1993): B. Porter, *The Absent-Minded Imperialists: Empire, Society, and Culture in Britain* (Oxford, 2004), p. ix. For postcolonialism generally, see R. J. C. Young, *Postcolonialism: An Historical Introduction* (Oxford, 2001). John MacKenzie, however, is no Saidist; nor is A. G. Hopkins, who nevertheless believes that 'images of empire and the imperial ideal...entered the British soul and influenced its character' in a lasting way. A. G. Hopkins, 'Back to the Future: From National History to Imperial History', *Past & Present*, 164/1 (1999), 214.

[5] See esp. Porter, *Absent-Minded Imperialists* and—though more cautiously—B. Nasson, *Britannia's Empire: Making a British World* (Stroud, 2004); R. Price, 'One Big Thing: Britain, Its Empire, and Their Imperial Culture', *Journal of British Studies* (*JBS*), 45/3 (2006), 602–27. A cautious note was also earlier struck by P. J. Marshall, 'Imperial Britain', *Journal of Imperial*

It is unlikely that the differences between these two schools of thought will ever be resolved. For they approach the same question—what has been the impact of empire on the home population of the colonizing society?—with very different methodologies. The one reads deep meaning in the culture of the imperial society, scouring it for the almost Freudian slips and symptoms of deep-seated and largely unconsciously held attitudes and assumptions. It is these, the postcolonialists, who are most likely to stress the pervasive influence of empire, manifested in such attitudes as racism. The other, more empirically minded school examines the more readily available evidence of school textbooks, novels, the popular culture of film and television, and the utterances of public figures. It is on the basis of this latter approach that some—by no means all—have concluded that the British empire has left surprisingly few marks on British society, at least among the general population.

Theorists and scholars of nationalism and ethnicity have recently begun to look more closely at the actual way in which national and other collective identities play out in the everyday lives of individuals. There is talk of 'banal nationalism', the way in which, on a daily basis, 'the nation is indicated, or "flagged", in the lives of its citizenry'.[6] On stamps and coins, in the national flags flown on private homes and in filling stations, in the statues and monuments that, barely noticed, are scattered throughout the major cities, in daily school rituals, such as the 'pledge of allegiance' in US public schools, the nation is repeatedly and routinely drummed into the consciousness of people—but at so banal a level as to be virtually unnoticed. This is 'mindless', as opposed to 'mindful', nationalism. It involves not simply the collective amnesia with regard to certain past events that Ernest Renan saw as necessary for the existence of nations, but a further act of forgetting, a

---

and Commonwealth History (JICH), 23/3 (1995), esp. 380, 392–3—though Marshall stressed more the lack of overt discussions of the empire in public life, and the relative ease with which Britain wound up its empire, than the absence of an impact on British society, which indeed he regarded as profound (385). For a judicious survey of the whole debate on the influence of empire on British society, see S. J. Potter, 'Empire, Cultures and Identities in Nineteenth- and Twentieth-Century Britain', History Compass, 5/1 (2007), 51–71; see also Duncan Bell, 'Empire and International Relations in Victorian Political Thought', Historical Journal, 49/1 (2006), 292–4; R. Drayton, 'Putting the British into the Empire', JBS 44 (2005), 187–94. A fair-minded and plausible account, indicating the many connections between empire and British society, is Thompson, The Empire Strikes Back?.

[6] M. Billig, Banal Nationalism (London, 1995), 6.

parallel 'forgetting of the present' that results from frequent, daily repetition.[7] That does not, however, mean that the attitudes and sentiments of nationalism are not latently there, waiting to be activated, as for instance in times of national emergency.

It has similarly been argued that there is a perceptual gap between the pronouncements of nationalist statesman and intellectuals and the 'everyday ethnicity' of ordinary people as they go about their daily lives. People have many other identities than national ones—as spouses, friends, co-workers, members of different classes and religions. For much of the time national and ethnic identities are not particularly 'salient' to individuals in the business of getting on with their lives. But several things—an openly nationalist mayor intent on favouring a particular national group, a flare-up of ethnic violence across the border—can bring home to individuals the fact of their ethnicity or nationhood and propel them into action.[8]

We need to bear this in mind when considering the question of empire and identities. Nation and empire are at one level divergent but, at other levels, also convergent phenomena.[9] Just as there is banal nationalism, there can also be 'banal imperialism'. The way in which the British empire affected the sense of identity of the various groups within Britain cannot be gained from any simple source, whether conscious recollection and self-identification or the assertions of statesmen and other public figures. We have to consider the multiplicity of ways—public and private—in which the empire impacted on the lives of individuals and shaped their sense of themselves.[10] It is even possible that we have to go beyond the individual altogether—whether as one or many—and consider identity as a matter of structure or position, rather than of consciousness. There is no guarantee that even then we will come up with definite and incontestable conclusions. But we will at least have indicated the 'field of meaning' within which individuals in

---

[7] M. Billig, *Banal Nationalism* (London, 1995), 38.

[8] For the general argument, see Rogers Brubaker, *Ethnicity without Groups* (Cambridge, Mass., 2004). For a detailed application in one case, the town of Cluj in Transylvania, see R. Brubaker, M. Feischmidt, J. Fox, and L. Grancea, *Nationalist Politics and Everyday Ethnicity in a Transylvanian Town* (Princeton, 2006).

[9] See further on this, see K. Kumar, 'Empires and Nations: Convergence or Divergence?', in George Steinmetz (ed.), *Sociology and Empire* (Durham, 2011).

[10] A sensitive study that indicates how this might be done is L. Colley, *Captives: Britain, Empire, and the World, 1600–1850* (New York, 2004); see also M. Jasanoff, *Edge of Empire: Conquest and Collecting in the East 1750–1850* (New York, 2005).

Britain were able to understand themselves and form some idea of their collective identities.

Nationalism and Imperialism

Benedict Anderson, in his influential *Imagined Communities*, suggests that the European imperial experience was largely a matter of class, 'as suggested by the equanimity with which metropolitan popular classes eventually shrugged off the "losses" of the colonies ... In the end, it is always the ruling classes, bourgeois certainly, but above all aristocratic, that long mourn the empires.'[11] A similar suggestion had been made by George Orwell in the 1940s when he remarked that 'it is quite true that the English are hypocritical about their Empire. In the working class this hypocrisy takes the form of not knowing that the Empire exists.'[12] More recently Bernard Porter has mounted a full-scale assault on the idea that the empire was a formative experience of British society as a whole. He too argues that it was mainly the people who ran the empire, the public-school educated upper-middle and upper classes—the 'Prefects', he calls them—who were most affected by it and who most regret its passing.

[T]he empire, huge and significant as it was, did not require the involvement of any large section of British society for it to live and even grow. So long as a minority of men (and their female helpmeets) was committed enough to actually

---

[11] B. Anderson, *Imagined Communities: Reflections on the Origins and Spread of Nationalism* (rev. edn., London, 2006), 111.

[12] G. Orwell, 'The Lion and the Unicorn: Socialism and the English Genius' (1941), in S. Orwell and I. Angus (eds.), *The Collected Essays, Journalism and Letters of George Orwell*, 3 vols. (Harmondsworth, 1970), ii. 80. On working-class 'indifference' to empire, specifically at the time of the Boer War, see R. Price, *An Imperial War and the British Working Class: Working Class Attitudes and Reactions to the Boer War 1899–1902* (London, 1972). That the working class was more interested in social reform at home than in empire abroad is also argued by H. Pelling, 'British Labour and British Imperialism', in his *Popular Politics and Society in Late Victorian Britain* (London and New York, 1968), 82–100. J. Rose generally endorses this picture of working-class indifference to, and ignorance of, empire, but some of his evidence, for example, the popularity of the stories of the imperialist G. A. Henty, and the vivid impression left by imperial exhibitions such as the great Wembley Exhibition of 1924, allows for an alternative account: Rose, *The Intellectual Life of the British Working Classes* (New Haven, 2002), 321–64. A more complex picture of the relation of the working class to the British Empire is provided by Thompson, *The Empire Strikes Back?*, 64–95. For a vigorous repudiation of the idea that the working classes were not caught up in imperialism, see MacKenzie, *Propaganda and Empire*, 61–2, and *passim*.

ruling it, the rest of the population could be left to concentrate on other things. The empire made no great material demands on most people, at least none that they were aware of, and did not need their support or even their interest. All that was needed was a minimum of apathy.[13]

One should note that it is quite possible to take the view that the empire was an upper-middle/upper-class affair—that 'the British Empire was first and foremost a class act'[14]—without concluding that it *therefore* had little effect on the rest of the population. That is roughly speaking the position of David Cannadine in his engaging *Ornamentalism* (2001). Cannadine sees the empire as reflecting and promoting the hierarchical structures of British society itself, thereby establishing a correspondence and consistency between empire and domestic society to create 'one vast interconnected world'. The fact of class rule did not cut off the rest of the population from the empire, any more than it did from British society as a whole. Quite the contrary. The British people, of all classes, shared a vision of British society as ordered, graded, and hierarchical. This was the vision of society that shaped the empire, an empire constructed in the image of the home society. There was a 'shared sense of Britishness' that linked metropole and colony, centre and periphery. The British saw their hierarchical society mirrored in the practices and institutions of empire: the same system of honours, the same cult of monarchy, the same ceremonials and rituals, the same forms of deference. Both parts of this common British world reacted upon each other in a mutually reinforcing pattern. 'The British exported and projected vernacular sociological visions from the metropolis to the periphery, and they imported and analogized them from the empire back to Britain, thereby constructing comforting and familiar resemblances and equivalences and affinities.'[15]

Cannadine's Burkean picture of British society no doubt exaggerates the consensus and underplays the conflicts and contestations between groups and regions over the past two centuries. But it has the merit of recognizing— what the Marxist model of class conflict often disguises or ignores—the very

---

[13] Porter, *Absent-Minded Imperialists*, 307. This is a view that, without the extensive documentation that Porter provides, has been common among a number of recent commentators— see e.g. D. Miller, 'Reflections on British National Identity', *New Community*, 21/2 (1995), 159.

[14] D. Cannadine, *Ornamentalism: How the British Saw Their Empire* (Oxford, 2001), 10.

[15] Ibid. 122. The view of British society contained in this account was first elaborated in D. Cannadine, *The Rise and Fall of Class in Britain* (New York, 1999). For further exploration of the idea of a common 'British world', see C. Bridge and K. Fedorowich, (eds.), *The British World: Diaspora, Culture and Identity* (London, 2003).

real linkages between different groups in society, no matter what their differences of perception and interest. A ruling-class model of society does not, and should not, portray classes in isolation or separation from each other; rather, particularly through the concept of ideology, it indicates the manner in which society comes to be perceived, at every level, as a more or less coherent and integrated whole, with each part having its allotted place and function. That is what Marx himself showed in his major works, and it is what his most gifted disciples, such as Antonio Gramsci with his concept of 'hegemony', also stressed.[16] If British society was hierarchically ordered, and if this structure came to be reflected in the dominant culture of the time, then one would expect all groups to be affected by this perception, however unequal their actual condition. 'False consciousness', perhaps; but real nonetheless.

The relation between socialism and nationalism illustrates this graphically. By the early twentieth century powerful socialist movements and parties had developed in Germany, France, and Italy. Even in Britain a largely non-Marxist but significant labour movement had come into being. Though not exclusively class-based, these movements all invoked the working class in their ideologies and looked to the working class for their core membership. The working class was announced to be the class of the future, the class that would dissolve all classes. If war were to break out between the capitalist nations, the working classes were enjoined not to take part; such wars would be capitalist wars, fought in the interests of the capitalists, not of the working class. The working class had no nation; its movement and aspirations were international, expressed in the successive Socialist Internationals.

What happened in 1914, when war did indeed break out between the capitalist nations? With remarkably few exceptions—the Italian and American socialists—the vast majority of socialist and labour parties committed themselves to the war effort on behalf of their own nations. Nationalism

---

[16] It is this understanding that seems to be lacking in E. P. Thompson's hugely influential *The Making of the English Working Class* (London, 1963), which studies the working class more or less in isolation from other classes. In his later work, especially on the 18th century, Thompson was acute in his analysis of class interaction and in the shared perceptions of different groups. He seems to have assumed—wrongly, in my view—that this pattern was decisively broken in the 19th century. See K. Kumar, 'Class and Political Action in Nineteenth-Century England', in *The Rise of Modern Society* (Oxford, 1988), 131–68.

triumphantly trumped socialism, a defeat from which the socialist movement never really recovered. Nationalism showed itself to have become the
dominant ideology in Europe by the early twentieth century, an ideology
that absorbed and overshadowed all others, and that drew in all groups and
classes. 'Nationalism', as Oliver Zimmer writes of this period, 'provided the
most powerful source of moral authority—and thus of political mobilization—for those wishing to gain political recognition and success. Thus
conflicts over politics tended to take the form of struggles over the definition of national identity. Nationalism became an integral part of political
culture.'[17]

Britain was not of course immune from these powerful currents. Irish
nationalism had already by the end of the nineteenth century joined the
ranks of 'historic' nationalisms, along with the Poles, the Germans, the
Italians, and the Hungarians. Welsh nationalism too, fuelled by the rapid
industrialization and urbanization of South Wales, the equally explosive
growth of religious nonconformity, and the revitalization of Welsh culture
through the eisteddfodau and the choral festivals, began to stir. 'By the early
1880s, a sense of Welsh nationality and of national distinctiveness within the
wider framework of the United Kingdom was present as never before.'[18]
Jogged by Irish nationalism, and claiming a like Celtic ancestry and culture,
Scottish nationalism also began its slow and erratic ascent in the 1880s, with
the formation of an all-party Scottish Home Rule Association—and the
establishment of a separate Scottish Football League—in 1886.[19]

Scottish and Welsh nationalism never matched the fire and energy of Irish
nationalism; and for Scots and Welsh independence from the United Kingdom was never a seriously considered goal until late in the twentieth
century. Moreover, whatever the feeling about the United Kingdom and
their place within it, there was little inclination to dispense with the
empire—even in the case of the Irish, until they achieved independence in
1922. For much of the time Celtic nationalism and British imperialism
marched together, often framed within the idea of an imperial federation.
'Scotland within the Empire' was the slogan of the Scottish National Party,

[17] O. Zimmer, *Nationalism in Europe, 1890–1940* (Basingstoke, 2003), 34. See also
E. Hobsbawm, *Nations and Nationalism since 1780: Programme, Myth, Reality* (2nd edn.,
Cambridge, 1992), 101–30; Anderson, *Imagined Communities*, 83–111.

[18] K. O. Morgan, *Rebirth of a Nation: A History of Modern Wales* (Oxford, 1998), 90.

[19] C. Harvie, *Scotland and Nationalism; Scottish Society and Politics 1707 to the Present*,
(4th edn., London, 2004), 15–20.

formed in 1934, and Irish nationalists such as Erskine Childers were fervent imperialists, as were many Irish Home Rulers.[20] Celtic nationalism in fact fared best, and was most actively fomented, in the overseas empire, among the emigrant communities of Scots and Irish in Canada, Australia, and New Zealand (not to mention the former American colonies). 'Indeed', says Raphael Samuel, 'it is possible to see the growth of Empire and the ethnic revival of the 1870s and 1880s as two sides of the same coin; each, after its own fashion, worshipped at the feet of race-consciousness'.[21]

Elsewhere in the empire, however, a different and, from the point of view of its rulers, more ominous form of nationalism was finding its voice. In 1885 the first meeting of the Indian National Congress took place in Bombay, spurred on by furious European reaction to a bill (the Ilbert Bill) that would have put Indian judges on the same footing as European ones in the Bengal Presidency, and which therefore involved the possibility that Europeans might be tried by an Indian judge without a jury. Moderate at first, Indian nationalism took on increased fervour under the new Viceroy, Lord Curzon, with his high-handed behaviour and indifference to Indian sensibilities. In a pattern that became familiar from a host of anti-colonial nationalisms in the twentieth century, Western-educated professionals and intellectuals turned the ideas of the West against the legitimacy of its own rule.[22]

---

[20] For the Irish leader John Redmond's embrace of empire, from the 1880s onwards, see Marshall, 'Imperial Britain', 388. This view survived independence: the 'vision of empire or Commonwealth as a union of free peoples in which the Irish could play a full and distinctive part was still alive in the 1920s, when the Cosgrave government in the Irish Free State was maintaining Ireland's Commonwealth membership'. Ibid. 389; see also D. McMahon, 'Ireland and the Empire-Commonwealth, 1900–1948', in J. M. Brown and Wm. R. Louis (eds.), *Oxford History of the British Empire (OHBE)*, iv. *The Twentieth Century* (Oxford, 1999), 147–54.

[21] R. Samuel, 'Four Nations History', in Samuel, *Theatres of Memory*, 2 vols. (London, 1998), ii. *Island Stories: Unravelling Britain*, 35; see also D. S. Forsyth, 'Empire and Union: Imperial and National Identity in Nineteenth Century Scotland', *Scottish Geographical Magazine*, 113/1 (1997), 6–12; Thompson, *The Empire Strikes Back?*, 199–200; T. M. Devine, 'The Break-Up of Britain? Scotland and the End of Empire', *Transactions of the Royal Historical Society (TRHS)*, 6/16 (2006), 166, 170.

[22] A. Seal, *The Emergence of Indian Nationalism: Competition and Collaboration in the Later Nineteenth Century* (Cambridge, 1968), 163–70, 346–51; P. Spear, *A History of India* (rev. edn., Harmondsworth, 1981), 158–80. It is worth noting that the Indian National Congress was actually founded by an Englishman, Allan Octavian Hume—son of the great mid-Victorian anti-imperialist Joseph Hume—a retired administrator who believed that the best way of preserving the permanence of British rule in India was to give qualified Indians some share in the running of the country. See K. Tidrick, *Empire and the English Character* (London, 1990), 223–4.

As elsewhere, nationalism and imperialism in India went hand in hand, the one modifying the goals and tactics of the other. The practices and policies of the imperial state shaped the responses of the nationalists, which in turn led to attempts to conciliate and, as far as possible, neutralize nationalist demands.[23] What one has to see is that this pattern was one that also applied, *mutatis mutandis*, to the United Kingdom, John Bull's 'other empire'. Over the course of the centuries the English had in effect constructed two types of empire. The first was the 'inner empire', the result of the Anglo-Norman conquest of Wales and Ireland and the later shotgun marriage with Scotland. This was the land empire of the United Kingdom, what some eighteenth-century writers called 'the Empire of Great Britain' or 'the British Empire in Europe'. The other was the more familiar overseas empire whose construction began with the sixteenth-century settlements in North America.[24] These two empires interacted in complex ways with each other—for instance, working-class movements in Britain could receive moral and material support from other parts of the empire, and vice versa; but so too British workers could react with hostility to the threat of cheap colonial labour, as in South Africa, and seek to resist competition from workers and industries elsewhere in the empire, as with the Indian textile industry.[25]

The two empires were not strictly parallel or symmetrical, of course. Most importantly, the native peoples of the United Kingdom shared in the rule of the overseas empire in a way that was not true of the native peoples of that empire, 'the British empire' as normally understood. Scots above all, but also Irish and Welsh, played key roles in the running of the empire, as administrators, soldiers, missionaries, merchants, engineers, doctors, botanists, explorers, and educators. This was bound to give them a feeling of having a stake in the empire, and to mute any national consciousness that might have arisen out of a sense of resentment at English domination of the British Isles. Pride in the empire, and a real share in its fruits, was by no

[23] See esp. A. Seal, 'Imperialism and Nationalism in India', in J. Gallagher, G. Johnson, and A. Seal (eds.), *Locality, Province and Nation: Essays on Indian Politics 1870–1940* (Cambridge, 1973), 1–28; see also J. Breuilly, *Nationalism and the State* (2nd edn., Chicago, 1994), 170–83.

[24] See for the general argument, K. Kumar, *The Making of English National Identity* (Cambridge, 2003), 35–8, 180, and *passim*. For the key medieval period, see R. R. Davies, *The First English Empire: Power and Identities in the British Isles 1093–1343* (Oxford, 2000).

[25] See Thompson, *The Empire Strikes Back?*, 64–82.

means restricted to the English.[26] Moreover, the British did not just collectively rule and run the empire; they to a good extent also occupied it, in the
form of settlements of British people that formed extensions of Britain
throughout the world, often displacing the native inhabitants—above all in
Canada, Australia, New Zealand, and South Africa, but also in significant
sections of East Africa.

Still there was never any real doubt that the British empire was an *English*
empire, founded originally by the English and developed largely according
to the pattern of English practices and institutions. In that sense the overseas
empire was the continuation of the original English empire—the 'inner
empire' of Great Britain—by other means (as Seeley, among others, had
noted).[27] It was English common law, English administration, the English
parliamentary system, the English monarchy, English education, English
culture, and the English language that were diffused throughout the empire
(though Scottish educational and ecclesiastical practices also left their mark).
If, as Niall Ferguson has contended, the British empire was one of the first
and most powerful sponsors of globalization, it took the form, as he rightly
notes, of 'Anglobalization'—the worldwide spread of an essentially English
system of values and institutions.[28]

One of the consequences of English domination of the empire, as of the
United Kingdom, was that they were obliged, by that very fact, to play down

[26] See J. M. MacKenzie, 'Essay and Reflection: On Scotland and Empire', *International History Review*, 15/4 (1993), 714–39; id., 'Empire and National Identities: The Case of Scotland', *TRHS* 6/8 (1998), 221–8; M. Fry, *The Scottish Empire* (East Linton, 2001); T. M. Devine, *Scotland's Empire 1600–1815* (London, 2003); K. Jeffery, (ed.), *'An Irish Empire'? Aspects of Ireland and the British Empire* (Manchester, 1996); K. Kenny (ed.), *Ireland and the British Empire* (Oxford, 2004); A. Jones and B. Jones, 'The Welsh World and the British Empire, c. 1851–1939: An Exploration', *JICH* 31/2 (2003), 57–81; G. Williams, *When Was Wales?* (Harmondsworth, 1991), 221–6; Hopkins, 'Back to the Future', 212.

[27] See J. R. Seeley, *The Expansion of England* (1883; Chicago, 1971), 13.

[28] N. Ferguson, *Empire: How Britain Made the Modern World* (London, 2004), p. xxiv. A. G. Hopkins has suggested that this is a general feature of all forms of globalization, that they all carry the 'imprint of nationality', and that they are all in that sense species of 'national globalization'. 'Links across space and cultures could be sustained only by generating common core values and a lingua franca, and these were put in place by a few dominant nations with the power to spread their own diasporas while also inspiring imitation and instilling deference in other societies... From constitutions to consumer tastes, from weights to measures, and from the creation of postal services to the colonization of time, it was the national stamp that sealed global connections.' A. G. Hopkins, 'The History of Globalization—and the Globalization of History?', in Hopkins (ed.), *Globalization in World History* (London, 2002), 31–2.

their own role as a nation. This is common among all imperial peoples, from Romans to Russians. To stress one's own ethnicity, to beat the nationalist drum, is a dangerous strategy for rulers concerned with the management of highly diverse peoples and cultures, as is the case with all empires. 'Mere' ethnicity or nationality has to be seen as something suited to other, 'lesser', peoples; imperial peoples have larger concerns, whether it be peace, religion, or, in a more secular vein, *la mission civilisatrice*.[29] English nationalism therefore, in comparison with nationalisms elsewhere, even in the United Kingdom, remained low-keyed and severely underdeveloped. In an era of nationalism, for the English at least, empire meant the suppression of a strong sense of national identity.[30]

The great nineteenth-century Russian historian Vassily Kliuchevsky once wrote that 'all of Russian history is the history of a country that colonizes itself'.[31] He was referring to the seemingly inexorable movement of the Russian people across the vast inland space of the Eurasian steppe, a movement seen as almost natural and foreordained. One effect of this, frequently noted by commentators on Russia, was that Russians found it difficult to separate themselves from their creation, or to think of themselves as a distinct nation in relation to the other peoples of the empire.[32]

Compared to the Russians, the English had a far more restricted inland space in which to expand. But, having filled that, they found ample scope for their colonizing impulse overseas. They too can be said to have been a people who colonized themselves. They too found it difficult to separate themselves from their creation, whether it was the United Kingdom or the British empire. The most obvious and telling evidence of this is the difficulty

[29] A typical view was that, as Harold Nicolson put it in explaining why the British, unlike the French, Germans, and Italians, had not established a cultural institution for promoting their way of life, the 'genius of England [*sic*], unlike that of lesser countries, spoke for itself'. Another diplomat added that 'good wine, we optimistically feel, needs no bush' Quoted in Frances Donaldson, *The British Council: The First Fifty Years* (London, 1984), 11–12. In the climate of the 1930s, with the competition offered by Russian communism and Italian and German fascism, such insouciance, it was felt, was no longer justified, and the British Council was established in 1934 'to make the life and thought of the British peoples more widely known abroad'.

[30] See K. Kumar, 'Nation and Empire: English and British National Identity in Comparative Perspective', *Theory and Society*, 29/5 (2000), 575–608; id. 'Empire and English Nationalism', *Nations and Nationalism*, 12/1 (2006), 1–13.

[31] Quoted in C. K. Woodworth, 'Ocean and Steppe: Early Modern World Empires', *Journal of Early Modern History*, 11/6 (2007), 507.

[32] Kumar, 'Nation and Empire', 584–8.

most English have of distinguishing themselves from British—compared to all the other peoples in 'the British world'.[33]

All this can help us understand the differential impact of the empire on the peoples of Britain in the twentieth century. For much of the time the common designation of 'British' served as an adequate badge of identity for most people. But there were always fault lines; and with the end of empire they were bound to show themselves more clearly. By the end of the twentieth century commentators could talk about 'the break-up of Britain'. There were many reasons for this; but the experience of empire, and of its passing, was one it was impossible to ignore.

Empire and National Identities to the Second World War

In the final volume of Paul Scott's 'Raj Quartet', Guy Perron, one of the central characters, reflects that 'for at least a hundred years India has formed part of England's idea about herself and for the same period India has been forced into a position of being a reflection of that idea'. But the nature of that part had changed dramatically since about 1900, 'certainly since 1918'. From being based upon a moral right of possession it had moved to its direct opposite: the duty to let go of India. 'The part played since then by India in the English idea of Englishness has been that of something we feel it does us no credit to have. Our idea about ourselves will now not accommodate any idea about India except the idea of returning it to the Indians in order to prove that we are English and have demonstrably English ideas.'[34] These reflections occurred on the morrow of the Labour Party's victory at the 1945 election and the commitment to Indian independence as soon as possible.

These thoughts express admirably some of the complexities of the relationship between empire and identities in the first half of the twentieth century. The century began with Britain at the height of imperial power. Not much more than halfway through most of that empire had disappeared. From seeing themselves at the centre of the world the British—and most notably the English—had to reconcile themselves to a position on the sidelines. On the way they had to change from a situation where the empire

---

[33] See the surveys discussed in Christopher G. A. Bryant, *The Nations of Britain* (Oxford, 2006), 4–7.

[34] P. Scott, *A Division of the Spoils* (London, 1977), 105.

was England or Britain writ large to one where the changes in the empire were ricocheting back on Britain itself, forcing profound modifications in its self-conception.

Here the parallels between the inner empire of the United Kingdom and the outer overseas empire continued to show themselves. At the beginning of the century all the nations of the United Kingdom—even those that experienced nationalist stirrings—shared in the imperial enterprise and identified themselves with it. As nationalist movements seeking independence grew within the empire, and as the empire itself weakened through war and economic dislocation, the nations of the United Kingdom lost confidence in their imperial mission, and in their right and ability to hold on to empire. The Irish were the first to break away, using the anti-imperialist rhetoric common to all nationalist movements. But the other Celtic nations also felt the 'demonstration effect' of the rising tide of nationalism in the post-1918 world.[35] In the latter part of the twentieth century, with the empire gone and Europe beckoning, they could contemplate, for the first time in more than two centuries, exit from the United Kingdom. Nor were the English themselves immune from these currents. Reacting partly against Scottish and Welsh nationalism, the English—or at least some of them—also began to reconsider their place in the United Kingdom, and wonder whether they too might not be better off without it.

Actually Guy Perron dates the onset of the new attitude somewhat too early. The importance of the empire to the British gained in significance during the First World War and was strengthened by the post-war settlement. The contribution of troops from all the corners of the empire to the war effort was not lost on the British public—episodes such as the Gallipoli landing and the deaths of so many Australian and New Zealand soldiers there were especially telling. After 1918, with the addition of the League of Nations mandates in the Middle East—Egypt, Transjordan, Iraq, Palestine—together with Tanganyika and other African territories taken from the Germans, the British empire increased to its greatest extent ever, covering a quarter of the world's territory and incorporating nearly a quarter of the world's population.[36] Undoubtedly there were questions

---

[35] See J. Gallagher, 'Nationalism and the Crisis of Empire, 1919–1922', *Modern Asian Studies*, 15/3 (1981), 355–68.

[36] Although strictly speaking, as Ashley Jackson points out, it was in 1945, not in the wake of the First World War, that the British Empire achieved its greatest territorial extent ever, as

about the empire's future, posed especially by the nationalist movements within the empire. But there had always been questions, ever since the eighteenth century when Britain in effect lost one empire and acquired another. There was little in the debates following the First World War to suggest that the empire was in a course of dissolution and might be wound up in the next few decades.[37]

In fact, as John MacKenzie has argued, there was, compared with the period of anxiety before the First World War, increased confidence and increased interest in the empire in the 1920s and 1930s. It was in these decades that the empire began to impact most directly on popular consciousness, spurred on by such events as the great imperial Wembley Exhibition of 1924, the activities of the Empire Marketing Board, the Christmas Day broadcasts by the monarch to the empire, and the rise of a popular cinema of empire.[38] This was the period too when Britain's foreign trade also began to turn more decisively in the direction of the empire: trade with the empire in the 1930s for the first time topped 50 per cent of the total, matching and overtaking trade with the United States and Latin America. The British empire, after the struggles and turmoil of the First World War, seemed to have emerged strengthened and a more necessary presence in the world than ever before, given the dangers and instabilities of the post-war order. Such was the conviction of public figures such as H. G. Wells, Halford Mackinder, and Ernest Barker.[39]

Britain reconquered its own colonies lost earlier to the Japanese and Italians and acquired new territories—in Somaliland, Libya, Madagascar, southern Iran, and elsewhere—from its defeated enemies: Jackson, *The British Empire and the Second World War* (London, 2006), 5.

[37] C. Meier claims that after the First World War, 'the spectacle of internecine European warfare and the advent of Woodrow Wilson's idea of self-determination undermined the legitimacy' of the French and British empires, despite their massive post-war territorial gains: *Among Empires: American Ascendancy and Its Predecessors* (Cambridge, Mass., 2006), 154. But he gives no evidence for this. Concerns and anxieties about their empires, and the sense that they would inevitably go the way of all mortal things—what Meier calls 'the melancholy of empire'— were common among the French and the British (as among all imperial peoples) throughout the lives of their empires. But there is little evidence that this deepened particularly in the wake of the First World War. For the British Empire, see esp. J. Gallagher, *The Decline, Revival and Fall of the British Empire: The Ford Lectures and Other Essays*, ed. A. Seal (Cambridge, 1982), 86–99.

[38] MacKenzie, *Propaganda and Empire*, 256; id., 'The Popular Culture of Empire in Britain', in *OHBE* iv., 212–31.

[39] For Wells's view of the British empire, see his *Imperialism and the Open Conspiracy* (London, 1929); see also K. Kumar, *Utopia and Anti-Utopia in Modern Times* (Oxford, 1987), 194–205; D. Deudney, 'Greater Britain or Greater Synthesis? Seeley, Mackinder, and Wells on

Not that the Great War did not leave its mark on national consciousness. Students of post-war national identity in Britain have discerned a certain retreat, a certain turning in and turning away, from the turbulent events of world politics. The trauma of the First World War, the utterly unexpected savagery and brutality of the war in the trenches and in the unprecedented impact on civilian populations, had taken something of the glamour away from tales of glory and heroism. Manly attitudes of struggle and sacrifice yielded to a more 'feminized' view of the national character. There was a reaction against the blustering, aggressive, John Bull-ish image of the Englishman. This was the era of the cartoonist Sidney Strube's 'little man', and of the sense that Dicken's good-hearted and eccentric Mr Pickwick was closer to the average Englishman than the heroes of Rider Haggard's novels of adventure and derring-do. George Santayana's *Soliloquies in England* (1922), with its portrait of a gentle, modest, domestic England, whose heart was in the countryside, was a popular and influential work throughout the interwar period.[40]

But did this mean, as some have claimed, that this represented a retreat from empire, a decline in imperial consciousness? Only a very selective reading of the evidence can point this way. The intellectuals and publicists of the *Round Table*, which included some of the most prominent politicians from all parties, continued their work of educating the public in the task of empire, and in proclaiming the need for empire in a parlous world situation (the worldwide community of the British empire, Jan Smuts remarked, was the only truly successful League of Nations). If Strube and Santayana were popular, so too was the novelist and Governor-General of Canada, John Buchan, an ardent imperialist. Imperial adventure storywriters Edgar Wallace and Sapper were widely read. Kitchener, the hero of Omdurman, remained an emblematic figure of imperial glory in the 1920s and 1930s. The same period also saw the romanticization and idealization of T. E. Lawrence, as the tortured intellectual turned imperial warrior. School textbooks of history continued the pre-war theme of England and Britain's march to

Britain in the Global Industrial Era', *Review of International Studies*, 27/2, (2001), 203–7; for Barker, see his 'The Conception of Empire', in C.Bailey (ed.), *The Legacy of Rome* (Oxford, 1923), 35–60.

[40] On these changes in the image of the English between the wars, see A. Light, *Forever England: Femininity, Literature and Conservatism between the Wars* (London, 1991); P. Mandler, *The English National Character: The History of an Idea from Edmund Burke to Tony Blair* (New Haven, 2006), 143–76.

imperial greatness through the exploits of its famous heroes, from Drake and Hawkins to Clive and Kitchener. The 'cinema of empire', which reached its apogee in the 1930s, was almost wholly celebratory. As Valentine Cunningham has observed, the much-remarked 'collapse of the idea of heroism' in the wake of the Great War 'did not last very long'.[41]

Far-reaching changes in the structure of the empire itself seemed to promise it a longer, not a shorter, lease of life. The Statute of Westminster of 1931, in granting the dominions autonomy and equality within the British empire, seemed to provide a firm framework for future development. The Ottawa Agreements of 1932 established, in the most comprehensive way so far, the system of imperial preferences, linking all parts of the empire to each other as well as to the metropolis. India had been repeatedly promised dominion status since 1917, and the India Act of 1935, though rejected by the Congress leaders, was seen by many others in the party as well as by officials in London as representing a stepping-stone to full dominionhood.[42] The empire seemed to be set on a relatively smooth path towards its evolution into a commonwealth—but still a *British* Commonwealth.

John Darwin has in fact suggestively put forward the idea of a 'Third British Empire', built around the dominion principle that emerged during the interwar decades. In this view, 'the Empire offered a capacious mould into which the special identities of the Dominions could be poured. Like Britain, herself a four-nation state, they were synthetic nations united through common adherence to British ideals and institutions.' A shared 'Britannic identity' could unite all parts of the empire, offering 'a distinctive blend of national status and Imperial identity', 'a permanent reconciliation of national autonomy and Imperial identity'.[43] True the ideal could be most

[41] V. Cunningham, *British Writers of the Thirties* (Oxford, 1989), 156. See also A. May, 'Empire Loyalists and "Commonwealth Men": The Round Table and the End of Empire', in Ward (ed.), *British Culture and the End of Empire*, 37–44; Tidrick, *Empire and the English Character*, 228–32; MacKenzie, *Propaganda and Empire*, 174–97; J. M. MacKenzie, 'T. E. Lawrence: The Myth and the Message', in Robert Giddings (ed.), *Literature and Imperialism* (London, 1991), 156–66; J. Richards, *Films and British National Identity: From Dickens to Dad's Army* (Manchester, 1997), 31–59; J. Chapman, 'Cinemas of Empire', *History Compass*, 4/5 (2006), 814–19.
[42] J. M. Brown, 'India', in *OHBE* iv. 430; J. Gallagher and A. Seal, 'Britain and India between the Wars', *Modern Asian Studies*, 15/3 (1981), 406–7—though they stress the 'ambiguities' in the term 'dominion status'.
[43] J. Darwin, 'A Third British Empire? The Dominion Idea in Imperial Politics', in *OHBE* iv. 70–1, 85. See also Hopkins, 'Back to the Future', 218–20, 235–6; Brown, 'India', 435–6; C. Bridge and K. Fedorowich, 'Mapping the British World', in Bridge and Fedorowich (eds.), *British*

easily applied to the white dominions, with their shared British 'racial' heritage (which was why Seeley, the originator of the basic idea, had excluded India from 'Greater Britain'). But it was thought that it could in time also include other parts of the empire. The fact that nationalists in several of the colonies—including India—were attracted by this prospect made it seem all the more capable of realization. What had been granted the white dominions in 1931 could be the model for future settlements with other dependencies.

Equally importantly, perhaps, the dominion idea could be applied to the United Kingdom itself, as a constitutional device to sort out its own nationality problems ('Scotland within the Empire'). Proponents of the idea—frequently couched in the terms of 'federal Britain'—clearly recognized its potential in this regard.[44] Ironically, though the dominion ideal finally failed within the wider British empire, towards the end of the twentieth century it could reappear (if not so-called) as a possible solution to nationalist demands within the 'inner empire' of the United Kingdom. Yet again one sees the permeability of the boundary separating the domestic and the imperial, the constant interaction of ideas and events in the overseas empire and British society 'at home'.

World, 1–15. The Britishness of the dominions, and corresponding links with the British metropolis, were enhanced by the swelling tide of British migrants to the dominions after 1900, replacing the United States as the most popular destination. See Stephen Constantine, 'British Emigration to the Empire-Commonwealth since 1880: From Overseas Settlement to Diaspora?', in Bridge and Fedorowich (eds.), British World, 20–1; S. Constantine, 'Migrants and Settlers', in OHBE iv. 167.

[44] Such a link had been made since the late 19th century, especially in the context of discussions of Irish Home Rule: see J. Kendle, Federal Britain: A History (London, 1997), 46–78; V. Bogdanor, Devolution in the United Kingdom (Oxford, 2001), 19–54. At the time of furious debates over Irish Home Rule in the early 1900s, the Liberal Daily News linked Home Rule within the United Kingdom to the empire: 'The nationalities within the British Isles are the natural units for devolution and their nationalization does not take from but strengthens a common Imperial patriotism.' Daily News (5 Aug. 1910), quoted in P. Ward, Britishness since 1870 (London, 2004), 97. A similar point was made by a Scots nationalist, W. Scott Dalgleish, in 1883: 'the maintenance of [Scottish] nationality will not only be just to Scotland but will also strengthen the Empire, of which Scotland forms an integral part', quoted in Kendle, Federal Britain, 183 n. 15; see also Forsyth, 'Empire and Union', 11. For the idea of 'imperial federation', see D. Bell, The Idea of Greater Britain: Empire and the Future of World Order, 1860–1900 (Princeton, 2007), 12–20, 93–119. For discussions in the interwar period, largely centered on the ideas of the Round Table group, see Kendle, Federal Britain, 79–104; MacKenzie, 'On Scotland and the Empire', 738.

The Second World War and Its Aftermath: The Reaffirmation of Imperial Identities

The dominion idea, in its intended form, did not long survive the Second World War. Nor in the end did the empire, though the war was fought in part to preserve it and with it Britain's place in the world. The impact of the war on Britain was devastating, weakening it on all fronts, domestic as well as foreign. Although it took time for this to become clear, Britain lost its hegemonic position as a world power. Whether or not without the war the British empire—as the French or Dutch—might have survived for a considerable period longer is an interesting and by no means idle counterfactual question. But the fact was that the war did supervene, with consequences that were both a speeding up of pre-war developments and the result of dynamics specific to the war itself. Particularly important was the Japanese conquest of much of South East Asia, with repercussions throughout the European empires in Asia. The belief in European superiority was shattered forever. Nationalists throughout the region were encouraged and emboldened to pursue their dreams of complete independence. Nationalist struggles and the altered balance of world power—with the United States and the Soviet Union now the major players on the world stage—turned the stakes against the European empires.

But though we, from the vantage point of the present, might see the war as the decisive turning point, and the end of empire as inscribed in the logic of events, that was not necessarily how it appeared to contemporaries. Our tendency to read the twentieth-century history of empires teleologically—to see their end as somehow foreordained, and discernible in various stirrings at the very beginning of the century—tends to foreshorten their lives and to obscure their continuing impact on their own societies.[45] The British empire, as conventionally understood, did indeed come more or less to an end a mere two decades or so after the close of the Second World War. But, in the first place, that was not an outcome that seemed at all inevitable to contemporaries during and immediately after the war. In the second place,

---

[45] Cf. J. Gallagher: 'There is a general notion that [the] empire rose, flourished, declined, fell, and that in its fall lay its fulfillment. But this is a sentimental view, arising from a banal teleology. In fact, the movement towards decline was reversible and sometimes was reversed.' *Decline, Revival and Fall of the British Empire*, 86.

our telescoped vision of empire has the effect of preventing us from seeing its long afterlife in the metropolis, in British society itself.

From one point of view the Second World War can be thought of, not as administering the *coup de grâce*, but as the acme of empire.[46] If a 'Britannic identity' was one of the unifying marks of the empire, the Second World War saw Britishness reach a new peak and intensity of expression.[47] It was a Britishness that was freely and deliberately extended to all the subjects of the empire, through such media as the Empire (later Overseas) Services of the BBC, the Colonial Film Unit, the royal broadcasts at Christmas, and perhaps even more the films and broadcasts of the popular actor Leslie Howard—a virtual compendium of the best British qualities—to all the corners of the empire. Newsreels in Britain showed Australian, Canadian, New Zealander, South African, Indian, and West Indian servicemen coming to Britain as well as fighting in the war zones. Films such as *49th Parallel* (1941) showed the multinational empire in action against the threat of the Nazi's 'New World Order'. The common theme was of a loyal empire coming to Britain's aid in a time of dire emergency. The common image was that of 'one great family', as George V said in his Christmas broadcast of 1941, 'the family of the British Commonwealth and Empire'. There was a calculated stress on the *ordinary* people of the empire as of the nation, the men and women in the fields and factories as well as at the front. The spirit of the 'people's war' was complemented by that of the 'people's empire'.[48]

The Second World War also qualified somewhat the picture of a more inward-looking, peaceful, and quiet national character that had been one

---

[46] 'The Second World War saw the apotheosis of the British Empire': K. Jeffery, 'Second World War', in *OHBE* iv. 326. This is a view comprehensively and powerfully presented by Jackson, *British Empire and the Second World War.*

[47] See Kumar, *Making of English National Identity*, 233–8; R. Weight, *Patriots: National Identity in Britain 1940–2000* (London, 2003), 23–118; Mandler, *English National Character*, 187–95.

[48] W. Webster, *Englishness and Empire 1939–1965* (Oxford, 2007), 19–54; Toby Haggith, 'Citizenship, Nationhood and Empire in British Official Film Propaganda, 1939–1945', in R. Weight and A. Beach (eds.), *The Right to Belong: Citizenship and National Identity in Britain, 1930–1960* (London, 1998), 59–88; S. Nicholas, '"Brushing Up Your Empire": Dominion and Colonial Propaganda on the BBC's Home Services, 1939–1945', in Bridge and Fedorowich (eds.), *British World*, 207–30. Though Sonya Rose stresses divisions and exclusions in wartime consciousness, she too acknowledges that 'there was a left-leaning, populist, progressive shift in the dominant political culture that inundated the United Kingdom' in these years, leading to a 'utopian vision of renewal'. See Rose, *Which People's War? National Identity and Citizenship in Wartime Britain 1939–1945* (Oxford, 2004), 24–5; see also 69–70, 290–1.

significant development of the interwar years. It did so in a direction that laid the stress on more heroic, soldierly, and, in a word, imperial qualities. There could of course be no imitating the Nazis with their bullying and glorification of militarism. To that extent there was the 'pipe-and-slippers' Little Englander J. B. Priestley, with his nightly BBC radio 'Postscipts', to indicate continuity with the pre-war period. A 'tempered', restrained masculinity was celebrated as against the 'hyper-masculinity' of the Nazis.[49] But against this, or rather, perhaps, combining with this, was the ample figure of the cigar-smoking Winston Churchill, the epitome of empire, the Churchill who famously declared in 1942 that 'I have not become the King's First Minister in order to preside over the liquidation of the British Empire'. It was Churchill who most clearly embodied the imperial character of the war effort, and the aspiration to continue the empire in some form after the war.

The British people rejected Churchill in 1945; but did they also reject the empire at the same time? Anti-colonialism, championed by a few fringe groups on the Left, had not been popular during the war nor had it much impact immediately afterwards (despite, or perhaps because of, considerable popular confusion and ignorance about what the empire was, as we have seen).[50] The theme of the 'people's empire' continued in the popular culture of the post-war period, shown partly in the increasing preference for the term 'Commonwealth' over 'empire'. The Sunday Times in 1947 even proclaimed a 'Fourth British Empire of independent peoples freely associated', much what people had come to understand by the 'British Commonwealth of Nations'. Such a theme reached its climax with the great procession of representatives from the whole empire at the time of the coronation of Elizabeth II in 1953. 'The "people's empire" promoted in Coronation year emphasized the ideal of a multiracial community of equal nations that would maintain Britishness as a global identity through transforming and modernizing its imperial dimension.'[51]

In fact what is most apparent in the post-war period is not so much a resigned acceptance of the end of empire as a surge of energy and new

---

[49] Rose, Which People's War?, 151–96.

[50] S. Howe, Anticolonialism in British Politics: The Left and the End of Empire, 1918–1964 (Oxford, 1993), 82–142. In this, the British public was only reflecting the muted anti-colonialism of most of the major left-wing groups and parties, including the Communist Party, preoccupied as they were with the imperialism of the Axis powers rather than their own.

[51] Webster, Empire and Englishness, 8; see also 55–6, and, on the Coronation and empire, 92–118.

thinking, especially in official circles, as to how to reform the empire in order to preserve it. In that sense John Gallagher was right to say that 'in the short term, the impact of war considerably strengthened the empire'.[52] The new Labour government, especially in the persons of the Prime Minister Clement Atlee and the Foreign Secretary Ernest Bevin, had no intention of giving up on the empire. Burma and India might get their independence, though this was not the same as severing ties with them nor ceasing to expect continuing British influence upon them. But perhaps for the first time the government turned its serious attention to its African colonies, seeking to stimulate economic development there to offset the losses in the eastern empire. 'The same Labour Government which had liquidated most of British Asia went on to animate part of British Africa. Africa would be the surrogate for India, more docile, more malleable, more pious.'[53] In other areas too the British sought not so much to wind up their empire—that never seems to have been the goal of any important groups—as to allow it to continue by other, more indirect, means.[54]

The most radical attempt to renew the empire came with the British Nationality Act of 1948. Common citizenship, as the bond of solidarity, had been a major theme of both official and popular propaganda on the home front during the Second World War.[55] It was a long-standing promise also held out to other peoples of the empire, though in many cases slow in its fulfilment. Now, spurred on by the mobilization of the whole empire for the war effort, the British government at last delivered on that promise. At a stroke all members of the empire—all inhabitants of the dominions and

---

[52] Gallagher, *Decline, Revival and Fall of the British Empire*, 139. See also Jackson, *British Empire and the Second World War*, 527.

[53] Gallagher, *Decline, Revival and Fall of the British Empire*, 146; see also R. Hyam, *Britain's Declining Empire: The Road to Decolonisation 1918–1968* (Cambridge, 2006), 94–5, 162–7. For parallel attempts to regenerate the French empire after the war, see F. Cooper, 'Labor, Politics, and the End of Empire in French Africa', in Cooper, *Colonialism in Question: Theory, Knowledge, History* (Berkeley, Calif., 2005), 204–30.

[54] See J. Darwin, *Britain and Decolonisation: The Retreat from Empire in the Post-War World* (London, 1988), esp. chs. 3 and 4; W. R. Louis and R. Robinson, 'The Imperialism of Decolonization', *JICH* 22/3 (1994), 462–511; W. R. Louis, 'The Dissolution of the British Empire', in *OHBE* iv. 329–56. All these accounts emphasize Anglo-American cooperation as the basis of attempts to maintain worldwide British control even as Britain divested itself formally of many of its colonies.

[55] See A. Calder, *The People's War: Britain 1939–1945* (London, 1969); D. Morgan and M. Evans, *The Battle for Britain: Citizenship and Ideology in the Second World War* (London, 1993); Weight and Beach (eds.), *The Right to Belong*; Rose, *Which People's War?*, 1–28.

dependencies, as well as former colonies, such as India, which had achieved Commonwealth status—were made equal subjects, with the right to live and work in the United Kingdom. While each dominion was left free to create its own citizenship laws, the United Kingdom as the 'Mother Country' made it clear that all subjects of the Crown were equal in its eyes, and that it remained the centre to which all members of the empire would be drawn. As the Attorney General Sir Hartley Shawcross stressed, 'the Bill's whole purpose is to maintain the common status, and with it the metropolitan tradition that this country is the homeland of the Commonwealth.' The image of the family, common in the war, was once more drawn upon: the conception of an 'all-pervading common status, or nationality', said Lord Chancellor Jowitt, was 'the mark of something which differentiates the family from mere friends'.[56]

Conservative critics of the 1948 Nationality Act at the time thought that, with its exceptionally liberal immigration provisions, it was storing up trouble for the future; those on the Left have said that its liberal pretensions were undermined by a 'racialization' of immigration policy in the actual implementation of the Act, as well as by a discourse of race and nation that increasingly defined Britishness as whiteness against the threat of 'dark strangers'.[57] No one however has denied that the Act represented, realistically or not, an extraordinary declaration of faith in the British Empire, and an expression of the determination to continue it, albeit in transformed form, in the changed circumstances of the post-war world.

Empire and Identities After Empire

By the late 1960s most of Britain's formal empire had gone. But neither in the former colonies nor in the metropolis itself did that mean 'the end of empire'—not, at least, if that suggests the end of imperial impact and influence. One does not so easily shrug off more than three-and-a half hundred years of imperial existence. By comparison with some other

[56] K. Paul, *Whitewashing Britain: Race and Citizenship in the Postwar Era* (Ithaca, NY, 1997), 16–17.

[57] Ibid. 111–30; C. Waters, '"Dark Strangers" in Our Midst: Discourses of Race and Nation in Britain, 1947–1963', *JBS* 36/2, (1997), 207–38. But see also, for a contrary view that stresses continuing official commitment to the Commonwealth ideal in the 1950s, R. Hansen, *Citizenship and Immigration in Postwar Britain: The Institutional Foundations of a Multicultural Nation* (Oxford, 2000), chs. 1–2.

empires, such as the Chinese, that may not seem very long. But in modern conditions that may be long enough. 'The empires of our time were short-lived', says the protagonist Ralph Singh in V. S. Naipaul's novel *The Mimic Men*, 'but they have altered the world for ever; their passing away is their least significant feature'.[58]

The empire had given the British, and more specifically and especially the English, a sense of themselves. They were an imperial people, not a merely 'national' people. In the heyday of empire, all the peoples of the United Kingdom—Scots, Irish, and Welsh, as well as English—shared in the enterprise of empire. The empire, in this sense, was a force for convergence, enabling the creation of an overarching British identity that could incorporate not just the peoples of the 'inner empire' of the United Kingdom but also those of the 'outer empire', the overseas British empire.

But while the empire contained and controlled possible fragmentation, it also to some extent provided the pattern of a less cohesive post-imperial British state. Here, once again, the United Kingdom participated in some of the same developments as in the rest of the empire. Just as the requirements and practices of the empire called into being a series of nationalist movements that eventually took over rule as independent states, so—though never to the same extent—the character of the empire also led to the strengthening of distinct national identities within the United Kingdom itself. While never sufficient to threaten the unity of either the empire or the United Kingdom, the development of these national identities at home meant that there were national communities 'in waiting', capable of being mobilized and deployed when the need or the opportunity arose.

John MacKenzie has argued that, far from the empire stifling national identities in the British Isles, it had the effect—similar to what occurred elsewhere in the empire—of preserving and promoting them.[59] For the

---

[58] V. S. Naipaul, *The Mimic Men* (Harmondsworth, 1969), 32, For the various ways in which the end of empire impacted on British culture and society, ranging from the satire boom of the 1960s to the 'literature of decline' from the 1950s onwards, see the essays in Ward (ed.), *British Culture and the End of Empire*, esp. the 'Introduction' by Stuart Ward, 1–20.

[59] J. M. MacKenzie, 'Empire and National Identities: The Case of Scotland', *TRHS* 6/8, (1998), 229–31; see also id., 'On Scotland and the Empire', 738; id., '"The Second City of the Empire": Glasgow—Imperial Municipality', in Felix Driver and David Gilbert (eds.), *Imperial Cities* (Manchester, 1999), 215–37; Forsyth, 'Empire and Union', 10; Gwyn. A. Williams, 'Imperial South Wales', in G. A. Williams, *The Welsh in Their History* (London, 1982), 171–87. An instructive comparison with this process is the development of the identities of the Slav nations within the Austro-Hungarian empire, in response to domination by Germans and Magyars.

Scots, Welsh, and Irish, the cultivation of their distinct identities was a means of offsetting the dominance of the English—the old enemy in both the empire and the United Kingdom. The empire afforded them an opportunity to do so on a scale and in a manner impossible within the home country itself. Scots, Welsh, and Irish were able to carve out distinct 'niches' for themselves within the empire. Cities such as Belfast, Cardiff, Glasgow, and Dundee became in effect imperial cities, performing specific economic functions within the overall economy of the empire. Scottish, Welsh, and Irish regiments maintained and developed a sense of ethnic pride within the overall framework of the imperial armed forces—and were encouraged to do so, as a matter of *esprit de corps*. Colonial settlements of Scots, Welsh, and Irish all over the empire became in many ways the central breeding grounds of their respective nationalisms, maintaining strong connections with their home communities and supporting and promoting their distinctive identities.[60]

The end of empire did not eliminate the need for it, or something like it, as a wider theatre allowing the different nationalities of the United Kingdom to find and express their identities. This was as true for the English as the other nationalities, but characteristically the problem expressed itself differently in the two cases. For the other nationalities the difficulty remained as always the overwhelming preponderance of England, within the United Kingdom as within the empire. All attempts to 'federalize' Britain and the empire since the late nineteenth century had fallen foul of this basic asymmetry. The Kilbrandon Commission on the Constitution of 1973, the last serious attempt to consider a federal solution for Britain, pointed precisely to this obstacle in its conclusion that a United Kingdom federation was 'not a realistic proposition'.[61]

More recently it has been shown how the Soviet Union also played a major role in the creation of national identities within its borders, thus, as with the United Kingdom, establishing 'nations in waiting'—waiting for the break-up of the Soviet empire (which, as with the British empire, was not brought down by nationalism). See T. Martin, *The Affirmative Action Empire: Nations and Nationalism in the Soviet Union, 1923–1939* (Ithaca, NY, 2001).

[60] See, for the relevant historiography, J. MacKenzie, 'Irish, Scottish, Welsh and English Worlds? A Four Nations Approach to the British Empire', paper presented to the conference, 'Race, Nation, Empire: The Writing of Modern British Histories', University College, London, 24–26 Apr. 2008; see also the essays in Bridge and Fedorowich (eds.), *British World*.

[61] Kendle, *Federal Britain*, 8, 165, and *passim*. Kendle rightly stresses that most demands for 'home rule all round' since the 19th century have been basically demands for decentralization and devolution, rather than for true federalism. Almost no one was prepared to demand, or

But if not the empire, why not Europe? If, with the end of empire, the 'Celtic' nationalities had lost one of the principal reasons for remaining attached to the United Kingdom, as well as one of the central means by which they had been able to assert themselves against English dominance, might they be able to find in the developing European Union a functional alternative to the British empire? Could 'Scotland in Europe' substitute for 'Scotland within the Empire'?[62] Ireland seemed to have shown the way. Since its accession to the European Economic Community in 1973, it had blossomed economically and socially, reversing its former position as one of the most backward regions of Europe to become one of the most dynamic and progressive—a magnet for migrants not just from the European Union but from other parts of the world as well. Could not Scotland and Wales repeat the Irish miracle? Could they not also find salvation within Europe? And would that not, in a way, continue the old imperial story of small nations finding a protective niche and nest within the larger framework of a multinational empire? For 'British empire' read 'European Union'—an expansive, still growing, multinational entity that some have already begun to compare to the empires of old.[63]

The relation between empire and identities is one not so much of consciousness as of structure. People may or may not know much about the empire; as with national identity (of which it can of course be an element), their imperial identity may, as a matter of consciousness, be highly fuzzy or unstable. They may even deny point-blank that they have one. But we are given our identities as much as we choose them. To live in an empire, as in a nation, is to be located in set of institutions and practices which daily infuse in us a sense, however imperfectly understood or articulated, of who we are and to what we owe allegiance. It becomes part of our common understanding of the world, and of our place in it. We need be no more self-conscious about it than we are about being a man or a woman.

As John Seeley and later John Pocock so clearly showed, the United Kingdom and the British empire were entities that evolved together, in a 'symbiotic' relationship. The British empire was 'essentially an extension . . . of

concede, that the Westminster parliament should *divide* its sovereignty with the devolved units, whether in the empire or the United Kingdom—so denying a basic requirement of federalism.

[62] Cf. MacKenzie, 'On Scotland and the Empire', 739.

[63] See esp. J. Zielonka, *Europe as Empire: The Nature of the Enlarged European Union* (Oxford, 2007).

the complex of marches and polities by which the archipelago underwent consolidation'. Both were fundamentally achievements of the eighteenth century, and both have marched in step ever since. The identities of the different peoples of the United Kingdom were given—not chosen—by their place in the division of labour that constituted the running of the kingdom and the empire. The blows to the empire, especially as the result of the world wars of the twentieth century, were also blows to the unity and integrity of the United Kingdom. The peoples of the United Kingdom were to a good extent held together by the common enterprise of empire; with its demise, that glue has begun to melt. People begin to look elsewhere for the satisfactions of their interests. 'The connections between loss of empire, assimilation to Europe, and loss of Union are without doubt confused and contradictory, but they seem to exist.'[64]

In an oft-quoted passage, written at the height of the nationalist agitation of the late 1970s, the historian of empire Jan Morris observed:

In the days of the never-setting sun all the pride of Empire was there for the sharing, and to be part of one of the most vital and exciting of the world's Powers was certainly a compensation. But who gets satisfaction from the present state of the Union? Who is really content with this grubby wreck of old glories? Is there anyone, except those with a vested interest in the thing, who does not yearn for a new beginning?[65]

It was a diagnosis and a sentiment frequently expressed at the time, most powerfully in a work that became almost a rallying-cry in certain quarters,

[64] J. G. A. Pocock, 'The Limits and Divisions of British History: In Search of the Unknown Subject', *American Historical Review*, 87/2 (1982), 333–4; see also David McCrone, 'Unmasking Britannia: The Rise and Fall of British National Identity', *Nations and Nationalism*, 3/4 (1997), 579–96; Catherine Hall. 'Introduction', in Hall (ed.), *Cultures of Empire: A Reader* (Manchester, 2000), 2; I. McLean and A. McMillan, *State of the Union: Unionism and Its Alternatives in the United Kingdom since 1707* (Oxford, 2005), 239–56.
[65] J. Morris, 'The Hills are Alive with the Sound of Devolution', *Daily Telegraph* (24 Feb. 1979), quoted in Keith Robbins, ' "This Grubby Wreck of Old Glories": The United Kingdom and the End of the British Empire', *Journal of Contemporary History*, 15 (1980), 83; see also K. Robbins, *Great Britain: Identities, Institutions and the Idea of Britishness* (London, 1998), 302–7. K. Thomas, writing about the same time as Morris, remarked that 'it is no coincidence that the decades of imperial decline have seen a recurrence of separatist feeling in Wales and Scotland. The association with England has become something less obviously to be treasured.' Thomas, 'The United Kingdom', in R. Grew (ed.), *Crises of Political Development in Europe and the United States* (Princeton, 1978), 52–3.

Tom Nairn's *The Break-Up of Britain*.[66] In a similar vein Kenneth Morgan, at the end of his history of modern Wales, commented that 'the loss of empire...has wrought powerful changes in the psyche of the British people', among them the erosion of 'the certainty that had once attached to English and imperial values'. But he noted that the loss of confidence in these values and the other 'dissolving certainties' of late twentieth-century Britain have, if not for the English at least for the Welsh and perhaps others in the United Kingdom, been 'to some degree liberating and invigorating'. They have made Welsh nationalism and Welsh national identity, with their different values and different modes of attachment to place and race, more relevant than ever before.[67]

The 'break-up of Britain' has not so far occurred, nor may it, despite the fillip given to Scottish and Welsh nationalism by the substantial devolution measures introduced in 1997. 'Euroscepticism' remains strong throughout Britain, though certainly less so in Wales and Scotland than in England. Without Europe, without the shelter and support that the European Union makes possible, it is difficult to see how any of the constituent parts of the United Kingdom could make it on their own, least of all the smaller and less prosperous nations on the periphery. Nevertheless empire, or rather its demise, has done its work. It has loosened the bonds that held the nations of the United Kingdom together.[68] It has made it possible, perhaps for the first time since the union of 1707, to conceive of the dissolution of the British state. If, as John Pocock says, a truly 'British history' can be defined as 'the creation of an offshore empire', then 'a case might be made for holding that the history of Britain is coming to an end and is about to be written by the owls of Minerva'.[69]

But if British history comes to an end, what does this say about *English* history? Where do the English fit into this story? The English are the anomaly, the joker in the pack. It is they who masterminded the whole imperial venture, from the conquests of Wales and Ireland in the thirteenth century, to the forced incorporating union with Scotland in 1707, to the

---

[66] T. Nairn, *The Break-Up of Britain: Crisis and Neo-Nationalism* (1977; 3rd, expanded edn., Edinburgh, 2003).

[67] Morgan, *Rebirth of a Nation*, 419–21.

[68] Though one should note T. M. Devine's view that Scotland's disenchantment with the empire long pre-dated its end, starting with the economic and social crisis of the interwar period: 'Break-Up of Britain?', 174–80.

[69] Pocock, 'Limits and Divisions', 334.

global expansion of the empire from the eighteenth to the twentieth centuries. They did not do this alone, of course; the other peoples of both the
'inner' and the 'outer' empires were in most cases willing accomplices and
often beneficiaries. But the empire, just as the United Kingdom, carried an
English stamp, in its dominant culture and institutions. The English were
the imperial people par excellence, the ones who could afford to suppress
ethnic and national pride in pursuit of a wider and more-encompassing
imperial mission.

The end of empire was bound to affect the English even more than Welsh,
Scots, and Irish. Those others had to some extent created their identities
against the dominant English; without empire they felt free to accentuate
those identities and to find an alternative theatre of operations in Europe
and perhaps elsewhere as well (the continuing links with the former white
dominions might prove important in this respect). This left the English
feeling doubly exposed: the loss of the outer empire—the British empire—
was now also matched by the possible loss of the inner empire—the United
Kingdom. Moreover, if the Scots and Welsh had problems with Europe, the
English had, for good historical reasons, even greater ones, thus making the
European card even more difficult for them to play.[70]

The legacy of empire in the English case is an acute question of national
identity. The Scots, Welsh, and Irish seem relatively secure in theirs, in this
case their subordinate position in the United Kingdom and the empire has
served them well. Nothing creates identities better than exclusion and
opposition. The English were able to look with lordly disdain on 'mere'
nationalism—in their eyes, something akin to tribalism and best suited to
an earlier stage of civilisation. For them, the main opponents were other
imperial powers—France, Russia, Japan, perhaps Germany and the United
States. But imperial competition is of a different nature from national
competition. Nations look to a world of nations, equal in principle. Empires
seek universality—the realization, on a world scale, of the 'civilizing
mission' that most empires aspire to carry. Ideally there can be only one
empire—a world empire.[71]

The fact that the British empire came close to realizing that ideal only
makes things more difficult for the English once that empire has gone. If

---

[70] See K. Kumar, 'Britain, England and Europe: Cultures in Contraflow', *European Journal of
Social Theory*, 6/1 (2003), 5–23.

[71] See, further on this, Kumar, 'Empires and Nations'.

you have been lords of the world, it is a little hard to shrink to being a mere nation. The difficulty is compounded by the fact that the English, engaged in empire and other global enterprises, had no need for and therefore did not develop the resources of a tradition of reflection on national identity and national character (as David Hume put it, 'the English, of any people in the universe, have the least of a national character; unless this very singularity may pass for such'[72]). This was by no means disabling for much of the time—one might think it almost fortunate, given the excesses of nationalism in the last century or so. But it became problematic with the loss of empire, and the rise of nationalism in other parts of the United Kingdom. Whether or not the United Kingdom broke up, it seemed apparent that from now on the four nations would need to be more conscious of their own character and take more control of their own concerns. After 1997, the Scots, Welsh, and Northern Irish had their own parliaments, or something close to it; the English did not. To many in England this began to seem unfair and anomalous. One began to see a movement for the establishment of an English parliament, alongside the parliament at Westminster; even the rise of that historical oddity, English nationalism.[73]

'The danger for the English is that they will be left holding on to the symbols and institutions of Britain long after it has been cleared out of any emotional or political meaning...England should prepare itself for the abandonment of Britain and give some thought to its own political future.'[74] Is this what the four-hundred-year story of empire has come to? The empire reduced to its English core, the protective layers surrounding it one by one peeled away, leaving it to fend for itself? Certainly there is no reason to think that it could not survive in this form. England's wealth and population—far greater than that of Wales, Scotland, and Northern Ireland combined—are sufficient to allow it to compete on equal terms with virtually any nation on earth, only the very largest such as the United States and China perhaps excepted. Its membership of the European Union, for all its occasional holding back, gives it additional support and direction. Even the perhaps residual goodwill of the Commonwealth, and the sometimes misguided

---

[72] D. Hume, 'Of National Character' (1741), in E. F. Miller (ed.), *Essays, Moral, Political and Literary* (Indianapolis, 1987), 207.

[73] See, among others, M. Perryman, (ed.), *Imagined Nation: England after Britain* (London, 2008); D. Goodhart, *Progressive Nationalism: Citizenship and the Left* (London, 2006); A. Aughey, *The Politics of Englishness* (Manchester, 2007); Weight, *Patriots*, 706–26.

[74] D. Goodhart, 'England Arise', *Prospect*, 148 (July 2008), 5.

sense of kinship with the United States, can serve it well, in drawing upon a common store of basically English institutions and understandings with which to confront the problems of an increasingly disorderly and turbulent world.[75] If not the English themselves, the English inheritance in the world remains rich and powerful.

Nevertheless there may be good grounds for mourning the death—if that is what comes to pass—of the United Kingdom. It has been some kind of experiment in multinationalism, as was the larger British empire of which it was a part. In an increasingly multicultural world, marked by mass migrations and new intermixings of peoples, the wiser choice would seem to be the larger and more capacious political unit rather than the smaller and potentially more exclusive one. It may not be entirely a matter of intellectual fashions that empires are once more arousing serious scholarly interest. They embody a wealth of experience in the management of difference and diversity. The British empire was one of the most imposing of these attempts. It may be that not the least of its legacies are the lessons that can be learned from its history.

Select Bibliography

A. AUGHEY, *The Politics of Englishness* (Manchester, 2007).

V. BOGDANOR, *Devolution in the United Kingdom* (Oxford, 2001).

C. G. A. BRYANT, *The Nations of Britain* (Oxford, 2006).

R. COLLS, *Identity of Britain* (Oxford, 2002).

C. HALL and S. O. ROSE (eds.), *At Home with the Empire: Metropolitan Culture and the Imperial World* (Cambridge, 2006).

J. DARWIN, *Britain and Decolonisation: The Retreat from Empire in the Post-War World* (Basingstoke, 1988).

J. GALLAGHER, *The Decline, Revival and Fall of the British Empire: The Ford Lectures and Other Essays*, ed. Anil Seal (Cambridge, 1982).

J. KENDLE, *Federal Britain: A History* (London, 1997).

K. KUMAR, *The Making of English National Identity* (Cambridge, 2003).

J. MACKENZIE, *Propaganda and Empire: The Manipulation of British Public Opinion 1880–1960* (Manchester, 1984).

I. McLEAN and A. McMILLAN, *State of the Union: Unionism and the Alternatives in the United Kingdom since 1707* (Oxford, 2005).

---

[75] See the interesting remarks in Deudney, 'Greater Britain or Greater Synthesis?', 207–8; also Bell, *Idea of Greater Britain*, 266–72.

P. MANDLER, *The English National Character: The History of an Idea from Edmund Burke to Tony Blair* (New Haven, 2006).

D. MORLEY and K. ROBINS (eds.), *British Cultural Studies: Geography, Nationality, and Identity* (Oxford, 2001).

S. O. ROSE, *Which People's War? National Identity and Citizenship in Wartime Britain 1939–1945* (Oxford, 2004).

R. SAMUEL, *Island Stories: Unravelling Britain* (London, 1999).

A. S. THOMPSON, *The Empire Strikes Back? The Impact of Imperialism on Britain from the Mid-Nineteenth Century* (Harlow, 2005).

P. WARD, *Britishness since 1870* (London, 2004).

S. WARD (ed.), *British Culture and the End of Empire* (Manchester, 2001).

W. WEBSTER, *Englishness and Empire 1939–1965* (Oxford, 2007).

R. WEIGHT, *Patriots: National Identity in Britain 1940–2000* (London, 2002).

9

Afterword: The Imprint of the Empire

Andrew Thompson

All empires generate their own legacies. If the aftermath of the British empire left its mark abroad, did it also do so at home, however? If so, were the consequences of colonialism for Britain itself confined mainly to the years immediately after decolonization, or have they in fact proved more enduring? As the colonies broke free from the 'mother country' after 1945, what were the repercussions for the British people and their conceptions of themselves?

While the 1960s saw a highly charged debate about the specific issue of 'new' Commonwealth immigration, not until the 1980s was there a significant effort to analyse, and to try to come to terms with, the persistence of an imperial 'legacy' in Britain. By this time, the vast majority of Britain's formal colonial responsibilities had come to an end, yet to some at least it appeared that their influence tenaciously lived on. The release of several high-budget films and television programmes narrating the privileged lifestyles of white, settler elites in the empire provoked critics to speak of a 'Raj' revival. The Indian-born novelist Salman Rushdie led the way, declaring them to be mere 'heritage' productions, responsible for rehabilitating the empire's tarnished image. In Rushdie's view, these productions were best understood as an artistic counterpart to the rise of conservative ideologies, a form of escape from what he perceived to be the growing inequalities of Britain under the premiership of Margaret Thatcher. However, if sepia-tinted visions of the imperial past offered escapism, it was not only from 'domestic' poverty and social hardship. Anger amongst ethnic minorities at racial discrimination, particularly from the police, sparked riots and disturbances as far apart as Brixton, Birmingham, Liverpool, and Leeds, and in turn encapsulated for many white British people all that was undesirable about empire 'coming home'.[1]

To be sure, not all of the dramatizations of the 1980s that are associated with the 'nostalgia industry' were about the empire. The Granada TV production of *Brideshead Revisited* (screened in eleven episodes in 1981) and *Chariots of Fire* (of the same year) are cases in point. Yet Rushdie was by no means alone in highlighting this decade as a moment of 'imperialist nostalgia'—a condition diagnosed by one scholar as a desire 'to relive the glory days of empire while simultaneously mourning their demise',[2] and by another as 'an elegiac mode of perception' whereby people mourned the passing of a disappearing world that they themselves had transformed and destroyed.[3] Indeed, many critics were quick to point out that the injustices of empire were far less prominent in these films and TV serials than they had been in the novels which had inspired them, with the camera preferring the epic sweep and exotic spectacle of the British in power to the harsher realities of colonial relations.

Several of the productions in question were about the British ruling class in India. Among the best known are the television adaptation of Paul Scott's 'Raj Quartet' (1966–75), a fourteen-episode serial screened in 1984 as *The Jewel in the Crown*, and David Lean's film of E. M. Forster's *A Passage to India* (1924) of the same year.[4] Although apparently popular with audiences, such productions were roundly condemned by the critics for providing a 'comfort blanket' that, by glamorizing the Raj, served only to distract the British from the uncomfortable realities of their colonial past.[5] Neither production was entirely uncritical of empire—albeit Lean was accused of expunging much of the anti-imperial sentiment of Forster's novel. Yet, by focusing on the private lives of the British community, they did tend to

---

[1] On this point, see S. Marks, 'History, the Nation and Empire: Sniping from the Periphery', *History Workshop Journal*, 29/1 (1990), 111–19. Some of the contemporary explanations of these outbreaks of urban unrest treated race and law as the key variables, while others focused on inner city decay and unemployment. For the debates provoked by these riots, and their legacies, see J. Solomos, *Race and Racism in Britain* (3rd edn., Basingstoke, 2003), 142–71.

[2] H.-M. Teo, 'Wandering in the Wake of Empire: British Travel and Tourism in the Post-Imperial World', in S. Ward (ed.), *British Culture and the End of Empire* (Manchester, 2001), 169.

[3] R. Rosaldo, 'Imperialist Nostalgia', *Representations*, 26 (1989), 107–22, at 107.

[4] See also *The Flame Trees of Thika* (Thames Television, 1981); *Heat and Dust* (James Ivory, 1982); *The Far Pavilions* (1984); and *Out of Africa* (1985).

[5] Michael Binyon, 'It's All the Raj Again', *The Times* (23 Apr. 2005).

portray India primarily through European eyes.[6] It was Western rather than Eastern characters that formed the backbone of plots, and who had complexity and depth,[7] even if what was arguably the greatest screen portrayal of the British Raj at this time—Richard Attenborough's Academy award-winning *Gandhi* (1982)—was more attuned to Indian perspectives. Another notable exception was the long-running television drama *Tenko* (1981–4), which dealt with the experiences of British, Australian, and Dutch women captured after the fall of Singapore (1942) and held in a Japanese internment camp. *Tenko* presented a somewhat different view of empire by showing some of the class tensions that existed in an ostensibly homogenous Western settler population.

In hindsight, it is easier to see that the legacies of empire that surfaced in the 1980s often did so for particular reasons and in particular ways. Zimbabwean independence in 1980 brought the last of the British wars of decolonization to an end, while two years later military adventure in the South Atlantic provided the chance to show that, empire or not, 'Britain had not lost the capacity to solve the problems facing it'.[8] Certainly, compared with the 1980s, the twenty-first century's interest in empire has so far proved more wide-ranging and arguably far-reaching. Today, we are living at a time of growing public interest in the relationship between Britain's colonial past and its postcolonial present, which has manifested itself across the news and entertainment media, and which has been wrapped up in feelings of anger, shame, and guilt as well as pride and nostalgia.[9] In a multi-ethnic society, subject to historically unprecedented levels of immigration, and grappling with questions of race and religion, the cross-cultural encounters engendered by the rise and fall of the British empire seem to speak powerfully to a range of contemporary concerns.

[6] J. Wilson, 'Niall Ferguson's Imperial Passion', *History Workshop Journal*, 56/1 (2003), 175–83, at 179–80.
[7] W. Webster, 'Domesticating the Frontier: Gender, Empire and Adventure Landscapes in British Cinema, 1945–1959', *Gender and History*, 15/1 (2003), 85–107; and A. Blunt, '"Land of our Mothers": Home, Identity, and Nationality for Anglo-Indians in British India, 1919–1947', *History Workshop Journal*, 54/1 (2002), 49–72. As Blunt puts it, 'Eurasians were portrayed as "tragic figures" whose British ancestry was paramount, yet who were "ultimately out of place in both British and independent India", rather than as people of mixed descent struggling with a dual affinity with Britain and India' (53–4).
[8] See here Richard Whiting, Ch. 5 in this volume.
[9] A. Woollacott, 'Making Empire Visible or Making Colonialism Visible? The Struggle for the British Imperial Past', *British Scholar*, 1/2 (2009), 7–17.

The idea that the empire might provide a source of satisfaction or pride, which still had considerable purchase during the 1980s, is also now beginning to look more outdated.[10] This may owe something to the way in which disturbing aspects of British imperial past have and continue to be unearthed. There are many such examples. Revelations of widespread detention, torture, and killings in Kenya and Malaya during the 1950s have raised difficult questions about why such practices were sanctioned at the time and why they subsequently have taken so long to be revealed.[11] Following campaigns by former child migrants, the British and Australian governments have been moved to apologize formally for the transportation and treatment of thousands of juveniles who were separated from their families, settled in far-off countries, and sometimes abused by the institutions entrusted with their care.[12] The long campaign for the repatriation of cultural artefacts and human remains of Aboriginal people held by museums in England and Scotland has reminded the British public of the brutal circumstances in which these remains first came into Britain's possession.[13] And acts of public commemoration have exposed the difficulties of reconciling memory with history, particularly with respect to the sharply conflicting perspectives that still exist on subjects such as slavery and the slave trade.[14]

Demands for recognition, reparation, and restitution, whether in relation to settler brutality, child migration, cultural artefacts, or slavery, can easily catch politicians on the horns of a dilemma—whether to acknowledge or apologize for past colonial 'wrongs', in the hope of assuaging them, or whether to refuse to do so for fear of the electoral consequences of

---

[10] This is not, of course, to say that such an idea is discredited or defunct. Indeed, for the view that 'mourning' or 'melancholia' for the imperial past still prevents Britain from moving towards a healthier society, able to acknowledge and confront the depth and extent of racism, see Paul Gilroy's *After Empire. Melancholia or Convivial Culture* (London, 2004).

[11] On Mau Mau, see D. Branch, *Defeating Mau Mau, Creating Kenya: Counterinsurgency, Civil War and Decolonisation* (Cambridge, 2009); D. Anderson, *Histories of the Hanged: The Dirty War in Kenya and the End of Empire* (London, 2006); C. Elkins, *Imperial Reckoning: The Untold Story of Britain's Gulag in Kenya* (New York, 2005).

[12] S. Constantine, 'The British Government, Child Welfare and Child Migration to Australia after 1945', *Journal of Imperial and Commonwealth History* (*JICH*), 30 (2002), 99–132.

[13] A. S. Thompson, *Living the Past: Public Memories of Empire in Twenty-First Century Britain*, Trevor Reese Memorial Lecture 2007 (London, 2008).

[14] The territorial remains of empire also provide tangible links between the colonial past and the post- or neo-colonial present: the Chagos Islands are a case in point.

appearing to impugn the national 'character'.[15] More broadly, there is the issue of what might be called the 'inheritance' of colonial violence: can one posit a causal relationship between the coercion and repression that characterized colonial counter-insurgency campaigns, and the ethnic clashes in Africa and anti-immigrant violence in Europe, which we are witnessing today? Above all, it is the worldwide increase in the mobility of virtually all categories of migrants—legal and illegal; refugees and asylum-seekers; temporary guest workers and permanent residents—that has brought decolonization home to roost. The moment migratory flows (and the colonial encounter) reversed, and large numbers of people began to arrive in Britain *from* the Caribbean and South Asia, the rhetoric and reality of 'imperial' citizenship suddenly collided. During the 1960s and 1970s, British governments sought to tighten border controls in ways that increasingly privileged 'old' (white) over 'new' (non-white) Commonwealth citizens. Coded legal restrictions, previously used to keep 'coloured' people out of Britain's settler colonies (often through education or language tests), were now adopted in the United Kingdom, through voucher schemes, annual quotas, 'patrial' clauses, or work permits. In theory these immigration controls were meant to be accompanied by positive measures of integration for existing immigrants, including an end to discrimination in housing, employment and public services. In practice the notion of multiculturalism, as it took shape in Britain towards and after the end of empire, was a limited and arguably impoverished one.[16] In many ways it was redolent of the notion of 'indirect rule', in that it betrayed a liberal decolonizing establishment desperately

[15] On memory and forgetting, see P. Connerton, *How Societies Remember* (Cambridge, 1990); K. Hodgkin and S. Radstone (eds.), *Contested Pasts: The Politics of Memory* (London, 2003); M. Lake (ed.), *Memory, Monuments and Museums: The Past in The Present* (Melbourne, 2006); W. James and L. van de Vijver (eds.), *After the TRC: Reflections on Truth and Reconciliation in South Africa* (Claremont, 2000). On the issue of restitution specifically, see E. Barkan, *The Guilt of Nations. Restitution and Negotiating Historical Injustices* (New York, 2000).

[16] For a comparative study of the concept, see C. Joppke, 'Multiculturalism and Immigration: A Comparison of the United States, Germany and Great Britain', *Theory and Society*, 25 (1996), 449–500 (476–86 for the case of Britain specifically, where the author claims 'the legacy of empire created a unique linkage between immigration and multiculturalism'). For a selection of key texts, see T. Modood, *Multiculturalism: A Civic Idea* (Cambridge, 2007); B. Parekh, *Rethinking Multiculturalism: Cultural Diversity and Political Theory* (Basingstoke, 2000); S. Vertovec and S. Wessendorf (eds.), *The Multiculturalism Backlash: European Discourses, Polices and Practices* (London, 2010). For a recent, provocative contribution to the debate, which criticizes prevailing theory and practice, see Rumy Hasan's *Multiculuralism: Some Inconvenient Truths* (London, 2010).

trying to accommodate these newcomers to Britain's shores, yet equally reluctant to contemplate the type of inclusive measures and policies that might provoke the hostility of white workers whose concerns about living standards, housing, and jobs were being played upon by the controversial Conservative MP Enoch Powell.[17] Understood in this way, the lineage of today's debates about *British* citizenship is therefore very much a colonial one.

Reflecting on the remaking of British identity in the aftermath of decolonization, the historian and sociologist Mike Savage has recently used the term 'epoch descriptions' to describe how social knowledge and notions of identity have changed over time.[18] Savage cites 'affluence' in the 1960s, 'post-industrialism' in the 1970s and 1980s, and 'globalization' in the 1990s as descriptions that have come to define the meaning of social change. Should 'postcolonialism' be included in this list? After all, for several disciplines in the humanities it would appear to be among the most influential of interpretations of how the past continues to shape the present, especially the 'political' present. In the words of one leading contributor to the field, postcolonialism might usefully be thought of as a 'politics and philosophy of activism that contests disparity, and so continues in a new way the anti-colonial struggles of the past'.[19] Empire, according to such a view, was essentially a matter of power: conquest, coercion, unequal authority, and extra-judicial repression were of its very essence. The registers of this power, however, were as much cultural and psychological as they were military, political, and economic, the implication being that the (ongoing) challenge of 'decolonization' has been, and continues to be, as much one of liberating people's minds as of repelling foreign armies, dismantling their bureaucracies, or controlling their corporations.

This idea of a distinctive 'colonial condition' has been explored by successive phases of postcolonialist writing. Octave Mannoni's 'colonial complex' (1956) referred to a dependency engendered on the part of colonized people's by their domination by colonial Europeans, while Frantz Fanon's 'colonial pathology' (1961) centred on a psychic disorder at the

---

[17] On Powell, immigration, and the 20 April 1968 'Birmingham' or 'Rivers of Blood' speech, see S. Heffer, *Like the Roman: the Life of Enoch Powell* (London, 2008 ed.), 449–59.

[18] M. Savage, *Identities and Social Change in Britain since 1940: The Politics of Method* (Oxford, 2010).

[19] R. Young, *Postcolonialism: An Historical Introduction* (Oxford, 2003), 4.

heart of colonialism marked by 'a furious determination to deny the other person of all attributes of humanity'.[20] More recently, the Kenyan author Ngũgĩ wa Thiong'o, who lost his stepbrother and whose mother was tortured during the Mau Mau Emergency, has spoken of a 'cultural bomb' unleashed by imperialism on Africa, the effect of which has been to annihilate a people's belief in 'their names, their languages, in their environment, in their heritage of struggle, in their unity, in their capacities and ultimately in themselves'.[21]

The view that colonialism had a profoundly dehumanizing effect, fundamentally changing how people perceived themselves, has thus been widely applied to the colonized.[22] There has been much less consideration of its relevance for the colonizers. Indeed, even as it became fashionable towards the end of the last century to speak of Britain's former colonies as 'post-colonial' societies, there remained a marked reluctance to apply this way of thinking to Britain itself. One of the first people to do so was the Indian political and social theorist Ashis Nandy. Focusing on the relationship between mass violence, nationalism, and culture, Nandy provided a systematic exposition of what he called the 'cultural pathologies of colonialism' for the Europeans. His book, *The Intimate Enemy* (1983), turned the spotlight from the colonized to the colonizing societies in order to question the 'folk wisdom' that the only sufferers of colonialism were subject communities.[23] It advanced the view that the colonizers were just as much affected by the ideology of colonialism, with the British in particular having been 'overwhelmed by their experience of being colonial rulers'.[24] Indeed, according to Nandy, colonialism did long-term cultural damage to Britain. It brought into prominence the least tender and humane parts of its political culture, openly sanctified forms of institutionalized violence, justified a limited

---

[20] Octave Mannoni, *Prospero and Caliban: The Psychology of Colonization* (London, 1956); Frantz Fanon, *The Wretched of the Earth*, trans. Constance Farrington (New York, 1963), and *Black Skin White Masks*, trans. Charles Markmann (New York, 1967).

[21] Ngũgĩ Wa Thing'o, *Decolonising the Mind: The Politics of Language in African Literature* (London, 1986), 3; See also Ngũgĩ Wa Thiong'o, *Dreams in a Time of War: A Childhood Memoir* (London, 2010).

[22] A. Césaire, *Discourse on Colonialism*, trans. J. Pinkham (New York, 1972 edn.), 20.

[23] A. Nandy, *The Intimate Enemy: The Loss and Recovery of Self under Colonialism* (Oxford, 1983), 29–48, at 30.

[24] Ibid. 32.

cultural role for women, applied a colonial concept of hierarchy to British society, and produced a false sense of cultural homogeneity.[25]

The question of whether Britain's empire was ultimately enriched or corrupted by the exercise of power does, of course, pre-date the advent of postcolonial studies. Generations of anti-imperialists grappled with this very issue. In fact, it could be argued that, over the centuries, British radicals and other critics of empire focused their gaze as much on the adverse social and political consequences of colonization for Britain—arising from authoritarian, militaristic, and capitalist rule—as they did on the violence and disruption inflicted on indigenous peoples.[26]

That said, contemporary postcolonialist writing clearly provides us with a much more developed framework for thinking about the current legacies of empire for Britain itself. To what extent, then, do the chapters in this volume lend credence to Nandy's view that the entanglements of empire were sufficiently dangerous, damaging, and divisive to have been a lasting, negative influence on the Britain we know today? From the preceding pages emerge three key challenges. First, there is the paradox that Britain's international position since 1945 is widely perceived to have declined while British politicians have nonetheless continued to envisage Britain's national security in global terms.[27] Second, there is the difficulty that Britain has experienced in matching a multiracial vision of the Commonwealth with a multiracial vision of Britain. Third, there is the increasing uncertainty surrounding the sense of British nationality as the empire receded, when that identity, and the identities of the constituent parts of the United

---

[25] Ibid. 32–5.

[26] A point well made by Miles Taylor's excellent essay, '*Imperium et Libertas*: Rethinking the Radical Critique of Imperialism during the Nineteenth Century', *JICH* 19/1 (1991), 1–23. On critics of empire, see also: B. Porter, *Critics of Empire: British Radical Attitudes to Colonialism in Africa, 1895–1914* (London, 1968); S. Howe, *Anticolonialism in British Politics: The Left and the End of Empire, 1918–1964* (Oxford, 1993); A. S. Thompson, 'The Language of Imperialism and the Meanings of Empire: Imperial Discourse in British Politics, 1895–1914', *Journal of British Studies* (*JBS*), 36/2 (1997), 147–77; and P. J. Cain, *Hobson and Imperialism: Radicalism, New Liberalism, and Finance 1887–1938* (Oxford, 2002).

[27] There is a large literature on the subject of decline, deftly introduced by Jim Tomlinson's essay in this volume. See also R. English and M. Kenny, 'British Decline or the Politics of Declinism', *British Journal of Politics and International Relations*, 1/2 (1999), 252–66, and their edited book, *Rethinking British Decline* (Basingstoke, 2000). On the economy specifically, see P. Clarke and C. Trebilcock (eds.), *Understanding Decline: Perceptions and Realities of British Economic Performance* (Cambridge, 2007).

Kingdom from which it was fashioned, had been so intimately tied up with a wider imperial consciousness for much of the twentieth century. In each of these ways, this volume suggests, the empire can be seen to have dug deeper under the skin of British society, with its imperial legacies continuing to work persistently and sometimes powerfully into the present day.

Debates about Britain's international involvements have made media headlines as a result of the protracted conflicts in Afghanistan and the Middle East. Today's experience of being a 'nation at peace and an army at war' is very much redolent of the earlier colonial counter-insurgency campaigns fought by the British army.[28] After serving in Palestine during the closing years of the League of Nations' mandate, Trevor Hall, a soldier in the Royal Artillery, recorded how 'the dangers from explosive devices and sniper bullets were ever present', and how 'daily we [learned] of assassinations, of bombings and attacks by guns, grenades and mortars'.[29] Hall could equally have been describing the situation in Iraq or Afghanistan fifty years later. Members of today's armed forces share with previous generations of soldiers the certainty of regular deployment to brutal conflicts in unknown foreign lands, in which they face the prospect of losing their life or returning home seriously disabled, as well as the uncertainty of what victory might mean and of how British forces might leave.[30]

There are also differences, of course. In the early twenty-first century news is conveyed far more quickly and effectively to the population at large than it was during the wars of decolonization. Moreover, since the Falklands War in 1982, the bodies of soldiers killed in action have been brought home. Those killed in Iraq and Afghanistan, for example, have been repatriated to Britain via RAF Lyneham. The residents of nearby Wootton Bassett, the small Wiltshire town which has become a focal point for these homecomings, have turned out to pay their respects and to bear witness to the human

---

[28] See e.g. the 150-foot-wide stone structure erected in the heart of England at Alrewas, Staffordshire, in 2007 to commemorate the 15,000-plus members of the armed services who have lost their lives since the Second World War. This monument will increasingly see the names of those who were killed in Iraq, Afghanistan, and the Falklands match the numbers from the Korean War (1950–3) and Northern Ireland (from 1969).

[29] T. Hall, *Enduring the Hour: A British Soldier in Palestine, 1946–1947* (Lincolnshire, 2005), 9 and 44.

[30] For an interesting commentary on the parallels between British military interventions in Iraq in 2003 and 1914, see esp. Charles Townshend's *When God Made Hell: The British Invasion of Mesopotamia and the Creation of Iraq, 1914–1921* (London, 2010).

cost of a protracted postcolonial conflict. Questions of why Britain has intervened militarily in Iraq and Afghanistan, and whether it is engaged in conflicts it can never win, have hung over these occasions, albeit the full implications of these questions have been tempered by the desire to show solidarity with the relatives of those men and women who have given their lives. Furthermore, to a greater extent than during the end days of empire, the conduct of serving British troops in the city of Basra and Helmand province has also come under close scrutiny. Indeed, calls for retrospective public enquiries into the killing of unarmed men by British forces looking for Communist insurgents in Malaya in 1948, and legal battles begun by survivors of torture in Kenyan detention camps in 1959 who now demand compensation, have eerily coincided with present-day investigations by journalists and human rights activists into the actions of servicemen allegedly operating outside the law in the Middle East.

While the Falklands War—justified in terms of the principle of self-determination for the Falkland islanders—arguably signified the advent of a 'post-imperial Conservatism',[31] New Labour's rhetoric of liberal interventionism or 'moralising internationalism', accompanying more recent conflicts in Iraq and Afghanistan, has harkened back to an imperial past. Britain's choice of allies may now be the United States and Europe, rather than the Commonwealth. But, as Philip Murphy observes, Britain in the early twenty-first century still seems to feel that it has wider responsibilities to discharge in the world. This type of rhetoric could, to be sure, be read simply as politicians playing to the electoral gallery. Yet it might also point to a belief among a post-war generation of political and military leaders that Britain's imperial past has equipped them with the judgement and experience necessary to resolve certain types of dispute and to exercise leadership on an international stage. As this volume has shown, several of the difficulties and dilemmas faced by politicians today were faced by their predecessors during the era of decolonization, not the least the question of whether universal principles of political organization (democratic representation especially) are applicable to all societies irrespective of their racial, ethnic, and linguistic complexion. Understood thus, the empire, long after the end of formal decolonization, remains a vital source of military and political experience—a point of reference not easily erased. Or, as Kumar less

---

[31] On this point, see Richard Whiting, Ch. 5 in this volume.

positively puts it, 'One does not so easily shrug off three-and-a-half hundred years of imperial existence.'

Not surprisingly, many of the contributors to this volume refer to the
challenge, in an increasingly secular society, of managing the raft of contentious religious and racial issues inherited from an imperial past. British
Christianity was reshaped by the history of immigration from the West
Indies, with the creation of many more Pentecostal and charismatic congregations. The arrival of South Asian immigrants further turned Britain
into a religiously diverse society—British Muslims now attend prayers at the
mosque at a 'stunningly higher rate' than Christians attend church.[32] For
much of the last two centuries, Europe's multinational empires similarly
had to manage their intrinsically diverse subject populations, as well as the
movement of people within and beyond their boundaries. As Western
governments grapple with the effects of ethnic diasporas, complex international migrations, and the resulting intermixing of peoples, what lessons,
if any, can they learn from this aspect of empire?[33]

Arguably the biggest single change to Britain since the Second World War
has been the transformation of the ethnic complexion of its population.[34]
The racial and religious diversity brought about by 'new' Commonwealth
immigration has changed the appearance of many parts of the United
Kingdom, and led to major differences in the way we live. Here it needs to
be understood that decolonization had a profound effect on public as well
as official responses to immigration. The link between, on the one hand, the
British government's capacity to provide for immigrants from its former
empire and, on the other, perceptions of its commitment to leading a
multiracial Commonwealth, was highly significant. Debates about immigration policy during the 1950s and 1960s were continually being weighed
against the effects they were likely to have on inter-Commonwealth relations. Thus, in spite of a distinct lack of enthusiasm for immigration from

[32] See Jeffrey Cox, Ch. 3 in this volume.

[33] J. Darwin, *After Tamerlane: The Global History of Empire since 1405* (London, 2007).

[34] For an introduction to post-war immigration, see R. Winder, *Bloody Foreigners: The Story
of Immigration to Britain* (London, 2004), and J. Walvin, *Passage to Britain: Immigration in
British History and Politics* (Harmondsworth, 1984). For the issue of race relations, see K. Paul,
Whitewashing Britain: Race and Citizenship in the Postwar Era (Ithaca, NY, 1997), and I. Spencer,
British Immigration Policy since 1939: The Making of a Multi-Racial Britain (London, 1997). But
arguably the best overall study of the social history of Commonwealth immigrants remains that
by Dilip Hiro, *Black British, White British* (London, 1971).

the dependent empire, what was referred to as 'Commonwealth sentiment' initially tempered vocal demands for the introduction of controls, with the government stating that Commonwealth citizens should not be treated differently to British nationals.

However, whilst it was important to show that 'new' Commonwealth immigrants would be treated equally and without discrimination, in prac- tice this meant that they could expect to gain access to statutory services and little more. Prior to the 1960s, 'integration' or 'assimilation' (the two words were used interchangeably because the assumptions upon which they were based were both widespread and unchallenged) rested on the belief that immigrants would, as time passed, naturally adapt to a British way of life by relying upon existing local services and the goodwill of the British people.[35] This represented the long-standing view that immigrants would be able to 'pull themselves up by their own bootstraps and to integrate themselves'. Yet, by the mid-1960s, it was becoming increasingly evident that reliance upon local efforts, the virtues of British citizens, and the good behaviour of Commonwealth citizens was not sufficient to prevent much-feared 'social problems' from posing a threat to good race relations. The inadequacy of the government's policy up to this time was starkly summarized by Britain's first Minister for Integration, Maurice Foley, on a tour of local authorities in 1965: 'Previously it had been assumed that immigrants would adjust without any help, that the social services could cope without difficulty with the burdens, and that British people as a whole were tolerant. It was becoming increasingly obvious that none of these assumptions were well founded.'[36]

Britain has never had an interventionist integration policy. Rather it has opted for a combination of a stringent immigration policy, regulated access to statutory services, and a legal framework for anti-discrimination. During the 1950s and 1960s, integration as a policy was politically expedient but amounted to very little. While an 'inclusive formal nationality policy' stressed that all members of the empire shared a universal British national- ity, and hence had the right to enter the United Kingdom, this was at odds

---

[35] E. Passmore, 'The Politics of Immigration and Welfare in the Context of Decolonisation: A Comparative Analysis of Immigrant Housing Policy in Britain and France during the 1950s and 1960s' (MA Research Thesis, University of Leeds, 2006).

[36] E. Passmore and A. S. Thompson, 'Multiculturalism, Decolonisation and Immigration: Integration Policy in Britain and France after the Second World War', in K. Fedorowich and A. S. Thompson (eds.), *Empire, Identity and Migration in the British World* (Manchester, forthcoming).

with what has been termed an 'informal national identity', more narrow and exclusive, and based on 'a racialized understanding of the world's population'.[37] These rival conceptions of British identity were not without serious social consequences in the post-war era. The intellectual mood of the time, in which the idea of 'one nation, one culture' seemed dangerous and wrong, ostensibly gave 'dignity to difference'. Yet concerns have since grown over the effects of the doctrine of multiculturalism, which, despite being deeply entrenched in our liberal democracy, is felt by some to be leading to greater segregation rather than integration. One of the most significant developments in recent years is the advent of new communication technologies— the Internet, mobile phones, and satellite television. While uniting people globally, these technologies are often perceived to divide them locally by strengthening non-national affiliations, and thereby to have changed, or at least to be in the process of changing, the terms of the debate about multiculturalism. In the words of one commentator, 'There is no nation. There are merely people-in-proximity.'[38] Multiculturalism, and the specific set of circumstances from which it arose, is thus increasingly coming under scrutiny both from academics interested in the subject of immigration as well as those working in the field of 'race relations'.[39]

What has proved difficult to disentangle, however, is the relationship between Britain's long imperial involvement and specific manifestations of domestic racial prejudice. How far have the latter been an inevitable consequence of the former? We must tread cautiously here. The history of Commonwealth migration needs to be set in the wider context of twentieth-century immigration to Britain. There were strains of 'indigenous racism' in which 'colonial mentalities' played a relatively minor role, with anti-alien sentiment expressed towards European (and especially Jewish) immigrants throughout the nineteenth and well into the twentieth century. Moreover, as the contributors to this volume rightly emphasize, racial discourses in twentieth-century Britain were neither singular nor static. For example, we have seen how the ethnocentric narratives that persisted in missionary

---

[37] K. Paul, '"British Subjects" and "British Stock": Labour's Postwar Imperialism', *JBS* 34/2 (1995), 236–9.

[38] J. Sacks, 'Wanted: A National Culture', *The Times* (20 Oct. 2007), 23.

[39] For the view that multiculturalism is not a meaningful concept, and that 'no one could possibly be a multiculturalist in any interesting or coherent sense', see Stanley Fish, 'Boutique Multiculturalism, or Why Liberals Are Incapable of Thinking about Hate Speech', *Critical Inquiry* (Winter 1997), 378–95, at 384.

societies and literature during the interwar era gradually gave way after the Second World War to a new emphasis on 'Third Worldism', championed by development experts in organizations like the Student Christian Movement, Oxfam, Voluntary Service Overseas, and Christian Aid, noticeably more secular in orientation than their missionary forebears, and for whom professionalism dictated a separation from religious ideals.[40]

That said, one is still struck by the deep and sometimes painful sense of not belonging expressed by African-Caribbean and South Asian immigrants arriving from Britain's colonies and former colonies after 1945. The former, in particular, had expected to be welcomed by the 'mother country', only to find that, despite the rhetoric of a wider imperial citizenship that the Colonial Office and the BBC had voiced during the war,[41] there was in peacetime little apparent appetite on the part of the host population to accept that non-white immigrants had any place in a post-war Britain. Indeed, if anything, they were identified as a threat to a 'Britishness' that was still widely conceived in insular, 'all-white', and 'nativist' terms. Difficulties in race relations manifested themselves not only in terms of segregated housing; under pressure from white parents, some local authorities actually began dispersing South Asian children in their schools at this time.

This failure to develop a more expansive British identity during the era of decolonization—subsequently reinforced by trends in global identity politics, including rising levels of remittances and return migration, so-called heritage tourism, and the outreach policies of the Indian and Pakistani states—goes some way to explain why the British 'brand' of multiculturalism is under strain. Multiculturalism, it is now widely argued, has neither been able to address questions of social inclusion in housing, employment, and education, nor to arrest a growing ethnic segregation. Implicit in this failure is the fact that for many on the Left the whole point of shedding the empire was precisely to concentrate attention on Britain itself, while those on the Right who resisted were the least likely to want to 'expand' an identity in cultural and racial terms.[42] New Commonwealth immigration

[40] See Cox, Ch. 3 in this volume.

[41] S. O. Rose, *Which People's War? National Identity and Citizenship in Britain, 1939–1945* (Oxford, 2004), 281–5.

[42] For the differing views within the Tory Party on Britain's 'lingering obligations' to refugees from its former colonies, see B. Harrison, *Finding a Role? The United Kingdom 1970–1990* (Oxford, 2010), 17.

is therefore yet another illustration of what we have already flagged as a key characteristic of Britain's twentieth-century imperial experience, namely, the 'pervasive influence' of the empire upon British life, coupled nonetheless with the 'tentative embrace' of that empire by the 'mother country'.

This volume has also highlighted how the history of Britain's empire is closely entwined with issues of identity in contemporary society and politics. Empire structured the development of national identities in the first half of the twentieth century. After the end of formal empire in the second half of that century, 'Britishness' had to find new moorings. In the immediate aftermath of victory in the Second World War, this did not pose too much of a problem—the years of struggle from 1939 to 1945 forged a collective sense of self in Britain in a way that even its long imperial involvement arguably never did. But the loss of the colonies took away something of real significance that the English, Scots, Welsh, and (more ambiguously) the Irish had shared. Previously a force for convergence, which contributed to the creation of an overarching identity that could incorporate the different nationalities of the United Kingdom, the diminishing sense of the British as an imperial people meant that there was little left (bar Europe) within which to subsume those nationalities. It is perhaps for partly this reason that Kumar concludes that 'the relation between empire and identities is one not so much of consciousness as of structure'. Britain, like France, is still coping with the differential impact of empire upon its peoples today. Since the possibility of the 'break-up of Britain' was first mooted in the 1970s, we have witnessed renewed assertions of 'Englishness' (in particular in the sphere of mass sport), the greater propensity of a post-imperial Scotland, and, to a lesser extent, Wales, to find salvation within Europe, and a growing sense of uncertainty as to what will continue to hold the constituent parts of the United Kingdom together. As the bonds within the United Kingdom have loosened, and the whole notion of a 'British' identity has consequently been called into question, one might even be tempted to speculate who will be left calling themselves 'British' in twenty or thirty years' time. Perhaps it will be only the Ulster Unionists, still in some minds 'colonists' or a 'frontier' people,[43] and some of Britain's

[43] The imperial mentality of Ireland's Unionists is a complex subject, but for commentary upon it, see esp. P. Clayton, *Enemies and Passing Friends: Settler Ideologies in Twentieth Century Ulster* (London, 1996); C. Falles, *The Birth of Ulster* (London, 1996 edn.); M. Ignatieff, *Blood and Belonging: Journeys into the New Nationalism* (London, 1994), ch. 6; A. Jackson, 'Irish Unionists

ethnic minorities, another product of the empire.[44] Whatever the future may bring for the British peoples, it is clear that the legacies of their empire are not only still with them, they may yet have fully to unfold.

and the Empire, 1880–1920: Classes and Masses', in K. Jeffery (ed.), *An Irish Empire? Aspects of Ireland and the British Empire* (Manchester, 1996); J. Loughlin, 'Imagining "Ulster": The North of Ireland and British National Identity, 1880–1921', in S. J. Connolly (ed.), *Kingdoms United? Ireland and Great Britain from 1500: Integration and Diversity since 1500* (Dublin, 1999).

[44] On British identities among Britain's ethnic minorities, see T. Modood, R. Berthoud et al., *Ethnic Minorities in Britain: Diversity and Disadvantage* (London, 1997). For a collection of, and reflection upon, oral histories of first generation Asian migrants, see A. S. Thompson with R. Begum, *Discovering Asian Views of Britishness: A Study of First Generation Asian Migrants in Greater Manchester*, Asylum and Migration Working Paper Series, Institute of Public Policy Research (London, 2004).

INDEX

Briane, Sir Bernard 113
'Break-up of Britain' 310, 325, 327, 344
Brideshead Revisited (1981) 102, 331
Brighton 137, 138, 279
Bristol 29, 144, 295
Britain's international role 8, 14, 23, 30–2, 33–4,
  50–1, 58, 64, 65, 68, 71, 72, 74, 161, 181–4, 226,
  254, 256, 257, 293, 310–11, 316, 337–40
Britannic identity 314–15, 317
British Broadcasting Corporation (BBC) 122,
  129, 136, 139, 146, 148, 317, 318, 343
British Council of Churches 107, 111, 115
British Empire Cancer Research Campaign 265
British Empire and Commonwealth
  Museum 295
British Empire Exhibition 265
British Empire Games–*see* Commonwealth 11
British Empire Society for the Blind 265
British Empire Union 269
British exports 56, 62, 227–8, 238, 281
British Guiana 61, 150
British history 2–3, 21, 84–5, 124, 246, 251–2, 325
British identity 19, 27, 65, 101, 127, 128, 133, 136,
  141, 144, 149, 150, 154, 155, 157, 159, 207, 208,
  258, 259, 260, 287, 303, 309–10, 312, 317, 318,
  320, 335, 337–8, 341–2, 343–5
British intelligence 46, 70
British industry 49, 56, 215, 247–8, 288
British Library 295
British Medical Association 265
British Muslims 117–18, 119, 156, 340
British Nationality Act (1948) 125, 319, 320
British Somaliland 29, 46
British Union of Fascists 177
British World 123, 149, 150, 156, 251, 260, 267,
  303, 310
Brixton 330
Brown, Callum 84, 85
Brown, George 65, 202
Buchan, John 313
Burgess, Anthony 289
Burma 43, 48, 272, 319
Burton, Richard 95
Bush, George W. 73
Butler, R. A. 132, 183, 191
Buxton, Dorothy 103

Caillard, Sir Vincent 211, 212
Cain, P. J. and Hopkins, A. G. 230
Caird, James 241
Callaghan, James 68, 69, 193
Calvert, Phyllis 276
Cameron, James 286
Canada 10, 16, 24, 40, 42, 50, 51, 87, 122, 135,
  217, 220, 224, 261, 262, 266, 276, 306, 308,
  313, 317
Cannadine, David 251–2, 303
Cardiff 138, 144, 280, 322

Caribbean–*see* also West Indies 16, 113, 123, 126,
  148, 149, 150, 234, 255, 281, 334
Carrington, Lord 172, 204–5
Carter, Jimmy 71
Castle, Barbara 194, 197
Catholic Agency for Overseas Development
  (CAFOD) 112, 113
Celtic nationalism 305–6, 323
Central African Federation 167, 188–91, 193, 199
Ceylon 61
Chadwick, Owen 85
Chamberlain, Austen 41–2
Chamberlain, Joseph 15, 166, 213
Chamberlain, Mary 152
Chamberlain, Neville 45, 47–8, 176
Chariots of Fire (1981) 331
Charmley, John 178–9
Chataway, Christopher 129, 130, 133, 148
Child migrants 267–8, 332
Childers, Erskine 306
Children 7, 82, 89, 95, 96, 101, 103–4, 109, 113, 143,
  153, 267–70, 289
China 20, 30, 31, 36, 37, 57, 70, 76, 79, 90, 93, 98,
  100, 103, 105, 207, 208, 280, 327
China Inland Mission 89, 90, 106
Cholmondeley, Hugh (Baron Delamere) 284
Christian globalisation–*see also* Globalisation
  77, 78
Christian universalism 25, 95, 97
Christianization–*see also* Churches and
  Missionaries 77–8, 79, 82
Christian Aid 110, 112, 113, 343
Church of England 81, 82, 84, 102, 116
Church of Scotland (*see also* United Free
  Church of Scotland) 81, 106
Church Missionary Society 86, 97, 104, 106, 114
Churches 28, 77, 80, 83, 85, 97, 102, 103, 104,
  108, 269
Comaroff, Jean and John 95
Churchill, Winston 18, 39, 47, 50, 52, 57, 58, 166,
  168, 169, 171, 175, 176, 177, 181, 182, 217, 318
Citrine, Walter 282
'Civilizing Mission' 4, 274, 290, 309, 326
Cold War 52, 55, 66, 67, 71, 72, 236
Colombo Plan (1950) 236
Colonial Advisory Committee 282
Colonial civil servants 168, 169–70, 271, 288–9
'Colonial complex' 335
'Colonial condition' 335
Colonial Development Act (1929) 218
Colonial Development and Welfare Act (1940)
  235–6
Colonial Development Commission 287
Colonial Film Unit 317
Colonial Office 200, 223, 265, 282, 298, 343
'Colonial pathology' 335
Colonial seamen 131, 138, 280–1
Colonial soldiers–*see also* Indian army 255, 317

Printed in Great Britain
by Amazon